OTHER TITLES OF INTEREST

CODING AND REIMBURSEMENT

CPT Coders Choice , Thumb Indexed
CPT TimeSaver, Ring Binder, Tab Indexed
CPT & HCPCS Coding Made Easy!
HCPCS Coders Choice
Health Insurance Carrier Directory
ICD-9-CM, Coders Choice, Thumb Indexed
ICD-9-CM, TimeSaver, Ring Binder, Tab Indexed
ICD-9-CM COding Made Easy!
Physicians Fee Guide
Make Medicare Work for You
RBRVS: Impact and Implications
Reimbursement Manual for the Medical Office
Understanding Medical Insurance

PRACTICE MANAGEMENT

365 Ways to Manage the Business Called Private Practice
A Practical Guide to Financial Management of the Laboratory
Choosing and Using a Medical Office Computer
Computerizing Your Medical Office
Designing and Building Your Professional Office
Effective Laboratory Supervision
Encyclopedia of Practice and Financial Managment
Managing Medical Office Personnel
Marketing Healthcare
Marketing Strategies for Physicians
Medical Practice Handbook
Medical Staff Privileges
On-Line Systems: How to Access and Use Databases
Patient Satisfaction
Performance Standards for the Laboratory
Physician's Office Laboratory
Professional and Practice Development
Promoting Your Medical Practice
Remodeling Your Professional Office
Starting in Medical Practice

D1403776

AVAILABLE FROM YOUR LOCAL MEDICAL
BOOK STORE OR CALL 1-800-MED-SHOP

OTHER TITLES OF INTEREST

FINANCIAL MANAGEMENT

A Physician's Guide to Financial Independence
Business Ventures for Physicians
Financial Planning Workbook for Physicians
Financial Valuation of Your Practice
Personal Money Management for Physicians
Personal Pension Plan Strategies for Physicians
Securing Your Assets
Selling or Buying a Medical Practice

RISK MANAGEMENT

Belli: For Your Malpractice Defense
Law, Liability and Ethics for Medical Office Personnel
Malpractice Depositions
Malpractice: Managing Your Defense
Medical Risk Management
Preventing Emergency Malpractice
Testifying in Court

DICTIONARIES AND OTHER REFERENCE

Drug Interactions Index
Isler's Pocket Dictionary
Medical Accronyms and Abbreviations
Medical Phrase Index
Medical Word Building
Medico-Legal Glossary
Spanish/English Handbook for Medical Professionals

MEDICAL REFERENCE AND CLINICAL

Anesthesiology: Problems in Primary Care
Cardiology: Problems in Primary Care
Gastroenterology: Problems in Primary Care
Medical Procedures for Referral
Neurology: Problems in Primary Care
Orthopaedics: Problems in Primary Care
Patient Care Emergency Handbook
Patient Care Flowchart Manual
Patient Care Procedures for Your Practice
Pulmonary Medicine: Problems in Primary Care
Urology: Problems in Primary Care

**AVAILABLE FROM YOUR LOCAL MEDICAL
BOOK STORE OR CALL 1-800-MED-SHOP**

REIMBURSEMENT MANUAL
for the
MEDICAL OFFICE

A Comprehensive
Guide To Coding,
Billing & Fee
Management

Second Edition

Davis, James B.
  Reimbursement Manual for the Medical Office

Library of Congress Catalog Card Number: 92-050000

ISBN 1-878487-37-X

PMIC (Practice Management Information Corporation)
4727 Wilshire Blvd, Suite 300
Los Angeles, California 90010
1-800-**MED-SHOP**

Printed in the United States of America

FOREWORD & ACKNOWLEDGMENTS

Most health care professionals would prefer to practice medicine and ignore the subjects of coding, billing and insurance. Unfortunately, many do exactly that, with serious detrimental economic impact to their practices. For every single physician the insurance carriers can uncover who is abusing the system by over-charging or unbundling, I can find ten who are undercharging or not charging at all for billable services.

Tremendous changes in health care reimbursement are already under way. Those professionals who 1) acknowledge that the change will occur, 2) understand that the change is irreversible, and 3) begin preparing for the change now, will, in most cases, find themselves far more successful than they are now. Part of preparing for this change is to take control of your own reimbursement process. This means that you have to understand and manage properly each step of the process. examining each piece separately. Reimbursement management is a like a puzzle with a lot of pieces. This book is about the puzzle and how to solve it. Understanding and managing each step of the process puts you in control of your reimbursement, which is exactly how it should be.

I would like to thank the over 100,000 medical professionals and medical institutions who have helped make PMIC the leading publisher and distributor of practice management and reimbursement texts in the country. Your comments, criticisms and suggestions have been invaluable in our product development process. In addition I wish to thank the many office managers, consultants, insurance and government agency staffs, and others who provided valuable information and suggestions as well as critical review.

DISCLAIMER

This publication is designed to offer basic information regarding coding and billing of medical services, supplies and procedures using the CPT, HCPCS and ICD-9-CM coding systems and additional information regarding forms, insurance claims processing and superbill design. The information presented is based on the experience and interpretations of the author. Though all of the information has been carefully researched and checked for accuracy and completeness, neither the author nor the publisher accept any responsibility or liability with regard to errors, omissions, misuse or misinterpretation.

THE AUTHOR

James B. Davis has been in the health care field for over 20 years working closely with medical professionals, hospitals and insurance carriers. He founded one of California's most successful medical billing companies in 1978. In 1986 he founded PMIC, which has become the nation's leading publisher and distributor of practice management and reimbursement books for medical professionals.

He has given seminars to hundreds of health care professionals on the subjects of data processing and reimbursement management. He is the author, editor or publisher of the *Health Insurance Carrier Directory*, the *Reimbursement Manual for the Medical Office, CPT & HCPCS Coding Made Easy!, ICD-9-CM Coding Made Easy!, 365 Ways to Manage the Business Called Private Practice* and PMIC's industry standard *ICD-9-CM, 9th Revision, 4th Edition*.

He is a member of the Medical Group Management Association, the Direct Marketing Association, the International Customer Service Association, the American Medical Publishers Association, the Professional Association of Healthcare Office Managers, the American Association for Medical Transcriptionists and the Healthcare Convention and Exhibitors Association.

CONTENTS

CONTENTS

CONTENTS

INTRODUCTION
AND
OVERVIEW

CHAPTER SUMMARY

Reimbursement management is like a puzzle with a lot of pieces. While difficult already, tremendous changes are coming. Those health care professionals who prepare for these changes *now* will continue to enjoy economic success and prosperity in the future. This chapter is an introduction to the process of reimbursement management. The knowledge learned in dealing with tens of thousands of health care professionals nationwide through our publications and seminars, combined with the experience gained from processing over one billion dollars in medical bills for health care professionals, has provided us with some unique information and insight.

One very important thing we have learned is that *there is no single answer, system or formula for getting paid.*

- Coding is important, but you can have the right code and the wrong (too low) fee, and the insurance carriers will happily pay you less than they are paying other medical professionals for the very same service.

- Your codes and fees may be okay, but you may be losing charges, missing fee tickets, o billing insurance carriers improperly or inconsistently.

- Not participating in Medicare may allow you to bill higher fees, but it may not be in the best interest of your practice.

A system designed to bill quickly and accurately, to maximize prompt and accurate payments from insurance carriers, is the ultimate goal of your reimbursement management process. Plus, by designing a system which maximizes the patient's insurance benefits, you will be providing a valuable service which will help you attract new patients to your service, and keep your existing ones. This chapter defines the basic steps of coding and billing, the fundamental tools needed for coding and billing, some general policies that all practices need to have and provides a glossary of billing and insurance terminology.

KEY POINTS REGARDING REIMBURSEMENT MANAGEMENT

1. The practice must be well informed about current coding and billing issues.

2. The practice must use forms and documents which are current, accurate and conform to legal requirements.

3. The practice must have written policies and procedures which support the billing, coding and collections processes.

4. The practice must use current CPT, HCPCS and ICD-9-CM codes for procedure and diagnosis coding.

5. The practice must understand how insurance carriers work and develop effective strategies and systems that allow maximal reimbursement with minimal effort.

TOOLS FOR THE BUSINESS OF MEDICINE

Some wise person once said "Given the right tools, people can do anything!" While few would disagree with this statement, it is surprising how many medical offices do not have basic billing and coding tools. Regardless of whether you use a manual billing system, such as a pegboard or ledger card system, or a computer billing system using a service bureau or your own in-house computer, you need to make sure that your practice has the required tools for billing and coding.

BASIC TOOLS

The following are some of the basic tools needed by all medical professionals for coding, billing and reimbursement management.

- A thorough understanding of the billing process and billing terminology

- Good forms and documents

- Current reference materials

- Written policies and procedures covering billing

- CPT and HCPCS procedure coding expertise

- ICD-9-CM diagnosis coding expertise

- A fee schedule based on relative values

- A well designed SUPERBILL

- A thorough understanding of the insurance claims process

In this chapter we provide an overview of these fundamental tools. The following chapters provide detailed discussions of forms and documents, procedure and diagnosis coding, fee schedule management, superbill design and dealing with insurance carriers.

BASIC STEPS OF MEDICAL BILLING

Reimbursement management starts with the moment of the first patient contact and ends only when the patient's account balance is zero. In between, there are a series of important steps, each of which is critical for accurate billing and proper reimbursement. In order to maximize your reimbursement, you must be in control of each step of the reimbursement process. The basic steps defined in the next few pages will help you develop an appreciation for the complexity of the medical billing process and the importance of each step and can also be used as a guideline for developing your reimbursement management system.

PATIENT REGISTRATION COMPLETED OR UPDATED

- For all NEW patients, complete patient registration form with complete patient and third party billing information.

- If patient has moved, changed employers or changed insurance carriers, complete a new patient registration form.

SUPERBILL INITIATED

For ALL patients, fill out the patient identification portion, date, account number and prior balance portion of the superbill. Clip to patient's chart or otherwise deliver to provider.

SERVICES DOCUMENTED BY PROVIDER

Provider sees patient and performs procedure(s) and/or services(s).

- Checks off or writes in services/procedures provided on superbill.

- Checks off diagnosis code(s) applicable to the services/procedures provided.

- Indicates relationship (link) of diagnostic code(s) to procedure code(s).

- Optionally may put fees next to code, indicate next recall or appointment information and may include special instructions.

- Superbill delivered to person responsible for collecting payment at the time of service and/or billing the patient's insurance.

- Makes entries in the patient's medical record which clearly indicate the medical necessity for the services, procedures, and level of care provided.

SUPERBILL REVIEWED, PAYMENT COLLECTED

- Any questions (by the biller or the patient) or discrepancies are clarified with the provider BEFORE the patient leaves the office.

- The patient is given a copy of the superbill indicating all services/procedures performed along with prior balance, current payment and the total amount due.

- If practice collects payment at the time of service the patient is asked for payment:

    -- If payment is made by cash, a receipt must be issued.

    -- If payment is made by check, the payment and check number should be indicated on all copies of the superbill.

    -- If payment is made by credit card, the credit card slip must be filled out and signed by the responsible party. In addition, if the total exceeds a specified amount, the practice must obtain telephone approval for the charge.

- Patient is informed that he/she must must file a claim with their insurance carrier (unless the practice files claims for all patients).

BILLING SYSTEM UPDATED

- Superbill reviewed for complete and accurate procedure and diagnosis coding. Any missing or incorrect codes are corrected. Procedures and/or diagnoses written in text are coded.

- Pegboard entry or ledger card entry made for manual office.

- Forms completed for batch entry to computer service bureau.

- Transactions input into on-line computer system or to the practice's own computer system.

INSURANCE CLAIM FORM PREPARED

- For practices which do not use an in-house computer or computer service bureau, all insurance claims must be typed.

- For computerized practices, or those using computer service bureaus, the preparation of insurance claim forms is a by-product of posting.

- For practices' using electronic claims, filing the claim may be processed and transmitted as a by-product of posting or may require a separate (additional) entry, depending on the system used, and the recipient of the electronic claim.

DOCUMENTS FILED FOR REVIEW AND FOLLOWUP

- All superbills are batched by date of service and filed for a specified period.

- Copies of all insurance claims are filed in an open claims file for review and disposal when payment is received.

PAYMENT RECEIVED FROM INSURANCE CARRIER

- Copy of claim retrieved from open claims file.

- Payment & explanation of benefits (EOB) reviewed against original claim.

- If payment in full, or acceptable to practice standards, post payment.

- Bill patient for balance due if any, or bill patient's secondary insurance carrier with copy of EOB from primary carrier attached.

- If payment less than expected or unsatisfactory, or if insurance carrier down-coded procedures, initiated appeal. Refile claim with copy of appeal letter in open claims file.

INQUIRY LETTER FROM INSURANCE CARRIER RECEIVED

- Pull original claim copy from open claims file and review based on carrier inquiry.

- Make necessary corrections and mail a copy of the corrected claim with a copy of the inquiry to the insurance carrier.

- Refile the claim with a copy of the inquiry in the open claims file.

DENIAL RECEIVED FROM INSURANCE CARRIER

- Pull original claim copy from open claims file and review based on carrier inquiry.

- If denial based on coding, informational or billing error, correct and re-bill to insurance carrier.

- Refile the claim with a copy of the denial in the open claims file.

- If denial is based on eligibility, exclusion or preexisting condition, bill the patient.

PATIENTS BILLED

- All patients who do not pay at the time of service are billed, ideally within seven days.

- All patients who have a balance remaining after insurance payment are billed.

- Accounts receivable reports or ledger card aging system maintained.

PATIENT PAYS THE BILL

- Payment posted to pegboard, ledger or computer system.

- Open item manually (ledger) or automatically (computer) removed from the aging system.

- Partial payments posted to pegboard, ledger or computer system and aging maintained.

REVIEW ACCOUNTS RECEIVABLE

- Maintain and review accounts receivable frequently.

- Take appropriate collection action on overdue accounts.

COLLECTION EFFORTS

- Send customized or form collection letters or notices, each notice slightly more serious and demanding.

- Call the patient and make arrangements for full payment, negotiate a reduced payment or a series of payments.

- Have your attorney write a simple demand for payment to the patient.

- Send the account to a formal collection agency, notify the patient that you will no longer provide services.

ACCOUNT CLOSED

Each of the above steps and processes must be completed totally and successfully in order for the subsequent actions and processes to be completed. While you may consider some of these steps to be technically more important than others, the bottom line is that in terms of billing and reimbursement, they are all equally important.

FORMS AND DOCUMENTS

In addition to the forms and documents required to maintain the patient's medical record, there are numerous forms and documents required for accurate coding and billing. The following forms and documents are considered fundamental and essential to all medical practices:

- Patient Registration Form

- Release and Assignment of Benefits

- Insurance Preauthorization or Certification Form

- Superbill

- HCFA1500 Insurance Claim Form

- Medicare Surgery Financial Disclosure Form

- Medicare Medical Necessity Form

REFERENCE MATERIALS

Every practice needs current reference materials. These references include procedure and diagnostic codes, relative value scales, worker's compensation fee schedules and other basic references. The following reference materials are considered fundamental and essential to all medical practices:

- *Physician's Current Procedural Terminology* (CPT) <u>Current Edition</u>

- *International Classification of Diseases, 9th Revision, <u>4th</u> Edition* (ICD-9-CM)

- Insurance Carrier Names & Addresses (for claim filing)

- Medicare Fee Schedule

- Relative Value System (for fee calculation)

- Workers Compensation Fee Schedule (for your state)

- HCPCS National Level 2 Medicare procedure codes

- HCPCS Local Level 3 Medicare procedure codes

- Medical Dictionaries and Terminology references

- "HOW TO" coding and billing reference materials

POLICIES AND PROCEDURES

For each step of the reimbursement management process, you must have clearly defined, written policies and procedures explaining exactly how your practice handles any given situation. In addition, you need written policies and procedures explaining how and when each of your forms and documents is completed and dispensed with. Some questions related to reimbursement policies that you need answers to, include:

- Are patients informed when they make an appointment as to what estimated costs will be and if they are expected to pay?

- For patients with insurance:

  -- Does the practice file insurance claims for all patients for all services?

  -- Does the practice file insurance claims for selected patients and/or services

  -- Does the practice accept assignment of benefits?

    -- always?
    -- most of the time?
    -- occasionally? (under what conditions?)

- For Medicare patients:

  -- Does the practice participate in Medicare?

  -- How do we handle deductibles and coinsurance?

  -- Are we complying with all current regulations?

- For Medicaid patients:

  -- Does the practice accept Medicaid patients?

  -- Are we filing claims properly within the time periods specified?

SYSTEMS DEVELOPMENT AND DESIGN SEQUENCE

The success of any reimbursement management system depends on the ability to understand, design, develop, implement, control and manage each step. There is a specific learning process and a sequence of events and steps which must take place before subsequent steps can be developed. This book was written with this learning and sequencing process in mind. If you find upon review that you already have an understanding of the basics, then proceed directly to the specific chapters in the book that are of interest.

THE ULTIMATE GOAL

The ultimate goal of any billing system is to bring the account balance to zero as soon as possible. A system designed to bill quickly and accurately, to maximize prompt and accurate payments from insurance carriers and/or patients, will accomplish this goal. Plus, by designing a system which maximizes patient's insurance benefits, you will be providing a service which will help you attract new patients to your service, and keep your existing ones.

BILLING AND INSURANCE TERMINOLOGY

Managing the reimbursement process requires a fundamental working knowledge of the words and acronymns used by medical professionals, government agencies and insurance carriers to describe services, benefits and reimbursement policies. While many publications place the terminology section in an appendix at the back of the book, we feel that you should have an opportunity to review and learn the terminology before you encounter it within the text itself.

AAPCC: Average Adjusted Per Capita Cost

ACCIDENT AND HEALTH INSURANCE: Insurance under which benefits are payable in case of disease, accidental injury or accidental death.

ACTUAL CHARGE: One of the factors determining a physician's payment for a service under Medicare; equivalent to the billed or submitted charge. See Customary, Prevailing and Reasonable.

ADJUSTED AVERAGE PER CAPITA COST (AAPC): An estimate of the average per capita cost incurred by Medicare per beneficiary in the fee-for-service system, adjusted by county for age, sex, and program entitlement.

ADJUSTED HISTORICAL PAYMENT BASIS (AHPB): The average historical payment in a specific locality for a specific service.

ADMINSTRATIVE AGENT: See CARRIER.

AFDC: Aid to Families with Dependent Children

AHPB: Adjusted Historical Payment Basis

ALLOWED CHARGE (APPROVED CHARGE): Payment for a physician service under the customary, prevailing and reasonable system; includes the payment from Medicare and the beneficiary's coinsurance, but not any balance bill. See Balance Bill; Coinsurance; Customary, Prevailing and Reasonable.

ANNUAL DEDUCTIBLE: See DEDUCTIBLE.

APPROVED CHARGE: See ALLOWED CHARGE or REASONABLE CHARGE.

ASSIGNMENT (MEDICARE): A decision made in advance of billing to accept the Medicare allowed charge and subsequent payment as payment in full.

ASSIGNMENT OF BENEFITS: A procedure whereby the subscriber authorizes the carrier to make payment of allowable benefits directly to the provider.

ASSISTANT-AT-SURGERY: An individual who actively assists in performing a surgery.

BALANCE BILL/EXTRA BILL: Physician's charges exceeding the Medicare allowed charge.

BALANCE BILLING: Billing the beneficiary for any fee in excess of that allowed by the insurance carrier.

BENEFICIARY: A person eligible to receive benefits under a health care plan.

BENEFICIARY SURVEY: A 1988 survey of a national sample of beneficiaries regarding assignment, participation, balance billing, and understanding of the Medicare program.

BLUE CROSS: Nonprofit, community service organizations, providing in-hospital health care services to their subscribers.

BLUE SHIELD: Nonprofit voluntary organization which provides subscribers with coverage for expenses (other than hospital costs). May also serve as the carrier for programs like Medicare.

BMAD: Part B Medicare Annual Data Files

CAPITATION: A census-driven reimbursement system wherein a health plan provides medical services for a fixed monthly fee. Contracting providers may be reimbursed in the same manner.

CARRIER: The insurance company which writes and administers the health insurance policy.

CARRIER (MEDICARE): A private contractor who administers claims for Part B Medicare services.

CBS: Current Beneficiary Survey

CF: Conversion Factor

CHAMPUS [Civilian Health and Medical Program of the Uniformed Services]: A federally funded comprehensive health benefits program designed to provide eligible beneficiaries a supplement to medical care in military and Public Health Service facilities.

CHARGE REDUCTION (MEDICARE): The percentage difference between a provider's billed charge and the Medicare allowed charge.

CLAIM: A demand to the carrier, by the insured person, for payment of benefits under a policy.

CLAIM FORM: A form used to present claim information in an organized manner to the carrier. See HCFA1500.

CLAIMS EXAMINER: The carrier's employee who is responsible for handling claims as they are received from patients and medical offices.

CMP: Competitive Medical Plan

COB: See COORDINATION OF BENEFITS

COBRA: Consolidated Omnibus Budget Reconciliation Act of 1985. P.L. 99-272, enacted April 1986

CODING: A mechanism for identifying and defining medical services.

COINSURANCE: A provision of a plan by which the beneficiary shares in the cost of certain covered expenses on a percentage basis. Also known as copayment.

COMMON WORKING FILE (CWF): A new HCFA data reporting system which will combine Part A and Part B claims in a common file.

COMPETITIVE MEDICAL PLAN (CMP): A health plan that is eligible under TEFRA 1982 to enter into a Medicare risk contract in return for a capitation payment, but which does not satisfy the requirements to be a federally qualified HMO. See Capitation, Federally Qualified HMO.

COMPREHENSIVE MEDICAL INSURANCE: A policy designed to give the protection offered by both a basic and a major medical health insurance policy.

CONVERSION FACTOR (CF): A dollar value, specific to the four general categories of service: medical, surgical, lab and radiology, that is used with a relative value scale to calculate fees for services and procedures.

COPAYMENT: See COINSURANCE.

COORDINATION OF BENEFITS [COB]: A provision in an insurance plan that when a patient is covered under more than one group plan, benefits paid by all plans will be limited to 100 percent of the actual charge.

COST OF PRACTICE INDEX (MEDICARE): A measurement of the differences across geographic areas of the cost of operating a medical practice.

CPR: Customary, Prevailing and Reasonable

CPT [CURRENT PROCEDURAL TERMINOLOGY]: A system of procedure codes and descriptions published annually by the American Medical Association. This procedure coding system is accepted by virtually all commercial insurance carriers and is required by Medicare and Medicaid.

CROSS-OVER PATIENT: A patient who has both Medicare and Medicaid coverage.

CURRENT PROCEDURAL TERMINOLOGY: See CPT.

CUSTOMARY CHARGE: The provider's standard charge for a given service. Typically calculated by insurance carriers as the provider's median charge for the service over a prior 12 month period.

CUSTOMARY, PREVAILING AND REASONABLE (MEDICARE): Current method of payment for physician services by Medicare. Payment for service is limited to the lowest of 1) the billed charge, 2) the customary charge, or 3) the prevailing charge in the community.

CWF: Common Working File

DEDUCTIBLE: A stipulated amount which the covered person must pay toward the cost of medical treatment before the benefits of the program go into effect.

DEDUCTIBLE CARRYOVER: A feature whereby covered charges in the last three months of the year may be carried over to be counted toward the next year's deductible.

DEFRA: Deficit Reduction Act of 1984. P.L. 98-369, enacted July 1984.

DEPENDENTS: The spouse and children of the insured as defined in the insurance contract.

DIAGNOSIS RELATED GROUPS (DRGs): A system of classifying medical cases for payment on the basis of diagnoses. Used under Medicare's prospective payment system (PPS) for inpatient hospital services.

DISABILITY INCOME INSURANCE: A form of health insurance that provides periodic payments to replace income when the insured is unable to work as a result of illness, injury or disease.

DOWNCODING: A process used by insurance carriers to reduce the value of billed procedures by changing the codes submitted to ones of lower value. Procedure code and procedure description mismatch, and diagnosis code not supporting the level of care are the two most common opportunities for insurance carrier down-coding.

DRG: See DIAGNOSIS RELATED GROUPS

DUAL ELIGIBLES: Medicare beneficiaries who also receive the full range of Medicaid benefits offered in their state.

ELECTRONIC CLAIM: A claim form which is processed and delivered from one computer to another via some form of magnetic media (magnetic tape, diskette) or via telecommunciations (telephone link).

EM: Evaluation and Management

EMC: Electronic Media Claim

ENROLLEE: See INSURED.

EOB [EXPLANATION OF BENEFITS]: A form included with a check from the insurance carrier which explains the benefits that were paid and/or charges that were rejected.

EOMB: Explanation of Medicare Benefits

EVALUATION AND MANAGEMENT SERVICES: Nontechnical services provided by most physicians for the purpose of diagnosing and treating diseases and counseling and evaluating patients.

EXCLUSIONS: Specific services or conditions which the policy will not cover or which are covered at a limited rate.

EXPLANATION OF BENEFITS: See E.O.B.

FEDERALLY QUALIFIED HMO: An HMO that has satisfied certain federal qualifications pertaining to organizational structure, provider contracts, health service delivery information, utilization review/quality assurance, grievance procedures, financial status, and marketing information.

FEE FOR SERVICE (FFS): Refers to paying medical providers for individual services rendered. UCR, CPR and Fee Schedules are examples of fee for service systems.

FEE SCHEDULE: A list of predetermined payments for medical services.

FEE SCHEDULE PAYMENT AREAS: Geographic areas within which payment under the fee schedule will be equal. Analogous to localities under current payment policies. See Geographic Adjustment Factor.

FFS: Fee-for-Service

FISCAL INTERMEDIARY (FI): A private contractor who administers claims for Part A services (for example hospital and nursing home) and some Part B services (such as hospital outpatient departments).

FMAP: Federal Medical Assistance Percentage

GAF: Geographic Adjustment Factor

GAMING: Gaining advantage by using improper means to evade the letter or intent of a rule or system.

GEOGRAPHIC ADJUSTMENT FACTOR (GAF): The adjustment made to a service's fee in the Medicare Fee Schedule to determine the correct payment in each fee schedule payment area. As defined in OBRA89, the geographic adjustment factor is created by combining three separate adjustment factors, one for each component of the Medicare Fee Schedule: physician work, practice expense, and malpractice expense. The adjustment factors for physician work, practice expense, and malpractice are based on the same measures that underlie the GPCI. See Fee Schedule Payment Areas, Geographic Cost of Practice Index.

GEOGRAPHIC COST OF PRACTICE INDEX (GPCI): An index summarizing the prices of inputs to physician services in an area relative to national average prices. The GPCI is based on three components, reflecting the opportunity cost of physician work, the costs of goods and services that comprise practice expenses, and malpractice expenses. The GPCI is a single measure that combines these three fixed shares, while the GAF of the Medicare Fee Schedule allows for each service to reflect different shares, creating a GAF for each service. See Geographic Adjustment Factor.

GLOBAL SERVICE: A group of clinically related services that are treated as a single unit for the purpose of coding, billing and payment.

GPIC: Geographic Cost of Practice Index

HARVARD RELATIVE VALUE STUDY: A study completed at Harvard University to develop a resource-based relative value scale.

HCFA [HEALTH CARE FINANCING ADMINISTRATION]: The U.S. Government agency with responsibility for the Medicare and Medicaid programs.

HCFA1500: A universal insurance claim form that is mandated for Medicare billing and generally accepted by all insurance carriers.

HCPCS [HCFA COMMON PROCEDURE CODING SYSTEM]: A three-level coding system, consisting of CPT, National or Level 2, and Local or Level 3 codes used to report and bill services provided to Medicare patients. See Coding, Current Procedural Terminology.

HEALTH PROFESSIONAL SHORTAGE AREAS (HPSAs): Replaces Health Manpower Shortage Areas (HMSAs). A Health Professional Shortage Area means any of the following: 1) an urban or rural area; 2) a population group; or 3) a public nonprofit private medical facility.

HHS: Department of Health and Human Services (also referred to as DHHS)

HMO [HEALTH MAINTENANCE ORGANIZATION]: An organization that provides comprehensive health services to its members in return for a fixed prepaid fee.

HPSA: Health Professional Shortage Area

ICD-9-CM [INTERNATIONAL CLASSIFICATION OF DISEASES]: A standardized system of describing diagnoses by code numbers developed and maintained by the World Health Organization.

INDEMNITY SCHEDULE: See SCHEDULE OF ALLOWANCES.

INDEPENDENT PRACTICE ASSOCIATION (IPA): An HMO which contracts directly with physicians who continue to practice in their private offices and are paid on a fee-for-service basis.

INSURANCE CLERK: One of the health care professional's employees who has been assigned the very important job of managing insurance claims in the medical office.

INSURED: The person who represents the family unit in relation to the insurance program. Usually the employee whose employment makes this coverage possible.

INSURER: See CARRIER.

INTERNATIONAL CLASSIFICATION OF DISEASES: See ICD-9-CM.

IPA: See Independent Practice Association

LCL: Lowest Charge Level Limit

LEVEL 2 CODES: See HCPCS

LEVEL 3 CODES: See HCPCS

LIMITED LICENSE PRACTITIONER (LLP): A professional licensed to perform certain health services in independent practice; for example, podiatrists, dentists, optometrists and chiropractors.

LLP: Limited License Practitioner

LOCAL CODES: See HCPCS

LONG-TERM DISABILITY INCOME INSURANCE: A provision to pay benefits to a covered disabled person as long as he or she remains disabled, up to a specified period.

INTERMEDIARY: An insurance carrier, or data processing company, designed to receive and process Medicare or Medicaid claims on behalf of the government.

MAAC [MAXIMUM ALLOWABLE ACTUAL CHARGE]: A limitation on billed charges for Medicare services provided by non-participating physicians.

MAF: Medical Assistance Facility

MAJOR MEDICAL INSURANCE: Health insurance to finance the expense of major illnesses and injuries. Major medical policies usually include a substantial deductible clause. Above the initial deductible, major medical insurance is characterized by large benefit maximums.

MAXIMUM FEE SCHEDULE: A compensation arrangement in which a participating physician agrees to accept the Schedule of Allowances as his total fee for covered services.

MAXIMUMS: The top limit of the amount a carrier will pay for a specific benefit or policy during a specified time period.

MCCA: Medicare Catastrophic Coverage Act of 1988, P.L. 100-360, enacted July 1, 1988 and repealed December 13, 1989.

MEDICAID: A state/federal government sponsored medical assistance program to enable eligible recipients to obtain essential medical care and services .

MEDICARE: A federal health insurance program for people 65 or over and for disabled persons with chronic renal disorders.

MEDICARE CATASTROPHIC COVERAGE ACT OF 1988: P.L. 100-330, enacted and repealed in 1989. Established ICD-9-CM coding requirements for all Medicare claims.

MEDICARE FEE SCHEDULE (MFS): A fee schedule developed by the PPRC and proposed for use by Medicare to pay for physician services. The MFS is based on RBRVS, a conversion factor and a geographic multiplier.

MEDICARE ECONOMIC INDEX (MEI): An index that tracks changes over time in physician practice costs and general earnings levels. A limitation on prevailing charges for Medicare services. See Prevailing Charge.

MEDIGAP INSURANCE: Health insurance policies provided by private carriers providing benefits not covered by Medicare, such as deductibles and coinsurance.

MEI: Medicare Economic Index

MFS: Medicare Fee Schedule

MODEL FEE SCHEDULE: The sample fee schedule developed by HCFA in 1990 from Phase I of the Hsaio study.

MODIFIERS: Codes used supplementally with CPT or HCPCS codes to indicate that the service has been changed in some way.

MSA: Metropolitan Statistical Area

MUA: Medically Underserved Area

NATIONAL CODES: See HCPCS

NATIONAL PRACTITIONER DATA BANK: A permanent record maintained by the U.S. Public Health Service of disciplinary actions taken against physicians and all payments made on behalf of physicians for actual or potential malpractice claims.

NO-FAULT INSURANCE: Automobile insurance that provides coverage against injury or loss without the need to determine responsibility for an accident.

NONPARTICIPATING PHYSICIAN (MEDICARE): A physician who does not sign a Medicare participation agreement, and therefore is not obligated to accept assignment on all claims. Frequently defined as NONPAR. See Participating Physician.

OBRA 80: Omnibus Budget Reconciliation Act of 1980. P.L. 96-499, enacted December 1980.

OBRA 86: Omnibus Budget Reconciliation Act of 1986. P.L. 99-509, enacted October 1986.

OBRA 87: Omnibus Budget Reconciliation Act of 1987. P.L. 100-203, enacted December 1987.

OBRA 90: Omnibus Budget Reconciliation Act of 1990. P.L. 101-508, enacted November 1990.

OIG: Office of the Inspector General

OUTCOME: The consequences of a medical intervention on a group of patients.

OVERVALUED PROCEDURE: A procedure considered to be overpriced based on its relative value.

PAR: Participating Physician and Supplier Program

PART A (MEDICARE): The Medicare Hospital Insurance program which covers hospital and related post-hospital services. As an entitlement program, it is available without payment of a premium. Beneficiaries are responsible for an initial deductible per spell of illness and coinsurance for some services.

PART B (MEDICARE): The Medicare Supplementary Medical Insurance program (SMI), which covers the costs of physician services, outpatient lab, x-ray, DME and certain other services. As a voluntary program, PartB requires payment of a monthly premium. Beneficiaries are responsible for a deductible and coinsurance payment for most covered services.

PARTICIPATING PHYSICIAN: A physician who signs a participation agreement, agreeing to accept assignment on all Medicare claims for a period of one year. Frequently referred to as PAR.

PARTICIPATING PHYSICIAN AND SUPPLIER PROGRAM (PAR): a program which provides financial and administrative incentives for physicians and suppliers to agree in advance to accept assignment on all Medicare claims for a period of one year.

PCF: Patient Compensation Fund

PEER REVIEW ORGANIZATION (PRO): An organization that reviews the medical necessity and the quality of care provided to Medicare beneficiaries.

PHYSICIANS PRACTICE COST AND INCOME SURVEY (PPCIS): A survey sponsored by HCFA of a national sample of physicians regarding practice characteristics, costs and reimbursement, conducted by the National Opinion Research Center in 1984 with a follow-up in 1987.

PLI: Professional Liability Insurance

POLICY HOLDER: See INSURED.

PPO: Preferred Provider Organization

PPRC: Physician Payment Review Commission

PPS: Prospective Payment System

PRACTICE EXPENSE: The cost of nonphysician resources incurred by the physician to provide physician services. Examples are salaries and the cost of fringe benefits received by nurses, physician assistants and receptionists who are employed by the physician, and the expenses associated with purchase and use of medical equipment and supplies in the physician's office.

PRACTICE GUIDELINES: Clinical recommendations for patient care, based on knowledge of effectiveness of medical practices and procedures.

PREAUTHORIZATION: See PRECERTIFICATION.

PRECERTIFICATION: The process of obtaining permission to perform a service from the insurance carrier before the service is performed.

PREDETERMINATION: The process of obtaining an estimate of what an insurance carrier will pay for service(s) before the service(s) is/are performed.

PREMIUM: An amount paid periodically to purchase medical insurance benefits.

PREVAILING CHARGE: One of the factors determining a physician's payment for service under Medicare. Currently set at the 75th percentile of customary charges for all physicians in a locality.

PRIMARY CARRIER: The insurance carrier which has first responsibility under Coordination of Benefits.

PROOF OF ELIGIBILITY: Evidence of eligibility provided by a patient in a public assistance program.

PRO: See Peer Review Organization

PROCEDURE CODING: See coding.

PROFESSIONAL COMPONENT: The part of the relative value or fee for a procedure that represents physician work.

PROFESSIONAL LIABILITY INSURANCE (PLI): The insurance physicians must purchase to help protect themselves from the financial risks associated with malpractice claims and awards.

ProPAC: Prospective Payment Assessment Committee

PROOF OF ELIGIBILITY: Evidence of eligiblity for insurance benefits.

PROVIDER: The person in relation to the insurance program who provides covered services and supplies to the beneficiary.

QA: Quality Assurance

QMB: Qualified Medicare Beneficiary

RBRVS [RESOURCE BASED RELATIVE VALUE SCALE]: A government mandated relative value system, based on a study conducted at Harvard University, that is to be used for calculating national fee schedules for services provided to Medicare patients.

REASONABLE CHARGE: The amount Medicare will pay for a covered service. This is usually the lowest of the actual, customary and prevailing charges.

RELATIVE VALUE SCALE: An index that assigns specific numeric values to medical services. Multiplying the relative value by a conversion factor results in a fee.

RELEASE OF INFORMATION: The patient's signature indicating consent to the release of information necessary for settlement of his or her insurance claim.

RESOURCE BASED RELATIVE VALUE SCALE: See RBRVS

RESOURCE COSTS: The costs of the inputs used by an efficient physician to provide a service or procedure, including both the costs of the physician's own time and effort and the costs of nonphysician inputs.

RVS: Relative Value Scale

RVU: Relative Value Unit

SCHEDULE OF ALLOWANCES: A list of specific amounts which the carrier will pay toward the cost of medical services provided.

SECONDARY CARRIER: The insurance carrier which is second in responsibility under Coordination of Benefits.

SMI [SUPPLEMENTARY MEDICAL INSURANCE]: Medicare Part B which helps pay for services other than hospital (Part A) services.

SMS: Socioeconomic Monitoring System

SOCIOECONOMIC MONITORING SYSTEM (SMS): A system of annual and supplemental surveys of physicians directed by the American Medical Association Center for Health Policy Research. The SMS provides information on a range of characteristics including physician's earnings, expense, work patterns, and fees.

SPECIALTY DIFFERENTIAL: The difference in the relative value or amount paid for the same service when performed by different specialists.

SSI: Supplemental Security Income

SUBSCRIBER: See INSURED.

SUPERBILL: A multi-part form which provides sufficient information so that patients may file their own insurance claim forms.

SUPPLIER: Providers, other than practitioners, of health care services. Under Medicare, these include independent labs, durable medical equipment suppliers, ambulance services, orthotists, prosthetists, and portable X-ray providers.

TABLE OF ALLOWANCES: See SCHEDULE OF ALLOWANCES.

TECHNICAL COMPONENT: The part of the relative value or fee for a procedure that represents the costs of doing the procedure excluding physician work.

TEFRA: Tax Equity and Fiscal Responsibility Act of 1982. P.L. 97-248, enacted September 1982.

TW: Total Work

UCR [USUAL, CUSTOMARY AND REASONABLE]: A method of determining benefits by comparing the physician's charges to those of his or her peers in the same community and specialty.

UI: Urban Institute

UNBUNDLING: The process of coding, billing and requesting payment for services that are generally included in a global charge.

UPCODING: The process of selecting a code for a service that is more intense, extensive, or has a higher charge, than the service actually provided.

UNDERWRITER: See CARRIER.

URVG: Uniform Relative Value Guide

UTILIZATION REVIEW: The process of reviewing services provided to determine if those services were medically necessary and appropriate.

VOLUME (BEHAVIORAL) OFFSET: The change in the volume of services that occurs in reaction to a change in fees. A 50 percent volume offset means that half of the savings from fee reductions will be offset by increase volume of services.

VOLUME PERFORMANCE STANDARD (VPS): A mechanism included in OBRA89 to adjust fee updates based on how annual increases in actual expenditures compare to previously determined performance standard rates of increase.

WORKERS' COMPENSATION: State laws which provide coverage of medical expenses for employees who are injured during performance of their work.

IMPORTANT FORMS AND DOCUMENTS

CHAPTER SUMMARY

The output or results of any management information system depends on the quality of the data input into the system. The quality of the input is dependent on the method of collecting the data as well as the quality of the people using and managing the system. In the computer field, this is often referred to by the acronym GIGO, which translates into "Garbage In, Garbage Out".

In order to collect the data required for creating accounts, posting charges, and billing patients and insurance carriers properly, the practice must develop, maintain and use proper billing forms and documents. The two most important points to remember regarding collecting this data are that the best time to obtain billing information is when the patient is first seen, plus, the success of the billing system is dependent on the quality of the data collected.

There are sometimes logistical problems involved in the data collection process. Some medical practices, such as independent laboratories, *never* see the patient. Hospital consultations, emergency room services, inpatient surgeries without pre-operative office visits are all examples of situations where the patient is not seen in the office prior to provision of services and may not be seen in the office after provision of services. This means that either the physician must collect the necessary forms, including signatures, required to bill the patient and/or insurance carriers or the billing personnel must develop a telephone and form letter approach to collecting the required billing data from the patient and/or the hospital and/or the referring physician.

The wellmanaged practice will not only make sure that they are using proper forms and documents, but will also develop systems to make sure that all required forms and documents are procured, are complete, and are filed appropriately.

KEY POINTS REGARDING FORMS AND DOCUMENTS

1. Billing forms and documents provide the fundamental information needed for you to bill insurance carriers and/or patients.

2. Some documents, such as release and assignment forms, are required by law.

3. The best time to collect billing information is the first time you see the patient.

4. Forms and documents management can make a significant difference in your reimbursement.

5. Good forms and documents management puts you in control of the reimbursement process.

OVERVIEW OF IMPORTANT FORMS AND DOCUMENTS

PATIENT REGISTRATION — a form used to record basic patient data such as name, address, phone numbers, employer, insurance carrier, member and group numbers, next of kin, etc.

RELEASE & ASSIGNMENT BENEFITS — a form which authorizes the practice to release information regarding diagnosis and treatment to the patient's insurance carrier. May be part of patient registration form or superbill. May be permanent or temporary.

PREAUTHORIZATION FORM — a form used to record information regarding a planned procedure or service which requires approval by the patient's insurance carrier or a government agency such as Medicare and Medicaid.

CERTIFICATION FORMS — a form used to record information obtained from the patient's insurance carrier which verifies coverage.

SUPERBILL	also known as an encounter form, visit slip, fee ticket, charge slip, etc. and used to record the services performed, the reason (diagnosis) for the service and may include recall, next appointment, release and assignment, and payment receipt as well.
INSURANCE FORM	a form used to bill the patient's insurance carrier. The HCFA 1500 is the most common form, however there are still different forms required by some states. The most common form exception is Medicaid.
MEDICARE SURGICAL FINANCIAL FORM	a form used by NON-PAR physicians to notify Medicare patients that the fee for a non-emergency surgical procedure will be $500.00 or more. The form is not required if the fee is less than $500.00 or if the NON-PAR physician is accepting assignment.
MEDICARE MEDICAL NECESSITY FORM	a notice given to the Medicare patient in advance of treatment indicating that Medicare is likely to deny payment for the stated services, and making the patient financially responsible if Medicare does deny payment.

Each of these forms and documents is discussed in detail in this chapter along with samples and illustrations.

THE PATIENT REGISTRATION FORM

The Patient Registration Form is usually the first document that is completed by the patient or patient's representative. This form is used to collect all information necessary to identify the patient to your practice, bill charges to the patient, insurance carrier(s) and/or other third parties. The form may also include additional information such as the patient's, or guarantor's employment, referral information, emergency notification and almost any other information the practice may want to collect at this time. If you are using a computer or billing service, the form will usually include spaces for account numbers and various codes to indicate assignment, account types, etc.

We strongly recommend that all patient registration documents be printed on two-part carbon-less forms. This provides a copy for billing purposes and a copy for the medical records. In addition, patients should be asked occasionally if they have moved, changed jobs, changed insurance carriers, etc. so that a new registration form can be completed for the practice's records.

The Patient Registration Form may be combined with a Superbill, see chapter **Designing a Better SUPERBILL,** and/or a Release and Assignment Form. The more forms you can combine, the less pieces of paper you will have to keep track of. Plus, your forms cost will be reduced.

The sample patient registration form on the facing page, provides an example of a form designed specifically for use with computer systems. Note that in addition to having wide spaces for the practice or patient to write in information, all of the coding choices for billing codes, account types, and relationships are printed on the form. The form is also designed in the specific input order of the computer system used by this practice which makes data entry easier.

THE PATIENT REGISTRATION FORM

PLEASE PRINT

PATIENT REGISTRATION
•PROFESSIONAL DATA SYSTEMS   #302 3/83

DATE		NEW	ADD	CHANGES

PRACTICE	ACCOUNT NUMBER	LAST NAME		FIRST NAME	MI
	AFFIX LABEL HERE				

STREET ADDRESS	APT. #	CITY, STATE	ZIP CODE

SEX	BIRTH DATE	SOCIAL SECURITY NUMBER	HOME TELEPHONE NUMBER	BILLING CODES	TYPE
			( )		

DEPENDENT NAME	BIRTH DATE	REL.	DEPENDENT NAME	BIRTH DATE	REL.
1.			2.		

INSURANCE COMPANY (PRIMARY)

CODE	NAME

INSURANCE COMPANY ADDRESS

MEMBER OR MEDICARE NUMBER	GROUP NUMBER

SUBSCRIBER'S NAME (IF NOT PATIENT)	REL

INSURANCE COMPANY (SECONDARY)

CODE	NAME

INSURANCE COMPANY ADDRESS

MEMBER/POLICY NUMBER	GROUP NUMBER

SUBSCRIBER'S NAME (IF NOT PATIENT)	REL.

EMPLOYMENT INFORMATION

EMPLOYER NAME	WORK TELEPHONE ( )
STREET ADDRESS	OCCUPATION
CITY, STATE	ZIP CODE

THIRD PARTY BILLING (OR REMARKS)

THIRD PARTY NAME

STREET ADDRESS

CITY, STATE	ZIP CODE

REFERRED BY

NAME	TELEPHONE ( )	REF. CODE	DR.

(FOR PRACTICE USE ONLY)   EMERGENCY NOTIFICATION

DRIVER'S LICENSE NUMBER	NAME	RELATIONSHIP
TELEPHONE ( )	STREET ADDRESS	CITY, STATE	ZIP CODE

BILLING CODES

20.	BILL PATIENT ONLY	36-46	BILL INSURANCE ONLY (AA)
21	BILL 3RD PARTY	36	BILL PATIENT & INS. (AA)
31	BILL PATIENT & INS. (NA)	46	NO STATEMENT - NO INS.
21-31	BILL 3RD PARTY & INS. (NA)		

TYPE = ACCOUNT TYPE CODES

A INDUSTRIAL	N MEDICARE & PVT.	X TWO PVT INS.
G MEDI-MEDI	P NO INSURANCE	Y PVT & MEDI-CAL
I ONE PVT INS.	W MEDI-CAL	Z MEDICARE

REL = RELATIONSHIP CODES

3—PATIENT IS MALE SPOUSE	5—PATIENT IS MALE CHILD	7—PATIENT IS MALE OTHER
4—PATIENT IS FEMALE SPOUSE	6—PATIENT IS FEMALE CHILD	8—PATIENT IS FEMALE OTHER

PDS COPY

RELEASE AND ASSIGNMENT FORM

This form is frequently separated into two different forms, a release form and an assignment form, however, our experience is that a combination form works just fine. This form is extremely important for two reasons. First, it authorizes the practice to release medical information to insurance carriers and administrators; and, second, it directs the insurance carrier to send payment directly to the practice.

In today's litigious environment, it is critical that the practice protect itself in every way from potential lawsuits. Failure to obtain a release signature prior to filing an insurance claim, or even prior to verifying benefits or requesting preauthorization, could result in a serious invasion of privacy lawsuit by a patient. We strongly advise that for diagnoses of a sensitive nature, such as mental illness, alcoholism, drug addiction, and AIDS, that you bypass the patient's employer totally if possible and deal directly with the insurance carrier. The sample form is designed to cover all the critical points of the release and assignment processes.

Note that our sample form includes four important elements; namely: 1) release authorization, 2) assignment of benefits, 3) conditional lifetime authorization, and 4) authorization to use a copy of the form in lieu of the orginal. This particular form has been used for several years by Professional Data Systems, our medical billing service, to file insurance claims nationwide. However, forms, requirements and wording may vary from state to state, so you should check with your state's insurance commissioner for specific requirements.

RELEASE AND ASSIGNMENT FORM

RELEASE AND ASSIGNMENT

TO MY INSURANCE CARRIER(S):

1. I authorize the release of any medical information necessary to process my insurance claim(s).

2. I authorize and request payment of medical benefits directly to my physicians.

3. I agree that this authorization will cover all medical services rendered until such authorization is revoked by me.

4. I agree that a photocopy of this form may be used in lieu of the original.

_____   _____/_____/_____
Signed (Patient or representative)   **Date**

_____
Patient's Name (Printed)

PREAUTHORIZATION FORM

Preauthorization, also known as precertification, is the process of obtaining permission to perform a procedure or service from the insurance carrier before the service is performed. Preauthorization is required by Medicare for selective procedures, Medicaid for elective procedures, and by many other insurance plans as well. The most common targets of preauthorization requirements are overutilized procedures, elective surgeries and non-emergency hospital admissions. Failure to obtain preauthorization in advance of performing procedures may result in denial of your claims, delays, or reduction of payments by as much as 50 percent.

Most patients do not read their insurance contracts, therefore they do not know if and when preauthorization is required. That means that it is your responsibility to know (or find out), if you want to get paid properly. The sample form on the facing page, known officially as a Treatment Authorization Request (TAR), is used as a preauthorization form for California Medicaid (Medi-Cal).

PREAUTHORIZATION FORM

CONFIDENTIAL PATIENT INFORMATION

STATE

SERVICE CATEGORY

TYPEWRITER ALIGNMENT
Elite Pica

F.I. USE ONLY

FOR F.I. USE ONLY

C C N

TREATMENT AUTHORIZATION REQUEST
STATE OF CALIFORNIA DEPARTMENT OF HEALTH SERVICES

TYPEWRITER ALIGNMENT
Elite Pica

(PLEASE TYPE) FOR PROVIDER USE (PLEASE TYPE)

VERBAL CONTROL NO.

TYPE OF SERVICE REQUESTED
DRUG OTHER

REQUEST IS RETROACTIVE?
YES NO

IS PATIENT MEDICARE ELIGIBLE?
YES NO

PROVIDER PHONE NO.
AREA

PATIENT'S AUTHORIZED REPRESENTATIVE (IF ANY) ENTER NAME AND ADDRESS

PLEASE TYPE YOUR NAME AND ADDRESS HERE

PROVIDER NAME AND ADDRESS

PROVIDER NUMBER

FOR STATE USE

PROVIDER; YOUR REQUEST IS:

APPROVED AS REQUESTED   DENIED   DEFERRED

APPROVED AS MODIFIED (ITEMS MARKED BELOW AS AUTHORIZED MAY BE CLAIMED)   JACKSON VS RANK PARAGRAPH CODE

NAME AND ADDRESS OF PATIENT

PATIENT NAME (LAST, FIRST, M.I.)

MEDI-CAL IDENTIFICATION NO

STREET ADDRESS

SEX   AGE   DATE OF BIRTH

CITY, STATE, ZIP CODE

PHONE NUMBER
AREA (   )

PATIENT STATUS:
HOME   BOARD & CARE
SNF/ICF   ACUTE HOSPITAL

By

MEDI-CAL CONSULTANT
ID #   DATE

REVIEW COMMENTS INDICATOR

COMMENTS/EXPLANATION

DIAGNOSIS DESCRIPTION:

ICD-9-CM DIAGNOSIS CODE

MEDICAL JUSTIFICATION:

RETROACTIVE AUTHORIZATION GRANTED IN ACCORDANCE WITH SECTION 51003 (B)

1 2 3 4 5 6

LINE NO	AUTHORIZED YES	NO	APPROVED UNITS	SPECIFIC SERVICES REQUESTED	UNITS OF SERVICE	PROCEDURE OR DRUG CODE	QUANTITY	CHARGES
1								$
2								$
3								$
4								$
5								$
6								$

TO THE BEST OF MY KNOWLEDGE, THE ABOVE INFORMATION IS TRUE, ACCURATE AND COMPLETE AND THE REQUESTED SERVICES ARE MEDICALLY INDICATED AND NECESSARY TO THE HEALTH OF THE PATIENT.

SIGNATURE OF PHYSICIAN OR PROVIDER   TITLE   DATE

AUTHORIZATION IS VALID FOR SERVICES PROVIDED
FROM DATE   TO DATE

TAR CONTROL NUMBER
OFFICE   SEQUENCE NUMBER

19005602

NOTE: AUTHORIZATION DOES NOT GUARANTEE PAYMENT. PAYMENT IS SUBJECT TO PATIENT'S ELIGIBILITY. BE SURE THE IDENTIFICATION CARD IS CURRENT BEFORE RENDERING SERVICE.   SEND TO FIELD SERVICES (F.I. COPY)   SEE YOUR PROVIDER MANUAL FOR ASSISTANCE REGARDING THE COMPLETION OF THIS FORM   50 1 12 87

PRECERTIFICATION FORM

More and more insurance carriers are requiring precertification, as a condition of their policies, before they will agree to reimburse for certain hospital admissions, inpatient and/or outpatient surgeries, and elective procedures. The purpose of precertification is to reduce health care costs by reducing or eliminating unnecessary procedures and services.

The process of pre-certification generally involves informing the insurance carrier of your specific plans for a patient and the insurance carrier granting permission for the procedure if covered under the patient's insurance plan. With over 2,000 insurance carriers, and tens of thousands of different insurance plans, it is impossible to know in advance the specific requirements with regard to precertification for them all. While the requirements are clearly spelled out in the patient's insurance policy, the patient's generally never read the policies and they don't usually have them when they come to your office.

While precertification may appear to be an administrative burden, it is in reality an important tool in your reimbursement management process. Even if pre-certification is not specifically required by an insurance carrier, the process can be used to verify benefits and coverage in all or selective situations.

The form on the facing page is an example of a precertification form which also may be used to verify benefits and coverage. See the chapter **Dealing with Insurance Carriers** for further discussion of this process.

PRE-CERTIFICATION FORM

InsuranceCarrier_____

Certification for [ ] admission and/or [ ] surgery and/or [ ] _____

PatientName_____

StreetAddress_____

City/State/Zip_____

Telephone _____Date of birth _____

SubscriberName_____

Employer_____

Member No. _____ Group No. _____

Admittingphysician_____

Provider No. _____

Hospital/Facility_____

Planned Admission/Procedure Date _____

Diagnosis/Symptoms_____

Treatment/Procedure_____

Estimated Length of Stay _____

ComplicatingFactors_____

Second Opinion Required [ ] Yes [ ] No If yes, [ ] Obtained

Corroborating physician _____

Insurance Carrier Representative _____

Approval [ ] Yes [ ] No If yes, Certification No. _____

If No, Reason(s) for Denial _____

SUPERBILL

The Superbill, also known as a Charge Ticket, Visit Slip, Encounter Form, Fee Ticket, etc., is the most common method of recording services, procedures and supplies. The form may be used as a substitute for an insurance claim form and may be used to record other information, such as next appointment, recall, payment receipt, etc.

The sample superbill on the facing page is designed for a practice that is using a computer billing system and has repetitive patients. Practices with repetitive patients should collect patient registration information on another form in order to have more space available on the superbill for procedures and diagnoses. See the chapter **Designing a Better SUPERBILL** for a complete discussion of this topic along with sample superbills by specialty.

SUPERBILL

DATE OF SERVICE	ACCOUNT NUMBER			INTERNAL MEDICINE GROUP	4186

ACCOUNT NAME (LAST, FIRST)

INTERNAL MEDICINE GROUP
4727 Wilshire Boulevard
Los Angeles, CA 90010
(708) 920-0700
LICENSE: P12345
FEIN: 95-4210732

TIME

☐ NEW PATIENT   ☐ ASSIGNED?

DX #1	DX #2	DX #3	DX #4

✓	CODE	DESCRIPTION	E/M	DX	FEE	✓	CODE	DESCRIPTION	DX	FEE	✓	CODE	DESCRIPTION	DX	FEE
		OFFICE VISITS NEW PATIENT						INJECTIONS AND IMMUNIZATIONS					LABORATORY (Cont'd)		
	90000	Brief	99201				90702	Immunization; DT				84295	Blood Sodium		
	90010	Limited	99202				90703	Immunization; Tetanus Toxoid				84450	SGOT		
	90015	Intermediate	99203				90724	Immunization; Influenza				84460	SGPT		
	90017	Extended	99204				90782	Injection, IM/SQ				84478	Blood Triglycerides		
	90020	Comprehensive	99205				90784	Injection, IV				85014	Hematocrit		
		OFFICE VISITS ESTABLISHED PATIENT					90788	Injection, Antibiotic				85022	Automated Hemogram		
	90030	Minimal	99211									85031	Manual Hemogram		
	90040	Brief	99212									85048	White Blood Cell Count		
	90050	Limited	99213									85580	Blood Platelet Count		
	90060	Intermediate	99214					RADIOLOGY				85610	Prothrombin Time		
	90070	Extended	99215				71010	X-Ray Exam Chest				85651	RBC Sedimentation Rate		
	90080	Comprehensive					71020	X-Ray Exam Chest				86585	Skin Test, TB		
		CONSULTATIONS INITIAL										87060	Culture, Throat or Nose		
	90605	Intermediate	99242												
	90610	Extended	99243					LABORATORY							
	90620	Comprehensive	99244				80019	Lab Panel 19+ Tests					SUPPLIES		
							80052	Premarital Profile				99070	Supplies & Materials		
							80070	Thyroid Panel							
							80072	Arthritis Panel							
		PROCEDURES					80060	Hypertension Panel							
	10060*	Drain Skin Lesion					80061	Lipid Profile					MISCELLANEOUS		
	20550*	Injection, Tendon Sheath					81000	Urinalysis				99361	Med Conference, 30 Min		
	36415*	Routine Venipuncture					82270	Stool for Occult Blood				99362	Med Conference, 60 Min		
	45330	Sigmoidoscopy					82310	Calcium				99371	Telephone Call, Brief		
	93000	EKG Complete					82465	Serum Cholesterol				99372	Telephone Call, Intermediate		
	93040	Rhythm EKG with Report					82565	Blood Creatinine				99000	Specimen Handling		
	94010	Spirometry Complete					82643	Ria for Digoxin				99080	Special Reports		
							82951	Glucose Tolerance Test							
							83718	Blood Lipoprotein							
							84075	Alkaline Phosphatase							

UNLISTED PROCEDURE	CODE	DESCRIPTION	FEE

DIAGNOSIS   ICD-9 CM

☐ Abnormal loss weight 783.2	☐ B.neoplasm lg bowel 211.3	☐ Diaphragmatic hernia 553.3	☐ Hypercholesterolemia 272.0	☐ Myeloma multiple 203.0	☐ Pneumonia, org NOS 486
☐ acute bronchitis 466.0	☐ Bronchitis NOS 490	☐ Diverticula colon 562.1	☐ Hyperlipidemia 272.4	☐ MI unsp 410.90	☐ Polycythemia vera 283.4
☐ Acute URI NOS 465.9	☐ Bronchitis obstr chr 491.2	☐ Diverticulitis colon 562.11	☐ Hypertension benign 401.1	☐ MI old 412	☐ Polymyalgia rheum 725
☐ Allergic rhinitis 477.9	☐ Calculus kidney 595.0	☐ Diverticulosis colon 562.10	☐ Hypertension essential 401.0	☐ Nasopharyngitis acute 460	☐ Preop chest xray/EKG V99.99
☐ Alzheimer's disease 331.0	☐ Cardiomyopathies 425.4	☐ Dizziness & giddiness 780.4	☐ Hypertension NOS 401.9	☐ Neuralgia, neuritis 792.2	☐ Prostate hyperplasia 600
☐ Anemia iron def unsp 280.9	☐ Cataract NOS 366.9	☐ Duodenal ulcer unsp 532.9	☐ Hypertens heart dis NOS 402.90	☐ Obesity 278.0	☐ Pul heart dis unsp 416.9
☐ Anemia unsp 285.9	☐ Cerebrovasc dis other 437.0	☐ Dyspepsia 536.8	☐ Hypopotassemia 276.8	☐ Osteoarthrosis unsp 715.90	☐ Pyrexia unk origin 780.6
☐ Anemia protein def 281.9	☐ Cerebral Thrombosis 434.0	☐ Edema 782.3	☐ Hypothyroidism unsp 244.9	☐ Osteoporosis NOS 733.00	☐ Renal failure 586
☐ Angina pectoris unsp 413.9	☐ Cerebrovasc dis NOS 437.9	☐ Emphysema other 492.8	☐ Impacted cerumen 380.4	☐ Osteoarthrosis gen 715.0	☐ Rheumatoid arthritis 714.0
☐ Anxiety state NOS 300.00	☐ Chest pain NEC 786.59	☐ Esophagitis 530.1	☐ Intermed cor syndrome 411.1	☐ Other abn blood chem 790.6	☐ Rhythm disord, other 427.89
☐ Aortic valve disord 424.1	☐ Chest pain unsp 786.50	☐ Gastritis unsp 535.5	☐ Intest obstruction NOS 560.9	☐ Other comp med care 999.9	☐ Senile dementia 290.0
☐ Aortcoronary bypass V45.81	☐ Chr airway obstr NEC 496	☐ Gen osteoarthrosis 715.09	☐ Intracereb hemorr 431	☐ Other bursitis 727.3	☐ Sx: abd pain, cramps 789.0
☐ Apoplexia 436	☐ Chr isch heart dis NEC 414.8	☐ Gout NOS 274.9	☐ Irritable colon 564.1	☐ Other cellulitis unsp 682.9	☐ Sx: nausea & vomiting 787.0
☐ Arrhythmia 427.9	☐ Chr renal failure 585	☐ Gouty arthritis 274.0	☐ Isch heart dis unsp chr 414.9	☐ Pain in limb 729.5	☐ Sx: headache face pain 784.0
☐ Arthropathy unsp 716.9	☐ Cirrhosis liver 471.5	☐ Heart dis isch NEC 411.8	☐ Isch heart dis chronic 414.0	☐ Painful respiration 786.52	☐ Sx: shortness breath 786.09
☐ ASCVD 429.2	☐ Constipation 564.0	☐ Heart fail congestive 428.0	☐ Kidney disord unsp 593.9	☐ Palpitations 785.1	☐ Syncope & collapse 780.2
☐ Asthma w/o status 493.90	☐ Contact dermatitis 692.9	☐ Heart failure NOS 428.9	☐ Lumbago 724.2	☐ Parkinson disease 332.0	☐ Systemic lupus eryth 710.0
☐ Atherosclerosis gen 440.9	☐ Convulsions, seizures 780.3	☐ Hematuria benign ess 599.7	☐ Lymphomas NEC 202.8	☐ Peptic ulcer unsp 533.9	☐ Thyrotoxicosis NOS 242.9
☐ Atrial fibrillation 427.31	☐ Cough 786.2	☐ Hemiplegia 342.9	☐ Malaise & fatigue 780.7	☐ Periph vasc dis unsp 443.9	☐ Trans cereb isch unsp 435.9
☐ Atrial flutter 427.32	☐ Cystitis unsp 595.9	☐ Hemorr GI tract unsp 578.9	☐ Melena blood in stool 587.1	☐ Pernicious anemia 281.0	☐ Unsp septicemia 038.9
☐ backache unsp 724.5	☐ Dehydration 276.5	☐ Hemorr rectum & anus 569.3	☐ Mitral valve disord 424.0	☐ Pharyngitis acute 462	☐ Unsp sinusitis chr 473.9
☐ B.hypertensive hrt dis 402.1	☐ Depress disord NEC 311	☐ Hemorrhoids unsp 455.6	☐ Mixed hyperlipid 272.2	☐ Phlebitis unsp 451.9	☐ Urinary tract infection 599.0
	☐ Diabetes w/comp NOS 250.00	☐ Herpes zoster 053.9	☐ Myalgia unsp 729.1	☐ Pleurisy unsp 511.9	

UNLISTED DIAGNOSIS	CODE	DESCRIPTION

REMARKS OR INSTRUCTIONS	

RELEASE & ASSIGNMENT	RECALL & RETURN	ACCOUNTING INFORMATION	
I authorize release of any information necessary to process my insurance claim and assign and request payment directly to my physicians.	RETURN	PRIOR BALANCE	
	☐ DAYS ☐ WEEKS ☐ MONTHS	TODAY'S CHARGES	
SIGNED		TOTAL DUE	
	NEXT APPOINTMENT	AM	AMOUNT PAID	
DATE	DATE _____ TIME _____ PM	NEW BALANCE	

REV. 01/92

INSURANCE CLAIM FORM

The HCFA1500 is the most commonly used insurance claim form. The form is mandated by Medicare and accepted by virtually all private insurance carriers. The notable exception to the use of the HCFA1500 is by Medicaid carriers, which are frequently data processing companies instead of insurance carriers.

See the chapter **Dealing with Insurance Carriers** for a complete discussion of the HCFA1500 and how to complete it properly.

INSURANCE CLAIM FORM

| PICA | | | | **HEALTH INSURANCE CLAIM FORM** | | PICA |

CARRIER

| 1. MEDICARE | MEDICAID | CHAMPUS | CHAMPVA | GROUP HEALTH PLAN | FECA BLK LUNG | OTHER | 1a. INSURED'S I.D. NUMBER | (FOR PROGRAM IN ITEM 1) |
| (Medicare #) | (Medicaid #) | (Sponsor's SSN) | (VA File #) | (SSN or ID) | (SSN) | (ID) | | |

2. PATIENT'S NAME (Last Name, First Name, Middle Initial)

3. PATIENT'S BIRTH DATE MM DD YY SEX M F

4. INSURED'S NAME (Last Name, First Name, Middle Initial)

5. PATIENT'S ADDRESS (No., Street)

6. PATIENT RELATIONSHIP TO INSURED Self Spouse Child Other

7. INSURED'S ADDRESS (No., Street)

CITY STATE

8. PATIENT STATUS Single Married Other

CITY STATE

ZIP CODE TELEPHONE (Include Area Code) ( )

Employed Full-Time Student Part-Time Student

ZIP CODE TELEPHONE (INCLUDE AREA CODE) ( )

9. OTHER INSURED'S NAME (Last Name, First Name, Middle Initial)

10. IS PATIENT'S CONDITION RELATED TO:

11. INSURED'S POLICY GROUP OR FECA NUMBER

a. OTHER INSURED'S POLICY OR GROUP NUMBER

a. EMPLOYMENT? (CURRENT OR PREVIOUS) YES NO

a. INSURED'S DATE OF BIRTH MM DD YY SEX M F

b. OTHER INSURED'S DATE OF BIRTH MM DD YY SEX M F

b. AUTO ACCIDENT? PLACE (State) YES NO

b. EMPLOYER'S NAME OR SCHOOL NAME

c. EMPLOYER'S NAME OR SCHOOL NAME

c. OTHER ACCIDENT? YES NO

c. INSURANCE PLAN NAME OR PROGRAM NAME

d. INSURANCE PLAN NAME OR PROGRAM NAME

10d. RESERVED FOR LOCAL USE

d. IS THERE ANOTHER HEALTH BENEFIT PLAN? YES NO **If yes**, return to and complete item 9 a-d.

READ BACK OF FORM BEFORE COMPLETING & SIGNING THIS FORM.

12. PATIENT'S OR AUTHORIZED PERSON'S SIGNATURE I authorize the release of any medical or other information necessary to process this claim. I also request payment of government benefits either to myself or to the party who accepts assignment below.

SIGNED DATE

13. INSURED'S OR AUTHORIZED PERSON'S SIGNATURE I authorize payment of medical benefits to the undersigned physician or supplier for services described below.

SIGNED

PATIENT AND INSURED INFORMATION

14. DATE OF CURRENT: MM DD YY ILLNESS (First symptom) OR INJURY (Accident) OR PREGNANCY(LMP)

15. IF PATIENT HAS HAD SAME OR SIMILAR ILLNESS GIVE FIRST DATE MM DD YY

16. DATES PATIENT UNABLE TO WORK IN CURRENT OCCUPATION MM DD YY MM DD YY FROM TO

17. NAME OF REFERRING PHYSICIAN OR OTHER SOURCE

17a. I.D. NUMBER OF REFERRING PHYSICIAN

18. HOSPITALIZATION DATES RELATED TO CURRENT SERVICES MM DD YY MM DD YY FROM TO

19. RESERVED FOR LOCAL USE

20. OUTSIDE LAB? YES NO $ CHARGES

21. DIAGNOSIS OR NATURE OF ILLNESS OR INJURY. (RELATE ITEMS 1,2,3 OR 4 TO ITEM 24E BY LINE)

1. |___.___ 3. |___.___

2. |___.___ 4. |___.___

22. MEDICAID RESUBMISSION CODE ORIGINAL REF. NO.

23. PRIOR AUTHORIZATION NUMBER

24.	A				B	C	D		E	F	G	H	I	J	K
	DATE(S) OF SERVICE				Place of Service	Type of Service	PROCEDURES, SERVICES, OR SUPPLIES (Explain Unusual Circumstances)		DIAGNOSIS CODE	$ CHARGES	DAYS OR UNITS	EPSDT Family Plan	EMG	COB	RESERVED FOR LOCAL USE
	From MM DD YY		To MM DD YY				CPT/HCPCS	MODIFIER							
1															
2															
3															
4															
5															
6															

PHYSICIAN OR SUPPLIER INFORMATION

25. FEDERAL TAX I.D. NUMBER SSN EIN

26. PATIENT'S ACCOUNT NO.

27. ACCEPT ASSIGNMENT? (For govt. claims, see back) YES NO

28. TOTAL CHARGE $

29. AMOUNT PAID $

30. BALANCE DUE $

31. SIGNATURE OF PHYSICIAN OR SUPPLIER INCLUDING DEGREES OR CREDENTIALS (I certify that the statements on the reverse apply to this bill and are made a part thereof.)

SIGNED DATE

32. NAME AND ADDRESS OF FACILITY WHERE SERVICES WERE RENDERED (If other than home or office)

33. PHYSICIAN'S, SUPPLIER'S BILLING NAME, ADDRESS, ZIP CODE & PHONE #

PIN# GRP#

(APPROVED BY AMA COUNCIL ON MEDICAL SERVICE 8/88)

PLEASE PRINT OR TYPE

FORM HCFA-1500 (12-90)
FORM OWCP-1500 FORM RRB-1500

MEDICARE SURGICAL FINANCIAL DISCLOSURE FORM

OBRA 86 established the requirement for NON-PAR physicians who do not submit an assigned claim for non-emergency surgical procedures with a fee of $500.00 or more to disclose certain financial information in writing to the Medicare beneficiary. The provision does not apply if the NON-PAR physician accepts assignment, or if the fee is less than $500.00.

Failure to obtain the patient's signature in advance of procedures subject to this regulation will result in the physician being required to refund all money collected in excess of the Medicare payment. Failure to refund the money may result in fines of up to $2000.00 per procedure and/or exclusion from the Medicare program. HCFA recommends the general format and wording on the facing page for this form.

MEDICARE SURGICAL FINANCIAL DISCLOSURE FORM

Dear Patient:

I do not plan to accept assignment for your surgery. The law requires that where assignment is not taken and the charge is $ 500.00 or more, the following information must be provided prior to surgery. These estimates assume that you have met the $ 75.00 annual Part B Medicare deductible.

Type of surgery   _____

Estimated charge $ _____

Medicare estimated payment $ _____

Your estimated payment $ _____

___/___/___   _____
Date   Beneficiary Signature

MEDICARE MEDICAL NECESSITY FORM

Medicare does not pay for procedures, supplies and/or services that are considered by Medicare criteria to be "not reasonable and necessary" for the stated diagnosis. This provision also applies to procedures, supplies and/or services that are unproven, experimental and/or investigational.

Note that this provision does not apply to services that are generally excluded or non-covered items such as personal comfort items, routine physicals, eyeglasses, hearing aids, cosmetic surgery, etc., or to certain services, such as those involving injections given by a paramedical or to services performed by physician extenders, such as physician assistants and other allied health professionals.

If Medicare does not pay, the patient is required to pay in some situations, and in others, the physician is not paid at all. Medicare regulations specify refund of any patient payments in these situations unless the patient was notified in advance that Medicare was not likely to pay for the specific service and the patient agreed to pay the physician directly. HCFA has developed acceptable wording for the advance notice and financial agreement form as illustrated on the sample form on the facing page.

MEDICARE MEDICAL NECESSITY FORM

PHYSICIAN NOTICE

Medicare will only pay for services that it determines to be "reasonable and necessary" under section 1862(a)(1) of the Medicare law. If Medicare determines that a particular service, although it would otherwise be covered, is "not reasonable and necessary" under Medicare program standards, Medicare will deny payment for that service. I believe that, in your case, Medicare is likely to deny payment for:

_____

_____

for the following reasons:

_____

_____

BENEFICIARY AGREEMENT

I have been notified by my physician that he or she believes that, in my case, Medicare is likely to deny payment for the services identified above, for the reasons stated. If Medicare denies payment, I agree to be personally and fully responsible for payment.

_____   ____/____/____

Signed (Beneficiary Signature)   **Date**

PROCEDURE CODING WITH CPT & HCPCS

CHAPTER SUMMARY

This section deals with one of the most important parts of the reimbursement puzzle: how to use CPT and HCPCS to code properly for the procedures and services you perform and the supplies and materials you use or distribute. Selection of the proper coding system and the proper code has a tremendous impact on your reimbursement. Prior to 1983 there were over 120 different coding systems in use in the United States. In order to bill insurance claims properly, the medical practice had to keep track of numerous codes and coding systems, as well as special claim forms in many cases. The complexity of the coding issue was one of the reasons that many practices started giving their patients superbills so that the patient could bill their own insurance.

This section provides a fundamental understanding of the CPT and HCPCS coding systems, including format and conventions. Steps for accurate and precise coding are defined along with critical coding and billing issues such as the use of modifiers, levels of service, multiple procedures, etc. Following the general discussion of CPT and HCPCS, a discussion of each of the specialty sections appears.

CPT

CPT is an acronym for Current Procedural Terminology. This coding system is a derivation of the California Relative Value System (CRVS) originally published by the California Medical Association in 1956. *Physicians' Current Procedural Terminology*, Fourth Edition, commonly known as CPT-4 or just plain CPT, is a listing of over 7,000 codes and descriptions used for reporting medical services and procedures performed by physicians and other medical professionals. The purpose of the coding system is to provide a uniform language that accurately describes medical, surgical, and diagnostic services, and provides an effective means for reliable nationwide communication among physicians, patients, and insurance carriers. CPT 1992 is the most recent revision of a work that first appeared in 1966.

CPT codes and terminology serve a variety of important functions in the field of medical nomenclature for the reporting of physician procedures and services under government and private health insurance programs. CPT is also used for administrative management purposes such as claims processing and for the development of guidelines for medical care review.

Medical nomenclature and procedural coding is a rapidly changing field. As new procedures are developed, old procedures become obsolete, and existing procedures are modified to reflect changes in medical practice. The American Medical Association revises and publishes CPT on an annual basis. The changes that appear in each revision are prepared by the CPT Editorial Panel with the assistance of physicians representing all specialties of medicine. A thorough understanding of CPT is critical to your reimbursement. Medicare and Medicaid programs mandate use of CPT codes and, with few exceptions, most commercial insurance carriers also use CPT codes. Most of the exceptions to the use of CPT codes are found in the processing of worker's compensation claims and in the billing of some HMOs which use CRVS as the basis for determining reimbursement.

HCPCS

HCPCS is an acronym for HCFA Common Procedure Coding System. This coding system was developed in 1983 by the Health Care Financing Administration (HCFA) for the purpose of standardizing the coding systems used to process Medicare claims on a national basis. The HCPCS coding system is used to bill Medicare primarily for supplies, materials and injections. It is also used to bill for certain procedures and services which are not defined in CPT.

HCPCS is a three level coding system which incorporates CPT, National and Local codes. HCPCS codes must be used when billing Medicare carriers and, in some states, Medicaid carriers. Some private insurance carriers also allow or mandate the use of HCPCS codes, mostly those that are also processing Medicare claims. There are three common problems associated with HCPCS coding; namely, 1) there is a general lack of knowledge and understanding about exactly how and when to use the HCPCS National Level 2 or Local Level 3 codes instead of CPT, and 2) the use, interpretation and reimbursement policies for HCPCS National Level 2 codes vary from carrier to carrier, and 3) the assignment, use, interpretation, reimbursement, and combination of HCPCS Local Level 3 codes and modifiers varies greatly from carrier to carrier.

KEY POINTS REGARDING CPT & HCPCS

1. All CPT codes are five digit numeric codes.

2. CPT codes describe procedures, services and supplies.

3. CPT codes are five digit, numeric codes.

4. With few exceptions, CPT codes are accepted or required by all insurance carriers.

5. CPT codes are self-defined. With the exception of a few codes which contain the term SPECIFY in the description, each code has only one meaning.

6. CPT codes are revised annually in December. Hundreds of CPT codes are added, changed or deleted each year. You need to purchase a new copy each year.

7. CPT 1992 deleted all visit codes based on level of service and replaced them with Evaluation and Management codes.

8. HCPCS codes are five digit, alphanumeric codes. The first digit is a letter between A and Z, and the second through fifth digits are numbers.

9. The HCPCS coding system includes two-digit modifiers at the National and Local levels which may be alphabetic or alphanumeric.

10. HCPCS codes describe supplies, materials and services provided by medical professionals.

11. The HCPCS coding system is a three-level system consisting of CPT Level 1, National Level 2 and Local Level 3 codes.

12. HCPCS codes are mandatory for billing Medicare carriers and some Medicaid carriers as well.

13. HCPCS codes are revised annually in March. Typically hundreds of codes are added, changed or deleted. You need to obtain a copy of the revised codes each year.

14. HCPCS codes follow a specific hierarchy of selection and use. Local Level 3 takes precedence over National Level 2 and National Level 2 takes precedence over CPT Level 1.

15. HCPCS coding can make a significant difference in your reimbursement from Medicare carriers.

16. CPT and HCPCS coding can make a 25 percent difference, (plus or minus) in your reimbursement.

17. Accurate CPT and HCPCS coding puts you in control of the reimbursement process.

PREPARING FOR CPT AND HCPCS CODING

Proper preparation for using CPT and HCPCS in your practice is a three-step process. Even if your practice is already using CPT and HCPCS, you should review the following steps and take appropriate action where necessary.

EVALUATE YOUR RESOURCES

CODING MATERIALS

Do you have a copy of CPT? Do you have enough copies for each person involved in the coding and billing process? Are you using the most current edition of CPT? Do you purchase new copies of the CPT every year? Do you have a copy of HCPCS? Do you have enough copies for each person involved in the coding and billing process? Are you using the most current edition of HCPCS? Do you purchase new copies of the HCPCS every year?

CODING EXPERTISE

Do you have staff with sufficient coding expertise to review and implement proper CPT and HCPCS coding on a continual basis? Does the expert coder have enough time to develop and manage the CPT and HCPCS coding process?

REVIEW PROCEDURE STATEMENTS AND CODES

PROCEDURE STATEMENTS

Are your procedure statements in the medical records accurate and precise? Are they easy to read? Do they include enough information for the coder to clearly define the level of service?

SUPERBILL

Are you using a fee ticket or superbill to record your charges? If yes, does the superbill have CPT codes in addition to any office codes you may use? Are the CPT codes current, accurate and complete? Is there space on the superbill to indicate a modifier? Do your superbills include both Visit codes (for non-Medicare patients) and Evaluation and Management codes (for Medicare patients)? Do your superbills include a space to record elapsed Visit time for the 1992 Evaluation and Management codes? Do you include HCPCS codes on your superbill for supplies, materials and injections for Medicare patients? Are the HCPCS codes current, accurate and complete?

TRAINING AND DEVELOPMENT

PURCHASE MATERIALS

Following the review steps previously outlined, purchase sufficient copies of the most current CPT and HCPCS codes for you and your staff.

TRAIN YOURSELF AND YOUR STAFF

If your review reveals a lack of coding expertise, plan to send the person(s) designated to be the practice's expert coder to CPT and HCPCS coding seminars. We strongly recommend that the health care professional also attend an introductory coding seminar if not welltrained in the area of CPT and HCPCS coding.

IMPROVE YOUR PROCEDURAL STATEMENTS

If the coding review reveals problems with illegible or difficult to read procedural statements, imprecise or inaccurate statements, or lack of ability to clearly define issues such as level of service, take steps to improve your charting in this area. Not only will this make coding easier for your staff, but it will improve your reimbursement, plus it will help protect you if you are audited.

CORRECT DEFICIENCIES IN YOUR SUPERBILL

Redesign your superbill to provide the ability to use CPT and HCPCS codes properly, including using modifiers where required. Make sure you include the ability to write-in CPT or HCPCS codes and descriptions which are not listed, plus link your CPT and HCPCS codes to ICD-9-CM codes as required under current Medicare regulations.

CREATE A MASTER CPT AND HCPCS CODES LIST

In addition to keeping your CPT and HCPCS books handy and listing the CPT and HCPCS codes you use frequently on your superbill, you should prepare and maintain an extended list of CPT and HCPCS codes. Flag CPT and HCPCS codes which often require a modifier to alert staff to look for one. Add new codes to the list and keep track of the number of times each procedure or service is performed. Review your superbills occasionally to see if you are writing in a lot of unlisted CPT or HCPCS codes and procedures. Add these codes to your master list for inclusion on your superbill the next time you print it.

STRUCTURE OF CPT

CPT is a systematic method for coding procedures and services performed by physicians and other health care professionals. Each procedure or service is identified with a five digit numeric code. The use of CPT codes simplifies the reporting of services. With this coding and recording system, the procedure or service rendered by the physicians is accurately identified.

The main body of CPT is divided into six sections. Within each section are subsections with anatomic, procedural, condition, or descriptor subheadings. The procedures and services with their identifying codes are presented in numeric order except for codes found in the EVALUATION AND MANAGEMENT section (99200-99499). These codes are located at the beginning of the CPT because they are used by all medical professionals and they are the most frequently used codes. The six SECTIONS of CPT are:

EVALUATION AND MANAGEMENT   99200 to 99499

ANESTHESIOLOGY	00100 to 01999
SURGERY	10000 to 69999
RADIOLOGY	70000 to 79999
PATHOLOGY AND LABORATORY	80000 to 89999
MEDICINE	90000 to 99199

For ease of use, the first and last code numbers plus the subsection name, appear at the top of each page of the CPT while the continuous page numbers appear on the lower, outer margin of each page along with the section name. Examples of CPT codes from each of the sections include:

EVALUATION AND MANAGEMENT SERVICES

99201 Office or other outpatient visit for the evaluation and management of a new patient, which requires these three components:

- a problem focused history;
- a problem focused examination; and
- straightforward medical decision making.

Counseling and/or coordination of care with other providers or agencies are provided consistent with the nature of the problem(s) and the patient's and/or family's needs.

Usually, the presenting problem(s) are self limited or minor. Physicians typically spend 10 minutes face-to-face with the patient and/or family.

ANESTHESIOLOGY

00955 Continuous epidural analgesia, for labor and vaginal delivery

SURGERY

44950 Appendectomy; for ruptured appendix with abscess or generalized peritonitis

RADIOLOGY

73050 Radiologic examination; acromioclavicular joints, bilateral, with or without weighted distraction

PATHOLOGY AND LABORATORY

80062 Cardiac evaluation (including coronary risk) panel

MEDICINE SERVICES

93000   Electrocardiogram, routine ECG with at least 12 leads; with interpretation and report

STRUCTURE OF HCPCS

HCPCS is a systematic method for coding supplies, materials, injections and services performed by physicians and other health care professionals. Each supply, material, injection or service is identified with a five digit alphanumeric code. With the HCPCS coding system, the supplies, materials, injections and services rendered to Medicare patients can be accurately identified. There are three levels of codes within the HCPCS coding system.

HCPCS LEVEL 1: CPT

The major portion of the HCPCS coding system, referred to as Level 1, is CPT. Most of the procedures and services you perform, even to Medicare patients, are billed using CPT codes. However, as mentioned previously, one of the major deficiencies of CPT is that it has limited code selections to describe supplies, materials and injections.

HCPCS LEVEL 2: NATIONAL CODES

HCPCS National Level 2 codes are alphanumeric codes which start with a letter followed by four numbers. The range of National Level 2 codes is from A0000 through V0000. There are also National Level 2 modifier codes. National Level 2 codes are uniform in description throughout the United States when describing covered services to Medicare intermediaries. However, due to carrier discretion, the processing and reimbursement of National Level 2 codes is not necessarily uniform.

There are over 2,400 HCPCS National Level 2 codes covering supplies, materials, injections and services. A fundamental understanding of how and when to use HCPCS National Level 2 or Local Level 3 codes can have a significant impact on your Medicare reimbursement. The majority of physicians will only use codes from the Medical and Surgical Supplies section and Drugs Administered by Other Than Oral Method, commonly referred to as "A" codes and "J" codes.

SECTIONS

The main body of HCPCS National Level 2 codes is divided into 18 sections. The supplies, materials, injections and services are presented in numeric order. The 18 major sections of HCPCS are:

TRANSPORTATION SERVICES	A0000-A0999
CHIROPRACTIC SERVICES	A2000-A2999
MEDICAL AND SURGICAL SUPPLIES	A4000-A4999
MISCELLANEOUS AND EXPERIMENTAL	A9000-A9999

ENTERAL AND PARENTERAL THERAPY	B4000-B9999
DENTAL PROCEDURES	D0000-D9999
DURABLE MEDICAL EQUIPMENT (DME)	E0000-E9999
REHABILITATIVE SERVICES	H5000-H6000
DRUGS ADMINISTERED OTHER THAN ORAL METHOD (INJECTIONS)	J0000-J8999
CHEMOTHERAPY DRUGS	J9000-J9999
ORTHOTIC PROCEDURES	L0000-L4999
PROSTHETIC PROCEDURES	L5000-L9999
MEDICAL SERVICES	M0000-M9999
PATHOLOGY AND LABORATORY	P0000-P9999
TEMPORARY CODES	Q0000-Q0099
DIAGNOSTIC RADIOLOGY SERVICES	R0000-R5999
VISION SERVICES	V0000-V2799
HEARING SERVICES	V5000-V5999

Specific examples of HCPCS National Level 2 codes include:

MEDICAL AND SURGICAL SUPPLIES

A4338   Indwelling catheter, foley type, two-way latex with coating (Teflon, Silicone, Silicone Elastomer, or Hydrophilic, etc.)

DRUGS ADMINISTERED OTHER THAN ORAL METHOD (INJECTIONS)

J0120   Injection, tetracycline, up to 250mg

ORTHOTIC PROCEDURES

L0500   Lumbar-sacral-orthosis (LSO), flexible, (lumbo-sacral surgical support), custom fitted

TEMPORARY CODES

Q0034 Administration of influenza vaccine to Medicare beneficiaries by participating demonstration sites

VISION SUPPLIES

V2620 Prosthetic, eye, glass, stock

HCPCS LOCAL LEVEL 3

HCPCS Local Level 3 codes are also alphanumeric codes which start with a letter followed by four numbers. The range of Local Level 3 codes is from W0000-Z0000. Local Level 3 codes are established and maintained by your local Medicare intermediary and will vary from state-to-state. Local Level 3 codes are often used to describe new procedures, services or supplies, or to describe procedures and services which have been deleted from CPT, but which the local intermediary still recognizes and reimburses. Local Level 3 codes may be obtained from your local Medicare intermediary. HCPCS Local Level 3 codes are categorized into ranges of alphanumeric codes as follows:

MEDICAL SERVICES	W0000-W9999
SURGICAL SERVICES	X0000-X9999
RADIOLOGY SERVICES	Y0000-Y9999
PATHOLOGY & LABORATORY	Z0000-Z9999

It should be noted that Medicare carriers do not always follow the above ranges when assigning HCPCS Local Level 3 codes. Specific examples of HCPCS Local Level 3 codes from various Medicare carriers across the nation include:

W0020 Brief examination, two or more patients in same facility (SNF, ECF), per patient

W0565 EKG with limited exercise test, master two-step, with interpretation and report

X5888 Laparoscopy, with fulguration of oviducts and D & C

X0014 Insertion of automatic defibrillator with major cardiac surgery

Y0112 Cat scan, using non-ionic contrast, i.e. omnipaque, isovue; enhanced, abdomen

Y0112 Weekly radiation therapy management, intermediate, superficial orthovoltage

Z0045 Acid Phosphatase, by RIA

HOW TO USE CPT

A medical professional using CPT for coding selects the name and associated code of the procedure or service that most accurately identifies and describes the service(s) performed. In surgery, this may be an operation; in medicine, an office visit, hospital visit, consultation or diagnostic procedure; in radiology, an x-ray. The professional selects names and codes for additional services or procedures and, when necessary, selects and lists modifiers for additional or reduced services, or for extenuating circumstances. Any services or procedures coded in this manner would also be documented in the patient's medical record.

It is important to recognize that the listing of a service or procedure and its code number in a specific section of this book does not restrict its use to a specific specialty group. Any procedure or service in any section of this book may be used to designate the services rendered by any qualified physician or other medical professional. The codes and descriptions listed in CPT are those that are generally consistent with contemporary medical practice and being performed by medical professionals in clinical practice. Inclusion in CPT does not represent endorsement by the American Medical Association of any particular diagnostic or therapeutic procedure. Inclusion or exclusion of a procedure does not imply any health insurance coverage or reimbursement policy.

FORMAT AND CONVENTIONS

CPT procedure terminologies have been developed as stand-alone descriptions of medical procedures. However, some of the procedures in CPT are not printed in their entirety but refer back to a common portion of the procedure listed in a preceding entry. This is evident when an entry is followed by one or more indentations. Any terminology after the semicolon has a subordinate status as do the subsequent indented entries. For example:

25100   Arthrotomy, wrist joint; for biopsy

25105   for synovectomy

Note that the common part of code 25100 (that part before the semicolon) should be considered part of code 25105.

GUIDELINES

Specific "Guidelines" are presented at the beginning of each of the six sections. These Guidelines define items that are necessary to appropriately interpret and report the procedures and services contained in that section. Guidelines also provide explanations regarding terms that apply only to a particular section.

STARRED PROCEDURES

The star "*" is used to identify certain surgical procedures. A detailed description of this reporting mechanism is found in the SURGERY Guidelines of CPT and in the SURGERY section below.

MODIFIERS

A CPT modifier provides the means to indicate that a service or procedure that has been performed has been altered by some specific circumstance but not changed in its definition or code. The proper use of modifiers reduces the need for separate procedure listings to describe the modifying circumstance. Typical uses of modifiers are to indicate that:

- A service or procedure has both a professional and technical component.

- A service or procedure was performed by more than one physician and/or in more than one location.

- A service or procedure has been increased or reduced.

- Only part of a service was performed.

- An adjunctive service was performed.

- A bilateral procedure was performed.

- A service or procedure was provided more than once.

- Unusual events occurred.

A complete listing of CPT modifiers is found in Appendix A of the CPT book. In addition, a list of modifiers common to each of the six sections described above are located in the Guidelines of each section.

APPENDICES

Following the six main sections listing the CPT codes and descriptors, there are three appendices and an alphabetical index.

APPENDIX A is a complete list of CPT modifiers and definitions.

APPENDIX B is a summary listing of all additions, deletions and revisions contained in the current edition. Appendix B is very useful for determining which of the codes that your practice uses may need revision.

APPENDIX C contains a listing of all additions and revisions for users who have previously purchased the CPT on magnetic tape or diskette. The listing includes 28-character "short descriptions" which are particularly useful for billing.

ALPHABETICAL INDEX

A complete alphabetical index is found in the back of the CPT. The index includes listings by procedure and anatomic site. Procedures and services commonly known by their eponyms or other designations are also included.

HOW TO USE THE CPT ALPHABETICAL INDEX

When you are using the alphabetic index to locate CPT codes, always use the following search sequence:

- Look for the PROCEDURE or SERVICE performed.

- Look for the ORGAN involved.

- Look for the CONDITION treated.

- Look for SYNONYMS, EPONYMS or ABBREVIATIONS.

In using the CPT index, it is important to understand how entries to the index have been made. Generally, entries made will fall into one or more of the categories described on the next page.

MAIN TERMS

1) PROCEDURE OR SERVICE

Pin traction

    elbow fracture   24580-24581
    supra-condylar or transcondylar fracture   24531-24542

Note that in the example above, the procedure/service was listed as the heading and a "range" of codes followed. The range of codes directs the coder to the appropriate section of the CPT where additional information on procedures may be obtained.

2) ORGAN

Bile duct

    exploration of 47700
    removal of stone 43264-47554

3) CONDITION

Tumor; see also lesion

    abdominal wall   22900
    adrenal   60545

         aural glomus 69550-69554
         bladder 51530-52240

4) SYNONYMS, EPONYMS AND ABBREVIATIONS

    Bowel; see also intestine/Intestine; see also bowel
    Mitchell procedure 28296
    EEG see electroencephalogram
    HAI test 86280

MODIFYING TERMS

A main term may be followed by a series of up to three indented terms that modify the main term. When modifying terms appear, they should be reviewed carefully, as these subterms do have an effect on code selection.

CROSS REFERENCES

Cross references direct the user to review additional information. There are two types of cross references used in the CPT index.

1) "SEE"   Directs the user to refer to the term listed after the word "SEE." This type of reference is used primarily for synonyms, eponyms and abbreviations.

2) "SEE ALSO"   Directs the user to look under another main term if the procedure is not listed under the first main entry.

HOW TO USE HCPCS

HCPCS codes must be used when coding and billing supplies, materials, injections and certain services provided to Medicare patients. For health care professionals, the most commonly used HCPCS codes are for medical/surgical supplies and injections. Many of the HCPCS codes describe equipment sold or rented as durable medical equipment and/or medical/surgical appliances.

The listing of a supply, material, injection or service and its code number in a specific section of HCPCS does not usually restrict its use to a specific profession or specialty group. However, there are some HCPCS codes which are by definition profession or specialty specific. The codes and descriptions listed in HCPCS are generally consistent with contemporary medical practice as defined by HCFA. Inclusion in HCPCS does not represent endorsement by any medical association of any particular supply, material, injection or service. Inclusion of a supply, material, injection or service does not imply any health insurance coverage or reimbursement policy. HCPCS National Level 2 codes are intended by HCFA to be implemented identically on a national basis. However, as HCFA also allows some "carrier discretion" with respect to administering the Medicare program, there are variations on a national level in terms of acceptance and reimbursement of these codes.

FORMAT AND CONVENTIONS OF HCPCS

HCPCS procedure terminologies have been developed as stand-alone descriptions of medical supplies, materials, injections and services by HCFA. HCPCS codes are published by many different publishers. Most either publish the HCPCS codes in the identical format published by HCFA, including errors, or they modify the format to be more like that of CPT. The HCPCS published annually by PMIC follows the format and conventions of CPT exactly, which allows the user to easily switch back and forth from one system to another.

GUIDELINES

There are no guidelines published with the HCFA version of HCPCS codes and descriptions. Information regarding the use of HCPCS codes is derived from Medicare bulletins published by Medicare intermediaries, books on Medicare rules and regulations, and books on coding such as this one.

HCPCS MODIFIERS

In addition to the specific uses of modifiers as described previously, HCPCS modifiers include the following additional uses:

- A service was supervised by an anesthesiologist.

- A service was performed by a specific medical professional, for example, a clinical psychologist, clinical social worker, nurse practitioner, or physician assistant.

- A service was provided as part of a specific government program.

- A service was provided to a specific side of the body.

- Equipment was purchased or rented.

- Single or multiple patients were seen during nursing home visits.

In addition to HCPCS National Level 2 modifiers revised and published by HCFA, Medicare intermediaries also create Local Level 3 modifiers to use within their own systems. These modifiers usually begin with W, X, Y or Z. A list of Local Level 3 modifiers can be obtained from your Medicare intermediary. It is important to note that HCPCS modifiers can be combined with CPT codes when reporting services to Medicare.

CODING RULES FOR HCPCS

All three levels of HCPCS must be considered when providing services to Medicare patients. Improper coding on your Medicare claims can result in denial, reduced payments, or delayed payments plus the possibility of audits and fines. While CPT will cover the great majority of procedures and services provided by most health care professionals, there are specific instances where NATIONAL codes should be used for maximum reimbursement.

MEDICAL AND SURGICAL SUPPLIES

One of the most important uses for HCPCS National Level 2 codes is to report the provision of medical and surgical supplies to Medicare patients. CPT lists only one code, 99070, for medical and surgical supplies, with instructions to specify. This is precisely what the HCPCS National Level 2 coding system does....it lists specific codes for thousands of medical and surgical supplies.

HCPCS CODE OVERLAP

As may be expected there is some overlap between CPT Level 1, National Level 2 and Local Level 3 codes and in some cases you may have to choose which of the three coding levels to use. The following rules represent how such coding situations should be handled.

KEY POINTS REGARDING HCPCS CODE OVERLAP

1. Local Level 3 codes always have the highest priority. If there is a choice between a Local Level 3 code and either a CPT Level 1 code or National Level 2 code, use the Local Level 3 code.

2. National Level 2 codes have the next highest priority. If there is a choice between a National Level 2 code and a CPT Level 1 code, use the National Level 2 code.

3. For CPT supply, materials or injection codes which contain the instructions SPECIFY, try to locate a National Level 2 or Local Level 3 code which describes the specific supply, material or injection.

FORMAT OF HCPCS CODES

All HCPCS National 2 and Local Level 3 codes begin with a letter followed by four numbers. For example: A0010, J1070 and W0010. The letter/number series A0000-V5999 is used for HCPCS National 2 codes and the letter/number series W0000-Z9999 is reserved for HCPCS Local Level 3 codes assigned by Medicare carriers.

Each letter/number range includes a series of related procedures, services or supplies. For example the code range A0000 through A0999 describes "transportation services including ambulance" while the code series V5000-V5999 describes "hearing services".

CODING AND BILLING ISSUES

The following coding and billing issues apply generally to all specialties and professions. There are additional specialty specific issues defined in each of the five sections of CPT discussed immediately following this general section. We recommend that you review the general information carefully before proceeding to the section of the book that discusses your specialty or area of interest.

SUPPORTING DOCUMENTATION

One of the most important issues related to CPT and HCPCS coding and billing is that you have medical record support for the procedures, services and supplies that you bill. Documentation can "make or break" you in the case of an audit by Medicare or a private carrier. The current emphasis on "fraud" and "abuse" by Medicare, Medicaid and private carriers necessitates a review of documentation by all medical professionals.

Use the following list to review the documentation policies, procedures and standards of your practice:

- Are your medical records maintained in a current, uniform, legible and consistent manner?

- Do all entries include the date, provider name, chief complaint, clinical findings, diagnosis or impression, tests and medications ordered, procedures performed and instructions given to the patient?

- Are all entries signed or countersigned by the responsible provider?

- Are all laboratory, x-ray and other test results recorded properly?

- Are consultations and advice given to patients by telephone documented accurately and consistently?

- Do your entries clearly document the need for the level of service you are billing for?

- Does the working diagnosis clearly support the need for the procedures or services provided?

SPECIAL MEDICARE CONSIDERATIONS

To satisfy Medicare requirements, there must be sufficient documentation in the medical record to verify the services billed and the level of care required. Section 1833(e) of Title XVIII, Social Security Act requires "available information that documents a claim." If there is no documentation to justify the services or level of care, the claim cannot be considered for Medicare benefits. If there is insufficient documentation to support claims that have already been paid by Medicare, the reimbursement will be considered an overpayment and a refund will be requested by Medicare. Medicare has the authority to review any information, including medical records, when such information pertains to a Medicare claim.

BILATERAL MODIFIER USAGE

With the exception of the Radiology Section, all procedure codes which defined bilateral procedures were deleted from the 1990 edition of CPT. This was the stated intent of the AMA for several previous editions of CPT. The modifier -50 was added to CPT previously for the purpose of reporting bilateral procedures. Practices that have been using bilateral procedure codes need to revise their code listings and superbills to reflect the deletion of these codes and start using modifier -50 as indicated in the claim example below.

21. DIAGNOSIS OR NATURE OF ILLNESS OR INJURY. (RELATE ITEMS 1,2,3 OR 4 TO ITEM 24E BY LINE)					
1. V54 . 0			3. ___ . ___		
2. ___ . ___			4. ___ . ___		

24. A DATE(S) OF SERVICE						B Place of Service	C Type of Service	D PROCEDURES, SERVICES, OR SUPPLIES (Explain Unusual Circumstances)		E DIAGNOSIS CODE
From MM	DD	YY	To MM	DD	YY			CPT/HCPCS	MODIFIER	
03	15	92				21		20680		1
03	15	92				21		20680	50	1

Note that what you could bill before previously with a single line on a claim form now requires two separate lines as defined in the CPT.

UNLISTED PROCEDURES OR SERVICES

The AMA and HCFA recognize that there may be services or procedures performed by medical professionals that are not found in CPT or HCPCS. Therefore, a number of specific code numbers have been included for reporting unlisted procedures. When an unlisted procedure code is used, the service or procedure must be described and a report describing the service or procedure must be attached to the insurance claim. Many practices abuse the unlisted procedure codes because 1) it is easier to use an unlisted procedure code than locate a specific code, and 2) they are using outdated copies of the CPT or HCPCS and are unaware that specific procedure codes do exist for the procedures or services they are providing. Using unlisted procedure codes increases the practice workload as detailed reports must be submitted to explain to insurance carriers what services were actually provided. This in turn delays reimbursement as the carriers must process these claims manually instead of through their normal claim processing system. Avoid whenever possible the use of unlisted procedure codes. Make sure you obtain a new copy of the CPT and HCPCS annually in order to update your code lists.

HCPCS contains numerous codes defined as unlisted supplies, materials and services. These codes are not usually allowed or paid for. Consult your local Medicare intermediary before using any of these codes.

CPT CHANGES, ADDITIONS AND DELETIONS

Every year hundreds of codes are added, changed or deleted from CPT. A summary of these changes is found in Appendix B of your CPT and provides a quick reference for coding review. In addition to the appendix, these modifications are identified throughout the CPT. It is imperative that you purchase a new copy of the CPT each and every year in order to make sure that you are using the most current codes. Using current CPT codes is important for two reasons:

1. Since coding directly affects reimbursement, using out-of-date codes may result in lower payments.

2. Using out-of-date codes may expose you to audit liability.

ADDITIONS TO CPT

New CPT codes are identified with a small black circle placed to the left of the code number. Examples of new CPT codes in the 1992 CPT include:

*   36535   Removal of implantable venous access port and/or subcutaneous reservoir

*   65125   Modification of ocular implant (eg, drilling receptacle for prosthesis appendage)(separate procedure)

This special identification of new codes appears only in a single edition of CPT. In the following edition, these codes will no longer have a small black circle to the left of the code number.

CHANGES TO CPT

Changes in CPT code definitions are identified with a small black triangle placed to the left of the code number. Examples of changed CPT code definitions in the 1992 CPT include:

▲ 15760   Graft; composite (full thickness of external ear or nasal ala), including primary closure, donor area

▲ 45378   Colonoscopy, fiberoptic, beyond splenic flexure; diagnostic, with or without colon decompression

This special identification of changed codes appears only in a single edition of CPT. In the following edition, these codes will no longer have a small black triangle to the left of the code number.

DELETIONS FROM CPT

Deleted codes are enclosed within parenthesis, along with a reference to replacement codes. Examples of deleted CPT codes and definitions in the 1992 CPT include:

(61331 has been deleted. To report use 61330 with modifier -50)

(90000-90080 have been deleted. To report, see 99201-99215)

This special identification of deleted codes appears only in a single edition of CPT. In the following edition, there will be no reference at all to these codes.

HCPCS CHANGES, ADDITIONS AND DELETIONS

Every year hundreds of codes are added, deleted or changed from HCPCS National Level 2. As there is no standardized format for HCPCS National Level 2, your awareness of these changes will depend on first, having a copy of the current HCPCS codes, and second, the reporting format chosen by the publisher of the HCPCS you use.

The HCPCS National Level 2 code book published annually by PMIC uses the same notation as CPT; namely, black circles, black triangles, and parentheses to indicate new codes, changes and deletions. It is imperative that you purchase a new copy of HCPCS National Level 2 each year in order to make sure you are using the most current codes. Using current HCPCS National Level 2 codes is important for two reasons:

1) Using out-of-date HCPCS codes may result in a delay, reduction or denial of your Medicare claims.

2) Using out-of-date HCPCS codes may result in non-compliance with Medicare rules and regulations, exposing you to fines and penalties.

STARRED PROCEDURES

The star "*" is used in CPT to identify certain relatively small surgical services that involve a readily identifiable surgical procedure but include variable preoperative and postoperative services. Examples of this type of service include: incision and drainage of an abscess, injection of a tendon sheath, manipulation of a joint under anesthesia, dilation of the urethra, etc.

Because of the indefinite pre- and postoperative services the usual "package" concept for surgical services cannot be applied. These procedures are identified in CPT by a star (*) following the procedure code number. See the SURGERY section below for a complete discussion of how to code starred procedures. HCPCS has no equivalent to the CPT starred procedure code.

NEW PATIENT VERSUS ESTABLISHED PATIENT

CPT Visit codes in the range 90000-90699 and Evaluation and Management codes in the range 99200-99499 require that you distinguish between new patients and established patients. The designation of new or established does not preclude the use of a specific level of service.

HCPCS Visit codes, M0000-M0999, do not distinguish between new and established patients.

NEW PATIENT OR INITIAL VISIT

Prior to 1992, CPT defined a NEW patient as "one who is new to the physician and whose medical and administrative records need to be established." In the 1992 edition of CPT, a NEW patient was re-defined as "one who has not received any professional services from the physician within the past three years." The following chart provides some perspective on the (confusing) array of codes which may be reported for visit or evaluation and management services.

CPT CODES FOR NEW PATIENTS OR INITIAL CARE

	MINIMAL	BRIEF	LIMITED	INTERMED	EXTENDED	COMPRE	COMPLEX
OFFICE	-----	90000	90010	90015	90017	90020	-----
	-----	99201	99202	99203	99204	99205	-----
HOME	-----	90100	90110	90115	90117	-----	-----
	-----	99341	99342		99353	-----	-----
HOSPITAL	-----	90200	-----	90215	-----	90220	-----
	-----	99221	-----	99222	99223		-----
SNF/ICF	-----	90300	-----	90315	-----	90320	-----
	99302	-----	-----	-----	99303	-----	
RESTHOME	-----	90400	90410	90415	-----	90420	-----
		99321		99322		99323	
E.R.	90500	90505	90510	90515	90517	90520	-----
	99281	99282	99283	99284	99285		
CONSULT	-----	-----	90600	90605	90610	90620	90630
	-----	-----	99241	99242	99243	99244	99245[1]
	-----	-----	99251	99252	99253	99254	99255[2]
	-----	-----	99271	99272	99273	99274	99275[3]
EYE SVC	-----	90000	90010	92002	90017	92004	-----
		99201	99202	92002	99204	92004	

[1] Office Consultations
[2] Initial Inpatient Consultations
[3] Confirmatory Consultations

Codes in the above chart which are placed between columns illustrate the lack of a direct crosswalk between the Visit and Evaluation and Management codes.

ESTABLISHED PATIENT OR FOLLOW-UP VISITS

Prior to 1992, CPT defined an ESTABLISHED patient as "a patient whose medical and administrative records are available to the physician." In the 1992 CPT, an ESTABLISHED patient was re-defined as "one who *has* received services from the physician within the past three years." The chart on the following page provides some perspective on the (confusing) array of coding choices available.

CPT CODES FOR ESTABLISHED PATIENTS/SUBSEQUENT VISITS

	MINIMAL	BRIEF	LIMITED	INTERMED	EXTENDED	COMPRE	COMPLEX
OFFICE	90030	90040	90050	90060	90070	90080	-----
	99211	99212	99213	99214	99215		-----
HOME	90130	90140	90150	90160	90170	-----	-----
	99351		99352		99353	-----	-----
HOSPITAL	-----	90240	90250	90260	90270	90280	-----
	-----	99231			99232	99233	-----
SNF/ICF	-----	90340	90350	90360	90370	-----	-----
	-----	99311	99312	99313		-----	-----
RESTHOME	90430	90440	90450	90460	90470	-----	-----
	99331		99332		99333	-----	-----
E.R.	90530	90540	90550	90560	90570	90580	-----
	99281	99282	99283	99284	99285		
CONSULT	-----	90640	90641	90642	-----	-----	90643
	-----	99212	99213	99214	-----	-----	99215[1]
	-----	99261	99261	99261	-----	-----	99263[2]
EYE SVC	90030	90040	92012	90070	92014	-----	-----
	99211	99212	92012	99214	92014	-----	-----

---

[1] Office consultations.
[2] Hospital consultations.

Codes in the above chart which are placed between columns illustrate the lack of a direct cross-walk between the Visit and Evaluation and Management codes.

VISIT CODES LEVELS OF SERVICE

Prior to 1992 CPT defined six levels of service to differentiate the variations in skill, effort, time, responsibility and knowledge required for proper examinations, evaluations, treatment, conferences, preventive health supervision and other medical services. Each level of service may be used by all physicians. In the 1992 CPT, all Visit codes were replaced by Evaluation and Management services. The new codes are not defined as brief, intermediate, or comprehensive; however, these terms are used extensively in the definitions of the components of these services. (See VISITS/EVALUATION AND MANAGEMENT SERVICES).

MINIMAL LEVEL OF SERVICE

A level of service supervised by a physician but not necessarily requiring his presence. To report a MINIMAL level of service, document the procedure or service as well as who, if other than the physician, performed the service (nurse, physician's assistant, etc.).

Examples of MINIMAL services as defined in CPT include:

Routine immunization for tetanus.
Blood pressure check.
Removal of sutures from a laceration.

BRIEF LEVEL OF SERVICE

A level of service pertaining to the evaluation and treatment of a condition requiring only an abbreviated history and examination. To report a BRIEF service, the following must be performed and documented:

* abbreviated history
* examination
* evaluation and treatment

Examples of BRIEF services as defined in CPT include:

Examination of acute tonsillitis.
Examination of minor trauma.
Concurrent hospital care for a minor secondary diagnosis.

LIMITED LEVEL OF SERVICE

A level of service pertaining to the evaluation of a circumscribed acute illness or to the periodic reevaluation of an existing problem. To report a LIMITED service, the following must be performed and documented:

* evaluation of acute illness or interval history and exam
* review of effectiveness of past management
* ordering and evaluation of tests
* adjustment of therapeutic management
* discussion of findings and/or management

Examples of LIMITED services as defined in CPT include:

Treatment of an acute respiratory infection.

Review of interval history, physical status and control of a diabetic patient.

Review of hospital course, studies, orders and chest recovering from acute congestive failure including revision of orders and limited exchange with nursing staff.

INTERMEDIATE LEVEL OF SERVICE

A level of service pertaining to the evaluation of a new or existing condition complicated with a new diagnostic or management problem not necessarily relating to the primary diagnosis. To report an INTERMEDIATE service, the following must be present or performed and documented:

- More than one diagnosis
- History and physical
- Ordering and evaluation of tests
- Ordering of therapeutic management or conference with patient, family or hospital staff regarding medical management

Examples of INTERMEDIATE services as defined in CPT include:

The evaluation of a patient with arteriosclerotic heart disease with recent onset of unstable angina including detailed interval history and physical, ordering of appropriate tests, and discussion of new therapeutic management.

Review of interval history, re-exam of musculoskeletal systems and abdomen, discussion of findings, and adjustment of therapeutic program in a patient with arthritic disorders with recently developed gastric complaints.

Conference with patient and/or family to review studies, hospital course, and findings in a young adult with acute hepatitis secondary to drug abuse.

EXTENDED LEVEL OF SERVICE

A level of service requiring an unusual amount of effort or judgment. To report an EXTENDED service, the following must be performed and documented:

- Detailed history taken
- Medical records reviewed
- Physical examination
- Formal conference with patient, family or staff

Examples of EXTENDED services as defined in CPT include:

Re-exam of neurological findings, detailed review of hospital studies and course, and formal conference with patient and family jointly concerning findings and plans in a diagnostic problem of suspected intracranial disease in a young adult.

Detailed intensive review of studies and hospital course and thorough re-exam of pertinent physical findings of a patient with a recent myocardial infarction with complications requiring constant physician bedside attention.

Review of results of diagnostic evaluation, performance of a detailed exam and a thorough review of physical findings, lab studies, x-rays, diagnostic conclusions and recommendations for treatment of complicated chronic pulmonary disease.

FREQUENCY DISTRIBUTION OF OFFICE MEDICAL SERVICES

NEW PATIENTS[1]

CODE	DESCRIPTION	PERCENT
90000	Office and other outpatient medical service, new patient; brief service	6.01
90010	limited service	15.90
90015	intermediate service	23.13
90017	extended service	4.97
90020	comprehensive service	49.98

ESTABLISHED PATIENTS[2]

CODE	DESCRIPTION	PERCENT
90030	Office and other outpatient medical service, established patient; minimal	1.11
90040	brief service	2.13
90050	limited service	10.13
90060	intermediate service	41.06
90070	extended service	35.11
90080	comprehensive service	10.46

[1] Sample size: 28,675 Visit transactions
[2] Sample size: 181,111 Visit transactions

SOURCE: Medical Fees in Southern California, 1990, PMIC Corporation

COMPREHENSIVE LEVEL OF SERVICE

A level of service providing an in-depth evaluation of a patient with a new or existing problem requiring the development or complete re-evaluation of medical data. To report a COMPREHENSIVE service, the following must be performed and documented:

- Record the chief complaint(s) and present illness
- Record the family history and the patient's past medical history and personal history
- A system review
- A complete physical examination
- Ordering of appropriate tests and procedures

PLACE (LOCATION) OF SERVICE

CPT makes specific distinctions for place (location) of service for codes in the Visit codes and the Evaluation and Management codes. HCPCS also includes codes that refer to specific locations of service. The place of service can have considerable impact on reimbursement. The following list defines CPT and HCPCS code ranges for specific places of service:

Office [And Other Outpatient]	90000-90080
	99201-99215
	A2000
	M0005-M0009
	M0702-M0710
Home Services	90100-90170
	99341-99353
	M0019
Hospital [Inpatient]	90200-90292
	99221-99238
	M0021-M0029
	M0722-M0730
Consultations	99241-99245
	99251-99255
	99261-99263
SNF, ICF, Long-Term Care	90300-90370
	99301-99315
	M0039
Nursing Home, Custodial Care, Etc.	90400-90470
	99321-99333
	M0049
Emergency Room [Assigned Physician]	90500-90580
	99281-99288
	M0059

HOSPITAL CARE

Hospital services frequently cause reimbursement problems for health care professionals. The three most common coding errors are:

• More than one physician submits an initial hospital care code for the same patient.

• Follow-up hospital visits are coded and billed incorrectly.

• Concurrent care visits by multiple specialists are not coded and billed properly.

If more than one provider is involved in the process of hospitalizing a patient, for example, surgeon and internist, the physicians must decide which is going to actually admit the patient and bill for the admission. If both do, the first claim in will be processed and paid, and the second will be rejected.

There are legitimate reasons for visiting a patient more than once daily while hospitalized. Many practices do not realize that subsequent hospital visit codes are for "daily" services. If the physician sees the patient twice in one day, providing a brief level of service each time, the practice may submit two 90240 codes for the same day. This coding is incorrect and will usually result in either the entire claim being returned for clarification, or the second visit being denied as an apparent duplication.

CPT clearly defines subsequent hospital care as "each day", meaning daily services. If you see the patient twice in one day, providing the equivalent of "brief" services each time, you would code and bill the service using the appropriate Visit or Evaluation and Management code for "limited" or "intermediate" services depending upon the cumulative level of service provided.

Prior to publication of the 1992 CPT, concurrent care was reported by 1) adding modifier -75 to the basic service and 2) reporting ICD-9-CM diagnosis code(s) that differ from any other professionals providing similar services concurrently to the same patient. Modifier -75 was deleted from the 1992 CPT. Therefore, the diagnosis code becomes the key factor in reporting (and being reimbursed for) concurrent care services.

FREQUENCY DISTRIBUTION OF HOSPITAL SERVICES CODES

INITIAL HOSPITAL CARE[1]

CODE	DESCRIPTION	PERCENT
90200	Initial hospital care; brief	2.96
90215	intermediate	13.07
90220	comprehensive	83.97

FOLLOW-UP HOSPITAL CARE[2]

90240	Subsequent hospital care; brief	0.05
90250	limited	10.17
90260	intermediate	43.46
90270	extended	42.77
90280	comprehensive	3.55

[1] Sample size: 7,599
[2] Sample size: 86,896

SOURCE: Medical Fees in Southern California, 1990, PMIC Corporation

---

HOSPITAL DISCHARGE

The CPT codes for hospital discharge services are Visit code 90292 and Evaluation and Management code 99238, defined as Hospital discharge day management. This service includes final examination of the patient, discussion of the hospital stay, instructions for continuing care, and preparation of discharge records. Many insurance carriers do not recognize and/or do not reimburse this CPT code. Options for the use of code 90292 or 99238 include the use of one of the other hospital daily services codes from the Visit series 90240-90280 or the Evaluation and Management series 99231-99233 and perhaps using a code which has a higher value than your routine hospital Visit.

EMERGENCY SERVICES

Proper coding for services performed in the emergency department depends on whether or not the physician is assigned to the emergency department. If the physician is assigned to the emergency department, emergency services would be coded from the Visit codes 90500-90590 or the Evaluation and Management codes 99281-99285.

For services performed in the emergency department at the request of, or for the convenience of the patient or physician, use Visit codes 90000-90080 or Evaluation and Management codes 99201-99215 to report. Note that Visit codes 99062-99065, previously used to report emergency care facility services when the non-hospital based physician is called to the emergency facility to provide services, were deleted from the 1992 CPT.

REFERRAL

A referral is the transfer of the total care or specific portion of care of a patient from one physician to another. A referral is not a consultation. If a patient is referred to you for total care or a portion of their care, you would use Visit or Evaluation and Management service codes to report. If a patient is sent to you for a consultation, you would use Visit or Evaluation and Management consultation codes to report, but you would assume no responsibility for the patient's care.

Many physicians, when sending thank you or cover letters for consultations, begin the letter with the phrase "Thank you for your referral of....". This can cost your practice significant revenues if claims examiners spot this phrase and decide to down-code what was truly a consultation to a routine office or hospital visit code.

SEPARATE OR MULTIPLE PROCEDURES

It is appropriate to designate multiple procedures that are rendered on the same date by separate entries. For example: if a proctosigmoidoscopy was performed in addition to a hospital visit, the proctosigmoidoscopy would be considered a SEPARATE procedure and listed in addition to the hospital visit on the claim form. Another example would be individual medical psychotherapy rendered in addition to a brief subsequent hospital service. In this instance, both services would be reported.

MULTIPLE SURGICAL PROCEDURES

It is common for several surgical procedures to be performed at the same operative session. When multiple procedures are performed on the same day or at the same session, the "major" procedure or service is listed first followed by secondary, additional, or "lesser" procedures or services. Modifier -51 is added to all procedures following the first one.

CONSULTATIONS   90600-90630

A consultation includes services rendered by a physician whose opinion or advice is requested by a physician or other appropriate source for the further evaluation and/or management of the patient. When the consulting physician assumes responsibility for the continuing care of the patient, any subsequent service rendered by him will cease to be a consultation. CPT defines five levels of initial consultations.

LIMITED CONSULTATION

VISIT CODE   90600

In a limited consultation the physician confines his service to the examination or evaluation of a single organ system. To report a LIMITED consultation, the following must be performed and documented:

- Documentation of complaint(s)
- Documentation of present illness
- Pertinent examination
- Review of medical data
- Establishment of a management plan
- Written report

EVALUATION AND MANAGEMENT CODE   99241
                                                                  or 99251

CPT Visit code 90600 cross-walks directly to Evaluation and Management code 99241 for office consultations and code 99251 for initial inpatient consultations. To report either of these services, the following key components must be performed and documented:

- A problem focused history
- A problem focused examination
- Straightforward decision making

INTERMEDIATE CONSULTATION

VISIT CODE   90605

To report an INTERMEDIATE consultation, the following must be performed and documented:

- Examination or evaluation of organ system
- Partial review of general history
- Recommendations
- Written report

EVALUATION AND MANAGEMENT CODE

99242
or 99252

CPT Visit code 90605 cross-walks directly to Evaluation and Management code 99242 for office consultations and code 99252 for initial inpatient consultations. To report either of these services, the following key components must be performed and documented:

- An expanded problem focused history
- An expanded problem focused examination
- Straightforward decision making

EXTENDED CONSULTATION

VISIT CODE

90610

An extended consultation involves the evaluation of problems that do not require a comprehensive evaluation of the patient as a whole. To report an EXTENDED consultation, the following must be performed and documented:

- Documentation of a history of the chief complaint(s)
- Past medical history
- Review and evaluation of past medical data
- Plan of investigative and/or therapeutic management
- Written report

EVALUATION AND MANAGEMENT CODE

99243
or 99253

CPT Visit code 90610 cross-walks directly to Evaluation and Management code 99243 for office consultations and code 99253 for initial inpatient consultations. To report either of these services, the following key components must be performed and documented:

- A detailed history
- A detailed examination
- Medical decision making of low complexity

COMPREHENSIVE CONSULTATION

VISIT CODE

90620

A comprehensive consultation involves an in-depth evaluation of a patient. To report a COMPREHENSIVE consultation, the following must be performed and documented:

- Documentation of chief complaints and present illness
- Family history, past medical history and personal history
- System review
- Physical examination
- Review of all previous tests and procedures

- Establishment or verification of a management plan
- Written report

EVALUATION AND MANAGEMENT CODE

**99244
or 99254**

CPT Visit code 90620 cross-walks directly to Evaluation and Management code 99244 for office consultations and code 99254 for initial inpatient consultations. To report either of these services, the following key components must be performed and documented:

- A comprehensive history
- A comprehensive examination
- Medical decision making of moderate complexity

COMPLEX CONSULTATION

VISIT CODE

90630

The complex consultation is defined by CPT as an uncommonly performed service. To report a COMPLEX consultation the following must be performed and documented:

- Documentation of chief complaints and present illness
- Family history, past medical history and personal history
- System review
- Physical examination
- Review of all previous tests and procedures
- Establishment or verification of a management plan
- In-depth evaluation of a critical problem requiring unusual knowledge, skill and judgment

EVALUATION AND MANAGEMENT CODE

**99245
or 99255**

CPT Visit code 90625 cross-walks directly to Evaluation and Management code 99245 for office consultations and code 99255 for initial inpatient consultations. To report either of these services, the following key components must be performed and documented:

- A comprehensive history
- A comprehensive examination
- Medical decision making of high complexity

Note that while CPT defines the complex consultation as "an uncommonly performed service," the frequency distribution table below indicates that this code is billed for almost 60 percent of initial consultations. This frequency distribution reveals a significant variation in the actual coding and billing practices of physicians as compared to that defined by CPT.

FREQUENCY DISTRIBUTION OF CONSULTATION CODES

INITIAL CONSULTATIONS[1]

CODE	DESCRIPTION	PERCENT
90600	Initial consultation; limited	1.89
90605	intermediate	1.62
90610	extended	5.03
90620	comprehensive	37.22
90630	complex	54.24

FOLLOW-UP CONSULTATIONS[2]

90640	Follow-up consultation; brief	0.10
90641	limited	57.73
90642	intermediate	14.02
90643	complex	28.15

[1] Sample size: 42,850
[2] Sample size: 21,111

SOURCE: Medical Fees in Southern California, 1990, PMI Corporation

---

CONSULTATION FOLLOW-UP

VISIT CODES   90640-90643

A follow-up consultation involves the consultant's reevaluation of a patient on whom he has previously rendered his opinion or advice. The consultant provides no patient management or treatment. If the physician assumes responsibility for any portion of the patient's continuing care, report using the appropriate Visit codes.

EVALUATION AND MANAGEMENT CODES   99212-99215

The 1992 CPT deleted all codes for follow-up "office" consultations. These services are now reported using the established patient visit codes. The 1992 CPT added new codes for hospital inpatient consultations, including codes for reporting subsequent hospital consultations.

CONFIRMATORY CONSULTATIONS

90650-90654
99271-99275

Confirmatory consultation codes are used when the consultation is requested by the patient, or other agency. Typically the consultation will involve a second or third opinion on the necessity or appropriateness of a medical treatment or surgical procedure recommended by another physician.

Note that there are special modifiers in the CPT and HCPCS coding systems that are used to modify these codes. Use the guidelines on the following page when adding modifiers to mandated consultations.

- If the second opinion is mandated by a professional review organization, use CPT modifier -32 if the patient IS NOT a Medicare patient and HCPCS modifier -SF if the patient IS a Medicare patient.

- Many Medicare intermediaries have assigned Local Level 3 modifiers for second opinions requested by the patient. Check with your local Medicare intermediary before reporting these services.

CRITICAL CARE BILLING

TIME VERSUS PROCEDURES

Due to the current methods of valuing cognitive services versus technical procedures, medical professionals must occasionally choose between two coding and billing methods for the same service. This billing problem will be resolved as the values of cognitive services are increased based on the newer relative value studies being completed.

TIME BASED BILLING

The codes listed in the critical care section of CPT are reported based on elapsed time, in hourly, or half-hourly, increments. These services are defined as including CPR, cardio-version, placement of catheters, etc. These codes are billed in the following manner:

21. DIAGNOSIS OR NATURE OF ILLNESS OR INJURY. (RELATE ITEMS 1,2,3 OR 4 TO ITEM 24E BY LINE)						
1. 427 . 5			3.			
2.			4.			

24. A DATE(S) OF SERVICE						B Place of Service	C Type of Service	D PROCEDURES, SERVICES, OR SUPPLIES (Explain Unusual Circumstances) CPT/HCPCS MODIFIER	E DIAGNOSIS CODE
From MM	DD	YY	To MM	DD	YY				
03	15	92				21		99291	1
03	15	92				21		99292	1
03	15	92				21		99292	1

PROCEDURE BASED BILLING

Another way of reporting critical care services is to itemize the actual procedures and services performed. This often results in a significant increase in reimbursement when combined to time-based billing.

21. DIAGNOSIS OR NATURE OF ILLNESS OR INJURY. (RELATE ITEMS 1,2,3 OR 4 TO ITEM 24E BY LINE)			
1. 427 . 5	3. |___ . ___		2
2. |___ . ___	4. |___ . ___		2

24. A DATE(S) OF SERVICE						B Place of Service	C Type of Service	D PROCEDURES, SERVICES, OR SUPPLIES (Explain Unusual Circumstances) CPT/HCPCS | MODIFIER	E DIAGNOSIS CODE
From MM	DD	YY	To MM	DD	YY				
1 03	15	92				21		92950	1
2 03	15	92				21		92960	1
3 03	15	92				21		93503	1

SUPPLIES AND MATERIALS SUPPLIED BY PHYSICIAN

CPT provides 28 specific codes for identifying certain supplies and materials provided by the physician. HCPCS provides over 2,000 specific codes for identifying supplies, materials and equipment on Medicare claims. These codes are used to bill for supplies and materials that are not included in the definition of the basic service.

92390 - 92396   These codes are used to bill for the provision of spectacles, contact lenses, low vision aids and ocular prosthesis.

95120 - 95170   These codes are used to bill for the provision of allergenic extracts and stinging insect venoms.

96545   Provision of chemotherapy agent. CPT codes 96400-96530 are used to bill for administration. These codes include preparation of chemotherapy agent(s) and administration but do not include supply of the specific agent.

99070   Supplies and materials provided by the physician. This global code is used to identify virtually all other materials and supplies, such as sterile trays, drugs, cast or strap materials, etc. over and above those usually included with the office visit or service rendered.

This code is valid only for private insurance carriers and some Medicaid carriers. This code is not to be used to bill Medicare carriers for materials and supplies. Use the appropriate National Level 2 HCPCS code to bill Medicare.

Some private insurance carriers, mostly those that are also Medicare carriers, allow or require use of HCPCS codes when billing for supplies and materials for patients. If you are having reimbursement problems with a private carrier for supplies and materials, contact their provider relations department and inquire about the use of HCPCS codes on private claims.

While some Medicaid carriers require HCPCS codes for billing of supplies, it is not unusual to find a completely different internal coding system required for Medicaid claims. Check with your local Medicaid carrier if you are not sure.

A4000-A4999   Medical and surgical supplies such as bandages, syringes, catheters, urinary supplies, ostomy supplies, surgical trays and various miscellaneous supplies commonly provided to patients.

B4000-B9999   Enteral and parenteral therapy supplies such as feeding kits, formulae, and infusion pumps.

E0000-E9999   Durable medical equipment such as ambulation devices, commodes, decubitus care equipment, heat/cold application equipment, bath and toilet aids, hospital beds and accessories, oxygen and related respiratory equipment, TENS, wheelchairs and accessories, oxygen supplies and equipment, and artificial kidney machines and accessories.

L0000-L4999   Orthotic supplies, materials and devices such as cervical collars, body jackets, surgical supports, correction pads, and orthopedic footwear.

L5000-L9999   Prosthetic supplies, materials and devices and fittings such as artificial limbs, terminal devices (hooks, hands, gloves), externally powered devices, batteries, breast prostheses, elastic supports.

V2000-V2900   Vision supplies, materials and devices such as spectacles, contact lenses and eye prostheses.

V5000-V5399   Hearing services, materials and supplies such as audiologic assessment, fitting and/or repair of hearing aids, and supply of hearing aids.

99071   Educational supplies, such as books, tapes, and pamphlets, provided by the physician for the patient's education at cost to physician.

Educational materials are normally supplied at no charge to the patient. Most practices provide this type of material as a service to their patients. It is also an important component of the practice's marketing program.

78990 & 79900   These codes, found in the NUCLEAR MEDICINE sub-section of the RADIOLOGY section of CPT are used to report radium or other radio-elements when provided by the physician.

PROCEDURE DOWN-CODING

Down-coding, which is the process of changing the procedure code you submitted to one of a lower value, costs medical professionals and their patients millions of dollars annually. Insurance claims examiners are trained to match codes and descriptions. If they don't match, the claims examiner has an opportunity to substitute a code with a lower value, which of course means lower reimbursement.

DOWN-CODING DUE TO MISMATCH OF PROCEDURE CODE AND DESCRIPTION

An insurance claim form submitted with CPT code 90060 and defined on the claim form as "Office Visit" could easily be down-coded to lower valued codes such as 90050 or 90040 simply because the description given provides the opportunity to do so. Obviously there are many claims submitted by medical professionals that are undercoded, meaning that the practice is under-valuing its own services. In our experience of billing over one billion dollars for health care professionals over a period of ten plus years, we have never seen or heard of, an insurance carrier "up-coding" a procedure that was obviously under-coded by the practice. There are two significant steps you can take to minimize or eliminate down-coding.

1) You can minimize procedure down-coding by making sure that the descriptions you print on your insurance claims match those found in the CPT exactly. The problem with this option is that many of the descriptions far exceed the 28 characters found on each procedure line of the HCFA1500. Abbreviation of terminology only increases the possibilities of down-coding.

2) You can eliminate procedure down-coding by eliminating procedure descriptions from your insurance claim forms. With no description to match, the claims examiner must allow full value for the procedure you submitted.

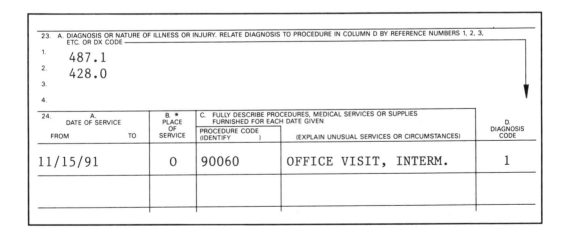

21. DIAGNOSIS OR NATURE OF ILLNESS OR INJURY. (RELATE ITEMS 1,2,3 OR 4 TO ITEM 24E BY LINE)								2
1. 487 .1				3. ____ . __				2
2. 428 .0 .				4. ____ . __				

24.	A						B	C	D		E
	DATE(S) OF SERVICE						Place of Service	Type of Service	PROCEDURES, SERVICES, OR SUPPLIES (Explain Unusual Circumstances)		DIAGNOSIS CODE
	From			To					CPT/HCPCS	MODIFIER	
	MM	DD	YY	MM	DD	YY					
1	03	15	92				11		90060		1,2
2											
3											

In support of this recommendation, please consider the following:

- The numeric CPT code, due to its universal acceptance by insurance carriers, precisely defines the procedure. CPT code 10120 means "Incision and removal of foreign body, subcutaneous tissues; simple" to any insurance carrier you submit it to. To list the actual definition is redundant (and in this example impossible to do in only 28 characters). To abbreviate, or restate the definition in any way, even if you actually call it something else, is providing the insurance claims examiner with an opportunity to down-code your claim.

- The national standards established by HCFA in 1983 for electronic transmission of Medicare claims provides no space within the electronic claim for a procedure description. All that is submitted is the procedure code(s), modifier code(s), fee(s) and diagnosis code(s). These code numbers precisely define what you did (CPT), any variations (MODIFIER), what you charged (FEE), and why you did it (ICD-9-CM). Nothing more is required. Electronic claims submission for Medicaid, Blue Cross and Blue Shield, and commercial insurance carriers generally use the HCFA standards or a modification of it.

- The December 1990 revision of the HCFA1500 form, first released in the fall of 1991, does not have any space for procedure descriptions, however, it has more space for procedure and diagnosis codes.

DOWN-CODING DUE TO MISMATCH OF PROCEDURE CODE AND DIAGNOSIS

As insurance carriers improve the sophistication of their claims processing systems, including implementation of automated pre- and post-payment review, you should expect to see more claims denied, returned, questioned or down-coded due to procedure code - diagnosis code mismatch. There are numerous ICD-9-CM codes that are gender, organ or system specific, and therefore usable only if the procedure matches the diagnosis. However, this type of mismatch is infrequent and not particularly significant. The four major coding issues related to ICD-9-CM and CPT are:

- Diagnosis codes must support the procedures billed.

- Diagnosis codes must support the need for the place (location) of service where the procedures were performed or services provided.

- Diagnosis codes must support the level of care billed.

- Diagnosis codes must support the frequency of services billed.

DOWN-CODING DUE TO LACK OF DOCUMENTATION OF KEY COMPONENTS

The 1992 CPT provides concise definitions of the key components required to report Evaluation and Management codes. We predict increased auditing activity by Medicare to monitor the transition period to the new codes. Your documentation must clearly support the Evaluation and Management codes reported for the visit.

Each Evaluation and Management code description consists of key components, contributory factors, and time. The performance of key components, either three of three, or two of three, must be documented for every service. Of the contributory factors, which include counseling, coordination, and nature of the presenting problem, only the last must be documented for every service. Counseling and/or coordination of care are not necessarily provided at every encounter and need to be documented only if actually provided.

The time spent either face-to-face with the patient and/or family or as unit/floor time for hospital care and hospital consultations should be noted for every service. This is particularly important in a situation where counseling and/or coordination of care takes up more than 50 percent of the face-to-face physician time. In this situation, time is considered the key or controlling factor, and the extent of counseling and/or coordination of care must be documented in the medical record.

Consider that in an eight or nine hour work day, there are a given number of time units which may be allocated to evaluation and management services. Obviously, the collective time reported (by choice of codes) can not exceed the amount of time available in the work day. As an example, Evaluation and Management code 99255, which is the highest level of inpatient consultation defined in the 1992 CPT, has an average time of 110 minutes. In an eight hour day, only four of these services could be reported by one individual, and that is only if he or she did not take lunch or breaks or spend time doing anything else. A maximum of three is more likely.

PURCHASED DIAGNOSTIC SERVICES - MEDICARE

It is common for physicians to bill patients and insurance carriers for diagnostic services that were procured or ordered on behalf of the patient but not actually provided by the ordering physician. It is also common for the ordering physician to "mark-up" the fee for the purchased service prior to billing. This is referred to as global billing.

Medical equipment companies, particularly those offering electrocardiography, pulmonary diagnostic equipment, and other diagnostic equipment, have used this global billing concept in the past as a method of selling physicians a new "profit center" for their practice. Some even provided technicians, who were not employees of the practice, to perform the diagnostic tests in the physicians office. OBRA 1987 placed severe restrictions on global billing of certain diagnostic tests as of March 1, 1988.

The Medicare regulations apply to diagnostic tests other than clinical laboratory tests including, but not limited to: EKGs, EEGs, cardiac monitoring, X-rays and ultrasound. Global billing is allowed only when the billing physician personally performs or supervises the diagnostic procedure. To qualify under the supervision definition, the person performing the test must be an employee or the physician or group. Ownership interest in an outside supplier does not meet the supervision requirement.

Billing for purchased services under the new requirement is complicated. You must provide the supplier's name, address, provider number and net charge on your claim form. In addition, you must typically include a HCPCS Local Level 3 modifier to indicate that the service was purchased. Billing for global services usually will also require a HCPCS Local Level 3 modifier to indicate that the service was not purchased. This requirement does not apply to the professional component of these services if provided separately. You may continue to bill for this service using modifier -26.

We strongly recommend that you discontinue billing for the technical component of diagnostic services that you did not provide or supervise as defined in this regulation. Not only are you no longer making any profit on the procedures, you are increasing your costs due to the increased reporting requirements. In addition, you are increasing your audit liability risk if you are not billing these services properly.

CPT MODIFIERS

A complete understanding of CPT modifiers and their appropriate use can make a significant difference in reimbursement. Improper use of modifiers can result in claim delays or claim denials. Too frequent use of modifiers can result in audit liability while the proper and judicious use of modifiers can result in higher reimbursement.

There are 26 modifiers listed in Appendix A of the CPT. In addition, pertinent modifiers are repeated in each SECTION of the CPT. The following is a list of the modifiers along with a brief description and billing considerations where appropriate.

-20 Microsurgery

Used when surgical services *require the use of an operating microscope*. It is not used to describe services performed with a magnifying surgical loupe.

-21 Prolonged Evaluation and management services

When the service(s) provided is prolonged or otherwise greater than that usually required for the highest level of Evaluation and management service within a given category, it may be identified by adding modifier -21 to the Evaluation and Management code number or by use of the separate five digit modifier code 09921. A report may also be appropriate.

-22 Unusual services

When the service(s) provided is/are *greater than usually required*. Report is required. Modifier -22 is one of the most frequently abused and misused modifiers. Many medical professionals routinely add on a modifier -22 as a means to increase reimbursement. Many insurance carriers routinely ignore this modifier for the same reason.

In most cases, it is more appropriate to choose a CPT code of a higher value than to use this modifier. If you do choose to use this modifier, make sure you send a cover letter or report with your insurance claim which explains why the services were unusual.

-23 Unusual anesthesia

Used to report that a procedure was *performed under general anesthesia* that is normally performed with no anesthesia.

-24 Unrelated Evaluation and Management service by the same physician during a postoperative period

The physician may need to indicate that an Evaluation and management service was performed during a postoperative period for a reason(s) unrelated to the original procedure. This circumstance may be reported by adding the modifier -24 to the appropriate level of Evaluation and Management service, or the separate five digit modifier 09924 may be used.

-25 Significant, separately identifiable Evaluation and Management service by the same physician on the day of a procedure

The physician may need to indicate that on the day a procedure or service identified by a CPT code was performed, the patient's condition required a significant, separately identifiable Evaluation and management service above and beyond the usual preoperative and post-operative care associated with the procedure that was performed. This circumstance may be reported by adding the modifier -25 to the appropriate level of Evaluation and Management service, or the separate five digit modifier 09925 may be used.

-26 Professional component

Used to report the *physician component* of a procedure which consists of a technical and a professional component. These are typically diagnostic procedures.

This modifier became more important with the implementation of the Medicare purchased diagnostic services regulations.

-32 Mandated services

Used to identify services that were *MANDATED by a third party*, such as a peer review organization or insurance carrier. This modifier is changed to HCPCS modifier -SF if the patient is a Medicare patient.

-47 Anesthesia by surgeon

Used to report regional or general *anesthesia provided by the surgeon*. Not to be used for local anesthesia and not to be used with the codes from the ANESTHESIA section.

-50 Bilateral procedure

Used to report *bilateral procedures requiring a separate incision* performed during the SAME operative session. Requires that the procedure code be listed two times, the second time with the modifier -50. With the exception of a few codes in the RADIOLOGY section, all codes with descriptions including the term "bilateral" were eliminated from the 1990 edition of CPT.

-51 Multiple procedures

When multiple procedures are *performed at the same operative session*, all secondary, additional, or lessor procedures are listed after the primary procedure with the addition of the modifier -51. This modifier must be used properly and carefully because it has a tremendous impact on reimbursement. See the SURGERY section for a complete discussion of the proper use of this modifier.

-52 Reduced services

Used to report that a service or procedure is *partially reduced or eliminated*. he intended use is to report the reduction of a service without affecting insurance carrier provider profiles. This is another modifier that is frequently misused. Many practices mistakenly use modifier -52 to mean "reduced fee" and use it as a discounting method. Not only is this incorrect, you may be seriously damaging your profile with the insurance carriers.

The proper use for modifier -52 is to report that a service was not completed, or some part of a multiple-part service was not performed. Frequently, a fee reduction is in order as well; however that is not the primary purpose of the modifier.

-54 Surgical care only

Used when one physician performs a surgical procedure and another provides preoperative and/or post-operative care.

-55 Postoperative management only

Used when one physician performs the postoperative care after another physician has performed the surgical procedure.

-56 Preoperative management only

Used when one physician performs preoperative care and evaluation prior to another physician performing the surgical procedure.

-62 Two surgeons

Used when the skills of two surgeons, *usually with different skills*, are required in the management of a specific surgical procedure.

-66 Surgical team

Used when *highly complex procedures* require the services of several physicians at the same time.

-75 Concurrent care, services rendered by more than one physician

Used when the patient's condition requires the services of more than one physician, *usually of different specialties*. For CPT visit codes this modifier is the key to proper reimbursement for concurrent care services. (This modifier was deleted from the 1992 CPT)

-76 Repeat procedure by same physician

Used when a procedure or service is repeated by the same physician.

-77 Repeat procedure by another physician

Used when a procedure is performed that was previously performed by another physician.

-78 Return to the operating room for a related procedure during the postoperative period

The physician may need to indicate that another procedure was performed during the post-operative period of the initial procedure. When this subsequent procedure is related to the first, and requires the use of the operating room, it may be reported by adding the modifier 78 to the related procedure, or by using the separate five digit modifier 09978. (For repeat procedures on the same day, see -76).

-79 Unrelated procedure or service by the same physician during the postoperative period

The physician may need to indicate that the performance of a procedure or service during the postoperative period was unrelated to the original procedure. This circumstance may be reported by using the modifier -79 or by using the separate five digit modifier 09979. (For repeat procedures on the same day, see -76).

-80 Assistant surgeon

Used to report services provided by the first assistant surgeon.

-81 Minimum assistant surgeon

Used to report minimal services provided by a second assistant surgeon.

-82 Assistant surgeon (qualified resident not available)

Use this modifier to report assistant surgeon services provided at teaching hospitals when a qualified resident surgeon was not available to assist.

-90 Reference (outside) laboratory

Used to indicate that laboratory procedures billed on a claim were performed by an outside laboratory.

-99 Multiple modifiers

Two or more modifiers may be necessary to completely delineate a service. In such situations modifier -99 should be added to the basic procedure, and other applicable modifiers may be listed as part of the description of the service.

HCPCS MODIFIERS

The HCPCS coding system includes modifiers at all three levels. HCPCS Level 1 modifiers are the same as CPT modifiers. HCPCS National Level 2 and Local Level 3 modifiers are two digit codes in either alpha or alphanumeric format.

NATIONAL LEVEL 2 MODIFIERS

The following list is the complete list of HCPCS National Level 2 modifiers and descriptions:

-AA **Anesthesia services by anesthesiologist**

When anesthesia services are *performed personally* by the anesthesiologist, add modifier -aa to the basic service.

-AB **Four or less concurrent services by CRNA or AA employed by anesthesiologist**

-AC **Four or less concurrent services by CRNA not employed by anesthesiologist**

-AD **Supervision of more than four concurrent anesthesia services by anesthesiologist**

-AE **Direction of residents in furnishing not more than two concurrent anesthesia services.**

Used to report supervision of residents in a teaching facility.

-AF **Anesthesia complicated by total body hypothermia.**

-AG **Anesthesia for emergency surgery on a patient who is moribund or who has an incapacitating systemic disease that is a constant threat to life.**

-AH   Clinical psychologist

-AJ   Clinical social worker

-AK   Nurse practitioner (team member service)

-AM   Physician (team member service)

-AN   Physician assistant for other assistant-at-surgery

-AP   Determination of refractive state was not performed

-AR   Ambulance - return trip

-AS   Physician assistant (assisting at surgery)(non-team member).

-AT   Acute treatment

When chiropractic manipulation, HCPCS code A2000, is performed for acute treatment, add modifier -AT.

-AU   Physician assistant (other than assistant at surgery)(team member)

-CC   Portable x-ray (system set)

-DD   Powdered enteral formula

Add this modifier to HCPCS codes B4100-B5999 when powdered enteral products are supplied.

-EJ   Subsequent EPO injection

-EM   Emergency reserve supply (ESRD)

-EP   Service provided as part of Medicaid early periodic screening, diagnosis and treatment (EPSDT) program

-ET   Emergency treatment

Used with codes D0000-D9999 for dental procedures performed in emergency situations.

-FP   Service provided as part of Medicaid family planning program

-LL   Lease/rental

When DME equipment rental is to be applied against the purchase price, add modifier -ll to the basic HCPCS code.

-LR   Laboratory round trip

-LS   FDA-monitored intraocular lens implant

-LT   Left side

Used to identify procedures performed on the left side of the body.

-MP   Multiple patients seen

Used with CPT Visit codes 90300-94070 to indicate that more than one patient was seen during the visit.

-MS   Maintenance/service on a capped rental item that has been rented for 15 months

-NH   Enteral supplies for NH (system set)

-NR   New when rented

When DME equipment which was new at the time of rental is subsequently purchased, add modifier -NR to the basic HCPCS code.

-NU   New equipment

-QB   Physician providing services in a rural HMSA

-QE   Prescribed amount of oxygen is less than one liter per minute

-QF   Prescribed amount of oxygen is greater than four liters per minute and portable oxygen also prescribed

-QG   Prescribed amount of oxygen is greater than four liters per minute

-QH   Conserving device is being used

-QI   Medical direction of own employees by anesthesiologist (three concurrent procedures)

-QJ   Medical direction of own employees by anesthesiologist (four concurrent procedures)

-QK   Medical direction of other than own employees by anesthesiologist (two concurrent procedures)

-QL   Medical direction of other than own employees by anesthesiologist (three concurrent procedures)

-QM   Medical direction of other than own employees by anesthesiologist (four concurrent procedures)

-QU   Physician providing services in an urban HMSA

-RP   Replacement and repair

Used with HCPCS codes E0000-E9999 and L0000-L9999 to indicate replace-ment of DME, orthotic and prosthetic devices which have been in use for some time.

-RR   Rental

Used with HCPCS codes E0000-E9999 to indicate that DME is rented.

-RT   Right side

Used to identify procedures performed on the right side of the body.

-SF   Second opinion ordered by a professional review organization

Used to record a second opinion ordered by a PRO. Reimbursement is 100 percent and there is no deductible or coinsurance.

-SP   Nursing home or SNF visit, single patient seen

-TC   Technical component

Technical component charges are institutional charges and are not billed separately by physicians.

-UE   Used durable medical equipment

-VP   Aphakic patient

LOCAL LEVEL 3 MODIFIERS

In addition to the above HCPCS National Level 2 modifiers, each Medicare carrier creates additional modifiers for their own purposes. These are known as HCPCS Local Level 3 modifiers. In many cases, these local modifiers are used in place of CPT modifiers or HCPCS National Level 2 modifiers. The same coding rule applies to modifiers as to base codes. HCPCS Local Level 3 modifiers take precedence over HCPCS National Level 2 modifiers which take precedence over CPT Level 1 modifiers. The following are examples of HCPCS Local Level 3 modifiers assigned by various local Medicare carriers:

-WA   Cosmetic surgery

-WC   Drug addiction

-XI   Administration of an FDA approved drug

-YB   No purchased services

VISITS/EVALUATION AND MANAGEMENT SERVICES

In response to legislation mandating physician payment reform, the 1992 edition of CPT included a completely new section called EVALUATION AND MANAGEMENT SERVICES. The codes in this section were developed by a special CPT editorial panel working in conjunction with the Physician Payment Review Committee (PPRC). The use of these codes was mandated by law for all Medicare claims for services rendered on or after January 1, 1992. Private carriers are not required to adopt or use these new codes; however, the historical trend is that new policies and procedures mandated by Medicare are followed shortly by Medicaid and private insurance. Due to the fact that there will be continued use of the CPT Visit and level of service codes, all of which were deleted from the 1992 CPT, this book presents a complete discussion of both systems and, where possible, shows the relationship between the new and previous codes.

GUIDELINES

CLASSIFICATION OF EVALUATION AND MANAGEMENT SERVICES

The CPT 1992 includes for the first time, a major section devoted entirely to Evaluation and management services. The new codes are more than a clarification of the old definitions; they represent a new way of classifying the work of physicians. In particular, they involve far more clinical detail than the old visit codes. For this reason, it is important to treat the new codes as a new system and not make a one-for-one substitution of a new code number for a code number previously used to report a level of service.

The EVALUATION AND MANAGEMENT section is divided into broad categories such as office visits, hospital visits and consultations. Most of the categories are further divided into two or more subcategories, For example, there are two subcategories or office visits (new and established patients) and there are two subcategories of hospital visits (initial and subsequent). The subcategories or services are further classified into levels of services that are identified by specific codes. This classification is important because the nature of physician work varies by type of service, place of service, and the patient's status.

The basic format of the levels of EVALUATION AND MANAGEMENT services is the same for most categories. First, a unique code number is listed. Second, the place and/or type of service is specified, eg. office consultation. Third, the content of the service is defined, eg. comprehensive history and comprehensive examination. Fourth, the nature of the presenting problem(s) usually associated with a given level is described. Fifth, the time typically required to provide the service is specified.

SUBSECTION INFORMATION

The EVALUATION AND MANAGEMENT section of CPT is divided into 11 subsections; namely:

Office or Other Outpatient Services   99201-99215

Hospital Inpatient Services	99221-99238
Consultations	99241-99275
Emergency Department Services	99281-99288
Critical Care Services	99291-99292
Nursing Facility Services	99301-99313
Domiciliary, Rest Home or Custodial Care Services	99321-99333
Home Services	99341-99353
Case Management Services	99361-99373
Preventive Medicine Services	99381-99249
Newborn Care	99431-99440

All subsections within the 1992 CPT EVALUATION AND MANAGEMENT section have extensive notes that should be reviewed carefully prior to selecting codes for services located within the section.

MATERIALS SUPPLIED BY PHYSICIAN

Supplies and materials provided by the physician over and above those usually included with the visit, evaluation and management, or other services rendered may be listed separately. List all drugs, trays, supplies and materials provided. See the section IMPORTANT CODING AND BILLING ISSUES for a discussion of how to code and bill properly for supplies and materials. Remember that HCPCS National Level 2 codes must be used instead of CPT codes when reporting supplies, materials, and injections to Medicare.

DEFINITIONS OF COMMONLY USED TERMS

Certain key words and phrases are used throughout the EVALUATION AND MANAGEMENT SECTION. The following definitions are intended to reduce the potential for differing interpretations and to increase the consistency of reporting by physicians in differing specialties.

NEW AND ESTABLISHED PATIENT

A new patient is one who has not received any professional services from the physician within the past three years. An established patient is one who has received professional services from the physician within the past three years. In the instance where a physician is on call for or covering for another physician, the patient's encounter will be classified as it would have been by the physician who is not available.

No distinction is made between new and established patients in the emergency department. Evaluation and Management services in the emergency category may be reported for any new or established patient who presents for treatment in the emergency department.

CONCURRENT CARE

Concurrent care is the provision of similar services, eg, hospital visits, to the same patient by more than one physician on the same day. When concurrent care is provided, no special reporting is required. Modifier -75 has been deleted from the 1992 CPT. Prior to 1992, modifier -75 was the key to successful reporting of visit codes for concurrent care. As this modifier has now been deleted, the key reporting component is the ICD-9-CM code reported to justify the visit or Evaluation and Management service.

LEVELS OF EVALUATION AND MANAGEMENT SERVICES

Within each category or subcategory of EVALUATION AND MANAGEMENT service, there are three to five levels of services available for reporting purposes. Levels of Evaluation and Management services are not interchangeable among the different categories or subcategories of service. For example, the first level of Evaluation and Management services in the subcategory of office visit, new patient, does not have the same definition as the first level of Evaluation and Management services in the subcategory of office visit, established patient.

The levels of Evaluation and Management services include examinations, evaluations, treatments, conferences with or concerning patients, preventive pediatric and adult health supervision, and similar medical services. The levels of Evaluation and Management services encompass the wide variations in skill, effort, time, responsibility and medical knowledge required for the prevention or diagnosis and treatment of illness or injury and the promotion of optimal health. Each level of Evaluation and Management services may be used by all physicians.

The descriptions of the Evaluation and Management codes include seven components; namely:

- History
- Examination
- Medical Decision Making
- Counseling
- Coordination of Care
- Nature of the Presenting Problem
- Time

KEY COMPONENTS

The first three of these components (history, examination and medical decision making) are considered the KEY components in selecting a level of Evaluation and Management services.

HISTORY

There are four types of history used to define specific Evaluation and Management services:

Problem Focused

Chief complaint;
brief history of present illness or problem.

Expanded Problem Focused

Chief complaint;
brief history of present illness;
problem pertinent system review.

Detailed

Chief complaint;
extended history of present illness;
extended system review;
pertinent past;
family and/or social history.

Comprehensive

Chief complaint;
extended history of present illness;
complete system review; **complete past;**
family and social history

You will also see the term "interval" used to describe a history that is a component of follow-up hospital care.

EXAMINATION

There are four types of examination used to defined Evaluation and Management codes:

Problem Focused

An examination that is limited to the affected body area or organ system.

Expanded Problem Focused

An examination of the affected body area or organ system and other symptomatic or related organ systems.

Detailed

An extended examination of the affected body area(s) and other symptomatic or related organ system(s).

Comprehensive

A complete single system specialty examination or a complete multi-system examination.

You will also see the term "interval" used to describe an examination that is a component of follow-up hospital care.

MEDICAL DECISION MAKING

Medical decision making refers to the complexity of establishing a diagnosis and/or selecting a management option as measured by:

1) The number of possible diagnoses and/or the number of management options considered;

2) The amount and/or complexity of medical records, diagnostic tests, and/or other information that must be obtained and analyzed;

3) The risk of significant complications, morbidity and or mortality, as well as co-morbidities, associated with the patient's presenting problem(s), the diagnostic procedure(s) and/or the possible management options.

Four types of medical decision making are defined in CPT: straightforward; low complexity; moderate complexity; and high complexity. In addition, some codes include choices or ranges of medical decision making; for example "straightforward or low" and "low to moderate."

Straightforward

Minimal number of diagnoses or management options
Minimal or no data to be reviewed
Minimal risk of complications and/or morbidity or mortality

Low Complexity

Limited number of diagnoses or management options
Limited amount and/or complexity of data to be reviewed
Low risk of complications and/or morbidity or mortality

Moderate Complexity

Multiple diagnoses or management options
Moderate amount and/or complexity of data to be reviewed
Moderate risk of complications and/or morbidity or mortality

High Complexity

Extensive diagnoses or management options
Extensive amount and/or complexity of data to be reviewed
High risk of complications and/or morbidity or mortality

Combinations

Note that combinations of the above may also be found in the code descriptions. For example, you will find codes where the level of medical decision making is defined as "straightforward or low", or "low to moderate complexity."

Comorbidities/underlying diseases are not considered in selecting an Evaluation and Management code *unless* their presence significantly increases the complexity of the medical decision making.

In converting the CPT Visit codes to Evaluation and Management codes, the most significant factor is medical decision making. (See the CPT CROSS-WALK charts beginning on page 91).

CONTRIBUTORY COMPONENTS

The next three components; counseling, coordination of care, and the nature of the presenting problem, are considered CONTRIBUTORY factors in the majority of encounters. Although counseling and coordination of care are important components of Evaluation and Management services, it is not required that either or both be provided at every patient encounter.

COUNSELING

Counseling is defined as a discussion with a patient and/or family concerning one or more of the following areas:

- diagnostic results, impressions, and/or recommended diagnostic studies;
- prognosis;
- risks and benefits of management (treatment) options;
- instructions for management (treatment) and/or follow-up;
- importance of compliance with chosen management (treatment) options;
- risk factor reduction; and
- patient and family education

Counseling is listed as one of the seven components of Evaluation and Management services; however, there are no specified measurements included in the definition of the services. In all cases where counseling is mentioned, the same phrase is repeated: "Counseling and/or coordination of care with other providers or agencies are provided consistent with the nature of the problem(s) and the patient's and/or family's needs."

COORDINATION OF CARE

There is no definition of coordination of care provided in the 1992 CPT. The only statement made is "Coordination of care with other providers or agencies without a patient encounter on that day is reported using the case management codes."

In the case where counseling and/or coordination of care dominates (more than 50%) the face-to-face physician/patient encounter, then TIME is considered the key or controlling factor to qualify for a particular level of Evaluation and Management services. The extent of counseling and/or coordination of care must be documented in the medical record.

NATURE OF THE PRESENTING PROBLEM

A presenting problem is a disease, condition, illness, injury, symptom, sign, finding, complaint, or other reason for encounter, with or without a diagnosis being established at the time of the encounter. There are five types of presenting problems that are used in defining the Evaluation and Management codes:

Minimal

A problem that may not require the presence of the physician, but service is provided under the physician's supervision.

Self-limited or Minor

A problem that runs a definite and prescribed course, is transient in nature and is not likely to permanently alter health status OR has a good prognosis with management and/or compliance.

Low Severity

A problem where the risk of morbidity without treatment is low; there is little to no risk of mortality without treatment; full recovery without functional impairment is expected.

Moderate Severity

A problem where the risk of morbidity without treatment is moderate; there is moderate risk of mortality without treatment; uncertain prognosis OR increased probability of prolonged functional impairment.

High Severity

A problem where the risk of morbidity without treatment is high to extreme; there is a moderate to high risk of mortality without treatment OR high probability of severe, prolonged functional impairment.

Combinations

Note that combinations of the above may also be found in the code descriptions. For example, you will find codes where the presenting problem(s) are defined as "moderate severity", or "high severity" or "moderate to high severity."

Other Definitions of Nature of the Presenting Problem

In addition to the above five specific definitions found in the 1992 CPT, there are other definitions found in the Evaluation and Management codes used to report Subsequent Hospital Care and Follow-up Inpatient Consultations. These definitions are:

Evaluation and Management Codes	Nature of Presenting Problem(s) Defined	Equivalent To
99231 or 99261	Stable, recovering or improving	Self-limited or minor
99232 or 99262	Inadequate response or minor complication	Low to moderate severity
99233 or 99263	Significant complication or new problem	Moderate to high severity

TIME

The inclusion of time in the definitions of the levels of Evaluation and Management services has been implicit in prior editions of CPT. The inclusion of time as an explicit factor beginning in CPT 1992 was done to assist physicians in selecting the most appropriate level of Evaluation and Management services. It should be recognized that the specific times expressed in the visit code descriptors are averages, and therefore represent a range of times which may be higher or lower depending on actual clinical circumstances.

Time is not a descriptive component for the emergency department levels of Evaluation and Management services because emergency department services are typically provided on a variable intensity basis, often involving multiple encounters with several patients over an extended period of time. Therefore, it is difficult for physicians to provide accurate estimates of the time spent face-to-face with the patient.

Studies to establish levels of Evaluation and Management services employed surveys of practicing physicians to obtain data on the amount of time and work associated with typical Evaluation and Management services. Since "work" is not easily identifiable, the codes must rely on other objective, verifiable measures that correlate with physicians' estimates of their "work". It has been demonstrated that physicians' estimations of intra-service time both within and across specialties, is a variable that is predictive of the "work" of Evaluation and Management services. This same research has shown there is a strong relationship between intra-service time and total time for Evaluation and Management services. Intra-service time, rather than total time, was chosen for inclusion with the codes because of its relative ease of measurement and because of its direct correlation with measurements of the total amount of time and work associated with typical Evaluation and Management services.

Intra-service times are defined as face-to-face time for office and other outpatient visits and as unit/floor time for hospital and other inpatient visits. This distinction is necessary because most of the work of typical office visits takes place during the face-to-face time with the patient, while most of the work of typical hospital visits takes place during the time spent on the patient's floor or unit.

FACE-TO-FACE TIME

For office and other outpatient visits and office consultations, the term face-to-face time is used. For coding purposes, face-to-face time for these services is defined as only that time that the physician spends face-to-face with the patient and/or family. This includes the time in which the physician performs such tasks as obtaining a history, performing an examination, and counseling the patient.

Physicians also spend time doing work before or after the face-to-face time with the patient, performing such tasks as reviewing records and tests, arranging for further services, and communicating further with other professionals and the patient through written reports and telephone contact.

This non face-to-face time for office services, also called pre- and post-encounter time, is not included in the time component described in the Evaluation and Management codes. However, the pre- and post- face-to-face work associated with an encounter was included in calculating the total work of typical services in physician surveys. Thus, the face-to-face time associated with the services described by any Evaluation and Management code is a valid proxy for the total work done before, during and after the visit.

UNIT/FLOOR TIME

For inpatient hospital care, initial and follow-up hospital consultations, and nursing facility assessments, the term unit/floor time is used. For coding purposes, intra-service time for these services is defined as unit/floor time, which includes the time that the physician is present on the patient's hospital unit and at the bedside rendering services for that patient. This includes the time spent in which the physician establishes and/or reviews the patient's chart, examines the patient, writes notes and communicates with other professionals and the patient's family.

In the hospital, pre- and post-time includes time spent off the patient's floor performing such tasks as reviewing pathology and radiology findings in another part of the hospital. This pre- and post-visit time is not included in the time component described in these codes. However, the pre- and post-work performed during the time spent off the floor or unit was included in calculating the total work of typical services in physician surveys. Thus, the unit/floor time associated with the services described by any code is a valid proxy for the total work done before, during, and after the visit.

DIAGNOSTIC TESTS OR STUDIES

The actual performance of diagnostic tests or studies for which specific CPT codes are available IS NOT included in the levels of Evaluation and Management services. Physician performance of diagnostic tests or studies for which specific CPT codes are available should be reported separately, in *addition* to the appropriate Evaluation and Management code.

UNLISTED SERVICE

An Evaluation and Management service may be provided that is not listed in the Evaluation and Management section of CPT. When reporting such a service, the appropriate "Unlisted" code may be used to indicate the service, identifying it by "Special Report". The "Unlisted Services" and accompanying codes for the evaluation and management section are:

99249   Unlisted preventive medicine service
99499   Unlisted evaluation and management service

SPECIAL REPORT

An unlisted service or one that is unusual, variable, or new may require a special report demonstrating the medical appropriateness of the service. Pertinent information should include an adequate definition or description of the nature, extent and need for the procedure; and the time, effort and equipment necessary to provide the service. Additional items which may be included are complexity of the symptoms, final diagnosis, pertinent physical findings, diagnostic and therapeutic procedures, concurrent problems, and follow-up care.

CLINICAL EXAMPLES

Clinical examples of the new CPT codes for Evaluation and Management services are intended to be an important element of the new coding system. The clinical examples, when used in conjunction with the revised Evaluation and Management descriptions and time guidelines provide a comprehensive and powerful new tool for physicians to report the services provided to their patients. At the time the 1992 CPT was published, the development and validation of the clinical examples had not been completed. See page XX of the Office Services section for clinical examples which were available at the time of publication of this work.

MODIFIERS

Listed services may be modified under certain circumstances. When applicable, the modifying circumstance against general guidelines should be identified by the addition of the appropriate modifier code, which may be reported in either of two ways. The modifier may be reported by a two digit number placed after the procedure code. Or, the modifier may be reported by a separate five digit code that is used in addition to the procedure code. Modifiers which may be used with Visit and Evaluation and Management codes are:

-21 Prolonged Evaluation and management services

-24 Unrelated Evaluation and management service by the same physician during a post-operative period

-25 Significant, separately identifiable Evaluation and management service by the same physician on the day of a procedure

-32 Mandated services

-52 Reduced services

-75 Concurrent care, services rendered by more than one physician

(Modifier -75 was deleted from the 1992 CPT)

-78 Return to the operating room for a related procedure during the postoperative period

-79 Unrelated procedure or service by the same physician during the postoperative period

CHOOSING EVALUATION AND MANAGEMENT CODES

Choosing the correct Evaluation and management code to report is a nine step process. The most important steps, in terms of both reimbursement and audit liability, are verifying compliance and documentation. The italicized items represent an example of the selection process.

1. **Identify the Category of Service**

   ☐ Office or Other Outpatient Services
   ☐ Hospital Inpatient Services
   ☐ Consultations
   ☐ Emergency Department Services
   ☐ Critical Care Services
   ☐ Nursing Facility Services
   ☐ Domiciliary, Rest Home or Custodial Care Services
   ☐ Home Services
   ☐ Preventive Medicine Services
   ☐ Newborn Care

2. **Identify the Subcategory of Service**

   ☐ New Patient
   ☐ Established Patient
   ☐ Initial Care
   ☐ Subsequent Care
   ☐ Follow-up

3. **Determine the Extent of History Obtained**

☐ Problem Focused
☐ Expanded Problem Focused
☐ Detailed
☐ Comprehensive

4. **Determine the Extent of Examination Performed**

☐ Problem Focused
☐ Expanded Problem Focused
☐ Detailed
☐ Comprehensive

5. **Determine the Complexity of Medical Decision Making**

☐ Straightforward
☐ Low Complexity
☐ Moderate Complexity
☐ High Complexity

6. **Record the Approximate Amount of Intra-Service Time**

☐ Face-to-face time for office visits and consults
☐ Unit or floor time for hospital care, hospital consults, and nursing facilities

If counseling and/or coordination of care exceeds 50 percent of the total face-to-face physician/patient encounter, then TIME is considered to be the key or controlling factor which qualifies the choice of a particular level of Evaluation and Management service. The extent of counseling and/or coordination of care must be documented in the medical record.

7. **Verify Compliance with Reporting Requirements**

All Three Key Components Required

To report services to new patients, initial care, office or confirmatory consultations, emergency department services, and comprehensive nursing facility assessments, all three key components must meet or exceed the stated requirements.

☐ History component met or exceeded
☐ Examination component met or exceeded
☐ Medical decision making component met or exceeded

Two of Three Key Components Required

To report services to established patients, subsequent or follow-up care, two of the three key components must meet or exceed the stated requirements.

☐ History component met or exceeded; and/or
☐ Examination component met or exceeded; and/or
☐ Medical decision making component met or exceeded

8. Verify Documentation

Make sure that the medical record includes proper documentation of the history, examination, medical decision making, the nature of the problem(s), the approximate amount of time, and when appropriate, the extent of counseling and/or coordination of care.

9. Assign the Code

EXAMPLE OF THE CODE SELECTION PROCESS

1.	Category of Service	*Office*
2.	Subcategory	*New patient*
3.	History	*Problem focused*
4.	Examination	*Problem focused*
5.	Medical Decision Making	*Straightforward*
6.	Intra-service Time	*10 minutes*
7.	Key Components	*Met or exceeded*
8.	Documentation	*Met or exceeded*
9.	Assign the Code	***99201***

OFFICE AND OTHER OUTPATIENT SERVICES

VISIT CODES   90000-90080

Visit codes in the range 90000-90080 are used to report services provided to new and established patients in the physician's office or in an outpatient or other ambulatory facility, including the emergency department when the physician is not assigned to the emergency department. A patient is considered an outpatient until admitted as an inpatient to a health care facility. The key coding issues are whether the patient is a new patient or established patient, and the level of service provided.

All CPT codes in this series were deleted from the 1992 CPT. These codes may not be used to bill Medicare for services rendered after January 1, 1992. However, these codes will be accepted by other insurance carriers until they have converted to the new 1992 CPT coding system.

EVALUATION AND MANAGEMENT CODES   99201-99215

Evaluation and management codes in the range 99201-99215 are used to report services provided to new and established patients in the office or other outpatient facility, including the emergency department when the physician is not assigned to the emergency department. The key coding issues are the extent of history obtained, the extent of examination performed, and the complexity of medical decision making. Additional reporting issues include counseling and/or coordination of care, the nature of presenting problem(s), and the face-to-face time spent with the patient and/or family.

Coding Rules

1) A patient is considered an outpatient until inpatient admission to a health care facility occurs.

2) If outpatient Evaluation and management services are provided in conjunction with, or result in, an inpatient admission, the service is reported using the codes for initial hospital care.

3) The codes in this section may also be used to report the services provided by a physician to a patient in an observation area of a hospital.

These codes were first implemented in the 1992 CPT. These codes must be used to bill Medicare for services rendered after January 1, 1992. These new codes will most likely be accepted by Medicaid and all other insurance carriers within a one year period. Watch your insurance carrier newsletters and Explanation of Benefits (EOBs) for notices regarding conversion.

CPT CROSS-WALK - OFFICE AND OTHER OUTPATIENT VISITS

NEW PATIENT

Visit	Description	Level	E/M	Time	Frequency
90000	Office visit	Brief	99201	10	100 %
90010		Limited	99202	20	100 %
90015		Intermediate	99203	30	100 %
90017		Extended	99204	45	100 %
90020		Comprehensive	99204	45	70 %
		or	99205[1]	60	30 %

[1] For code 90020 to cross-walk to code 99205, medical decision making must be of high complexity and the encounter time should average 60 minutes.

ESTABLISHED PATIENT

90030		Minimal	99211	5	100 %
90040		Brief	99212	10	100 %
90050		Limited	99213	15	100 %
90060		Intermediate	99214	25	100 %
90070		Extended	99215	40	100 %
90080		Comprehensive	99215[2]	40	100 %

[2] There are six visit codes but only five Evaluation and Management codes. Visit code 90080 is cross-walked to the same code as 90070, meaning that code 90080 has been permanently "down-coded" by definition.

The column titled "Frequency" in the above chart (and all following charts) is the percentage of cross-walk to from the "old" Visit code to the "new" Evaluation and Management code predicted by HCFA. For example, HCFA predicts that 70 percent of services formerly coded as 90020 will be coded as 99204 and 30 percent will be coded as 99205.

CLINICAL EXAMPLES FOR OFFICE EVALUATION AND MANAGEMENT SERVICES

An important element of the new CPT coding system is the clinical examples of each level of service. At the time of publication of the 1992 CPT, development and validation of the clinical examples was not complete. Therefore, there are no clinical examples in the CPT book. The following are clinical examples for office Evaluation and management services.

99201   NEW PATIENT, BRIEF SERVICE

Internal Medicine   *Office visit with an out-of-town visitor who needs a prescription refilled because she forgot her hay fever medication.*

Oral and Maxillofacial Surgery   *Office visit to advise for or against the removal of* wisdom teeth, for an 18-year -old male referred by an orthodontist.

99202   NEW PATIENT, LIMITED SERVICE

Dermatology   *Initial office visit, 16-year-old male with severe cystic acne, new patient.*

Internal Medicine   *Initial Evaluation and Management of recurrent urinary infection in female.*

Orthopedics   *First visit for Evaluation and management and counseling of 28-year-old male runner with knee and calf pain.*

Otolaryngology   *Initial office evaluation for gradual hearing loss, 58-year-old-male, history and physical exam, with interpretation of complete audiogram, air bone, etc.*

99203   NEW PATIENT, INTERMEDIATE SERVICE

Internal Medicine   *Initial office evaluation for diagnosis and management of painless gross hematuria in new patient, without cystoscopy.*

Orthopedics/ Physical Medicine   *Initial office visit for evaluation of 13-year-old female* with progressive *scoliosis.*

General Surgery   *Office visit for initial evaluation of a 48-year-old man with recurrent low back pain radiating to the leg.*

Urology   *Initial evaluation and management of recurrent renal calculi in 40-year-old male.*

Obstetrics/Gynecology   *Initial office evaluation of secondary amenorrhea, in 22-year-old new patient, pregnancy excluded.*

99204   NEW PATIENT, EXTENDED SERVICE

Thoracic Surgery
Initial office evaluation of a 50-year-old male with an aortic aneurysm with respect to recommendation for surgery.

Internal Medicine
Initial office evaluation of a 70-year-old patient with recent onset of episodic confusion.

Cardiology
Office visit for initial evaluation of a 63-year-old male with chest pain on exertion.

Urology
Initial evaluation and management of unexplained renal failure in a 40-year-old female.

Obstetrics/Gynecology
Initial office visit for 34-year-old patient with primary infertility, including counseling.

Rheumatology
Initial office evaluation of a 70-year-old female with polyarthralgia.

99205   NEW PATIENT, COMPREHENSIVE SERVICE

Hematology
Initial office visit for a 73-year-old male with an unexplained 20-pound weight loss.

Infectious Diseases
Initial office visit for a 24-year-old homosexual male who has fever, cough and shortness of breath.

Rheumatology
Initial office evaluation for a patient with systemic lupus erythematosus, fever, seizures and profound thrombocytopenia.

Initial office evaluation and management of a patient with systemic vasculitis and compromised circulation to the limbs.

99211   ESTABLISHED PATIENT, MINIMAL SERVICE

Internal Medicine
Cursory check in the office for an established patient with a hematoma one day after venipuncture.

99212   ESTABLISHED PATIENT, BRIEF SERVICE

Pediatrics/
Internal Medicine/
Family Practice
Office evaluation for possible purulent bacterial conjunctivitis with a 1-2 *day history of redness and* discharge for a 16-year-old female patient.

Internal Medicine
Office visit with a 65-year-old established patient with eruption on both arms from poison oak exposure.

| Family Practice/ Pediatrics | *Office visit, established visit for a 6-year-old child* with a sore throat and *headache.* |

99213   ESTABLISHED PATIENT, LIMITED SERVICE

| Family Practice/ Internal Medicine | *Follow-up visit with a 55-year-old male for* management of hypertension *and mild fatigue, on beta blocker/thiazide regimen.* |

| Gastroenterology | *Follow-up office visit for an established patient with stable cirrhosis of the liver.* |

| Pulmonary Medicine | *Quarterly follow-up office visit for a 45-year-old male, with stable chronic asthma, on steroid and broncho-dilator therapy.* |

| Rheumatology/ Orthopedics | *Office visit for an established patient with known osteoarthritis and painful swollen knees.* |

| Hematology/Oncology | *Routine, follow-up office evaluation at a three-month interval for a 77-year-old female with nodular small cleaved-cell lymphoma.* |

| Internal Medicine | *Follow-up visit for a 70-year-old diabetic hypertensive patient with recent change in insulin requirement.* |

99214   ESTABLISHED PATIENT, INTERMEDIATE SERVICE

| Family Practice/ Internal Medicine | *Office evaluation of a 28-year-old patient with* diarrhea and low grade *fever, established patient.* |

| Urology/ General Surgery/ Internal Medicine/ Family Practice | *Office evaluation of new onset RLQ pain in a 32-year-*old woman, *established patient.* |

| Cardiology | *Office visit for a 68-year-old male with stable angina, two months post-myocardial infarction, who is not tolerating his medications.* |

| Hematology/Oncology | *Weekly office visit for 5FU therapy for an ambulatory established patient with metastatic colon cancer and increasing shortness of breath.* |

| Neurology | *Follow-up office visit for a 60-year-old male whose post-traumatic seizures have disappeared on medication, and who now raises the question of stopping the medication.* |

| Rhematology | *Follow-up office visit for a 45-year-old patient with rheumatoid arthritis on gold, methotrexate, or immuno-suppressive therapy.* |

99215 ESTABLISHED PATIENT, EXTENDED SERVICE

Neurology   *Follow-up office visit for a 75-year-old patient with amyotrophic lateral schlerosis (ALS) who is no longer able to swallow.*

Rhematology   *Follow-up visit for a 40-year-old female with acute rheumatoid arthritis and deteriorating function.*

Internal Medicine   *Office visit for evaluation of recent onset of syncopal attacks in a 70-year-old female, established patient.*

General Surgery   *Office evaluation and discussion of treatment options for a 68-year-old male with a biopsy-proven rectal carcinoma.*

Infectious Diseases *Follow-up office visit for a 65-year-old male with a fever of recent onset while on outpatient antibiotic therapy for endocarditis.*

Hematology/Oncology *Office visit for restaging of an established patient with new lymphadenopathy one year post therapy for lymphoma.*

HOME MEDICAL SERVICES

VISIT CODES   90100-90170

Visit codes in the range 90100-90170 are used to report services provided in the patient's home for new patients and established patients. The key coding issues are whether the patient is a new patient or established patient, and the level of service provided.

All CPT codes in this series were deleted from the 1992 CPT. These codes may not be used to bill Medicare for services rendered after January 1, 1992. However, these codes will be accepted by other insurance carriers until they have converted to the new 1992 CPT coding system.

EVALUATION AND MANAGEMENT CODES   99341-99353

Evaluation and management codes in the range 99341-99353 are used to report services provided to new and established patients in the patient's home. The key coding issues are the extent of history obtained, the extent of examination performed, and the complexity of medical decision making. Additional reporting issues include counseling and/or coordination of care, and the nature of presenting problem(s). As of the publication of the 1992 CPT typical times had not been established for this category of services.

These codes were first implemented in the 1992 CPT. These codes must be used to bill Medicare for services rendered after January 1, 1992. These new codes will most likely be accepted by Medicaid and all other insurance carriers within a one year period. Watch your insurance carrier newsletters and Explanation of Benefits (EOBs) for notices regarding conversion.

CPT CROSS-WALK FOR HOME MEDICAL SERVICES

NEW PATIENT

Visit	Description	Level		E/M	Time	Frequency
90100	Home visit	Brief		99341	UNS[1]	100
90110[2]		Limited		99341	UNS	50
			or	99342	UNS	50
90115[2]		Intermediate		99342	UNS	50
			or	99343	UNS	50
90117		Extended		99343	UNS	100

ESTABLISHED PATIENT

Visit		Level		E/M	Time	Frequency
90130		Minimal		99351	UNS	100
90140[2]		Brief		99351	UNS	50
			or	99352	UNS	50
90150		Limited		99352	UNS	100
90160[2]		Intermediate		99352	UNS	50
			or	99353	UNS	50
90170		Extended		99353	UNS	100

[1] Typical times were not specified in the 1992 CPT.
[2] Cross-walk possible to more than one code. The code selection depends on the level of medical decision making, the nature of the problem(s), and time.

HOSPITAL SERVICES

VISIT CODES   90200-90292

Visit codes in the range 90200-90292 are used to report services provided in the inpatient hospital for new patients and established patients. The key coding issues are whether the service is an admission (initial care), follow-up visit (subsequent care) or discharge and the level of care provided.

All CPT codes in this series were deleted from the 1992 CPT. These codes may not be used to bill Medicare for services rendered after January 1, 1992. However, these codes will be accepted by other insurance carriers until they have converted to the new 1992 CPT coding system.

HCPCS VISIT CODES

HCPCS 1991 includes four codes, M0021-M0023 and M0029, which describe hospital visits which pertain to multiple visits per day and routine newborn care. Consult with your local Medicare intermediary before using these HCPCS codes for hospital services.

EVALUATION AND MANAGEMENT CODES   99221-99238

Evaluation and management codes in the range 99331-99238 are used to report services provided in the hospital. The key coding issues are the extent of history obtained, the extent of examination performed, and the complexity of medical decision making. Additional reporting issues include counseling and/or coordination of care, the nature of presenting problem(s), and the time spent at the bedside and on the patient's facility floor or unit.

Coding Rules

1)   The codes defined as Initial Hospital Care are used to report the first hospital inpatient encounter with the patient by the admitting physician.

2)   For initial inpatient encounters by physicians other than the admitting physician, use codes from the inpatient consultation or subsequent hospital care series as appropriate.

3)   When the patient is admitted to the hospital in the course of an encounter in another location for example, office, or hospital emergency department, all evaluation and management services provided by the reporting physician in conjunction with the admission are considered part of the initial hospital care when performed on the same date of service.

4)   The admitting physician should report all service related to the admission provided in all other locations.

5)   Evaluation and management services provided on the same date of service, in locations other than the hospital, that are related to the admission, are not reported separately.

These codes were first implemented in the 1992 CPT. These codes must be used to bill Medicare for services rendered after January 1, 1992. These new codes will most likely be accepted by Medicaid and all other insurance carriers within a one year period. Watch your insurance carrier newsletters and Explanation of Benefits (EOBs) for notices regarding conversion.

CPT CROSS-WALK FOR HOSPITAL SERVICES

INITIAL HOSPITAL CARE

Visit	Description	Level	E/M	Time	Frequency
90200	Initial Hospital	Brief	99221	30	100
90215	Initial hospital	Intermediate	99222	50	100
90220	Initial hospital	Comprehensive	99222	50	50
		or	99223[1]	70	50

[1] For code 90220 to cross-walk to code 99223, medical decision making must be of high complexity, the nature of the presenting problem must be of high severity and the encounter time should average 70 minutes.

SUBSEQUENT HOSPITAL CARE

Visit	Description	Level	E/M	Time	Frequency
90240	Hospital visit	Brief	99231	15	100
90250[2]	Hospital visit	Limited	99231	15	80[3]
		or	99232	25	20
90260[2]	Hospital visit	Intermediate	99231	15	50[3]
		or	99232	25	50
90270	Hospital visit	Extended	99232	25	100
90280	Hospital visit	Comprehensive	99233	35	100
90292	Hospital discharge		99238	--	

[2] Cross-walk possible to more than one code. The code selection depends on the level of medical decision making, the nature of the problem(s), and time.

[3] Based on predicted frequencies, 80% of visits formerly coded 90250 and 50% of visits formerly coded 90260 will be "down-coded" by the provider due to the inability to report the key components necessary to support the higher level codes.

SKILLED NURSING, INTERMEDIATE CARE, AND LONG-TERM CARE FACILITIES

VISIT CODES   90300-90370

Visit codes in the range 90300-90370 are used to report services provided in the skilled nursing, intermediate care, and long-term care facility for new patients and established patients. These services are defined as involving active, definitive, and professional care to patients confined in convalescent, rehabilitative or long-term care facilities. The key coding issues are whether the service is an admission (initial care), or follow-up visit (subsequent care), the level of care, and the number of patients seen per visit.

All CPT codes in this series were deleted from the 1992 CPT. These codes may not be used to bill Medicare for services rendered after January 1, 1992. However, these codes will be accepted by other insurance carriers until they have converted to the new 1992 CPT coding system.

When reporting these codes to Medicare include the HCPCS National Level 2 modifier -SP or -MP, or other Local Level 3 modifier specified by your local Medicare carrier.

EVALUATION AND MANAGEMENT SERVICES   99301-99313

Evaluation and management codes in the range 99301-99313 are used to report services provided in nursing facilities (formerly referred to as Skilled Nursing Facilities, Intermediate Care Facilities, and Long Term Care Facilities). The key coding issues are the extent of history obtained, the extent of examination performed, and the complexity of medical decision making. Additional reporting issues include counseling and/or coordination of care, the nature of presenting problem(s), and the time spent at the bedside and on the patient's facility floor or unit.

These codes are also used to report evaluation and management services provided to a patient in a psychiatric residential treatment center. If procedures such as medical psychotherapy are provided in addition to evaluation and management services, these are reported in addition to the evaluation and management services.

Nursing facilities included in this category are required to conduct assessments of each patient's functional capacity. Physicians have the primary responsibility for assuring that all patients receive thorough assessments and that medical care plans are instituted and/or revised as appropriate. Codes in this section apply to Comprehensive Nursing Facility Assessments and Subsequent Nursing Facility care. Both subcategories apply to new and established patients. Comprehensive Assessments may be performed at one or more sites during the assessment process; including the hospital, the office, a nursing facility, a domiciliary facility and/or the patient's home.

Coding rules

1.   When the patient is admitted to the nursing facility in the course of an encounter in another location, for example, the office or hospital emergency department, all evaluation and management services provided by the physician in conjunction with that admission

are considered part of the initial nursing facility care when performed on the same date as the admission.

2.   The nursing facility care level of service reported by the admitting physician should include the services related to the admission he or she provided in the other location(s).

3.   With the exception of hospital discharge services, evaluation and management service on the same date provided in locations other than the nursing facility that are related to the admission should not be reported separately.

4.   More than one comprehensive assessment may be necessary during an inpatient confinement.

These codes were first implemented in the 1992 CPT. These codes must be used to bill Medicare for services rendered after January 1, 1992. These new codes will most likely be accepted by Medicaid and all other insurance carriers within a one year period. Watch your insurance carrier newsletters and Explanation of Benefits (EOBs) for notices regarding conversion.

When reporting these codes to Medicare include the HCPCS National Level 2 modifier -SP or -MP, or other Local Level 3 modifier specified by your local Medicare carrier.

CPT CROSS-WALK FOR NURSING ASSESSMENTS (SKILLED NURSING FACILITY)

INITIAL CARE

Visit	Description	Level		E/M	Time	Frequency
90300[1]	Facility visit	Brief		99302	40	25
			or	99303	50	75
90315[1]		Intermediate		99302	40	25
			or	99303	50	75
90320		Comprehensive		99303	50	100

SUBSEQUENT CARE

Visit	Level		E/M	Time	Frequency
90340	Brief		99311	15	100
90350	Limited		99312	25	100
90360[1]	Intermediate		99301[2]	30	25
		or	99312	25	50
		or	99313	35	25
90370[1]	Extended		99301[2]	30	25
		or	99302[2]	40	25
		or	99313	35	50

[1] Cross-walk possible to more than one code. The code selection depends on the level of medical decision making, the nature of the problem(s), and time.

[2] More than one comprehensive assessment may be necessary during an inpatient confinement.

REST HOME OR CUSTODIAL SERVICES

VISIT CODES   90400-90470

Visit codes in the range 90400-90470 are used to report services provided in the domiciliary, rest home or custodial care facilities for new patients and established patients. These codes are used to bill for periodic services rendered to a patient who is institutionalized on a long-term basis. Codes may be used for new and established patients. Key coding issues are level of care and number of patients seen per visit.

All CPT codes in this series were deleted from the 1992 CPT. These codes may not be used to bill Medicare for services rendered after January 1, 1992. However, these codes will be accepted by other insurance carriers until they have converted to the new 1992 CPT coding system. When reporting these codes to Medicare include HCPCS modifier -SP or -MP to indicate single or multiple patients seen during the visit. Consult your local Medicare intermediary before using these modifiers.

EVALUATION AND MANAGEMENT CODES   99321-99333

Evaluation and management codes in the range 99321-99333 are used to report services provided to new and established patients in domiciliary, rest home or custodial care facility. The key coding issues are the extent of history obtained, the extent of examination performed, and the complexity of medical decision making. Additional reporting issues include counseling and/or coordination of care, the nature of presenting problem(s). As of publication of the 1992 CPT, typical times had not been established for this category of services.

These codes were first implemented in the 1992 CPT. These codes must be used to bill Medicare for services rendered after January 1, 1992. These new codes will most likely be accepted by Medicaid and all other insurance carriers within a one year period. Watch your insurance carrier newsletters and Explanation of Benefits (EOBs) for notices regarding conversion.

When reporting these codes to Medicare include HCPCS modifier -SP or -MP to indicate single or multiple patients seen during the visit. Consult your local Medicare intermediary before using these modifiers.

CPT CROSS-WALK FOR DOMICILIARY
(REST HOME/CUSTODIAL CARE) SERVICES

NEW PATIENT

Visit	Description	Level		E/M	Time	Frequency
90400	Facility visit	Brief		99321	UNS[1]	100
90410[2]		Limited		99321	UNS	50
			or	99322	UNS	50
90415[2]		Intermediate		99322	UNS	50
			or	99323	UNS	50
90420		Comprehensive		99323	UNS	100

ESTABLISHED PATIENT

90430		Minimal		99331	UNS	100
90440[2]		Brief		99331	UNS	50
			or	99332	UNS	50
90450		Limited		99332	UNS	100
90460[2]		Intermediate		99332	UNS	50
			or	99333	UNS	50
90470		Extended		99333	UNS	100

[1] Typical times were not specified in the 1992 CPT.

[2] Cross-walk possible to more than one code. The code selection depends on the level of medical decision making, the nature of the problem(s), and time.

EMERGENCY SERVICES

VISIT CODES   90500-90590

Visit codes in the range 90500-90590 are used to report services provided in the emergency department for new patients and established patients. These codes may be used only by physicians who are assigned to the emergency department. For patients seen in the emergency department by a physician not assigned to the emergency department, visit codes from the 90000-90080 series are used. Key coding issues are whether the patient is new or established and the level of care provided.

All CPT codes in this series were deleted from the 1992 CPT. These codes may not be used to bill Medicare for services rendered after January 1, 1992. However, these codes will be accepted by other insurance carriers until they have converted to the new 1992 CPT coding system.

EVALUATION AND MANAGEMENT CODES   99281-99288

Evaluation and management codes in the range 99281-99288 are used to report services provided to new or established patients in the emergency department. The key coding issues are the extent of history obtained, the extent of examination performed, and the complexity of medical decision making. Additional reporting issues include counseling and/or coordination of care, and the nature of presenting problem(s).

Time is not a descriptive component for Evaluation and Management services provided in the emergency department. These services are typically provided on a variable intensity basis, often involving multiple encounters with several patients over an extended period of time. Therefore, it is difficult for physicians to provide accurate estimates of the time spent face-to-face with the patient in the emergency department.

These codes were first implemented in the 1992 CPT. These codes must be used to bill Medicare for services rendered after January 1, 1992. These new codes will most likely be accepted by Medicaid and all other insurance carriers within a one year period. Watch your insurance carrier newsletters and Explanation of Benefits (EOBs) for notices regarding conversion.

CPT CROSS-WALK FOR EMERGENCY SERVICES

NEW PATIENT

Visit	Description	Level		E/M	Time	Frequency
90500	Emergency visit	Minimal		99291	UNS[1]	100
90505[2]		Brief		99281	UNS	50
			or	99282	UNS	50
90510[2]		Limited		99282	UNS	50
			or	99283	UNS	50
90515[2]		Intermediate		99283	UNS	50
			or	99284	UNS	50
90517[2]		Extended		99284	UNS	50
			or	99285	UNS	50
90520		Comprehensive		99285	UNS	100

ESTABLISHED PATIENT

Visit	Level		E/M	Time	Frequency
90530	Minimal		99281	UNS	100
90540[2]	Brief		99281	UNS	50
		or	99282	UNS	50
90550[2]	Limited		99282	UNS	50
		or	99283	UNS	50
90560[2]	Intermediate		99283	UNS	50
		or	99284	UNS	50
90570[2]	Extended		99284	UNS	50
		or	99285	UNS	50
90580	Comprehensive		99285	UNS	50

[1] Typical times were not specified in the 1992 CPT.
[2] Cross-walk possible to more than one code. The code selection depends on the level of medical decision making, the nature of the problem(s), and time.

CONSULTATIONS

VISIT CODES   90600-90654

Visit codes in the range 90600-90654 are used to report initial, follow-up and confirmatory consultation services provided in any location for new patients and established patients. A consultant is expected to render an opinion or advice only. If the consultant subsequently assumes responsibility for a portion of the patients care, he or she will be rendering concurrent care and should report using appropriate visit codes with modifier -75.

If the consultant has the case transferred to him or her, he or she should then use the appropriate visit codes, without modifier -75, for services rendered on and after the date of transfer. Key coding issues are whether the consultation is initial, follow-up or confirmatory and the level of service provided.

All CPT codes in this series were deleted from the 1992 CPT. These codes may not be used to bill Medicare for services rendered after January 1, 1992. However, these codes will be accepted by other insurance carriers until they have converted to the new 1992 CPT coding system.

EVALUATION AND MANAGEMENT CODES   99241-99275

Evaluation and management codes in the range 99241-992275 are used to report office, inpatient and confirmatory consultation services provided to new or established patients. The key coding issues are the location of the service, the extent of history obtained, the extent of examination performed, and the complexity of medical decision making. Additional reporting issues include counseling and/or coordination of care, the nature of presenting problem(s), and the time, depending on location, spent either face-to-face with the patient and/or family or at the bedside and on the patient's facility floor or unit.

Coding Rules

1)   The request for a consultation from the attending physician or other appropriate source, and the need for a consultation must be documented in the patient's medical record.

2)   The consultant's opinion and any services that were ordered or performed must be documented in the patient's medical record and communicated to the requesting physician or source.

3)   Consultations which are initiated by request from the patient and/or family may be reported using codes for confirmatory consultations or office services as appropriate.

4)   If a confirmatory consultation is required by a third party, such as a Peer Review Organization (PRO), modifier -32 should be added to the basic service.

5)   Any specifically identifiable procedure performed on or subsequent to the date of the initial consultation is reported separately.

6)   If the consultant subsequently assumes responsibility for management of all or a portion of the patient's condition(s), then either hospital services or office services are used as appropriate.

These codes were first implemented in the 1992 CPT. These codes must be used to bill Medicare for services rendered after January 1, 1992. These new codes will most likely be accepted by Medicaid and all other insurance carriers within a one year period. Watch your insurance carrier newsletters and Explanation of Benefits (EOBs) for notices regarding conversion.

CPT CROSS-WALK FOR OFFICE CONSULTATION SERVICES

INITIAL CONSULTATIONS

Visit	Description	Level	E/M	Time	Frequency
90600	Consultation	Limited	99241	15	100
90605		Intermediate	99242	30	100
90610		Extended	99243	40	100
90620		Comprehensive	99244	60	100
90625		Complex	99245	80	100

FOLLOW-UP CONSULTATIONS

Visit	Description	Level	E/M	Time	Frequency
90640	Follow-up	Brief	99212[1]	10	100
90641		Limited	99213[1]	15	100
90642		Intermediate	99214[1]	25	100
90643		Complex	99215[1]	40	100

[1] There are no codes in the new Evaluation and Management coding system for follow-up office consultations. These services are reported using follow-up office visit codes.

CPT CROSS-WALK FOR INPATIENT CONSULTATION SERVICES AND CONFIRMATORY CONSULTATIONS

INITIAL CONSULTATIONS

Visit	Description	Level	E/M	Time	Frequency
90600	Consult	Limited	99251	20	100
90605		Intermediate	99252	40	100
90610		Extended	99253	55	100
90620		Comprehensive	99254	80	100
90625		Complex	99255	110	100

FOLLOW-UP CONSULTATIONS

Visit	Description	Level	E/M	Time	Frequency
90640	Follow-up	Brief	99261	10	100
90641		Limited	99262	20	100
90642		Intermediate	99262	20	100
90643		Complex	99263	30	100

CONFIRMATORY CONSULTATIONS (OFFICE OR INPATIENT)

Visit	Description	Level	E/M	Time	Frequency
90650	Confirming	Limited	99271	15/20[1]	100
90651		Intermediate	99272	30/40[1]	100
90652		Extended	99273	40/55[1]	100
90653		Comprehensive	99274	60/80[1]	100
90654		Complex	99275	80/110[1]	100

[1] Location dependent. Use the value to the left for office confirmatory consultations and the value to the right for hospital confirmatory consulations.

PREVENTIVE MEDICINE SERVICES

VISIT CODES   90750-90778

Visit codes in the range 90750-90778 are used to report preventive medicine services provided to new and established patients. The key coding issues are whether a patient is a new patient or established patient, the age of the patient, and the level of service provided.

The codes and descriptions included under Preventive Medicine are designed to report routine examinations for adults and children as well as "well-baby" encounters when these procedures are performed in the absence of complaints. The extent of the physical examination largely depends on the age of the patient, the circumstances of the examination, and the abnormalities encountered. Ancillary studies involving laboratory, radiology, or other procedures are usually coded separately. The major problem with Preventive Medicine codes is that most insurance carriers do not provide coverage for well care.

All CPT codes in this series were deleted from the 1992 CPT. These codes may not be used to bill Medicare for services rendered after January 1, 1992. However, these codes will be accepted by other insurance carriers until they have converted to the new 1992 CPT coding system.

EVALUATION AND MANAGEMENT SERVICES   99381-99429

Evaluation and management codes in the range 99381-99429 are used to report routine evaluation and management of adults and children in the absence of patient complaints or counseling and/or risk factor reduction intervention services to healthy individuals. The key coding issues are whether the patient is a new patient or established patient, the age of the patient, the circumstances of the examination, and the nature of any abnormalities encountered, and for counseling services, whether the service was provided to an individual or to a group and the amount of time spent counseling.

These codes were first implemented in the 1992 CPT. These codes must be used to bill Medicare for services rendered after January 1, 1992. These new codes will most likely be accepted by Medicaid and all other insurance carriers within a one year period. Watch your insurance carrier newsletters and Explanation of Benefits (EOBs) for notices regarding conversion.

CPT CROSS-WALK FOR PREVENTIVE MEDICINE SERVICES

NEW PATIENT

Visit	Description	Level	E/M	Time	Frequency
90750	Initial Visit	18 - 39 Years	99385[1]	UNS[2]	
		40 - 64 Years	99386[1]	UNS	
		Over 65 Years	99387[1]	UNS	
90751		12 - 17 Years	99384	UNS	100
90752		5 - 11 Years	99383	UNS	100
90753		1 - 4 Years	99382	UNS	100
90754		Under 1 Year	99381	UNS	100
90755	Infant Care	To One Year	99438[3]	UNS	100
90757	Newborn Care Non-Hospital		99432[3]	UNS	100

ESTABLISHED PATIENT

Visit	Description	Level	E/M	Time	Frequency
90760	Interval Visit	18 - 39 Years	99395[1]	UNS	
		40 - 64 Years	99396[1]	UNS	
		Over 65 Years	99397[1]	UNS	
90761		12 - 17 Years	99394	UNS	100
90762		5 - 11 Years	99393	UNS	100
90763		1 - 4 Years	99392	UNS	100
90764		Under 1 Year	99391	UNS	100

[1] Note age range change resulting in two additional codes.
[2] Typical times were not specified in the 1992 CPT.
[3] These codes are found in the new category Newborn Care of the 1992 CPT.

NEWBORN CARE

Prior to publication of the 1992 CPT, newborn care services were reported using codes 90225 and 90282 from the Hospital care section of CPT and code 99152 from the Special Services and Report section. The 1992 CPT introduced a new subcategory of care for newborn services.

CASE MANAGEMENT SERVICES

VISIT CODES   98900-98922

Visit codes in the range 98900-98922 are used to report case management services which include team conferences and telephone calls. Case Management is defined as a process in which a physician is responsible for direct care of a patient, and for coordinating and controlling access to or initiating and/or supervising other health care services needed by the patient. Key coding issues are type of service, amount of time spent, and level of service provided.

The codes in this section define time specific medical conferences and telephone calls of various levels and replace similarly defined codes previously found in the Special Services and Reports section of CPT. Medicare will not pay for telephone calls; however, some insurance carriers do.

All CPT codes in this series were deleted from the 1992 CPT. These codes may not be used to bill Medicare for services rendered after January 1, 1992. However, these codes will be accepted by other insurance carriers until they have converted to the new 1992 CPT coding system.

EVALUATION AND MANAGEMENT SERVICES   99361-99373

Evaluation and management codes in the range 99361-99373 are used to report team conferences or telephone calls. The key coding issues are the type of service, the amount of time spent, and the level of service provided.

These codes were first implemented in the 1992 CPT. These codes must be used to bill Medicare for services rendered after January 1, 1992. These new codes will most likely be accepted by Medicaid and all other insurance carriers within a one year period. Watch your insurance carrier newsletters and Explanation of Benefits (EOBs) for notices regarding conversion.

CPT CROSS-WALK FOR NEWBORN CARE

Visit	Description Level	E/M	Time	Frequency
90225	History and Exam Normal Newborn Infant	99431	UNS1	100
90282	Hospital Visit Normal Newborn Infant	99433	UNS	100
99152	Newborn Resuscitation	99440	UNS	100

CPT CROSS-WALK FOR CASE MANAGEMENT SERVICES

CONFERENCES

Visit	Description	Level	E/M	Time	Frequency
98900	Conference with Patient/Family	30 Minutes	NONE[2]		
98902	Conference with Patient/Family	60 Minutes	NONE[2]		
98910	Conference with Medical Team	30 Minutes	99361	30	100
98912		60 Minutes	99362	60	100

TELEPHONE CALLS

98920	Telephone call	Brief	99371	UNS	100
98920		Intermediate	99372	UNS	100
98922		Complex	99373	UNS	100

[1] Typical times were not specified in the 1992 CPT.
[2] These two Case Management codes were deleted from the 1992 CPT. To report these services use the appropriate category and level of Evaluation and Management code(s).

SPECIAL SERVICES AND REPORTS 99000-99199

There are several codes listed in this category of the MEDICINE section of CPT which may be reported in addition to basic VISIT and/or EVALUATION AND MANAGEMENT services. The proper use of Special Services codes can result in a significant increase in reimbursement. Most of the codes in this section are "add on" codes. This means that they are used in addition to whatever other codes describe the procedures or services performed.

MISCELLANEOUS SERVICES

99024   Postoperative follow-up visit, included in global service

This code is used to track no-charge post-op visits. See the SURGERY section Guidelines.

99025   Initial (new patient) visit when starred (*) surgical procedure constitutes major service at that visit

See section titled "Starred Procedures" in the SURGERY section.

SERVICES RENDERED AFTER REGULAR OFFICE HOURS

99050   Services requested after office hours in addition to basic service

99052   Services requested between 10:00 PM and 8:00 AM in addition to basic service

99054   Services requested on Sundays and holidays in addition to basic service

Note that codes 99050, 99052 and 99054 are reported in addition to the basic Visit or Evaluation and Management services code.

SERVICES RENDERED AT SPECIAL LOCATION

99056   Services provided at request of patient in a location other than physician's office

Note that code 99056 is reported in addition to the basic visit or Evaluation and Management code.

OFFICE EMERGENCY SERVICES

99058   Office services provided on an emergency basis

The diagnostic codes used to bill for this service must clearly justify the nature of the emergency.

EMERGENCY ROOM SERVICES

The following codes were deleted in the 1992 edition of CPT and should not be used to bill Medicare for services rendered on or after January 1, 1992. However, these codes may be used to bill for services rendered to non-Medicare patients until otherwise notified by private insurance carriers.

99062   Emergency care facility services: when the non-hospital-based physician is in the hospital, but is involved in patient care elsewhere and is called to the emergency facility to provide emergency services

99064   Emergency care facility services: when the non-hospital-based physician is called to the emergency facility from outside the hospital to provide emergency services; not during regular office hours

99065   during regular office hours

PROLONGED SERVICES

99150   Prolonged physician attendance requiring physician detention beyond usual service (for example, operative standby, monitoring ECG, EEG, intrathoracic pressures, intravascular pressures, blood gases during surgery, standby for newborn care following cesarean section or maternal-fetal monitoring); 30 minutes to one hour

99151   more than one hour

99152   Newborn resuscitation: care of the high risk newborn at delivery including, for example, inhalation therapy, aspiration, administration of medication for initial stabilization (This code was deleted in the 1992 CPT)

CRITICAL CARE SERVICES

VISIT CODES   99160-99174

Visit codes in the range 99160-99174 are used to report services for specific conditions (usually) provided in a critical care area. Critical care includes the care of critically ill patients in a variety of medical emergencies that requires the constant attention of the physician. Cardiac arrest, shock, bleeding, respiratory failure, postoperative complications, or a critically ill neonate are examples of medical emergencies defined in CPT. Critical care is usually, but not always, given in a critical area, such as the coronary care unit, intensive care unit, respiratory care unit, or the emergency care facility.

The codes listed in this section are intended to include cardio-pulmonary resuscitation (CPR) and the variety of services commonly employed with this procedure as well as other acute emergency situations. Other services, such as catheter placement, cardiac output measurement, dialysis management, control of gastrointestinal hemorrhage, cardioversion, etc. are considered to be included when billing critical care services under these time-based codes.

Prior to billing for critical care services, review the section titled Important Coding and Billing Issues in order to clearly understand your coding options. Key coding issues include the condition of the patient (supported by diagnostic coding), the service(s) provided, and the amount of time spent. Follow-up critical care services may be reported using visit codes from this section or hospital visit codes from the series 90240-90280.

All CPT codes in this series were deleted from the 1992 CPT. These codes may not be used to bill Medicare for services rendered after January 1, 1992. However, these codes will be accepted by other insurance carriers until they have converted to the new 1992 CPT coding system.

EVALUATION AND MANAGEMENT CODES   99291-99292

Evaluation and management codes in the range 99291-99292 are used to report services for specific conditions (usually) provided in a critical care area. Critical care is defined in the new Evaluation and Management section identically to the previous visit definition provided above.

Prior to billing for critical care services, review the section titled Important Coding and Billing Issues in order to clearly understand your coding options. Key coding issues include the condition of the patient (supported by diagnostic coding), the service(s) provided, and the amount of time spent. Follow-up critical care services may be reported using Evaluation and management codes from this section or hospital Evaluation and management codes from the series 99231-99233.

Coding Rules

1) The critical care codes are used to report the total duration of time spent by a physician providing constant attention to a critically ill patient.

2) Code 99291 is used to report the first hour of critical care on a given day. It may be reported only once per day even if the time spent is not continuous on that day.

3) Code 99292 is used to report each additional 30 minutes beyond the first hour.

4) Other procedures which are not considered included in the critical care services, for example, suturing of lacerations, setting of fractures, reduction of joint dislocations, lumbar puncture, peritoneal lavage and bladder tap, are reported separately.

These codes were first implemented in the 1992 CPT. These codes must be used to bill Medicare for services rendered after January 1, 1992. These new codes will most likely be accepted by Medicaid and all other insurance carriers within a one year period. Watch your insurance carrier newsletters and Explanation of Benefits (EOBs) for notices regarding conversion.

CPT CROSS-WALK FOR CRITICAL CARE

Visit	Description	Level	E/M	Time	Frequency
99160	Initial Care	First Hour	99291	60	100
99162	Additional	Per 30 Minutes	99292	30	100

ANESTHESIA SERVICES

GUIDELINES

Proper reporting and billing of anesthesia services depends on the insurance carrier involved. As of April 1, 1989 anesthesia services covered under Medicare, are reported and billed using CPT codes from the ANESTHESIA section of CPT. For most other carriers, anesthesia services are billed using codes from the SURGERY section of CPT to describe the major surgical procedure. The reporting of anesthesia services is appropriate by or under the responsible supervision of a physician. These services may include general, regional, supplementation of local anesthesia, or other supportive services.

Following is a sample insurance claim illustrating how anesthesia for a TURP is billed to a group or private insurance carrier.

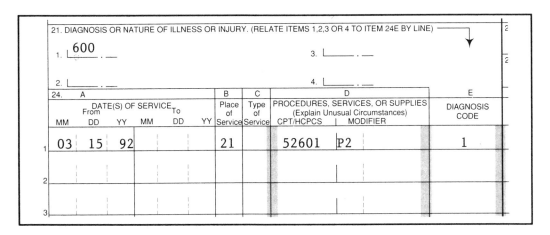

The same service provided to a Medicare beneficiary is billed as illustrated in the sample claim form below.

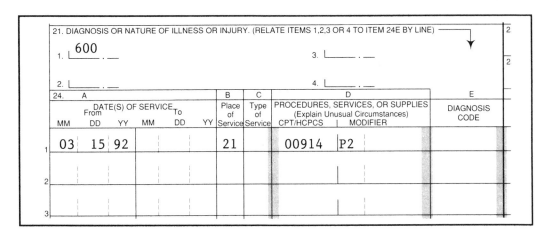

These services include the usual preoperative and postoperative visits, the anesthesia care during the procedure, the administration of fluids and/or blood incident to the anesthesia or surgery, and the usual monitoring procedures. Unusual forms of monitoring (eg, intra-arterial, central venous and Swan-Ganz) are not included.

SUBSECTION INFORMATION

The ANESTHESIA section of CPT is divided into 16 subsections; namely:

Head	00100-00222
Neck	00300-00352
Thorax (Chest Wall and Shoulder Girdle)	00400-00474
Intrathoracic	00500-00580
Spine and Spinal Cord	00600-00670
Upper Abdomen	00700-00796
Lower Abdomen	00800-00884
Perineum	00900-00955
Pelvis (Except Hip)	01000-01190
Upper Leg (Except Knee)	01200-01274
Knee and Popliteal Area	01300-01444
Lower Leg (Below Knee)	01460-01682
Upper Arm and Elbow	01700-01784
Forearm, Wrist and Hand	01800-01860
Radiological Procedures	01900-01922
Miscellaneous Procedure(s)	01990-01999

TIME REPORTING

Time for anesthesia procedures may be reported as is customary in the local area. Anesthesia time begins when the anesthesiologist begins to prepare the patient for the induction of anesthesia in the operating room or in an equivalent area and ends when the anesthesiologist is no longer in personal attendance, that is, when the patient may be safely placed under postoperative supervision.

PHYSICIAN'S SERVICES

Services rendered by anesthesiologists in the office, home, or hospital, consultation and other medical services are coded from the VISIT or EVALUATION AND MANAGEMENT section.

MATERIALS SUPPLIED BY PHYSICIAN

Supplies and materials provided by the physician over and above those usually included with the office visit or other services rendered may be listed separately.

SEPARATE OR MULTIPLE PROCEDURES

It is appropriate to indicate multiple procedures that are rendered on the same day by separate entries.

SPECIAL REPORT

A service that is rarely provided, unusual, variable, or new MAY require a special report in determining medical appropriateness of the service. This simply means that you may need to provide additional documentation either routinely, as when billing unlisted procedure codes or using modifier -22, or when requested to do so by an insurance carrier.

ANESTHESIA MODIFIERS

All anesthesia services are reported by use of the appropriate SURGERY or ANESTHESIA code plus the addition of a physical status modifier. The use of other optional modifiers may be appropriate.

PHYSICAL STATUS MODIFIERS

Physical Status modifiers are represented by the initial letter P followed by a single digit from 1 to 6 defined below.

-P1   A normal healthy patient.

-P2   A patient with a mild systemic disease.

-P3   A patient with severe systemic disease.

-P4   A patient with severe systemic disease that is a constant threat to life.

-P5   A moribund patient who is not expected to survive without the operation.

-P6   A declared brain-dead patient whose organs are being removed for donor purposes.

The six levels of Physical Status Modifiers are consistent with the American Society of Anesthesiologists (ASA) ranking of patient status. Physical status is included to distinguish between various levels of complexity of the service provided.

OTHER MODIFIERS

Under certain circumstances, medical services and procedures may need to be further modified. Other modifiers commonly used in ANESTHESIA include:

-22   Unusual services

-23   Unusual anesthesia

-32   Mandated services

-51   Multiple procedures

-75   Concurrent care, services rendered by more than one physician

       (modifier -75 was deleted from the 1992 CPT)

-AA   Anesthesia by anesthesiologist

-AB   Four or less concurrent services by CRNA or AA employed by anesthesiologist

-AC   Four or less concurrent services by CRNA not employed by anesthesiologist

-AD   Supervision of more than four concurrent anesthesia services by anesthesiologist

-AF   Anesthesia complicated by total body hypothermia

-AG   Anesthesia for emergency surgery on a patient who is moribund or who has an incapacitating systemic disease that is a constant threat to life

-QI   Medical direction of own employees by anesthesiologist (three concurrent procedures)

-OJ   Medical direction of own employees by anesthesiologist (four concurrent procedures)

-QK   Medical direction of other than own employees by anesthesiologist (two concurrent procedures)

-QL   Medical direction of other than own employees by anesthesiologist (three concurrent procedures)

-QM   Medical direction of other than own employees by anesthesiologist (four concurrent procedures)

QUALIFYING CIRCUMSTANCES FOR ANESTHESIA

Many anesthesia services are provided under particularly difficult circumstances depending on factors such as extraordinary condition of patient, notable operative conditions, and unusual risk factors. This section includes a list of important qualifying circumstances that significantly impact on the character of the anesthetic service provided. These procedures are not reported alone but would be reported as additional procedure codes. More than one code may be selected.

99100   Anesthesia for patient of extreme age, under one year and over seventy

99116   Anesthesia complicated by utilization of total body hypothermia

99135   Anesthesia complicated by utilization of controlled hypotension

99140   Anesthesia complicated by emergency conditions (specify)

In addition to the previous guidelines, it is common for anesthesia to be administered by Certified Registered Nurse Anesthetists either providing services independently or under the supervision of a physician.

SURGERY SERVICES

GUIDELINES

In addition to the common issues relevant to all physicians discussed in the INTRODUCTION to CPT, the SURGERY section contains definitions and items unique to that section.

PHYSICIANS' SERVICES

Services rendered by surgeons in the office, home or hospital, plus consultations and other medical services are reported using Visit or Evaluation and Management services codes. In addition, codes in the series 99000-99199, found in the category Special Services and Reports in the MEDICINE section, are also frequently used by surgeons.

LISTED SURGICAL PROCEDURES

The procedures listed in the SURGERY section include the operation, local, metacarpal/digital block or topical anesthesia when used, and normal, uncomplicated follow-up care. This concept is referred to as a PACKAGE for surgical procedures.

FOLLOW-UP CARE

FOR DIAGNOSTIC PROCEDURES

The follow-up care for diagnostic procedures, such as endoscopy and injection procedures for radiography, includes only that care related to recovery from the diagnostic procedure itself. Care of the condition for which the diagnostic procedure was performed or of other concomitant conditions is not included and should be listed separately.

FOR THERAPEUTIC SURGICAL PROCEDURES

The follow-up care for therapeutic surgical procedures includes only that care which is usually a part of the surgical service. Complications, exacerbations, recurrence of the presence of other diseases or injuries requiring additional services should be reported with the identification of appropriate procedures.

MATERIALS SUPPLIED BY PHYSICIAN

Supplies and materials provided by the physician over and above those usually included with the office visit or other services rendered should be listed separately. HCPCS codes should be used when appropriate.

MULTIPLE SURGICAL PROCEDURES

It is common for several surgical procedures to be performed at the same operative session. When multiple procedures are performed on the same day or at the same session, the "major" procedure or service is listed first followed by secondary, additional, or "lesser" procedures or services. CPT modifier -51 is added to all procedures following the first one.

Billing multiple procedures incorrectly can have a serious impact on your reimbursement. An inexperienced biller may simply list the procedures on the insurance claim in the order dictated or described in the operative report.

There are two critical decisions related to billing multiple surgical procedures; namely: 1) The order in which the procedures are listed on the claim form, and 2) whether or not to bill additional procedures at full or reduced fees.

ORDER OF LISTING

The first procedure to be listed when billing under the multiple procedure rule is the procedure with the highest fee. Additional procedures should be listed in descending order by fee. Modifier -51 should be added to each additional procedure.

21. DIAGNOSIS OR NATURE OF ILLNESS OR INJURY. (RELATE ITEMS 1,2,3 OR 4 TO ITEM 24E BY LINE)							
1. 952 . 10					3. ___ . ___		
2. ___ . ___					4. ___ . ___		

24. A DATE(S) OF SERVICE						B Place of Service	C Type of Service	D PROCEDURES, SERVICES, OR SUPPLIES (Explain Unusual Circumstances) CPT/HCPCS | MODIFIER	E DIAGNOSIS CODE
From			To						
MM	DD	YY	MM	DD	YY				
1	03	15	92				21		63046	
2	03	15	92				21		62223 | 51	
3	03	15	92				21		63048 | 51	

ALL insurance carriers will reduce the allowance for the additional procedures, typically by 50 percent for the second procedure, and 50 to 75 percent for the third and subsequent procedures. Listing the procedures in descending order by fee minimizes the possibility of an incorrect reduction.

BILLING FULL VERSUS REDUCED FEES

We recommend that you list your full fee for each procedure billed as part of multiple surgical procedures. This does not mean that you should expect to be reimbursed the full amount that you list as the total of all the multiple procedures. Our reasoning on this matter is simple. First, insurance carriers WILL reduce the allowances for the additional procedures. Listing full fees in descending order will result in the maximum allowable reimbursement for you or your patient. Second, there is no easy way to inform the insurance carrier that you have already reduced your fees.

At this time, the only way to inform the insurance carrier that you have reduced your fees for additional procedures is to include a statement to that effect somewhere on your claim form. Considering the circumstances under which your claim is processed, this method is very risky, often resulting in double reductions, and delayed or lost reimbursement.

This method of billing is not designed to <u>increase</u> your reimbursement but rather to <u>maximize</u> it. We also recommend that after you have received the maximum benefits from the insurance carrier, that the balance remaining, less any patient co-insurance or deductible requirements, be written off. We recognize that billing practices vary in different areas of the country and you should continue to use the method that is recommended or required by the insurance carriers in your area.

SEPARATE PROCEDURE

Some of the listed procedures are commonly carried out as an integral part of a total service, and as such do not warrant a separate identification. When, however, such a procedure is performed independently of, and is not immediately related to other services, it may be listed as a "separate procedure." Thus, when a procedure that is ordinarily a component of a larger procedure is performed alone for a specific purpose, it may be considered to be a separate procedure.

SUBSECTION INFORMATION

The SURGERY section of CPT is divided into 16 subsections; namely:

Integumentary System	10040-19499
Musculoskeletal System	20000-29999
Respiratory System	30000-32999
Cardiovascular System	33000-37799
Hemic and Lymphatic Systems	38000-38999
Mediastinum and Diaphragm	39000-39599
Digestive System	40000-49999
Urinary System	50000-53899
Male Genital System	54000-55899
Intersex Surgery	55970-55980
Female Genital Surgery	56000-58999
Maternity Care and Delivery	59000-59899

Endocrine System	60000-60699
Nervous System	61000-64999
Eye and Ocular Adnexa	65000-68899
Auditory System	69000-69999

Each sub-section of the SURGERY section of CPT is divided into organs then into procedures involving anatomic sites. Each anatomic site is further separated into surgical processes such as INCISION, EXCISION, REPAIR, REMOVAL, AMPUTATION, etc. The following subsections within the SURGERY section have NOTES that should be reviewed carefully prior to selecting codes for services located within the section:

Musculoskeletal	20000-29999
Vascular Injection Procedures	36000-37799
Endoscopy-cystoscopy, Urethroscopy, Cystourethroscopy	52000-52700
Maternity Care and Delivery	59000-58999

UNLISTED SERVICE OR PROCEDURE

A service or procedure may be provided that is not listed in the current edition of CPT. When reporting such a service, you may use the appropriate Unlisted Procedure code. You must include a report which clearly explains the service or procedure you are reporting.

SPECIAL REPORT

A service that is rarely provided, unusual, variable, or new MAY require a special report in determining medical appropriateness of the service. This simply means that you may need to provide additional documentation either routinely, as when billing unlisted procedure codes or using modifier -22, or when requested to do so by an insurance carrier.

MODIFIERS

Listed surgical services and procedures may be modified under certain circumstances. When applicable, the modifying circumstance is identified by adding the appropriate two digit modifier to the base procedure code(s). Virtually all of the 22 modifiers listed in Appendix A of the CPT may be applied to surgical procedures.

-20   Microsurgery

-22   Unusual Procedural Services

-26   Professional Component

-32   Mandated Services

-47   Anesthesia by Surgeon

-50   Bilateral Procedure

-51   Multiple Procedures

-52   Reduced Services

-54   Surgical Care Only

-55   Postoperative Management Only

-56   Preoperative Management Only

-62   Two Surgeons

-66   Surgical Team

-75   Concurrent Care, Services Rendered by More Than One Physician

       (Modifier -75 was deleted from the 1992 CPT)

-76   Repeat Procedure by Same Physician

-77   Repeat Procedure by Another Physician

-78   Return to the operating room for a related procedure during the post-operative period

-79   Unrelated procedure or service by the same physician during the post-operative period

-80   Assistant surgeon

-81   Minimum assistant surgeon

-82   Assistant surgeon (when qualified resident not available)

-99   Multiple modifiers

-LT   Procedure performed on left side of body

-RT   Procedure performed on right side of body

STARRED PROCEDURES

The star "*" is used in CPT to identify certain relatively small surgical services that involve a readily identifiable surgical procedure but include variable preoperative and postoperative services. Examples of this type of service include: incision and drainage of an abscess, injection of a tendon sheath, manipulation of a joint under anesthesia, dilation of the urethra, etc.

Because of the indefinite pre- and postoperative services, the usual "package" concept for surgical services cannot be applied. Such procedures are identified in CPT by a star (*) following the procedure code number. When a star (*) follows a surgical procedure code number, the following rules apply:

A. The service as listed includes the surgical procedure only. Associated pre- and postoperative services are not included in the service as listed.

B. Preoperative services are considered as one of the following:

1. When the starred (*) procedure is carried out at the time of an initial visit (new patient) and this procedure constitutes the major service at that visit, CPT code 99025 is listed instead of the usual office visit as an additional service.

2. When the starred (*) procedure is carried out at the time of an initial or other visit involving significant identifiable services (eg, removal of a small skin lesion at the time of a comprehensive history and physical examination), the appropriate visit is listed in addition to the starred procedure and its follow-up care.

3. When the starred (*) procedure is carried out at the time of a follow-up (established patient) visit and this procedure constitutes the major service at that visit, the service visit is usually not added.

4. When the starred (*) procedure requires hospitalization, an appropriate hospital visit is listed in addition to the starred (*) procedure and its follow-up care.

C. All postoperative care is added on a service-by-service basis (eg, office or hospital visit, cast change, etc).

D. Complications are added on a service-by-service basis (as with all surgical procedures).

Examples of "starred" procedures include:

10060* Incision and drainage of abscess (eg, carbuncle, suppurative hidradenitis, cutaneous or subcutaneous abscess, cyst, furuncle, or paronychia); simple or single

30903* Control nasal hemorrhage, anterior, complex (extensive cautery and/or packing) any method

59000* Amniocentesis, any method

SURGICAL DESTRUCTION

Surgical destruction is considered a part of a surgical procedure and the different methods of destruction are not usually listed separately unless the technique substantially alters the standard management of a problem or condition. Exceptions under these special circumstances are provided for by the addition of separate procedure codes.

WOUND REPAIR

The repair of wounds is classified in CPT as simple, intermediate or complex.

SIMPLE REPAIR

Simple repair codes are reported when the wound is superficial; ie, involving skin and/or subcutaneous tissues, without significant involvement of deeper structures, and which requires simple suturing. For closure with adhesive strips, list appropriate visit only.

INTERMEDIATE REPAIR

Intermediate repair codes are used to report the repair of wounds that, in addition to the above, require layer closure. Such wounds usually involve deeper layers such as fascia or muscle, to the extent that at least one of the layers requires separate closure.

COMPLEX REPAIR

Complex repair codes include the repair of wounds requiring reconstructive surgery, complicated wound closures, skin grafts or unusual and time consuming techniques of repair to obtain the maximum functional and cosmetic result. It may include creation of the defect and necessary preparation for repairs or the debridement and repair of complicated lacerations or avulsions.

STEPS FOR CODING WOUND REPAIRS

There are four steps required for the accurate reporting of wound repair codes.

1. The repaired wound(s) should be measured and recorded in centimeters, whether curved, angular or stellate.

2. When multiple wounds are repaired, add together the lengths of those in the same classification (see above) and report as a single item. When more than one classification of wounds is repaired, list the more complicated as the primary procedure and the less complicated as the secondary procedure, using modifier -51.

3. Decontamination and/or debridement is considered a separate procedure only when gross contamination requires prolonged cleansing, when appreciable amounts of devitalized or contaminated tissue are removed, or when debridement is carried out separately without immediate primary closure.

4. If the wound repair involves nerves, blood vessels and/or tendons, choose codes from the appropriate subsection of the SURGERY section (Nervous, Cardiovascular, Musculoskeletal) for repair of these structures.

The repair of these associated wounds is included in the primary procedure unless it qualifies as a complex wound, in which case modifier -51 applies. Simple ligation of vessels in an open wound is considered as part of an open wound closure. Simple "exploration" of nerves, blood vessels or tendons exposed in an open wound is also considered part of the essential treatment of the wound and is not a separate procedure unless appreciable dissection is required.

HCPCS codes for medical and surgical supplies, A4000-A4999, may be used to report supplies and materials provided to Medicare patients if the supplies and materials are not considered to be included with or part of the basic service(s) or procedure(s).

FREE SKIN GRAFTS   15000-15416

When coding free skin grafts, the choice of codes is based on the size and location of the defect (recipient area) and the type of graft to be used. The graft codes include simple debridement of granulations or recent avulsion.

When a primary procedure such as orbitectomy, radical mastectomy or deep tumor removal requires skin graft for definite closure, use codes from the appropriate anatomical subsection for the primary procedure and codes from the
series 15000-15416 for the skin graft. Note that the repair of a donor site requiring skin graft or local flaps should be coded as an additional procedure.

HCPCS codes for medical and surgical supplies, A4000-A4999, may be used to report supplies and materials provided to Medicare patients if the supplies and materials are not considered to be included with or part of the basic service(s) or procedure(s).

MUSCULOSKELETAL SYSTEM   20000-29999

The procedures and services listed in this section of CPT include the application and removal of the FIRST cast or traction device only. Subsequent replacement of the cast and/or traction device may be coded using the cast and strapping procedure codes appearing at the end of the section.

Most bone, cartilage and fascia graft procedures include obtaining of the graft by the operating surgeon. When a surgical associate obtains the graft for the operating surgeon, the additional service should be coded and reported separately using codes from the 20900-20926 range. In addition, a surgical modifier for assistant surgeon or co-surgeon should be included when billing the associate's services.

When coding the rereduction of a fracture and/or dislocation performed by the primary physician, add modifier -76 to the procedure code. If the rereduction were performed by another physician, then modifier -77 would be added to the procedure code.

There are numerous starred (*) procedures in this section of CPT indicating the opportunity of reporting an appropriate visit code in addition to the surgical procedure.

HCPCS codes for medical and surgical supplies, A4000-A4999, may be used to report supplies and materials provided to Medicare patients if the supplies and materials are not considered to be included with or part of the basic service(s) or procedure(s).

GRAFTS OR IMPLANTS   20900-20926

Codes for obtaining autogenous bone, cartilage, tendon, fascia lata grafts, or other tissues, through separate incisions are to be used only when graft is not already listed as part of basic procedure.

RECONSTRUCTION OF ORAL   21079-21299
AND FACIAL DEFORMITIES

CPT 1991 included extensive revision of codes in the range 21079-21299. Forty-eight new codes were added to this section and six were changed. Codes 21079-21089 describe professional services for the rehabilitation of patients with oral, facial or other anatomical deformities by means of prostheses such as an artificial eye, ear or nose or intraoral obturator to close a cleft. These codes should be used only when the physician, not an outside laboratory, actually designs and prepares the prosthesis.

APPLICATIONS OF CASTS   29000-29799

Codes in this section are used only when the cast application or strapping is a replacement procedure performed during or after the period of follow-up care. An additional visit code, dependent on location, is reportable only if significant identifiable other services are provided at the time of the cast application or strapping. For coding cast or strap application in situations not involving surgery, for example, casting of a sprained ankle or knee, use the appropriate level of visit code plus code 99070 or equivalent HCPCS code to bill for casting materials.

HCPCS codes for medical and surgical supplies, A4000-A4999, may be used to report supplies and materials provided to Medicare patients if the supplies and materials are not considered to be included with or part of the basic service(s) or procedure(s).

ARTHROSCOPY   29799-29909

Per CPT definition, surgical arthroscopy ALWAYS includes a diagnostic arthroscopy and would therefore never be coded and billed in addition to the surgical procedure. However, there are several arthroscopy procedures defined as separate procedures, indicating that the codes may be used for reporting and billing if the diagnostic arthroscopy is the only procedure performed.

RESPIRATORY SYSTEM   30000-32999

Codes from this section of CPT are used to report invasive and surgical procedures performed on the nose; sinuses; larynx; trachea and bronchi; and the lungs and pleura.

There are numerous starred (*) procedures in this section of CPT indicating the possibility of reporting an appropriate visit code in addition to the surgical procedure. When coding endoscopic procedures from this section of CPT, code the appropriate endoscopy of each anatomic site examined.

CARDIOVASCULAR SYSTEM   33000-37799

Codes from this section of CPT are used to report invasive and surgical procedures performed on the heart and pericardium, including pacemakers or defibrillators; cardiac valves; coronary arteries; aorta; and arteries and veins.

For coding services such as monitoring, operation of pump and other non-surgical services performed during cardiovascular surgery, see the Special Services codes 99150, 99151, 99160-99162 or visit codes 99291-99292 and 99190-99192 from the EVALUATION AND MANAGEMENT or MEDICINE sections of CPT.

There are a few starred (*) procedures in this section of CPT indicating the possibility of reporting an appropriate visit code in addition to the surgical procedure. In addition, the complexity of procedures in this section would frequently require the presence of multiple assistant surgeons, co-surgeons and/or surgical teams.

VASCULAR INJECTION PROCEDURES   36000-37799

When using codes from this section, note that the listed procedures include local anesthesia, introduction of needles or catheter, injection of contrast medium with or without automatic power injection, and pre- and post-injection care specifically related to the injection procedure.

The most common code used in this section is code 36410* used to code for routine venipuncture for collection of specimen(s). Note that catheters, drugs and contrast media are not included in the codes contained in this section. These should be coded using CPT code 99070 or the appropriate HCPCS code for Medicare patients.

The codes listed in this section do not cover radiological vascular injections, injection procedures for cardiac catheterization or chemotherapy. Refer to the RADIOLOGY or MEDICINE sections of CPT for the appropriate codes for these procedures.

HCPCS codes for medical and surgical supplies, A4000-A4999, may be used to report supplies and materials provided to Medicare patients if the supplies and materials are not considered to be included with or part of the basic service(s) or procedure(s).

HEMIC AND LYMPHATIC SYSTEMS   38100-38999

Codes from this section of CPT are used to report invasive and surgical procedures performed on the spleen and lymph nodes. Bone marrow transplants are reported using codes 38230-38241 from this section.

MEDIASTINUM AND DIAPHRAGM 39000-39599

Codes from this section of CPT are used to report invasive and surgical procedures performed on the mediastinum and the diaphragm.

DIGESTIVE SYSTEM 40000-49999

Codes from this section of CPT are used to invasive and surgical procedures performed on the lips; mouth; tongue; dentoalveolar structures; palate; salivary gland; pharynx, adenoids and tonsils; esophagus; stomach; intestines; rectum; anus; liver; biliary tract; pancreas; and the abdomen, peritoneum, and omentum.

There are numerous starred (*) procedures in this section of CPT indicating the possibility of reporting an appropriate visit code in addition to the surgical procedure. When coding esophagoscopy procedures, code the appropriate endoscopy of each anatomic site examined.

URINARY SYSTEM 50000-53899

Codes from this section of CPT are used to report invasive and surgical procedures performed on the kidney; ureter; bladder; prostate (resection); and urethra.

There are numerous starred (*) procedures in this section of CPT indicating the possibility of reporting an appropriate visit code in addition to the surgical procedure.

URODYNAMICS 51725-51797

The codes in this section may be used separately or in various combinations. When multiple procedures are performed in the same session, modifier -51 should be added to the second and all subsequent codes. Procedures in this section are performed by, or under the direct supervision of, a physician. In addition, all materials and supplies, used in the provision of these services, such as instruments, equipment, fluids, gases, probes, catheters, technician's fees, medications, gloves, trays, tubing and other sterile supplies are considered to be included in the base code. Use modifier -26 to code and bill for interpretation of results or operation of equipment only.

CYSTOSCOPY, URETHROSCOPY, 52000-52710
and CYSTOURETHROSCOPY

The descriptions of codes in this section are listed so that the main procedure can be identified without having to list all of the minor related procedures performed at the same time.

An example of how codes in this section are defined includes:

52601   Transurethral resection of prostate, including control of postoperative bleeding, complete (vasectomy, meatotomy, cystourethroscopy, urethral calibration and/or dilation, and internal urethrotomy are included)

All of these secondary procedures are included in the single code 52601. If any of the secondary procedures requires significant additional time and effort, to the point of making the procedure "unusual", modifier -22 should be added with an appropriate increase in fee and a report explaining what made the procedure unusual.

MALE GENITAL SYSTEM   54000-55899

Codes from this section of CPT are used to report invasive and surgical procedures performed on the penis; testis; epididymis; scrotum; spermatic cord and prostate. There are several starred procedures in this section.

FEMALE GENITAL SYSTEM   56000-58999

Codes from this section of CPT are used to report invasive and surgical procedures performed on the perineum; vulva and introitus; vagina; cervix uteri; corpus uteri; oviduct and ovarium. In vitro fertilization is also reported using codes 58970-58976 from this section.

ENDOSCOPY-LAPAROSCOPY-HYSTEROSCOPY   58980-58994

The descriptions of codes in this section are listed so that the main procedure can be identified without having to list all of the minor related procedures performed at the same time. An example of how codes in this section are defined includes:

58992   Hysterscopy, diagnostic with lysis of intrauterine adhesions or resection of intrauterine septum (any method)

The secondary procedure(s) is/are included in the single code 58992. If any of the laparoscopy require mini-laparotomy (Hasson technique) or when the secondary procedures require significant additional time and effort, to the point of making the procedure "unusual", modifier -22 should be added with an appropriate increase in fee and a report explaining why the procedure was unusual.

MATERNITY CARE AND DELIVERY   59000-59899

Codes from this section of CPT are used to report routine maternity care and invasive and surgical procedures performed as part of prenatal, delivery and post-partum care. The services normally provided in uncomplicated maternity cases include antepartum care, delivery, and postpartum care. As of this writing, the most common method of billing for maternity care is the surgical package method using CPT code 59400.

ANTEPARTUM CARE

The definition of antepartum care for coding purposes includes the initial and subsequent history, physical examinations, recording of weight, blood pressures, fetal heart tones, routine chemical urinalysis, and routine visits. The 1990 edition of CPT established for the first time a definition of what are considered routine visits. Routine visits are defined as:

- Monthly visits up to 28 weeks gestation
- Biweekly visits up to 36 weeks gestation, and
- Weekly visits until delivery

Any other visits or services provided within this time period should be coded separately. Using 6 to 8 weeks gestation as the typical starting point, the above definition translates into between 9 and 11 routine visits per patient.

DELIVERY

Delivery services are defined as including hospital admission, the admission history and physical examination, management of uncomplicated labor, and vaginal or cesarean delivery. Three important changes in this definition occurred in the 1990 edition of CPT.

- The definition of delivery services now <u>includes</u> the hospital admission, and admission history and physical. Prior to these new definitions it was not unusual for obstetricians to code and charge a hospital admission based on community practices and insurance carrier allowances.

- Resuscitation of newborn infants when necessary, defined in previous editions, was deleted. By this new definition, if the delivering physician has to resuscitate the newborn infant, he/she may code this service as a separate procedure.

- Medical problems "complicating labor and delivery management" may require additional resources and should be reported using Visit or Evaluation and Management services codes.

POSTPARTUM CARE

Postpartum care is defined as hospital and office visits following vaginal or cesarean delivery. No number of visits is defined by CPT; however, the typical fee for total obstetrical care includes a single office follow-up visit six weeks postpartum.

COMPLICATIONS OF PREGNANCY

The services defined previously are for normal, uncomplicated maternity care. For medical complications of pregnancy, for example, cardiac problems, neurological problems, diabetes, hypertension, toxemia, hyperemesis, pre-term labor and premature rupture of membranes, use Visit or Evaluation and Management codes.

For surgical complications of pregnancy, such as appendectomy, hernia, ovarian cyst, Bartholin cysts, etc., use codes from the SURGERY section of CPT. Note that in either case, complications are not considered to be part of routine maternity care and should be coded and billed in addition to maternity codes.

PARTIAL MATERNITY SERVICES

Occasionally a physician may provide all or part of the antepartum and/or postpartum care but does not perform the actual delivery due to termination of the pregnancy by abortion, or referral to another physician for delivery. In this circumstance, the physician has the option of using the inclusive codes 59420 or 59430 from the Maternity Care and Delivery section or to code and bill for each Visit using codes from the 90000-90080 series or Evaluation and Management codes from the 99201-99215 series.

ENDOCRINE SYSTEM 60000-60699

Codes from this section of CPT are used to report invasive and surgical procedures performed on the thyroid gland, parathyroid, thymus, adrenal glands and carotid body.

NERVOUS SYSTEM 61000-64999

Codes from this section of CPT are used to report invasive and surgical procedures on the skull; meninges and brain; spine and spinal cord; and the extracranial nerves, peripheral nerves and autonomic nervous system.

EYE AND OCULAR ADNEXA 65000-68999

Codes from this section of CPT are used to report invasive and surgical procedures performed on the eyeball; cornea; anterior segment; posterior segment; and ocular adnexa.

AUDITORY SYSTEM 69000-69979

Codes from this section of CPT are used to report invasive and surgical procedures performed on the external ear; middle ear; inner ear and temporal bone.

RADIOLOGY SERVICES

GUIDELINES

Items used by all physicians in reporting their services are presented in the INTRODUCTION. Some of the commonalities are repeated here for the convenience of those physicians referring to this section on RADIOLOGY (including Nuclear Medicine and Diagnostic Ultrasound). Other definitions and items unique to Radiology are also listed.

SUBJECT LISTINGS

The codes in this section apply to radiological services performed by or under the responsible supervision of a physician.

SEPARATE OR MULTIPLE PROCEDURES

It is appropriate to designate multiple procedures that are rendered on the same date by separate entries.

SUBSECTION INFORMATION

The RADIOLOGY section of CPT is divided into 4 subsections; namely:

Diagnostic Radiology (Diagnostic Imaging)	70000-76499
Diagnostic Ultrasound	76500-76999
Radiation Oncology	77261-77999
Nuclear Medicine	78000-79999

Several of the subheadings or subsections have special needs or instructions unique to that section. The following subsections of the RADIOLOGY section have NOTES which should be reviewed carefully before choosing codes from the section:

Diagnostic Ultrasound	76500-76999
Therapeutic Radiology	77261-77799
Nuclear Medicine	78000-79999

COMPLETE PROCEDURES

Interventional radiologic procedures or diagnostic studies involving injection of contrast media include all usual preinjection and postinjection services, for example, necessary local anesthesia, placement of needle or catheter, injection of contrast media, supervision of the study, and interpretation of results. When one of these procedures is performed in full by a single physician, it is designated as a "complete procedure."

SUPERVISION AND INTERPRETATION ONLY

When a procedure is performed by a radiologist-clinician team, it is designated as "supervision and interpretation only" and the separate injection procedure is listed in the appropriate section of the SURGERY section of CPT. These codes are used only when a procedure is performed by more than one physician, for example, a radiologist-clinician team.

MODIFIERS

Listed surgical services and procedures may be modified under certain circumstances. When applicable, the modifying circumstance is identified by adding the appropriate two digit modifier to the base procedure code(s). Modifiers commonly used to report RADIOLOGY services include:

-22   Unusual services

-26   Professional component

-32   Mandated services

-51   Multiple procedures

-52   Reduced services

-62   Two surgeons

-66   Surgical team

-75   Concurrent care, services rendered by more than one physician

        (Modifier -75 was deleted from the 1992 CPT)

-76   Repeat procedure by same physician

-77   Repeat procedure by another physician

-78   Return to the operating room for a related procedure during the postoperative period

-79   Unrelated procedure or service by the same physician during the postoperative period

-80   Assistant surgeon

-90   Reference (outside) laboratory

-99   Multiple modifiers

-LT   Left side of body

-RT   Right side of body

BILATERAL PROCEDURE CODES

In the 1990 edition of CPT all codes containing the term "bilateral" were deleted with the exception of select codes within the RADIOLOGY section. In the 1992 edition, there were still a few codes in this section which included the term "bilateral" in the definition. As the stated intent of the AMA is to eliminate all "bilateral" CPT codes, you should watch this section of the CPT carefully with each new edition.

SPECIAL MEDICARE CONSIDERATIONS

Most of the codes in this section fall under the Medicare Purchased Diagnostic Services guidelines. Coding and reporting should be as instructed by your local Medicare carrier.

DIAGNOSTIC ULTRASOUND   76506-76999

The following definitions are important when choosing codes for diagnostic ultrasound services and procedures.

A-MODE   Implies a one-dimensional ultrasonic measurement procedure.

M-MODE   Implies a one-dimensional ultrasonic measurement procedure with movement of the trace to record amplitude and velocity of moving echo-producing structures.

B-SCAN   Implies a two-dimensional ultrasonic scanning procedure with a two-dimensional display.

REAL-TIME   Implies a two-dimensional ultrasonic scanning procedure with display of both two-dimensional structure and motion with time.

THERAPEUTIC RADIOLOGY   77261-77799

Services defined in this section of CPT include teletherapy and brachytherapy. To report Therapeutic Radiology services, the following must be performed and documented:

• The initial consultation
• Clinical treatment planning with/without simulation
• Medical radiation physics, dosimetry, treatment devices and special services
• Clinical treatment management procedures
• Normal follow-up care during treatment and for three months following completion of treatment

CONSULTATION OR CLINICAL MANAGEMENT

Preliminary consultations, evaluation of the patient prior to a decision to treat, or the provision of full medical care (in addition to treatment management), is reported using appropriate Visit or Evaluation and Management codes.

CLINICAL TREATMENT PLANNING   77261-77299

The clinical treatment planning process is a complex service including interpretation of special testing, tumor localization, treatment volume determination, treatment time/dosage determination, choice of treatment modality, determination of number and size of treatment ports, selection of appropriate treatment devices, and other procedures. CPT defines three distinct levels of clinical treatment planning: simple, intermediate and complex. Review this section of CPT for detailed definitions of these levels of service.

CLINICAL TREATMENT MANAGEMENT   77400-77499

Codes in this section presume treatment on a daily basis (4 or 5 fractions per week) with the use of megavoltage photon or high energy particle sources. Daily and weekly clinical treatment management are mutually exclusive for the same dates. CPT defines three distinct levels of clinical treatment management: simple, intermediate and complex. Review this section of CPT for detailed definitions of these levels of service.

NUCLEAR MEDICINE   78000-79999

Nuclear medicine procedures may be performed independently or in the course of overall medical care. If the physician providing nuclear medicine services is also responsible for the diagnostic work-up and/or follow-up care of the patient, Visit or Evaluation and Management codes should be reported in addition to the nuclear medicine procedures.

Radioimmunoassay tests are located in the clinical pathology section, code series 82000-84999. These codes can be used by any specialist performing such tests in a laboratory licensed and/or certified for radioimmunoassays. The reporting of these tests is not confined to clinical pathology laboratories alone.

Note that the services listed in this section DO NOT include the provision of radium or other elements. When those materials are supplied by the physician they should be listed as separate procedures using code 78990 for diagnostic radionuclide(s) and 79900 for therapeutic radionuclide.

HCPCS EQUIPMENT TRANSPORTATION CODES   R0070-R0076

HCPCS contains three codes, R0070, R0075 and R0076 to report transportation of portable x-ray equipment and personnel to home or nursing home. Consult your local Medicare intermediary before using these codes.

LABORATORY SERVICES

GUIDELINES

Items used by all physicians in reporting their services are presented in the INTRODUCTION. Some of the commonalities are repeated here for the convenience of those physicians referring to this section on PATHOLOGY AND LABORATORY. Other definitions and items unique to Pathology and Laboratory are also listed.

SERVICES IN PATHOLOGY AND LABORATORY

The procedures listed in this section of CPT are provided by a pathologist or by technologists under the responsible supervision of a physician.

SUBSECTION INFORMATION

The PATHOLOGY AND LABORATORY section of CPT is divided into 12 subsections; namely:

Automated, Multichannel Tests	80000-80019
Therapeutic Drug Monitoring	80031-80042
Organ or Disease Oriented Panels	80050-80099
Consultations (Clinical Pathology)	80500-80502
Urinalysis	81000-81999
Chemistry and Toxicology	82000-84999
Hematology	85000-85999
Immunology	86000-86999
Microbiology	87000-87999
Anatomic Pathology	88000-88299
Surgical Pathology	88300-88399
Miscellaneous	89000-89399

Several of the subheadings or subsections have special needs or instructions unique to that section. The following subsections of the PATHOLOGY AND LABORATORY section contain NOTES that should be reviewed carefully prior to choosing codes from those subsections:

Automated, multichannel tests	80002-80019
Chemistry and toxicology	82000-84999
Surgical pathology	88300-88399

MODIFIERS

Listed services and procedures may be modified under certain circumstances. When applicable, the modifying circumstances should be identified by the appropriate modifier code. Modifiers commonly used to report PATHOLOGY and LABORATORY procedures include:

-22 unusual services

-26 professional component

-32 mandated services

-52 reduced services

-90 reference (outside) laboratory

AUTOMATED, MULTICHANNEL TESTS   80002-80019

The following list contains those tests that can be and are frequently done as groups and combinations ("profiles") on automated multichannel equipment. For any combination of tests among those listed below, use the appropriate CPT code from 80002 to 80019. Code selection depends on the number of tests performed. Groups of the tests listed here are distinguished from multiple tests performed individually for immediate or "stat" reporting.

Albumin	*Lactic dehydrogenase (LDH)*
Albumin/globulin ratio	*Phosphatase, alkaline*
Bilirubin, direct	*Phosphorus (inorganic phosphate)*
Bilirubin, total	*Potassium*
Calcium	*Protein, total*
Carbon dioxide content	*SGOT*
Chlorides	*SGPT*
Cholesterol	*Sodium*
Creatinine	*Urea Nitrogen (BUN)*
Globulin	*Uric acid*
Glucose (sugar)	

ORGAN OR DISEASE PANELS 80050-80099

Codes for organ or disease oriented panels were included in CPT due to the increase use of general screening programs by physicians, clinics, hospitals, and other health care facilities. Other codes in this section define profiles that combine laboratory tests together under a problem oriented classification. Note that there is no expanded list of laboratory tests under each code as with the automated, multichannel test codes. This omission is deliberate on the part of CPT. As no two laboratories utilize the same array of tests in a particular panel, each laboratory should establish its own profile and accompany each reported panel by a listing of the components of that panel performed by the laboratory.

The lack of definitive codes for the ORGAN OR DISEASE ORIENTED PANELS results in confusion when coding and billing. Some Medicare carriers have defined specific tests that are considered to be components of these panels. However, in many cases the tests defined by the Medicare carrier are identical to those contained in the list of tests defined as part of AUTOMATED, MULTI-CHANNEL TESTS. One Medicare carrier defines CPT code 80058, Hepatic function panel, as including the following tests:

84155	Total protein	84075	Alkaline phosphatase
82040	Albumin	84450	SGOT
82465	Cholesterol	84460	SGPT
82251	Total and direct bilirubin		

The above tests are listed individually under AUTOMATED, MULTI- CHANNEL TESTS. Billed as a panel of 7 tests, using CPT code 80007, this service has a combined relative value of 1.2 laboratory units based on SysteMetrics/McGraw-Hill's Relative Value for Physicians. Billed as a Hepatic function panel, using CPT code 80058, the service has a combined relative value of 4.0 laboratory units.

PATHOLOGY CONSULTATIONS 80500-80502

To be considered a clinical pathology consultation, the following components must be present:

- The consultation must be requested from an attending physician
- The service must require additional medical interpretative judgement by the pathologist
- The pathologist must render a written report

Reporting of a test result(s) without medical interpretive judgment IS NOT considered a clinical pathology consultation.

SURGICAL PATHOLOGY 88300-88399

Surgical pathology procedure codes include accession, handling and reporting. The unit of service for codes 88300 through 88309 is the specimen. A specimen is defined as "tissue or tissues that is (are) submitted for individual and separate attention, requiring individual examination and pathologic diagnosis." The 1992 edition of CPT redefines codes 88300-88309 as LEVEL I through LEVEL VI and provides specific definitions of specimens and procedures for each level.

MEDICINE SERVICES

Prior to 1992, the MEDICINE section of CPT included codes for office, hospital and other visits, plus consultations, as well as diagnostic and therapeutic procedures. The MEDICINE section of CPT was traditionally placed in the front of the book because these codes are (were) used by all medical professionals. With the introduction of the new Evaluation and Management codes in the 1992 CPT, all visit codes in the range 90000-90699 were deleted and replaced by Evaluation and management codes in the range 99200-99499. The EVALUATION AND MANAGEMENT SECTION is located in the front of the CPT, where the MEDICINE section used to be. The remaining codes of the MEDICINE section was moved to its logical place at the back.

Due to the fact that the new Evaluation and Management codes are required only by Medicare at the time of this writing, this book includes a complete discussion of the visit codes in use prior to 1992 in the chapter titled VISITS/EVALUATION AND MANAGEMENT SERVICES. Medicine services are used to report diagnostic or therapeutic procedures. CPT codes for medicine services are in the range 90700 to 99199. HCPCS codes for medicine services are in the range M0000-M0999.

GUIDELINES

In addition to the standard definitions and general instructions found in the INTRODUCTION to CPT, the MEDICINE section of CPT includes specific items that are unique to that section. As previously discussed, HCPCS has no specific guidelines.

MULTIPLE PROCEDURES

It is appropriate to designate multiple procedures that are rendered on the same date by separate entries. For example: if individual medical psychotherapy (90841) is rendered in addition to subsequent hospital care (e.g 99231), the psychotherapy would be reported separately from the hospital visit.

SEPARATE PROCEDURES

Some of the listed procedures are commonly carried out as an integral part of a total service, and as such, do not warrant a separate identification. When, however, such a procedure is performed independently of, and is not immediately related to, other services, it may be listed as a "separate procedure." Thus, when a procedure that is ordinarily a component of a larger procedure is performed alone for a specific purpose, it may be reported as a separate procedure.

SUBSECTION INFORMATION

The MEDICINE section of (the 1992) CPT is divided into 18 subsections; namely:

Immunization Injections	90701-90749
Infusion Therapy (Excludes Chemotherapy)	90780-90781

Therapeutic or Diagnostic Injections	90782-90799
Psychiatry	90801-90899
Biofeedback	90900-90915
Dialysis	90935-90989
Gastroenterology	91000-92199
Ophthalmology	92002-92499
Special Otorhinolaryngologic Services	92502-92599
Cardiovascular	92950-93799
Non-Invasive Vascular Diagnostic Studies	93875-93979
Pulmonary	94010-94799
Allergy and Clinical Immunology	95000-95199
Neurology and Neuromuscular Procedures	95805-95999
Chemotherapy Administration	96400-96549
Special Dermatological Procedures	96900-96999
Physical Medicine	97010-97799
Special Services and Reports	99000-99199

Several of the subsections have special needs or instructions unique to that section. Subsections within the MEDICINE section that have special instructions are:

Psychiatry	90801-90899
Ophthalmology	92002-92499
Otorhinolaryngology	92502-92599
Pulmonary	94010-94799
Allergy and Clinical Immunology	95000-95199
Neurology and Neuromuscular	95819-95999

UNLISTED SERVICE OR PROCEDURE

A service or procedure may be provided that is not listed in this edition of CPT. When reporting such a service, the appropriate "Unlisted Procedure" code may be used to indicate the service. A report which describes the unlisted service or procedure should be sent with your insurance claim forms.

MODIFIERS

Listed services and procedures may be modified under certain circumstances. When applicable, the modifying circumstance is identified by the addition of the appropriate modifier code. The following modifiers are frequently used with MEDICINE services.

-22 Unusual services

-26 Professional component

-51 Multiple procedures

> This modifier may be used to report multiple medical procedures performed at the same session, as well as a combination of medical and surgical procedures.

-52 Reduced services

-76 Repeat procedure by same physician

-77 Repeat procedure by another physician

-90 Reference (outside) laboratory

-99 Multiple modifiers

SPECIAL REPORT

A service that is unlisted, rarely provided, unusual, variable, or new MAY require a special report in determining medical appropriateness of the service. This simply means that you may need to provide additional documentation either routinely, as when billing unlisted procedure codes or using modifier -22, or when requested to do so by an insurance carrier.

MATERIALS SUPPLIED BY PHYSICIAN

Supplies and materials provided by the physician over and above those usually included with the office visit or other services rendered may be listed separately. List all drugs, trays, supplies and materials provided. See the section Important Coding and Billing Issues a discussion of how to code and bill properly for supplies and materials. Remember that HCPCS codes must be used instead of CPT codes when reporting supplies, materials, and injections to Medicare.

VISITS

All Visit codes were deleted from the 1992 edition of CPT and replaced by Evaluation and Management codes. For a complete discussion of both coding systems please see the section titled VISITS/EVALUATION AND MANAGEMENT SERVICES.

IMMUNIZATION INJECTIONS   90701-90749

Immunizations are usually given in conjunction with a visit or evaluation and management service. When an immunization is the only service performed, a minimal service, CPT Visit code 90030 or CPT Evaluation and Management code 99211, may be listed in addition to the injection code. Immunization codes include the supply of materials. The use of these minimal service codes, billed in addition to the immunization injection code(s), is one of the most frequently overlooked opportunities to increase reimbursement.

INFUSION THERAPY   90780-90781

Infusion therapy procedures are used to report prolonged intravenous injections requiring the presence of a physician during the infusion. These codes are not used for intra-dermal, subcutaneous, intra-muscular, or routine IV drug injections. In addition, they are not used for chemotherapy. These codes are time specific codes covering the first hour, and each additional hour of therapy up to eight (8) hours.

THERAPEUTIC INJECTIONS   90782-90799

Therapeutic injection codes are used for reporting therapeutic injections of medication, via subcutaneous, intramuscular, intra-arterial or intravenous routes; intramuscular injection of antibiotic and intravenous therapy for intractable allergic disease. CPT lists only six codes for therapeutic injections. CPT instructs the user to "specify material injected" the medication or antibiotic used. Use CPT codes when reporting therapeutic injections to commercial insurance carriers (unless otherwise instructed by specific carriers). Note that these codes are NEVER used to report therapeutic injections to Medicare.

DRUGS ADMINISTERED   J0000-J8999
OTHER THAN ORAL METHOD

HCPCS lists over 400 codes which describe specific therapeutic injections, miscellaneous drugs and solutions, stinging insect venoms, and immuno-suppressive drugs. You must use these codes when reporting therapeutic injections provided to Medicare beneficiaries. Failure to use HCPCS codes instead of CPT codes for therapeutic injections may result in denial of your claim, reduced payment or delayed payment. Using HCPCS codes properly for therapeutic injections provided to Medicare beneficiaries can have a significant impact on your reimbursement.

The March 1990 revision of HCPCS included a fundamental change in the way HCPCS injection codes are described. The descriptions of all HCPCS codes in the range J0000-J9999 were changed from brand name to generic name. The PMIC version of HCPCS includes the brand name of the drug in bold letters within the description and a brand name and generic name index.

PSYCHIATRY   90801-90899

This subsection of CPT includes codes for reporting general psychiatric, clinical psychiatric, and psychiatric therapeutic services and procedures.

Hospital Care

Hospital care services reported by the attending physician in treating a psychiatric inpatient, may use the full range of hospital Visit or Evaluation and Management codes.

Case Management

If the physician is active in the leadership or direction of a treatment team, a code may be selected based upon the services provided that day using Case Management codes from the Visit range 98900-98902 or the Evaluation and Management series 99361-99362.

Separate Procedures

All procedures that are performed in addition to hospital care, such as electroconvulsive therapy or medical psychotherapy should be listed in addition to hospital care.

Psychiatric care may be reported without time dimensions, using the codes 90841 or 90845, or with time dimensions, using codes 90843 or 90844, based upon practices customary in the local area. The modifiers -52, reduced service, or -22, unusual service, may be used to bill for services that were less or more lengthy that the time-specified codes define.

PSYCHIATRIC CONSULTATIONS

Consultation for psychiatric evaluation of a patient includes examination of a patient and exchange of information with primary physician and others, such as nurses or family members, and preparation of report. Consultation services provided by psychiatrists are billed using CPT Visit or Evaluation and Management consultation codes. Psychiatric consultation services are limited to initial or follow-up evaluation and do not involve psychiatric treatment.

DIALYSIS   90935-90999

Services provided to renal dialysis patients are reported using codes from this section. All visit/evaluation and management services related to the patient's end stage renal disease that are rendered on a day when dialysis is performed and all other patient care services that are rendered during the dialysis procedure are included in the dialysis procedure codes.

Visit or Evaluation and Management services that are unrelated to the dialysis procedure that cannot be rendered during the dialysis session may be reported in addition to the dialysis procedure. The addition of Prolonged Detention codes 99150 or 99151 may be appropriate for dialysis services. Key coding issues include whether the patient is receiving hemodialysis or peritoneal dialysis and the location of the service.

Supplies provided to dialysis patients that are not considered to be included with the dialysis service or procedure are reported using CPT code 99070 or HCPCS codes E1500-E1699 for DME, and A4650-A5149 for supplies for ESRD.

OPHTHALMOLOGY   92002-92499

Ophthalmological diagnostic and treatment services are reported using codes in the range 92002-92499. Minimal, brief and limited office services, and hospital, home, extended care, emergency department and consultations are reported using CPT Visit or Evaluation and Management codes. See the section VISITS/EVALUATION AND MANAGEMENT services for a complete discussion of these services.

SPECIAL DEFINITIONS FOR OPHTHALMOLOGY SERVICES

INTERMEDIATE OPHTHALMOLOGICAL SERVICES

To report intermediate ophthalmological services, the following must be performed and documented:

- Evaluation of new or existing condition
- Complicated by new diagnostic or management problem (not necessarily related to the primary diagnosis)
- History
- General medical observation
- External ocular and adnexal examination
- Other diagnostic procedures as indicated
- May include the use of mydriasis
- Do not usually include determination of refractive state but may in an established patient under continuing active treatment

Examples of INTERMEDIATE ophthalmology services as defined in CPT include:

Review of history, external examination, ophthalmoscopy, biomicroscopy for an acute complicated condition, for example, iritis, not requiring comprehensive ophthalmological services.

Review of interval history, external examination, ophthalmoscopy, biomicroscopy and tonometry in established patient with known cataract not requiring comprehensive ophthalmological services.

COMPREHENSIVE OPHTHALMOLOGICAL SERVICES

A level of service in which a general evaluation of the complete visual system is made. To report comprehensive ophthalmological services the following must be performed and documented:

- Billed as a single service but may be performed at more than one session.
- History
- General medical observation
- External and ophthalmoscopic examination
- Gross visual fields
- Basic sensorimotor examination
- May (often) include(s), as indicated; biomicroscopy, examination with cycloplegia or mydriasis and tonometry
- <u>Always</u> includes initiation of diagnostic and treatment programs

Examples of COMPREHENSIVE ophthalmological services as defined in CPT include:

Services required for diagnosis and treatment of a patient with symptoms indicating possible disease of the visual system, such as glaucoma, cataract, or retinal disease, or to rule out disease of the visual system, new or established patient.

Initiation of diagnostic and treatment program includes the prescription of medication, lenses and other therapy and arranging for special ophthalmological diagnostic or treatment services, consultations, laboratory procedures and radiological services as may be indicated.

Prescription of lenses may be deferred to a subsequent visit, but in any circumstance is not reported separately.

Intermediate and comprehensive ophthalmological services are considered integrated services in which medical diagnostic evaluation cannot be separated from the examining techniques used. Service components, such as slip lamp examination, keratomy, ophthalmoscopy, retinoscopy, tonometry and motor evaluation are not reported separately.

SPECIAL OPHTHALMOLOGICAL SERVICES

A level of service in which a special evaluation of part of the visual system is made which goes beyond the services usually included under general ophthalmological services, or in which special treatment is given.

Flourescein angioscopy, quantitative visual field examination, or extended color vision examination should be specifically reported as special ophthalmological services.

DETERMINATION OF THE REFRACTIVE STATE

Prior to CPT 1992, determination of the refractive state was not considered a separate medical procedure or service entity. It was considered an integral part of the general ophthalmological services, carried out with reference to other diagnostic procedures. However, CPT 1992 includes a new code, 92015, to report determination of refractive state.

You should consult with your major insurance carriers prior to using this new code. Some insurance carriers, notably Medicare carriers, may require the use of HCPCS modifier -AP when using CPT codes 92004, 92012 or 92014. The modifier -AP is a HCPCS National Level 2 modifier defined as "determination of refractive state was not performed in course of diagnostic ophthalmological examination."

CONTACT LENS SERVICES   92310-92326

The prescription of contact lens is defined as specification of optical and physical characteristics, such as power, size, curvature, flexibility and gas-permeability. It is not considered a part of the general ophthalmological services. The fitting of contact lens includes instruction and training of the wearer and incidental revision of the lens during the training period. Follow-up of successfully fitted extended wear lenses is considered as part of a general ophthalmological service. The supply of contact lenses may be included as part of the service or fitting or may be billed separately using codes 92391 or 92396.

If contact lenses are included as part of the fitting code, use modifier -26 to indicate the service of fitting without supply. If the prescription and fitting is for only one eye, use modifier -52 to indicate reduced service.

SPECTACLE SERVICES (INCLUDING PROSTHESIS FOR APHAKIA)

Prescription of spectacles, when required, is an integral part of general ophthalmological services and is not reported separately. However, fitting of spectacles is a separate service, when provided by the physician, it is reported using codes from the 92340-92371 series. Presence of physician is not required during the fitting.

Supply of materials including spectacles, contact lenses, low vision aids, and ocular prosthesis are not considered part of the service of fitting spectacles and should be coded separately using codes 92390-92396.

HCPCS CODES FOR VISION SERVICES   V0000-V2799

There is a section of the HCPCS National Level 2 coding system which contains specific codes, from V0000 through V2799, for spectacles, contact lenses and eye prosthesis. With the exception of post-cataract lenses used as a prosthetic device, these services are generally not covered by Medicare; therefore you would not bill Medicare for these services or use the HCPCS codes to bill any other carrier for these services.

OTORHINOLARYNGOLOGIC SERVICES   92502-92599

Diagnostic or treatment procedures usually included in a comprehensive otorhinolaryngologic evaluation or office visit, are reported as an integrated medical service, using Visit or Evaluation and Management codes. Component procedures, such as otoscopy, rhinoscopy, tuning fork test, which may be provided as part of a comprehensive service are not reported separately.

Special otorhinolaryngologic services are those diagnostic and treatment services not usually included in a comprehensive otorhinolaryngologic evaluation or office visit. These services are reported separately. All services include medical diagnostic evaluation. Technical procedures (which may or may not be performed by the physician personally) are often part of the service, but should not be mistaken to constitute the service itself.

AUDIOLOGIC FUNCTION TESTS WITH MEDICAL DIAGNOSTIC EVALUATION

Audiometric tests described in codes 92551-92599 presume the use of calibrated electronic equipment. Other hearing tests, such as whispered voice, tuning fork etc., are considered part of the general otorhinolaryngologic services and are not reported separately. All codes in this section refer to testing of both ears. Use the modifier -52 "Reduced Service" if a test is applied to one ear instead of to two ears. Note that all codes, with the exception of 92559, apply to the testing of individuals. For testing of groups, use code 92559 and specify testing used.

HCPCS CODES FOR HEARING SERVICES   V5000-V5999

As with vision services, there is a section of the HCPCS National Level 2 coding system, which contains specific codes from V5000 through V5999 that describe hearing services such as audiometric exam, hearing aids, etc. None of
these services are covered by Medicare, therefore Medicare should not be billed for these services, and the HCPCS codes should not be used (unless otherwise instructed) to bill any other carrier.

CARDIOVASCULAR SERVICES   92950-93799

Codes in this section of CPT are used to report therapeutic services such as cardiopulmonary resuscitation (CPR), cardioversion and percutaneous transluminal coronary angioplasty (PTCA) and diagnostic procedures such as electrocardiography, echocardiography and cardiac catheterization.

HCPCS National Level 2 includes 13 codes, as of the 1991 edition, that describe specific cardiovascular services. Consult your local Medicare intermediary before using these codes.

SPECIAL MEDICARE CONSIDERATIONS

Many of the codes in this section fall under the Medicare Purchased Diagnostic Services guidelines. Coding and reporting should be as instructed by your local Medicare carrier.

NON-INVASIVE VASCULAR STUDIES   93850-93960

Vascular studies include patient care required to perform the studies, supervision of the studies and interpretation of the study results with copies for patient records of hard copy output with analysis of all data, including bidirectional vascular flow or imaging when provided.

The use of a simple hand-held or other Doppler device that does not produce hard copy output, or that produces a record that does not permit analysis of bidirectional vascular flow, is considered to be part of the physical examination of the vascular system and is not reported separately. To report unilateral non-invasive diagnostic studies, add modifier -52 to the basic code.

A Duplex Scan is defined as "An ultrasonic scanning procedure with display of both two-dimensional structure and motion with time and Doppler ultrasonic signal documentation with spectral analysis and/or color flow velocity mapping or imaging.

In the 1992 CPT all codes in this section were deleted and replaced by new codes.

SPECIAL MEDICARE CONSIDERATIONS

All of the codes in this section fall under the Medicare Purchased Diagnostic Services guidelines. Coding and reporting should be as instructed by your local Medicare carrier.

PULMONARY SERVICES   94010-94799

Pulmonary services include the laboratory procedure(s), interpretation, and physician's services (except surgical and anesthesia services) unless otherwise stated. It is common for pulmonologists to provide interpretation services only, under contract to medical facilities. Billing of interpretation only for pulmonary services would include the modifier -26 "Professional Component".

SPECIAL MEDICARE CONSIDERATIONS

Most of the codes in this section fall under the Medicare Purchased Diagnostic Services guidelines. Coding and reporting should be as instructed by your local Medicare carrier.

ALLERGY AND IMMUNOLOGY   95000-95199

Allergy and Clinical Immunology may include the performance and evaluation of sensitivity tests, the administration of allergenic extracts and/or medical conference services. It should be noted that the codes listed under this section are in addition to visits or consultations.

OTHER ALLERGY MEDICAL SERVICES

Use code 95105 to report Medical conference services related to explaining the use of mechanical and electrical devices, climato-therapy, breathing exercises and/or postural drainage.

To report summary conference or therapeutic conferences following completion of the diagnostic workup, including discussion, avoidance, elimination, symptomatic treatment and immunotherapy use Visit codes from the 90040-90070 series or Evaluation and Management codes from the 99241-99245 series.

For prolonged conferences use Case Management codes 99361 or 99362 from the 1992 CPT.

ALLERGEN IMMUNOTHERAPY   95115-95199

These codes include the professional services necessary for allergen immunotherapy. Office Visit or Evaluation and Management codes may be reported in addition to allergen immunotherapy if and only if other identifiable services are provided at that time.

HCPCS includes two codes, J7010 and J7020, to report provision of allergy vaccine to Medicare patients.

NEUROLOGY PROCEDURES   95819-95999

Codes in this section are used to report diagnostic tests that are (usually) performed in addition to a consultation. All EEG services listed include the tracing, interpretation and report. For interpretation of EEG only, add modifier -26 to the basic procedure code.

SPECIAL MEDICARE CONSIDERATION

Most of the codes in this section fall under the Medicare Purchased Diagnostic Services guidelines. Coding and reporting should be as instructed by your local Medicare carrier.

CHEMOTHERAPY ADMINISTRATION   96400-96549

Due to continued advances in chemotherapy techniques, the 1990 edition of CPT included 12 new codes for what is now called Chemotherapy Administration instead of Chemotherapy Injections. These procedures are independent of the patient's office visit. The injection procedures may occur independently, or on the same day as an office visit. Chemotherapy administration may be coded when administered by a physician or a qualified assistant under the supervision of a physician, excluding chemotherapy administered by hospital or home health agency personnel.

Regional (isolation) chemotherapy perfusion should be reported using existing codes for arterial infusion. Placement of the intra-arterial catheter should be reported using the appropriate code from the Cardiovascular Surgery section.

Another important note is that the injection procedure codes do not include provision of the chemotherapy agent. Code 96545 is used to report and bill for provision of the chemotherapy agent for non-Medicare patients. For Medicare patients, choose HCPCS codes from the series J9000-J9999 to bill for chemotherapy drugs. See the following page for an example of how to bill this service properly.

Preparation of chemotherapy agent(s) is included in the service for administration of the agent. Report separate codes for each parenteral method of administration employed when chemotherapy is administered by different techniques.

21. DIAGNOSIS OR NATURE OF ILLNESS OR INJURY. (RELATE ITEMS 1,2,3 OR 4 TO ITEM 24E BY LINE)						2:
1. XXX . XX			3. |_____ . __			2:
2. |_____ . __			4. |_____ . __			

24. A DATE(S) OF SERVICE						B Place of Service	C Type of Service	D PROCEDURES, SERVICES, OR SUPPLIES (Explain Unusual Circumstances) CPT/HCPCS | MODIFIER		E DIAGNOSIS CODE
	From			To						
MM	DD	YY	MM	DD	YY					
1 03	15	92				11		90050 |		1
2 03	15	92				11		96420 |		1
3 03	15	92				11		96545 |		1

CHEMOTHERAPY DRUGS   J9000-J9999

The codes listed in this section of HCPCS are for the cost of the chemotherapy drug only and do not include the administration of the drug.

PHYSICAL MEDICINE   97010-97799

CPT physical medicine codes are divided into three sections: Modalities, Procedures and Tests and Measurements. The physician or therapist is required to be in constant attendance when reporting codes for modalities and procedures. The procedure codes specify treatment to one area, initial 30 minutes, and provide codes to report each additional 15 minutes of treatment.

Other services performed by medical professionals specializing in physical medicine and/or physical therapy may include:

Muscle testing, range of joint motion, electromyography	95831-95869
Biofeedback training by EMG	90900
Transcutaneous Nerve Stimulation (TNS)	64550

HCPCS physical therapy codes, M0005-M0008, describe combinations of visits, modalities and procedures. Consult your local Medicare intermediary before using these codes.

SPECIAL PHYSICAL MEDICINE CODING ISSUES

Many worker's compensation and casualty insurance carriers use pre-CPT coding systems, such as CRVS, and do not use any form of diagnostic coding, relying instead on special reports to justify the procedures performed and services provided. As the majority of physical medicine services are performed for accidents and injuries, many work related, the medical professional performing these services must be informed of the specific reporting requirements in the area that they practice.

OSTEOPATHIC SERVICES   M0702-M0710

HCPCS provides codes for Osteopathic Manipulation Therapy (OMT) provided in the office or location other than hospital. Codes are included for brief, limited, intermediate, extended and comprehensive OMT. Consult your local Medicare intermediary prior to using these codes.

HOSPITAL OSTEOPATHIC   M0722-M0730
MANIPULATION THERAPY

HCPCS includes codes M0722-M0730 for brief, limited, intermediate, extended and comprehensive osteopathic manipulation therapy provided on an inpatient basis. Consult your local Medicare intermediary prior to using these codes.

CHIROPRACTIC SERVICES   90000-90699

Office visits and consultations by chiropractors are reported using Visit or Evaluation and Management codes. In addition, many chiropractors perform and report services using codes from the Physical Medicine series 97000-97799 and Radiology series 70000-79999 of CPT. CPT code 99080 is often used in conjunction with worker's compensation cases.

Manipulation of spine by chiropractor is billed to Medicare only using HCPCS National Level 2 code A2000. There are restrictions on the number of times the code may be used, a maximum reimbursement amount per year, and extensive supporting documentation is required as described below.

DOCUMENTATION OF TREATMENT PHASE

Proper documentation of the treatment phase is extremely important when submitting claims for chiropractic services to Medicare. The treatment phase consists of the date the course of treatment was initiated and the number of treatments rendered to date. Proper documentation enables Medicare to process your claims quickly and accurately. For payment of chiropractic claims, the following information must be on the HCFA1500 claim form.

1. The service must be manual manipulation of the spine. This service is reported by procedure code A2000.

2. The primary diagnosis must be subluxation of the spine, either so stated or identified by a term descriptive of the subluxation. The following diagnoses are acceptable because they would always involve a subluxation:

intervertebral disc disorders	722.0-722.9
curvatures of the spine	737.0-737.9
spondylolisthesis	738.4,756.12
nonallopathic lesions	739.1-739.4
spondylolysis	756.11

3. The level of subluxation must be stated.

4. The symptoms related to the level of subluxation must be given.

5. The date of the confirming x-ray must be on the claim. Note that the x-ray must have been taken within 12 months prior to or 3 months after the course of treatment was initiated.

6. The date this course of treatment was initiated and the number of treatments rendered since the start of this course must be on the claim.

SPECIAL SITUATIONS

If a patient returns with a new condition or injury, this represents a new treatment phase. The treatment phase information should reflect when you first saw the patient for this condition. Do not use the date you first saw the patient for an earlier course of treatment. Note on your HCFA1500 claim form that this is a new condition. Remember that a new documenting x-ray may be required.

In the case of chronic conditions, an x-ray older than 12 months may be acceptable. For coverage of chronic conditions such as scoliosis, spondylolysis, and spondylolisthesis, there must be a reasonable expectation that there is a restorative potential. Remember that maintenance care is not covered by Medicare.

SPECIAL SERVICES AND REPORTS

The procedures with code numbers 99000 through 99090 provide the reporting physician with the means of identifying the completion of special reports and services that are an adjunct to the basic services rendered. The specific number assigned indicates the special circumstances under which a basic procedure is performed.

The proper use of Special Services codes can result in a significant increase in reimbursement. Most of the codes in this section are "add on" codes. This means that they are used in addition to whatever other codes describe the procedures or services performed.

MISCELLANEOUS SERVICES

99000 Handling and/or conveyance of specimen transfer from the physician's office to a laboratory

99001 Handling and/or conveyance of specimen for transfer from the patient in other than a physician's office to a laboratory (distance may be indicated)

99002 Handling, conveyance, and/or any other service in connection with the implementation of an order involving devices (eg, designing, fitting, packaging, handling, delivery or mailing) when devices such as orthotics, protectives, prosthetics are fabricated by an outside laboratory or shop but which items have been designed, and are to be fitted and adjusted by the attending physician

For routine collection of venous blood, report CPT code 36415.

99024 Postoperative follow-up visit, included in global service

This code is used to track no-charge post-op visits. As a component of a surgical package, review the Guidelines of the SURGERY section.

99025 Initial (new patient) visit when starred (*) surgical procedure constitutes major service at that visit (See section titled Starred Procedures in the Surgery section of this chapter)

SERVICES RENDERED AFTER REGULAR OFFICE HOURS

99050 Services requested after office hours in addition to basic service

99052 Services requested between 10:00 PM and 8:00 AM in addition to basic service

99054 Services requested on Sundays and holidays in addition to basic service

Note that codes 99050-99054 are reported in addition to the visit or Evaluation and Management codes used to report the basic service(s).

SERVICES RENDERED AT SPECIAL LOCATION

99056   Services provided at request of patient in a location other than physician's office

Note that code 99056 is reported in addition to the visit or Evaluation and Management codes used to report the basic service(s).

OFFICE EMERGENCY SERVICES

99058   Office services provided on an emergency basis

The diagnostic codes used to bill for this service must clearly justify the nature of the emergency.

EMERGENCY ROOM SERVICES

These codes were deleted from the 1992 edition of CPT and should not be reported to Medicare. However, they may be reported to other carriers until notified otherwise.

99062   Emergency care facility services: when the non-hospital-based physician is in the hospital, but is involved in patient care elsewhere and is called to the emergency facility to provide emergency services

99064   Emergency care facility services: when the non-hospital-based physician is called to the emergency facility from outside the hospital to provide emergency services; not during regular office hours

99065   during regular office hours

SUPPLIES AND MATERIALS

99070   Supplies and materials (except spectacles), provided by the physician over and above those usually included with the office visit or other services rendered (list drugs, trays, supplies, or materials provided.) For spectacles, use codes 92390-92395

Remember that HCPCS National Level 2 or Local Level 3 codes are always used instead of CPT code 99070 when reporting supplies, materials and drugs to Medicare.

99071   Educational supplies, such as books, tapes, and pamphlets, provided by the physician for the patient's education at cost to physician

99075   Medical testimony

This code may be used to report medical testimony provided as part of malpractice, worker's compensation and casualty cases. If you appear as an expert witness, negotiate appearance and stand-by fees with the attorneys up front. Demand payment prior to appearance.

99078 Physician educational services rendered to patients in a group setting for example, prenatal, obesity, or diabetic instructions

SPECIAL REPORTS

99080 Special reports such as insurance forms, or the review of medical data to clarify a patient's status - more than the information conveyed in the usual medical communications or standard report form

This code is used frequently to report review of medical records in worker's compensation and casualty cases.

99082 Unusual travel (eg, transportation and escort of patient)

This code may also be used to report travel associated with medical testimony.

99090 Analysis of information data stored in computers (eg, ECGs, blood pressures, hematologic data)

PROLONGED SERVICES

99150 Prolonged physician attendance requiring physician detention beyond usual service, (for example, operative standby, monitoring ECG, EEG, intrathoracic pressures, intravascular pressures, blood gases during surgery, standby for newborn care following cesarean section or maternal-fetal monitoring); 30 minutes to one hour

99151   more than one hour

99152 Newborn resuscitation: care of the high risk newborn at delivery including, for example, inhalation therapy, aspiration, administration of medication for initial stabilization

This code was deleted from the 1992 CPT. To report use Evaluation and Management code 99440.

CRITICAL CARE SERVICES

See VISITS/EVALUATION AND MANAGEMENT SERVICES

TRANSPORTATION SERVICES

99082
A0000-A0999

CPT has only one code to report transportation services. If the medical professional accompanied the patient on a long hospital transfer by ambulance, air ambulance, or long distance by common carrier, CPT code 99082 is used in addition to any other services provided, to report this service.

HCPCS codes A0000-A0999 cover emergency ambulance service using surface, air or water transport, plus non-emergency transportation services. There are also specific Ambulance Service Modifiers and a waiting time table to be used with these codes.

MISCELLANEOUS AND EXPERIMENTAL   A9000-A9999

HCPCS contains codes which may be used to report miscellaneous and experimental services or procedures. Most of the codes in this section begin with the term "non-covered". As Medicare will not reimburse non-covered services, there would be no reason to use these codes unless specifically instructed to do so by your local Medicare intermediary.

DENTAL PROCEDURES   D0000-D9999

There are no CPT codes to report dental services. Most dental procedures are reported using Current Dental Terminology (CDT) published by the American Dental Association. However, there are HCPCS National Level 2 codes which describe dental services and procedures. These codes are generally non-covered by Medicare.

REHABILITATIVE SERVICES   H5000-H6000

The codes listed in this section of HCPCS National Level 2 describe residential care, group psychotherapy, special classes and other services which are generally non-covered by Medicare.

TEMPORARY CODES   Q0000-Q0099

Temporary codes are HCPCS codes assigned by HCFA on a temporary basis. These codes change frequently and may be deleted or replaced completely from one year to the next. For example, all "Q" codes describing electrocardiographic monitoring for 24 hours were deleted from the March 1990 revision of HCPCS National Level 2 because the 1990 edition of CPT contained new CPT codes describing these services.

DIAGNOSIS CODING WITH ICD-9-CM

CHAPTER SUMMARY

Health care professionals have long used various coding systems, such as RVS and CPT, to describe procedures, services and supplies. However, most described the reason for the procedure, service or supply with a diagnostic statement, i.e. the diagnosis in words. Of those health care professionals who do code the diagnosis, either due to a requirement for a computer billing system and/or electronic claims filing, many do not code completely or accurately. With the passage of the Medicare Catastrophic Coverage Act of 1988, diagnostic coding using ICD-9-CM became mandatory for Medicare claims. In the area of health care reimbursement rules and regulations, the typical progression is that changes required for Medicare are followed shortly by similar changes for Medicaid and private insurance carriers.

To some professionals, the requirement to use diagnostic coding may seem a burden or simply another excuse for Medicare intermediaries to delay or deny payment. However, it is important to understand that the proper use of coding systems for both procedures and diagnoses gives the professional absolute control over his or her billing and reimbursement. Accurate diagnosis coding is not easy. It requires a good working knowledge of medical terminology and a fundamental understanding of ICD-9-CM. In addition, the coder must know the rules and regulations required to comply with Medicare requirements for coding.

This chapter provides the information necessary to develop a fundamental understanding of ICD-9-CM coding as well as the steps needed to comply fully with the new Medicare rules and regulations governing ICD-9-CM coding.

KEY POINTS REGARDING ICD-9-CM

1. ICD-9-CM codes are three to five numeric or alphanumeric codes.

2. ICD-9-CM codes describe illnesses, injuries, signs and symptoms, and procedures.

3. With few exceptions, ICD-9-CM codes are accepted or required by all insurance carriers.

4. Most ICD-9-CM codes have a specific definition; however, some ICD-9-CM codes have more than one definition.

5. ICD-9-CM coding can make a significant difference in your reimbursement.

6. Accurate ICD-9-CM coding puts you in control of the reimbursement process.

PREPARING YOUR PRACTICE FOR ICD-9-CM CODING

Proper preparation for converting your practice to ICD-9-CM coding is a four-step process. Even if your practice is already using ICD-9-CM coding you will need to review the following steps and take appropriate action where necessary.

EVALUATE YOUR RESOURCES

CODING MATERIALS

Do you have a copy of ICD-9-CM? Do you have enough copies for each person involved in the coding and billing process? Are you using the 1979 2nd Edition of ICD-9-CM? If yes, do you have all the official addenda published since 1986?

CODING EXPERTISE

Do you have staff with sufficient coding expertise to prepare your practice for ICD-9-CM coding? Does the expert coder have enough time to develop and manage the ICD-9-CM coding process?

REVIEW CURRENT DIAGNOSTIC CODES AND STATEMENTS

DIAGNOSTIC STATEMENTS

Are your diagnostic statements in the medical record accurate and precise? Are they easy to read? Do you use a lot of "rule out" diagnostic statements?

SUPERBILL

Are you using a fee ticket or superbill to record your charges and diagnoses? If yes, does the superbill have ICD-9-CM codes in addition to written descriptions? Are the codes current, accurate and complete? Do you have the ability to code fifth digits where required? Is there a place on the superbill to relate the diagnosis code to a specific procedure?

TRAINING AND DEVELOPMENT

PURCHASE MATERIALS

Following completion of the steps outlined above, prepare your practice for ICD-9-CM coding by purchasing necessary materials, such as the new 3rd Edition of ICD-9-CM, or additional copies of ICD-9-CM, or the Official Addenda.

TRAIN THE STAFF

If the review reveals a lack of staff coding expertise, plan to send the person(s) designated to manage the practice's ICD-9-CM coding process to seminars for training. We strongly recommend that the health care professional also attend coding seminars if not well- trained in the area of diagnostic coding.

SUPPLEMENT THE STAFF

If the review reveals staff expertise, but lack of staff time, consider hiring additional full or part-time staff to perform the coding function, or to perform the functions of the practice's designated coder. Consider hiring someone from your hospital medical records department.

IMPROVE YOUR DIAGNOSTIC STATEMENTS

If the coding review reveals problems with illegible or difficult to read coding statements, excessive use of "rule out" statements, imprecise or inaccurate coding statements, try to improve your efforts in this area. Keep in mind that this not only makes coding easier for the staff, but it directly affects the practice's reimbursement.

CORRECT DEFICIENCIES IN YOUR SUPERBILL

Redesign your superbill to provide the ability to use ICD-9-CM codes properly, including fifth-digits where required, plus a means to relate the diagnoses specifically to the procedures, services, and/or supplies provided. Make sure you include the ability to write-in and code diagnoses which are not listed.

CREATE A MASTER LIST OF COMMONLY USED ICD-9-CM CODES

Prepare a list of the 50 to 100 diagnoses most frequently used by your practice. Make sure to include appropriate symptoms, signs and other conditions. Indicate the need for fifth digits by using a dash, box, or asterisk next to appropriate codes. Use this list to redesign your superbill or fee ticket. Make sure the health care professional and all staff involved with the coding and billing process are familiar with the list.

Review your superbills from time-to-time to determine if you are writing-in a lot of unlisted diagnoses. Add these codes to your ICD- 9-CM codes master list if they are being used frequently.

MEDICARE REQUIREMENTS FOR ICD-9-CM CODING

The Medicare Catastrophic Coverage Act of 1988 (P.L 100-330) required health care professionals to submit an appropriate diagnosis code (or codes), using the International Classification of Diseases, 9th Revision, Clinical Modification (ICD-9-CM) for each procedure, service, or supply billed under Medicare Part B. Even though the original law was subsequently repealed, the diagnosis coding requirement was maintained.

To comply with the regulations, health care professionals must convert the reason(s) for the procedures, services or supplies, performed or issued, from written diagnostic statements which may include specific diagnoses, signs, symptoms and/or complaints, into ICD-9-CM diagnosis codes. The Health Care Financing Administration originally set the implementation date for this requirement as April 1, 1989, however, it was subsequently delayed twice, until October 1989, at the request of the American Medical Association, to give health care providers additional time to prepare for the change.

HCFA GUIDELINES FOR USING ICD-9-CM CODES

The Health Care Financing Administration (HCFA) has prepared guidelines for using ICD-9-CM codes and instructions on how to report them on claim forms. In addition, HCFA has directed your Medicare intermediary to provide you with a written copy of these instructions. The basic HCFA guidelines are summarized below. However, it is very important that you obtain a copy of the guidelines from your Medicare intermediary as implementation of HCFA requirements varies from one intermediary to another.

1. Indicate on the claim form or itemized statement the appropriate code(s) from the ICD-9-CM code range 001.0 through V82.9 to identify diagnoses, symptoms, conditions, problems, complaints or other reason(s) for the procedure, service or supply provided.

A. In choosing codes to describe the reason for the encounter, the health care professional will frequently be using codes within the range from 001.0 through 999.9, the section of ICD-9-CM for the classification of diseases and injuries (e.g. infectious and parasitic diseases; neoplasms; signs, symptoms and ill-defined conditions). Codes that describe symptoms, as opposed to diagnoses, are acceptable if this is the highest level of certainty documented by the physician.

B. ICD-9-CM also provides codes to deal with visits for circumstances other than a disease or injury, such as a visit for a lab test only. These codes are found in the V-code section and range from V01.0 through V82.9.

2. The ICD-9-CM code for the diagnosis, condition, problem, or other reason for the encounter documented in the medical record as the main reason for the procedure, service or supply provided should be listed first. Additional ICD-9-CM codes that describe any current coexisting conditions are then listed. Do not include codes for conditions that were previously treated and no longer exist.

3. ICD-9-CM codes should be used at their highest level of specificity.

A. Assign three digit codes only if there are no four digit codes within the coding category.

B. Assign four digit codes only if there is no fifth digit subclassification for that category.

C. Assign the fifth digit subclassification code for those categories where it exists.

Claims submitted with three or four digit codes where four and five digit codes are available may be returned to you by the Medicare intermediary for proper coding. It is recognized that a very specific diagnosis may not be known at the time of the initial encounter. However, that is not an acceptable reason to submit a three digit code when four or five digits are available.

4. Diagnoses documented as "probable," "suspected," "questionable," or "rule out" should not be coded as if the diagnosis is confirmed. The condition(s) should be coded to the highest degree of certainty for the encounter, such as describing symptoms, signs, abnormal test results, or other reasons for the encounter.

5. Chronic disease(s) treated on an ongoing basis may be coded and reported as many times as the patient receives treatment and care for the condition(s).

6. When patients receive ancillary diagnostic services only during an encounter, the appropriate "V code" for the service should be listed first, and the diagnosis or problem for which the diagnostic procedures are being performed should be listed second.

A. V codes will be used frequently by radiologists who perform radiological examinations on referrals. For example, ICD-9-CM code V72.5, Radiological examination, not elsewhere classified, describes the reason for the encounter and should be listed first on the claim form or statement. If the reason for the referral is known, a second ICD-9-CM code which describes the signs or symptoms for which the examination was ordered should be listed.

B. Failure to list a second ICD-9-CM code in addition to the V code may result in claim delays or denials. The ICD-9-CM code V72.5, Radiological examination, not elsewhere classified, includes referrals for routine chest x-rays that are not covered by the Medicare program. Medicare intermediaries may establish screening programs to verify that the referrals were not for routine chest x-rays.

By supplying a second ICD-9-CM code to describe the reason for the referral, these claims can be clearly identified by the Medicare intermediary as referrals to evaluate symptoms, signs or diagnoses. The omission of a second ICD-9-CM code may lead to requests for additional information from Medicare intermediaries prior to processing the claim.

7. For patients receiving only ancillary therapeutic services during an encounter, list the appropriate V code first, followed by the ICD-9-CM code for the diagnosis or problem for which the services are being performed. For example, a patient with multiple sclerosis presenting for rehabilitation services would be coded using code V57.1, Other physical therapy, or code V57.89, Other care involving use of rehabilitation procedures, followed by code 340, multiple sclerosis.

8. For surgical procedures, use the ICD-9-CM code for the diagnosis for which the surgery was performed. If the postoperative diagnosis is known to be different at the time the claim is filed, use the ICD-9-CM code for the post operative diagnosis.

9. Code all documented conditions that coexist at the time of the visit that require or affect patient care, treatment or management. Do not code conditions that were previously treated and no longer exist.

COMPLETING THE HCFA1500 CLAIM FORM

Health care professionals using the Uniform Health Insurance Claim Form, HCFA 1500, to file claims for services provided to Medicare beneficiaries must list a minimum of one ICD-9-CM code and may list up to four total ICD-9-CM codes on the claim form. The ICD-9-CM code for the diagnosis, condition, problem or other reason for the encounter is listed first, followed by up to three additional codes that describe any coexisting conditions. At times, there may be several conditions that equally resulted in the encounter. In these cases, the health care professional is free to select the one that will be listed first.

The ICD-9-CM codes are listed in Box 23 of the HCFA 1500 claim form (see example). In addition, in Box 24 D of the HCFA 1500 claim form, you must indicate by a number from 1 to 4, or combination of numbers, which diagnoses from Box 23 support the procedure, service or supply listed in Box 24 C. Due to space limitations on the Uniform Insurance Claim Form, HCFA 1500, you may use only up to four ICD-9-CM codes for diagnoses, conditions, or signs and symptoms. Frequently the patient may have more than four conditions present at the time of the encounter, however, you must choose only four codes to be listed on the claim form.

If you strongly believe that additional diagnostic information is needed by the Medicare intermediary for proper claim processing you may attach additional supporting documentation to your manual claim. Keep in mind that in most cases the additional documentation will be ignored by the claims examiners, and, in other cases will result in reimbursement delay while someone reviews your documentation.

21. DIAGNOSIS OR NATURE OF ILLNESS OR INJURY. (RELATE ITEMS 1,2,3 OR 4 TO ITEM 24E BY LINE)				
1. 786 . 52			3. 410 . 9	
2. 413 . 9			4. ___ . __	

24. A DATE(S) OF SERVICE						B Place of Service	C Type of Service	D PROCEDURES, SERVICES, OR SUPPLIES (Explain Unusual Circumstances) CPT/HCPCS | MODIFIER		E DIAGNOSIS CODE
	MM	DD	YY	MM	DD	YY				
1	03	15	92				11		71020	1
2	03	15	92				11		93015	2
3	03	15	92				11		93307	3

PENALTIES FOR NON-COMPLIANCE

The Medicare Catastrophic Coverage Act of 1988 mandates submission of an appropriate ICD-9-CM diagnosis code or codes for each procedure, service, or supply furnished by the health care professional to Medicare Part B beneficiaries. The Act further specifies that compliance is mandatory and that penalties may be assessed for noncompliance. The penalties for noncompliance differ depending upon whether or not the health care professional has agreed to accept assignment or not.

1. For health care professionals who accept assignment on a Medicare claim and who fail to include ICD-9-CM codes as required, will have their claim(s) returned for proper coding and may be subject to post-payment review by the Medicare intermediary, as well as payment denials.

2. For health care professionals who do not accept assignment, the penalties are more severe.

A. If the original claim form does not include ICD-9-CM codes as required, and the health care professional refuses to provide the codes promptly on request to the Medicare intermediary, the professional may be subject to a civil monetary penalty in an amount not to exceed $ 2,000, per claim.

B. If the health care professional continuously fails to provide ICD-9-CM codes as requested, the professional may be subject to the sanction process described in section 1842 (j) (2) (A), which mandates that the professional may be barred from participation in the Medicare program for a period not to exceed five years.

HISTORICAL PERSPECTIVE

The International Classification of Diseases, 9th Revision, Clinical Modification (ICD-9-CM) is based on the official version of the World Health Organization's (WHO) 9th Revision, International Classification of Diseases (ICD-9). ICD-9 is designed for the classification of morbidity and mortality information for statistical purposes, and for the indexing of medical records by disease and operations, and for data storage and retrieval.

In use since January 1979, ICD-9-CM provides a diagnostic coding system which is more precise than those needed only for statistical groupings and trend analysis. Official addenda (updates) to ICD-9-CM were issued in October 1986, 1987, 1988 and 1989 by the Health Care Financing Administration. A special addendum was published by the U.S. Public Health Service in January 1988 containing codes for AIDS and AIDS related illnesses. A revised two-volume 3rd Edition, containing all revisions through 1988 was released in March 1989. The next revision, ICD-10, was due in 1990, however, current estimates is that the revision will not be available until 1992 or later.

USE OF ICD-9-CM CODES FOR PROFESSIONAL BILLING

Until passage of the Medicare Catastrophic Coverage Act of 1988, health care professionals were not required to report ICD-9-CM codes when billing government or private insurance carriers for reimbursement. The exception to this requirement was for those health care professionals who filed insurance claims electronically and those who used "code driven" computer billing services or computer systems. Most health care professionals simply included the text or description of the injury, illness, sign or symptom which was the reason for the encounter. Insurance carriers who used ICD-9-CM coding had to code the diagnostic statements prior to input into their computer systems for reimbursement processing.

A specific requirement of the Medicare Catastrophic Coverage Act of 1988 required health care professionals to include ICD-9-CM codes on their Medicare claim forms effective April 1, 1989. A two-month grace period, to June 1, 1989, was implemented at the request of the American Medical Association, to allow health care professionals additional time to develop the knowledge and systems necessary to implement the requirement. Traditionally in the area of issues related to reimbursement, rules and regulations mandated by HCFA for the Medicare program are followed shortly by similar rules for the Medicaid program and private insurance carriers.

IMPORTANT CODING & BILLING ISSUES

DIAGNOSES CODES MUST SUPPORT PROCEDURE CODES

Each service/procedure billed for a patient should be supported by a diagnosis that would substantiate those particular services or procedures as necessary in the investigation or treatment of their condition based on currently accepted standards of practice by the medical profession.

PLACE (LOCATION) OF SERVICE

The actual setting that the services are rendered in for particular diagnoses plays an important part in reimbursement. Many people became accustomed to using Emergency Rooms for any type of illness or injury. By utilizing highly specialized places of service for conditions that were not true emergencies, third party payers were being billed with CPT codes indicating emergency services were rendered.

Since the cost of services rendered on an emergency basis is considerably more expensive than those services in an non-emergency situation, third party payers began watching for those claims with diagnoses that did not indicate that a true emergency existed. Payment then was based on what the cost would have been had the patient been treated in the proper setting.

LEVEL OF SERVICE PROVIDED

The patient's condition and the treatment of that condition must be billed according to the criteria, as published by the AMA, for each level of service (i.e., minimal, brief, limited, intermediate, extended, comprehensive). Many practices bill the office visit level that they know will pay better rather than to consider the criteria that must be met to use a particular level of service. Again, the patient's diagnosis enters into this concept as well. As it is often the diagnosis that indicates the complexity of the level of service to be used.

FREQUENCY OF SERVICES

Many times claims are submitted for a patient with the same diagnosis and the same procedure(s) time after time. When the diagnosis indicates a chronic condition and the claims do not indicate any change in the patient's treatment or, gives any indication that the patient's condition has been altered (i.e., exacerbated, other symptomology) the third party payer may deny payment based on the frequency of services for the reported condition.

Currently, statistics are being tabulated from all claims submitted to Medicare or any other third party payer. These statistics will be used in the future as the basis of your fee profile for a prospective payment system. Again, this is why correct reporting by using the most appropriate codes is very important to the financial outlook of a provider.

DOWN CODING

Down coding is the process of reducing a code from one of a higher value to one of a lower value which results in lowered reimbursement. In the area of procedure coding, this process results in the loss of millions of dollars annually by health care professionals and their patients. With procedure coding, down coding claims is easily resolved by either providing a procedure description which matches that of Current Procedural Terminology (CPT) exactly, or, even better, by eliminating all procedure descriptions from your claim forms, which forces the insurance carrier to allow full value for your procedure, service, or supply.

With diagnosis coding, the issue is not mismatch of description to code, as the description is not required, but that the ICD-9-CM code(s) provide justification for the procedure, service or supply or the level of service provided. For example, if you submit an insurance claim form listing CPT code 90070, Office medical service, established patient; extended service, with an ICD-9-CM code of 487.1 Influenza with other respiratory manifestations, the insurance carrier will almost certainly down code the procedure to a lower level of service such as CPT code 90040 or 90050. A key point to remember is that if there are any current coexisting conditions which may complicate the treatment for the primary condition, it is very important to include the ICD-9-CM codes for the coexisting conditions which will help to justify the level of service provided.

CONCURRENT CARE

Reimbursement problems often arise when a patient is being treated by different professionals, within the same billing entity (medical group or clinic), for different problems at the same time. This is known as concurrent care. For example, a patient may be hospitalized by a clinic's general surgeon for an operation and may also be seen while hospitalized by the group's cardiologist for an unrelated cardiac condition.

If you submit claims for daily hospital visits by both of the above professionals without explanation, most insurance carriers would reject one daily visit as an apparent "duplication" of service. Prior to publication of the 1992 edition of CPT the key to obtaining proper reimbursement for concurrent care was to use the procedure modifier - 75, Concurrent Care submitted with a different ICD-9- CM code for the services provided by each physician, which support and justify the need for those services. Modifier -75 was deleted from the 1992 edition of CPT, therefore, the diagnosis becomes the qualifying factor for justification of concurrent care services.

ELECTRONIC CLAIMS

HCFA has issued instructions to all Medicare intermediaries requiring them to make the changes necessary to accommodate the new ICD-9-CM coding requirements in the electronic billing process. ICD-9-CM codes have been required for Medicare electronic claims processing since its implementation in 1983. Those professionals who use electronic claims processing, either with a computer billing service bureau or their own computer system, are already providing ICD-9-CM codes with their claims. However, as mentioned previously, most professionals are not coding to the degree of accuracy, certainty or specificity required by the new regulations, so review and changes to the diagnostic coding process will be required.

In addition, most previous electronic claim formats allowed diagnostic coding on a one to one basis with procedures. For example, if you listed six procedures or services in the electronic claim, you could list up to six different ICD-9-CM codes as well. Under the new format, you will be restricted to the same four ICD-9-CM codes allowed on the HCFA 1500 claim form with some provisions for listing additional diagnoses with the charge record as before. In most cases, this new requirement will result in program changes by your computer billing service bureau, your computer software vendor, or in-house programming staff. In addition, you will probably need to review and revise your input documents (superbills, fee tickets, visit slips, etc.) in order to assure compliance with the new coding format.

USE OF SUPERBILLS

As of October 1, 1990, health care professionals must file the HCFA1500 claim form for all Medicare patients, regardless of the participation status of the provider. Approximately 10 percent of all HCFA1500 claim forms are submitted with a superbill attached. In order to expedite the claims process for unassigned Medicare beneficiaries, you must provide the patient with a superbill (billing statement) which includes the ICD-9-CM codes listed in the proper order, along with a number next to each procedure code indicating the corresponding ICD-9-CM diagnosis code. Failure to provide this information will result in penalties as described above.

The use of superbills causes Medicare a great deal of aggravation plus costs a lot of money for special processing. Plus, claims with superbills are processed more slowly than regular claims. As of May 1, 1992, Medicare carriers will no longer accept superbills attached to HCFA1500 claim forms. This will benefit both Medicare carriers and health care professionals.

FORMAT OF ICD-9-CM

The International Classification of Diseases, 9th Revision, Clinical Modification was originally published as a three volume set (2nd edition). Newer versions of ICD-9-CM, Third Edition, are available as two separate books (Volume 1 and Volume 2) and as a single book containing Volume 1 and Volume 2, or Volumes 1, 2 and 3 depending on the publisher. The only difference between the newer Third Edition of ICD-9-CM and the previous Second Edition, is that the Third Edition has the Official Addenda from 1986 through 1988 incorporated in the revised publication.

THE TABULAR LIST (VOLUME 1)

The TABULAR LIST (VOLUME 1) is a numeric listing of diagnosis codes and descriptions consisting of 17 chapters which classify diseases and injuries, two sections containing supplementary codes (V codes and E codes) and six appendices.

The Classification of Diseases and Injuries includes the following 17 chapters:

CHAPTER 1   Infectious and Parasitic Diseases (001-139)

CHAPTER 2   Neoplasms (140-239)

CHAPTER 3   Endocrine, Nutritional and Metabolic Diseases, and Immunity Disorders (240-279)

CHAPTER 4   Diseases of the Blood and Blood-Forming Organs (280-289)

CHAPTER 5   Mental Disorders (290-319)

CHAPTER 6   Diseases of the Nervous System and Sense Organs (320-389)

CHAPTER 7   Diseases of the Circulatory System (340-459)

CHAPTER 8   Diseases of the Respiratory System (460-519)

CHAPTER 9   Diseases of the Digestive System (520-579)

CHAPTER 10   Diseases of the Genitourinary System (580-629)

CHAPTER 11   Complications of Pregnancy, Childbirth, and the Puerperium (630-676)

CHAPTER 12   Diseases of the Skin and Subcutaneous Tissue (680-709)

CHAPTER 13   Diseases of the Musculoskeletal System and Connective Tissue (710-739)

CHAPTER 14   Congenital Anomalies (740-759)

CHAPTER 15   Certain Conditions Originating in the Perinatal Period (760-779)

CHAPTER 16   Symptoms, Signs and Ill-defined Conditions (780-799)

CHAPTER 17   Injury and Poisoning (800-999)

Each chapter of the Tabular List (Volume 1) is structured with the following components:

SECTIONS: groups of three-digit code numbers

CATEGORIES: three-digit code numbers

SUBCATEGORIES: four-digit code numbers

FIFTH-DIGIT SUBCLASSIFICATIONS: five digit code numbers

The two supplementary classifications included in the Tabular List (Volume 1) are:

V CODES   Supplementary Classification of Factors Influencing Health Status and Contact with Health Services (V01-V82)

E CODES   Supplementary Classification of External Causes of Injury and Poisoning (E800-E999)

The six appendices included in the Tabular List (Volume 1) are:

APPENDIX 1   Morphology of Neoplasms

APPENDIX 2   Glossary of Mental Disorders

APPENDIX 3   Classification of Drugs by American Hospital Formulary Service List Number and their ICD-9-CM equivalents

APPENDIX 4   Classification of Industrial Accidents According to Agency

APPENDIX 5   List of Three-Digit Categories

APPENDIX 6   Supplementary Classification of External Causes of Injury and Poisoning

THE ALPHABETICAL INDEX (VOLUME 2)

The Alphabetic Index (Volume 2) of ICD-9-CM consists of an alphabetic list of terms and codes, two supplementary Sections following the alphabetic listing, plus three special tables found within the alphabetic listing.

The Alphabetic Index (Volume 2) is structured as follows:

MAIN TERMS: appear in **BOLDFACE** type

SUBTERMS: are always indented two spaces to the right under main terms

CARRY-OVER LINES: are always indented more than two spaces from the level of the preceding line

The supplementary sections following the Alphabetic Index (Volume 2) are:

TABLE OF DRUGS AND CHEMICALS

This table contains a classification of drugs and other chemical substances to identify poisoning states and external causes of adverse effects.

INDEX TO EXTERNAL CAUSES OF INJURIES & POISONINGS (E-CODES)

This section contains the index to the codes which classify environmental events, circumstances, and other conditions as the cause of injury and other adverse effects.

SPECIAL TABLES

The three special tables, located within the Alphabetic Index (Volume 2), and found under the main terms as underlined below, are:

Human Immunodeficiency Virus with Associated Conditions

Hypertension Table

Neoplasm Table

PROCEDURES: TABULAR LIST AND ALPHABETIC INDEX (VOLUME 3)

The Procedures: Tabular List and Alphabetic Index (Volume 3) consists of two sections of codes which define procedures instead of diagnoses. Frequently used incorrectly by health care professionals, codes from Volume 3 are intended only for use by hospitals. The new U.S. Government Printing Office printing of ICD-9-CM, Third Edition, does not include Volume 3.

TABULAR LIST OF PROCEDURES

Includes 16 chapters containing codes and descriptions for surgical procedures and miscellaneous diagnostic and therapeutic procedures.

ALPHABETIC INDEX TO PROCEDURES

Provides an alphabetic index to the Tabular List of Volume 3

ICD-9-CM CODING CONVENTIONS

The ICD-9-CM Tabular List (Volume 1) makes use of certain abbreviations, punctuation, symbols, and other conventions which must be clearly understood. The purpose of these conventions is to first, provide special coding instructions, and second, to conserve space.

INSTRUCTIONAL TERMS

Instructional terms define what is or what is not included in a given subdivision. This is accomplished by using both inclusion and exclusion terms.

INCLUDES: Indicates separate terms, as, modifying adjectives, sites and conditions, entered under a subdivision, such as a category, to further define or give examples of the content of the category.

Excludes   Exclusion terms are enclosed in a box and are printed in italics to draw attention to their presence. The importance of this instructional terms is its use as a guideline to direct the coder to the proper code assignment. In other words, all terms following the word EXCLUDES: are to be coded elsewhere as indicated in each instance.

NOTES   These are used to define terms and give coding instructions. Often used to list the fifth-digit subclassifications for certain categories.

SEE   Acts as a cross reference and, is an explicit direction to look elsewhere. This instructional term must ALWAYS be followed. (Cross references provide the user with other possible modifiers for a term, or, its synonyms.)

SEE A   Variation of the instructional term "SEE." This refers the coder to a specific category. You must ALWAYS follow this instructional term.

SEE ALSO   A direction given to look elsewhere if the main term or subterm(s) are not sufficient to code the information you have.

CODE ALSO   Identifies those instances where more than one code is required to fully describe a given condition.

USE CODE   Adds further information to give a better picture of ADDITIONAL diagnosis.

PUNCTUATION MARKS

( )   PARENTHESIS are used to enclose supplementary words which may be present or absent in a statement of disease without effecting the code assignment.

[ ]   SQUARE BRACKETS are used to enclose synonyms, alternate wordings or explanatory phrases.

:   COLONS are used after an incomplete phrase or term which requires one or more of the modifiers indented under it to make it assignable to a given category. EXCEPTION to this rule pertains to the abbreviation NOS.

}   BRACES are used to connect a series of terms to a common stem. Each term on the left of the brace is incomplete and must be completed by a term to the right of the brace.

ABBREVIATIONS

NOS   Not Otherwise Specified - equivalent to Unspecified. This abbreviation refers to a lack of sufficient detail in the statement of diagnosis to be able to assign it to a more specific subdivision within the classification.

NEC   Not Elsewhere Classified - used with ill-defined terms to alert the coder that a specified form of the condition is classified differently. The codes given for such terms should be used only if more precise information is not available. Secondly, NEC is used with terms for which a more specific category is not provided in the TABULAR LIST (VOLUME 1) and, no additional amount of information will alter the code selection.

SYMBOLS

§   The SECTION MARK symbol preceding a code indicates the presence of a footnote at the bottom of the page. It also indicates that the footnote is applicable to all of the subdivisions within that code.

☐   The LOZENGE symbol appearing in the left margin preceding a four-digit code indicates a change in the code number and its content that are not the same as the code number in ICD-9. May be ignored for coding purposes.

RELATED TERMS

AND   Whenever this term appears in a title, it should be interpreted as "and/or."

WITH   When this term is used in a title it indicates a requirement that both parts of the title must be present in the diagnostic statement.

ESSENTIALS OF ICD-9-CM CODING

Learning and following the basic steps of coding will increase your chances of better and faster reimbursement from third party payers, as well as, establish meaningful profiles for future reimbursement rates. To become a proficient coder, two basic principles must be considered.

- First, it is imperative that you use both the Alphabetic Index (Volume 2) and the Tabular List (Volume 1) when locating and assigning a code number. Attempting to code only from the Alphabetic Index (Volume 2) will cause you to miss any additional information provided only in the Tabular List (Volume 1), such as exclusions, instructions to use additional codes or the need for a fifth-digit.

- Second, the level of specificity is important in all coding situations. So, a three-digit code that has subdivisions indicates you must use the appropriate subdivision code. Also, any time a fifth-digit subclassification is provided, you must use the fifth-digit code.

NINE STEPS FOR ACCURATE AND PRECISE CODING

1. Locate the main term within the diagnostic statement.

2. Locate that main term in the Alphabetic Index (Volume 2). Keep in mind that the primary arrangement for main terms is by condition in the Alphabetic Index (Volume 2); main terms can be referred to in outmoded, ill-defined and lay terms as well as proper medical terms; main terms can be expressed in broad or specific terms, as nouns, adjectives or eponyms and can be with or without modifiers. Certain conditions may be listed under more than one main term.

3. Remember to refer to all notes under the main term. Be guided by the instructions in any notes appearing in a box immediately after the main term.

4. Examine any modifiers appearing in parentheses next to the main term. See if any of these modifiers apply to any of the qualifying terms used in the diagnostic statement.

5. Take note of the subterms indented beneath the main term. Subterms differ from main terms in that they provide greater specificity becoming more specific the further they are indented to the right of the main term in two-space increments and, they provide the anatomical sites affected by the disease or injury.

6. Be sure to follow any cross reference instructions. These instructional terms ("see" or "see also") must be followed to locate the correct code.

7. Confirm the code selection in the Tabular List (Volume 1). Make certain you have selected the appropriate classification in accordance with the diagnosis.

8. Follow instructional terms in the Tabular List (Volume 1). Watch for exclusion terms, notes and fifth-digit instructions that apply to the code number you are verifying.

   NOTE: It is necessary to search not only the selected code number for instructions but also, the category, section and chapter in which the code number is collapsible. Many times the instructional information is located one or more pages preceding the actual page you find the code number on.

9. Finally, assign the code number you have determined to be correct.

ITALICIZED ENTRIES; OTHER AND UNSPECIFIED CODES

During the process of selecting a code to identify a principal diagnosis it is important to remember that italicized entries or codes in slanted brackets cannot be used. In these instances, the etiology code would be sequenced first and the manifestation code be listed second. Subcategories for diagnoses listed as "Other" and "Unspecified" are referred to as residual subcategories. The subdivisions are arranged in a hierarchy starting with the more specific and ending with the least specific. In the Tabular List (Volume 1), in most instances, the four-digit subcategory .8 has been reserved for "Other" specified conditions not classifiable elsewhere and the four-digit subcategory .9 has been reserved for "Unspecified" conditions. Below is an example demonstrating this principle.

005   Other food poisoning (bacterial)

        Excludes: *salmonella infections (003.0-003.9)*
                    toxic effect of:
                          food contaminants (989.7)
                          noxious foodstuffs (988.0-988.9)

005.0   Staphylococcal food poisoning

               Staphylococcal toxemia specified as due to food

                              ▼
                              ▼
                              ▼

005.8   Other bacterial food poisoning
               Food poisoning due to Bacillus cereus

               Excludes: *salmonella food poisoning (003.0-003.9)*

005.9   Food poisoning, unspecified

The hierarchy from more specific to less specific is not consistently maintained at the fifth-digit level. The level of specificity at the fifth-digit level is usually (not always) indicated by the use of 0 and 9. The digit 9 identifies the entry for "Other specified" while the digit 0 identifies the "Unspecified" entry.

ACUTE AND CHRONIC CODING

Whenever a particular condition is described as both acute and chronic, code according to the subentries in the Alphabetic Index (Volume 2) for the stated condition. The following directions should be considered:

1. If there are separate subentries listed for acute, subacute and chronic, then use both codes sequencing the code for the acute condition first.

2. If there are no subentries to identify acute, subacute or chronic, ignore these adjectives when selecting the code for the particular condition.

3. If a certain condition is described as a subacute condition and the index does not provide a subentry designating subacute, then code the condition as if it were acute.

CODING SUSPECTED CONDITIONS

Whenever the diagnosis is stated as "questionable", "probable", "likely" or "rule out" it is advisable to code documented symptoms or complaints by the patient. The reason for this is that you do not want an insurance carrier to include a disease code in the patient's history if in fact the "suspected" condition is never proven. There are no "rule out" codes in the ICD-9-CM coding system. If your diagnostic statement is "Rule out Breast Carcinoma" and you use code 174.9 Malignant Neoplasm of Female Breast, Unspecified, the code definition does not include "rule out". Therefore, the insurance carrier processes the code 174.9 as is, which results in the patient having an insurance history of Malignant Neoplasm, Female Breast, Unspecified.

To avoid what could become a problem for you and your patient (including the potential of litigation), you should use codes for signs and symptoms in these cases. For example, use code 611.72 (Lump) or 611.71 (Breast Pain) if these symptoms exist and this is the highest degree of certainty you can code to. If the patient is asymptomatic but there is a family history of breast cancer then you should consider using a V-code, such as V16.3 (Family history of malignant neoplasm, breast) as your diagnosis code. There are also V-codes to indicate screening for a particular illness or disease. In the above example, code V76.1 (Special screening for malignant neoplasm, breast) could also have been used.

It is important to note that when you use a screening code from the V- code section you should also code signs or symptoms. The reason for doing so is because most health insurance carriers do not provide coverage for routine screening procedures or preventive medicine.

COMBINATION CODES

A combination code is used to fully identify an instance where two diagnoses or a diagnosis with an associated secondary process (manifestation) or complication is included in the description of a single code number. These combination codes are identified by referring to the subterms in the Alphabetic Index (Volume 2) and the inclusion and exclusion terms in the Tabular List (Volume 1).

Examples of commonly used combination codes include 034.0, Streptococcal sore throat and 404, Hypertensive heart and renal disease. Code 034.0 exists because the throat is often infected with Streptococcus and code 404 must be used whenever a patient has both heart and renal disease instead of assigning codes from categories 402 and 403. Two main terms may be joined together by combination terms listed in the Alphabetic Index (Volume 2) as subterms such as:

associated with	*in*
complicated (by)	*secondary to*
due to	*with*
during	*without*
following	

The listing for the above terms advises the coder to use one or two codes depending on the condition.

MULTIPLE CODING

The concept of multiple coding is encouraged when the use of more than one code number will fully identify a given condition. The use of multiple codes allows all the components of a complex diagnosis to be identified. However, the statement of diagnosis must mention the presence of all the elements for each code number used. Multiple coding is mandatory if the instructional terms are "Code Also", "Use Additional Code..." or "Note:...". In these cases the code for the etiology is listed first followed by the code for the manifestation.

Coding Examples

Cerebral degeneration in childhood with mental retardation

    330.9   Unspecified cerebral degeneration in childhood

    319   Unspecified mental retardation

Diabetic neuropathy

    250.60   Diabetes with neurological manifestations

    357.2   Polyneuropathy in diabetes

Even though mandatory multiple coding is always indicated by the presence of the instructional term "Code Also" in italics beneath the italicized code number and title for the manifestation, this does not always hold true under the code number for the etiology. Multiple coding is not to be used in those instances when a combination code accurately identifies all of the elements within the diagnostic statement.

CODING LATE EFFECTS

You use late effects coding when coding diagnostic statements that identify a residual effect (condition produced) after the acute phase of an illness or injury has ended. The proper coding sequence is the code number identifying the residual (the current condition) to be listed first with the code number identifying the cause (original illness/injury no longer present in its acute phase but which was the cause of the long term residual condition) listed second.

Coding Example

Hemiplegia due to previous cerebral vascular accident

    342.9   Hemiplegia, unspecified

    438   Late effects of cerebrovascular disease

Often, the diagnostic statement will contain key words to help identify a late effects situation. Look for words such as "late", "due to an old injury", "due to a previous illness/injury" and "due to an illness or injury occurring one year or more ago". In cases where these key words (phrases) are not included within the diagnostic statement, an effect is considered to be late if sufficient time has elapsed between the occurrence of the acute illness/injury and the development of the residual effect. Be sure to distinguish between a late effect and a historical statement in a diagnosis. Whenever the statement uses the terms "effects of old...," "sequela of...," or "residuals of...," then code as late effects. If the diagnosis is expressed in terms as "history of..." these are coded to personal history of the illness or injury and are coded to the V-Codes (V-10 to V-15).

CODING INJURIES

Injuries comprise a major section of ICD-9-CM. Categories 800-959 include fractures, dislocations, sprains and various other types of injuries. Injuries are classified first according to the general type of injury and within each type there is a further breakdown by anatomical site.

In cases where a patient has multiple injuries, the most severe injury is the principal diagnosis. Where multiple sites of injury are specified in the diagnosis, you should interpret the term "with" as indicating involvement of both sites, and interpret the term "and" as indicating involvement of either or both sites. You will also note that fifth-digits are commonly used when coding injuries to provide information regarding level of consciousness, specific anatomical sites and severity of injuries.

CODING FRACTURES

Some general rules to apply when coding fractures follow. Fractures can either be "open" or "closed." An "open" fracture is when the skin has been broken and there is communication with the bone and the outside of the body. Whereas, with a "closed" fracture the bone does not have contact with the outside of the body. Note the following descriptions as set forth in the ICD-9-CM at the four-digit subdivision level to help distinguish between an "open" and "closed" fracture.

CLOSED FRACTURES

comminuted	*impacted*	*depressed*
linear	*elevated*	*march*
fissured	*simple*	*fractured nos*
spiral	*greenstick*	*slipped epiphysis*

OPEN FRACTURES

compound	*puncture*	*infected*
missile	*with foreign body*	

If the diagnostic statement does not indicated whether a fracture is "open" or "closed", code it as if it were "closed." Fracture-dislocations are classified as fractures. Pathological fractures are classified to the condition causing the fracture with an additional code to identify the pathological fracture.

CODING BURNS

When coding burns, code only the most severe degree of burns when the burns are of the same site but of different degrees. In cases of burns where it is noted that there is an infection, assign the code for the burn and also the code to identify the infection (958.3). The percentage of the body surface involved with burns is specified by using Category 948. This code may be used as a solo code when the site of the burn is unspecified. There is also a fifth-digit subclassification included in Category 948 to identify the percentage of the total body surface involved with third degree burns. Use Category 949 only when neither the site nor the percentage of the body surface involved is specified in the diagnosis.

POISONING AND ADVERSE EFFECTS OF DRUGS

There are two different sets of code numbers to use to differentiate between poisoning and adverse reactions to the correct substances properly administered. First, you must make the distinction between poisoning and adverse reaction.

POISONING DEFINED

Poisoning by drugs includes accidental (given or taken in error) and purposeful (suicide or homicide). The statement of diagnosis will usually have descriptive terms that would indicate poisoning. Look for terms such as:

intoxication	*poisoning*	*wrong drug given/taken in error*
overdose	*toxic effect*	*wrong dosage given/taken in error*

Adverse effects of a medicine taken in combination with alcohol or, from taking a prescribed drug in combination with a drug the patient took on his/her own initiative (for example anti-histamines) are coded as poisonings. If you wish to code a manifestation of the poisoning as well, this code is always listed second, after listing the code identifying the poison first.

ADVERSE REACTION DEFINED

To be considered an adverse reaction, the drugs are prescribed for a therapeutic or diagnostic reason and either taken by the patient or given to the patient as prescribed. The adverse reaction could be due to an accumulative effect, drug interaction, a synergistic reaction, an allergic reaction or hypersensitivity. The World Health Organization (WHO) defines adverse drug reaction as any response to a drug "which is noxious and unintended and which occurs at doses used in man for prophylaxis, diagnosis or therapy". Notice that this definition does not include the terms "overdose" or "poisoning".

CODING POISONING BY DRUGS

To code poisoning by drugs, use the Alphabetic Index (Volume 2) which contains the Table of Drugs and Chemicals. This table includes one column to identify the poisoning code (960-989) and four columns of External Cause Codes to classify whether the poisoning was an accident, suicide, assault or undetermined.

The column labeled "Therapeutic Use" is not used for poisonings but in coding adverse reactions to correct substances properly administered. The External Cause Codes are optional but may be used if a facility's coding policy requires their use. Note that in the Alphabetic Index (Volume 2) that the subterm entry (DRUG) under the main term of poisoning refers the coder to the Table of Drugs and Chemicals for the code assignment. Because the Table of Drugs and Chemicals is so extensive, it is acceptable to code directly from the "Table" without verifying the code obtained in Volume 1.

Drugs not found in the Table of Drugs and Chemicals can be coded by referring to Appendix C, American Hospital Formulary Service, in the Tabular List (Volume 1). Locate the name of the drug and the AHFS number. Turn back to the Table of Drugs and Chemicals and find the subterm "AHFS LIST". Look through the list until you find the category that you are looking for.

CODING ADVERSE EFFECTS OF DRUGS

Two codes are required when coding adverse drug reactions to the correct substance properly administered. The first code is used to identify the manifestation or the nature of the adverse reaction such as urticaria, vertigo, gastritis, etc. The second code is required to identify the drug causing the adverse reaction. In ICD-9-CM, the only codes provided to identify the drug causing an adverse reaction to a substance properly administered are E930 through E949. Anytime a code is selected from the E930-E949 range it can never be sequenced first or used by itself.

LOCATING THE E CODE

Turn to the Table of Drugs and Chemicals in the Alphabetic Index (Volume 2). Earlier we noted that the column labeled "Therapeutic Use" is not used for coding instances involving poisoning. However, for adverse drug reactions the "Therapeutic Use" column is used to find the proper code within the range E930 through E949 to identify the drug.

DRUG INTERACTIONS

To properly code drug interactions, first code the manifestation. Then code each drug involved in the interaction using the E codes from the column labeled "Therapeutic Use" from the Table of Drugs and Chemicals.

Coding Example

> *Gastritis due to interaction between Motrin and Procainamide*

> 535.5   Gastritis [Manifestation first]

> E935.8   Other specified analgesics and antipyretics

> E942.0   Cardiac rhythm regulators

When a diagnostic statement does not state specifically the manifestation or nature of the adverse reaction, use the code provided to identify an adverse drug reaction of unspecified nature.... 995.2 Unspecified adverse effect of drug, medicinal and biological substance.

Coding Example

> *Allergic reaction to Motrin, proper dose*

> 995.2   Unspecified adverse effect of drug, medicinal and biological substance

> E935.8   Other specified analgesics and antipyretics

It is very important to remember that codes in the range 960 through 979 are never used in combination with codes in the range E930 through E949 because codes in the range 960-979 identify poisonings and codes in the range E930-E949 identify the external cause of adverse reactions to the correct substance properly administered.

CODING COMPLICATIONS OF MEDICAL AND SURGICAL CARE

A complication is the occurrence of two or more diseases in the same patient at the same time. Recent studies have revealed serious deficiencies in properly coding complications for insurance claims processing. Often the complication is never mentioned. Complications are responsible for many of the procedures that are ordered for patients, therefore the complication should be coded and submitted on your insurance claims.

POSTOPERATIVE COMPLICATIONS

Postoperative complications that affect a specific anatomical site or body system are classified to the appropriate chapter 1 through 16 of the Tabular List (Volume 1). Postoperative complications affecting more than one anatomical site or body system are classified in the chapter on injury and poisoning (Chapter 17, Categories 996-999). If the Alphabetic Index (Volume 2) does not provide a specific main term and subterm to identify a postoperative complication, classify the complication to categories 996-999.

Coding Example

Postcholecystectomy syndrome

> 576.0   Postcholecystectomy syndrome

The Alphabetic Index (Volume 2) specifically classifies the post- operative condition to one of the categories from 001 through 799. See main term "complication", subterms "surgical procedure" and "postcholecystectomy syndrome".

Coding Example

Postoperative wound infection

> 998.5   Postoperative infection

The Alphabetic Index (Volume 2) has a main term "infection" and subterms "wound, postoperative" for this condition. Note that this code appears in Chapter 17 within categories 996-999.

Coding Example

Postoperative atelectasis

> 997.3   Complications affecting body systems, not elsewhere classified, respiratory complications

Refer to the main term "atelectasis" in the Alphabetic Index (Volume 2). Note there is no subterm for postoperative beneath this main term. Therefore, you must presume this complication is classified to one of the categories in the range 969-999. You may also code 518.0 to identify the nature of the respiratory complication for statistical purposes; however, the code for the complication must be listed first.

COMPLICATIONS FROM MECHANICAL DEVICES

Subcategories in the range 996.0 through 996.5 are used to identify mechanical complications of devices. Mechanical complications are the result of a malfunction on the part of the internal prosthetic implant or device. Breakdown or obstruction, displacement, leakage, perforation or protrusion of the devices are all forms of mechanical complications.

Coding Examples

Displacement of cardiac pacemaker electrode

996.01   Mechanical complication of cardiac device, implant and graft due to cardiac pacemaker (electrode)

Protrusion of nail into acetabulum

996.4   Mechanical complications of internal orthopedic device, implant, and graft

Other complications of devices, such as infection or hemorrhage, are due to an abnormal reaction of the body to an otherwise properly functioning device. All complications involving infection are coded to category 996.7 Other complications of internal prosthetic device, implant and graft.

SPECIAL NOTES REGARDING CARDIAC COMPLICATIONS

In the case of cardiac complications, ICD-9-CM defines the "immediate postoperative period" as "the period between surgery and the time of discharge from the hospital". This definition is the basis of whether to code cardiac complications under subcategory 997.1 Complications affecting specified body systems, not elsewhere classified, cardiac complications or, under subcategory 429.4 Ill-defined descriptions and complications of heart disease, functional disturbances following cardiac surgery.

Code with subcategory 997.1 for a cardiac complication that occurs anytime between surgery and hospital discharge from any type of procedure performed. Subcategory 429.4 is used to code long term cardiac complications resulting from cardiac surgery.

It is important to distinguish between complications and aftercare. Aftercare is usually an encounter for something planned in advance (example, removal of Kirshner wire). Aftercare is classified using codes in the range of V51-V58. An encounter for a complication occurs from unforeseen circumstances, such as wound infection, resulting in complication of the patient's condition.

CODING CIRCULATORY DISEASES

Because of the variety of terms and phrases used by physicians to identify diseases of the circulatory system, you will often experience difficulty in coding. To accurately code disorders of the circulatory system, the coder must carefully read all inclusion, exclusion and "use additional code" notations contained in the Tabular List (Volume 1).

Fifth digit subclassifications are frequently used to code combination disorders or to provide further specificity in this section. This section of ICD-9-CM is used frequently by most specialties due to the prevalence of circulatory disorders in the United States.

DISEASES OF MITRAL AND AORTIC VALVES

Certain diseases of the mitral valve of unspecified etiology are presumed to be of rheumatic origin and others are not. None of the disorders of the aortic valve of unspecified etiology are presumed to be of rheumatic origin. When you have disorders involving both the mitral and aortic valves of unspecified etiology, then they are presumed to be of rheumatic origin.

Coding Examples

Mitral Valve Insufficiency

424.0   Other diseases of endocardium Mitral valve disorders

Mitral Valve Stenosis

394.0   Diseases of mitral valve Mitral Stenosis

Aortic Valve Insufficiency

424.1   Other diseases of endocardium Aortic valve disorders

ISCHEMIC HEART DISEASE

There are many synonyms used to indicate ischemic heart disease such as: coronary artery heart disease, ASHD, and coronary ischemia. Categories in the range 410-414, Ischemic Heart Disease, includes "that with mention of hypertension." Use an additional code to identify the presence of hypertension.

Coding Examples

Angina pectoris

413.9   Other and unspecified angina pectoris

Angina pectoris with essential hypertension

> 413.9   Other and unspecified angina pectoris
>
> 401.9   Essential hypertension Unspecified

MYOCARDIAL INFARCTION

A myocardial infarction is classified as acute if it is either specified as "acute" in the diagnostic statement or with a stated duration of eight weeks or less. When a myocardial infarction is specified as "chronic" or with symptoms after eight weeks from the date of the onset, it is coded to subcategory 414.8. If a myocardial infarction is specified as old or healed or otherwise diagnosed but is currently not presenting any symptoms, code using category 412.

Coding Examples

Myocardial infarction three weeks ago

> 410.90   Acute myocardial infarction unspecified site

Chronic myocardial infarction with angina

> 414.8   Other forms of chronic ischemic heart disease, Other specified forms of chronic ischemic heart disease
>
> 413.9   Angina pectoris Other and unspecified angina pectoris

Note that the October 1989 Addendum to ICD-9-CM added the requirement for fifth digit specificity to category 410, Acute myocardial infarction. The new fifth digits are:

0   episode of care unspecified
1   initial episode of care
2   subsequent episode of care

This is an excellent example of why you need to obtain updates to all of your coding resources as soon as they become available.

ARTERIOSCLEROTIC CARDIOVASCULAR DISEASE (ASCVD)

Arteriosclerotic cardiovascular disease (ASCVD) is classified to subcategory 429.2. Use an additional code to identify the presence of arteriosclerosis when coding ASCVD. Other forms of heart disease, categories 420-429, are used for multiple coding purposes to fully identify a stated diagnosis. The exception to this rule is if the Alphabetic Index (Volume 2) or Tabular List (Volume 1) specifically instructs you otherwise.

Coding Example

Arteriosclerotic heart disease with acute pulmonary edema

428.1   Heart failure Left Heart Failure

414.0   Coronary atherosclerosis

Arteriosclerotic heart disease with congestive heart failure

428.0   Congestive heart failure

414.0   Coronary atherosclerosis

CEREBROVASCULAR DISEASE

When coding cerebrovascular disease (codes 430-438) code the component parts of the diagnostic statement identifying the cerebrovascular disease unless specifically instructed to do otherwise in the Alphabetic Index (Volume 2) or Tabular List (Volume 1).

Coding Examples

Cerebrovascular arteriosclerosis with subarachnoid hemorrhage

430   Subarachnoid hemorrhage

437.0   Cerebral atherosclerosis

Cerebrovascular accident secondary to thrombosis

434.0   Cerebral thrombosis

Whenever there are conditions resulting from the acute cerebrovascular disease, code them if they are stated to be residual(s). If the resulting condition is stated to be transient, do not code them.

Coding Example

Cerebrovascular accident with residual aphasia

436   Acute, but ill-defined cerebrovascular disease

784.3   Aphasia

HYPERTENSIVE DISEASE

As with ischemic heart disease, conditions that are classified to cerebrovascular disease (codes 430-438) include "that with mention of hypertension." You must identify the hypertension with another code (401-405) and list it as the second code. Hypertensive disease is classified to the categories 401-405. The Table of Hypertension is located in the Alphabetic Index (Volume 2) under the main term "Hypertension". This Table contains subterms to identify types of hypertension and complications as well as three columns labeled "malignant", "benign" and "unspecified" as to whether malignant or benign.

	Malignant	Benign	Unspecified
Hypertension, hypertensive (arterial) (arteriolar) (degeneration) (disease) (essential) (fluctuating) (idiopathic) (intermittent) (labile) (low renin) (orthostatic) (paroxysmal) (primary) (systemic) (vascular)	401.0	401.1	401.9
with			
heart involvement (conditions classifiable to 428, 429.0–429.3, 429.8, 429.9 due to hypertension) (see also Hypertension, heart)	402.00	402.10	402.90
with kidney involvement— see Hypertension, cardiorenal			
renal involvement (conditions classifiable to 585,586,587) (see also Hypertension,,kidney)	403.00	403.10	403.90
with heart involvement—see Hypertension, cardiorenal			
failure (and sclerosis) (see also Hypertension, kidney)	403.01	403.11	403.91
sclerosis without failure (see also Hypertension, kidney)	403.00	403.10	403.90
accelerated (see also Hypertension, by type, malignant)	401.0	—	—
antepartum—see Hypertension complicating pregnancy, childbirth, or the puerperium			
cardiorenal (disease)	404.00	404.10	404.90
with			
heart failure (congestive)	404.01	404.11	404.91
and renal failure	404.03	404.13	404.93
renal failure	404.02	404.12	404.92
and heart failure (congestive)	404.03	404.13	404.93
cardiovascular disease (arteriosclerotic) (sclerotic)	402.00	402.10	402.90
with			
heart failure (congestive)	402.01	402.11	402.91
renal involvement (conditions classifiable to 403) (see also Hypertension, cardiorenal)	404.00	404.10	404.90
cardiovascular renal (disease) (sclerosis) (see also Hypertension cardiorenal)	404.00	404.10	404.90
cerebrovascular disease NEC	437.2	437.2	437.2
complicating pregnancy, childbirth, or the puerperium	642.2	642.0	642.9
with			
albuminuria (and edema) (mild)	—	—	642.4
severe	—	—	642.5
edema (mild)	—	—	642.4
severe	—	—	642.5
heart disease	642.2	642.2	642.2
and renal disease	642.2	642.2	642.2
renal disease	642.2	642.2	642.2

Hypertension is frequently the cause of various forms of heart and vascular disease. However, the mention of hypertension with some heart conditions should not be interpreted as a combination resulting in hypertensive heart disease. The combination is only to be made if there is a cause-and-effect relationship between hypertension and a heart condition classified to subcategories 428.0-428.9, 429.0-429.3 and 429.8-429.9.

First you need to be able to make a distinction between conditions specified as "due to" or "with" hypertension. Keep in mind that the phrase "due to hypertension" and the word "hypertensive" are to be considered synonymous.

Coding Examples

Hypertensive heart disease

> 402.90 Hypertensive heart disease, Unspecified, Without congestive heart failure

Heart disease due to hypertension

> 402.90 Hypertensive heart disease, Unspecified, Without congestive heart failure

Each of the above diagnostic statements indicate clearly a cause-and-effect relationship between hypertension and the condition by specifying that the condition is "due to". Therefore, both statements are coded using 402.90. If the phrase "with hypertension" is stated or, the diagnostic statement mentions the conditions separately then, you code the conditions separately.

Coding Example

Myocarditis with hypertension

> 429.0   Myocarditis unspecified

> 401.9   Essential hypertension Unspecified

As a cause-and-effect relationship is not indicated in the diagnostic statement the conditions are coded separately.

HIGH BLOOD PRESSURE VERSUS ELEVATED BLOOD PRESSURE

With the ICD-9-CM coding system there is a differentiation made between high blood pressure (hypertension) and elevated blood pressure without a diagnosis of hypertension. If the diagnostic statement indicates elevated blood pressure without the diagnosis of hypertension, it is coded to subcategory 796.2. If the diagnostic statement indicates high blood pressure or hypertension, it is coded to category 401.

DIABETES MELLITUS CODING

In 1980, the American Diabetic Association reclassified the types of diabetes mellitus to signify whether or not the patient is dependent on insulin for survival of life. Note the revisions (italicized portions) of the statements below for the fifth-digit subclassification.

0   Adult onset or unspecified as to type; insulin non-dependent
1   Juvenile type; insulin dependent regardless of the time-of-life onset

Do not assume a patient has insulin-dependent diabetes simply because the patient is receiving insulin, as some non-dependent diabetics may require temporary use when they encounter stressful situations such as surgery or physical or mental illness. Anytime diabetes is described as "brittle" or "uncontrolled" you should interpret it as diabetes mellitus complicated and assign code 250.9 with the appropriate fifth-digit, 0 or 1. However, if there is also a specific complication present, then assign the code identifying that specific complication.

CODING MENTAL DISORDERS

Appendix B of the Tabular List (Volume 1) contains a glossary of mental disorders. This glossary is not used for coding purposes but rather as a guide to provide a common frame of reference for statistical comparisons. The coder should choose code assignments based on the terminology used by the physician or psychiatrist and not by the coder's impression of the content of the categories and subcategories. The chapter on mental disorders has many fifth digit sub-classifications to watch for when selecting your code.

APPENDIX B

Ganser's syndrome (hysterical): A form of factitious illness in which the patient voluntarily produces symptoms suggestive of a mental disorder.[2]

Gender identity disorder—see gender identity disorder under Psychosexual identity disorders

Gilles de la Tourette's disorder or syndrome—see Gilles de la Tourette's disorder under Tics

Grief reaction—see depressive reaction, brief under Adjustment reaction

Gross stress reaction—see Stress reaction, acute

Group delinquency—see socialized conduct disorder under Conduct disorders

Habit spasm—see chronic motor tic disorder under Tics

Hangover (alcohol)—see Drunkenness, simple

Head-banging—see Stereotyped repetitive movements

Hebephrenia—see Schizophrenia, disorganized type

Heller's syndrome—see Psychosis, disintegrative

High grade defect—see Mental retardation, mild

Homosexuality: Exclusive or predominant sexual attraction for persons of the same sex with or without physical relationship. Record homosexuality as a diagnosis whether or not it is considered as a mental disorder.[1]

Hospital addiction syndrome—see Munchausen syndrome

Hospital hoboes—see Munchausen syndrome

Hospitalism: A mild or transient adjustment reaction characterized by withdrawal seen in hospitalized patients. In young children this may be manifested by elective mutism.[1]

Hyperkinetic syndrome of childhood: Disorders in which the essential features are short attention-span and distractibility. In early childhood the most striking symptom is disinhibited, poorly organized and poorly regulated extreme overactivity but in adolescence this may be replaced by underactivity. Impulsiveness, marked mood fluctuations, and aggression are also common symptoms. Delays in the development of specific skills are often present and disturbed, poor

Hypomanic personality—see Personality disorder, chronic hypomanic type

Hyposomnia—see Insomnia

Hysteria—see hysteria under Neurotic disorders

  anxiety—see phobia under Neurotic disorders

  psychosis—see Psychosis, reactive

  acute—see Psychosis, excitative type

Hysterical personality—see Personality disorder, histrionic type

Identity disorder: An emotional disorder caused by distress over the inability to reconcile aspects of the self into a relatively coherent and acceptable sense of self, not secondary to another mental disorder. The disturbance is manifested by intense subjective distress regarding uncertainty about a variety of issues relating to identity, including long-term goals, career choice, friendship patterns, values, and loyalties.[2]

Idiocy—see Mental retardation, profound

Imbecile—see Mental retardation, moderate

Impotence: A psychosexual dysfunction in which there is partial or complete failure to attain or maintain erection until completion of the sexual act.[2]

Impulse control disorder—see impulse control disorders under Conduct disorders

Inadequate personality—see Personality disorder, dependent type

Induced paranoid disorder—see Shared paranoid disorder

Inebriety—see Drunkenness, simple

Infantile autism—see Autism, infantile

Insomnia: A disorder of initiating or maintaining sleep.[2]

  persistent: A chronic state of sleeplessness associated with chronic anxiety, major or minor depressive disorders, or psychoses.[2]

  transient: Episodes of sleeplessness associated with acute or intermittent emotional reactions or conflicts.[2]

Intermittent explosive disorder: Recurrent episodes of sudden and significant loss of control of aggressive impulses, not accounted for

---

INFECTIOUS AND PARASITIC DISEASES

There are two categories for identifying the organism causing diseases classified elsewhere.

041   Bacterial infection in conditions classified elsewhere and of unspecified nature

079   Viral infection in conditions classified elsewhere and of unspecified nature

These codes may be used as either additional codes, or as solo codes depending on the diagnostic statement.

Coding Examples

Acute UTI due to Escherchia coli

599.0   Urinary tract infection, site not specified

041.4   Escherchia coli

Staphylococcus infection

041.1   Staphylococcus

Bacterial infection

041.9   Bacterial infection, unspecified

The basic coding principles regarding combination codes (one code accurately identifies the components of the condition) applies throughout the chapter on Infectious and Parasitic Diseases. In the Alphabetic Index (Volume 2), a subterm that identifies an infectious organism takes precedence in code assignment over a subterm at the same indentation level that identifies a site or other descriptive term.

Coding Example

Chronic syphilitic cystitis

095.8   Other specified forms of late symptomatic syphilis

Using the Alphabetic Index (Volume 2) to look up the main term "cystitis (bacillary)", you will note the subterms "Chronic 595.2" and "Syphilitic 095.8" at the same indentation level under the main term. Therefore, code 095.8 is assigned to this diagnostic statement as the organism has precedence over other descriptive terms or anatomical sites.

MANIFESTATIONS

Manifestations are characteristic signs or symptoms of an illness. Signs and symptoms that point rather definitely to a given diagnosis are assigned to the appropriate chapter of ICD-9-CM, for example, hematuria is assigned to the Genitourinary System chapter. However, Chapter 16, encompassing categories 780-799, includes ill-defined conditions and symptoms that may suggest two or more diseases or, may point to two or more systems of the body, and are used in cases lacking the necessary study to make a final diagnosis. Conditions found in Chapter 16 include:

1. Cases for which no more specific diagnosis can be made even after all facts bearing on the case have been investigated, for example, code 784.0 Headache.

2. Signs or symptoms existing at the time of initial encounter that proved to be transient and whose cause could not be determined, for example, code 780.2 Syncope and Collapse.

3. Provisional diagnoses in a patient who failed to return for further investigation or care, for example, code 782.4, Jaundice, unspecified, not of newborn.

4. Cases referred elsewhere for investigation or treatment before the diagnosis was made, for example, code 782.5, Cyanosis.

5. Cases in which a more precise diagnosis was not available for any other reason, for example, code 780.7, Malaise and Fatigue.

6. Certain symptoms which represent important problems in medical care and which it might be desired to classify in addition to a known cause, for example, code 780.0, Coma and Stupor.

In the latter case, if the cause of a symptom or sign is stated in the diagnosis, assign the code identifying the cause. An additional code may be assigned to further identify this symptom or sign if a need to further identify the symptom or sign has been identified. In such cases, the code identifying the cause will ordinarily be listed as the principal diagnosis.

CODING OF NEOPLASMS

The coding of neoplasms requires a good understanding of medical terminology. All neoplasms are classified to Chapter 2 of the Tabular List (Volume 1) under Neoplasms 140-239.

TABLE OF NEOPLASMS

The Table of Neoplasms appears in the Alphabetic Index (Volume 2) under the main term "Neoplasms". This Table gives the code numbers for neoplasms of anatomical site. For each anatomical site there are six possible code numbers according to whether the neoplasm in questions is either: 1) Malignant: Primary, Secondary or CA in situ, 2) Benign, 3) Of uncertain behavior, or 4) Of unspecified nature

INDEX TO DISEASES						Neoplasm
	Malignant					
	Primary	Secondary	Ca in situ	Benign	Uncertain Behavior	Unspecified
intestine, intestinal	159.0	197.8	230.7	211.9	235.2	239.0
large	153.9	197.5	230.3	211.3	235.2	239.0
appendix	153.5	197.5	230.3	211.3	235.2	239.0
caput coli	153.4	197.5	230.3	211.3	235.2	239.0
cecum	153.4	197.5	230.3	211.3	235.2	239.0
colon	153.9	197.5	230.3	211.3	235.2	239.0
and rectum	154.0	197.5	230.4	211.4	235.2	239.0
ascending	153.6	197.5	230.3	211.3	235.2	239.0
caput	153.4	197.5	230.3	211.3	235.2	239.0
contiguous sites	153.8	—	—	—	—	—
descending	153.2	197.5	230.3	211.3	235.2	239.0
distal	153.2	197.5	230.3	211.3	235.2	239.0
left	153.2	197.5	230.3	211.3	235.2	239.0
pelvic	153.3	197.5	230.3	211.3	235.2	239.0
right	153.6	197.5	230.3	211.3	235.2	239.0
sigmoid (flexure)	153.3	197.5	230.3	211.3	235.2	239.0
transverse	153.1	197.5	230.0	211.3	235.2	239.0
contiguous sites	153.8	—	—	—	—	—
hepatic flexure	153.0	197.5	230.3	211.3	235.2	239.0
ileocecum, ileocecal (coil) (valve)	153.4	197.5	230.3	211.3	235.2	239.0
sigmoid flexure (lower) (upper)	153.3	197.5	230.3	211.3	235.2	239.0
splenic flexure	153.7	197.5	230.3	211.3	235.2	239.0
small	152.9	197.4	230.7	211.2	235.2	239.0
contiguous sites	152.8	—	—	—	—	—
duodenum	152.0	197.4	230.7	211.2	235.2	239.0
ileum	152.2	197.4	230.7	211.2	235.2	239.0
jejunum	152.1	197.4	230.7	211.2	235.2	239.0
tract NEC	159.0	197.8	230.7	211.9	235.2	239.0

DEFINITIONS OF SITES AND BEHAVIORS OF NEOPLASMS

PRIMARY   Identifies the stated or presumed site of origin

SECONDARY Identifies site(s) to which the primary site has spread (direct extension) or metastasized by lymphatic spread, invading local blood vessels, or by implantation as tumor cells shed into body cavities.

BENIGN   Tumor does not invade adjacent structures or spread to distant sites but may displace or exert pressure on adjacent structures.

IN-SITU   Tumor cells that are undergoing malignant changes but are still confined to the point of origin without invasion of surrounding normal tissue (non-infiltrating, non-invasive or pre-invasive) carcinoma.

UNCERTAIN The pathologist is not able to determine whether the tumor is benign
BEHAVIOR   or malignant because some features of each are present.

UNSPECIFIED Neither the behavior nor the histological type of tumor are specified
NATURE   in the diagnostic statement. This type of diagnosis may be encountered when the patient has been treated elsewhere and comes in terminally ill without accompanying information, is referred elsewhere for work-up, or no work-up is performed because of advanced age or poor condition of the patient.

STEPS TO CODING NEOPLASMS

1. ICD-9-CM disregards classification of neoplasms by histological type (according to tissue origin) with the exception of lymphatic and hematopoietic neoplasms, malignant melanoma of skin, lipoma, and a few common tumors of bone, uterus, ovary, etc. All other tumors are classified by system, organ or site. The existence of these exceptions makes it necessary to first consult the Alphabetic Index (Volume 2) to determine whether a specific code has been assigned to a specified histological type. For example, Malignant melanoma of skin of scalp is coded 172.4 although the code specified in the "Malignant: Primary Column" of the Neoplasm Table for skin of scalp is 173.4.

2. The General Alphabetical Index (Volume 2) also provides guidance to the appropriate column for neoplasms which are not assigned a specific code by histological type. For example, if you look up Lipomyoma, specified site in the Alphabetic Index (Volume 2), you will find "See Neoplasm, connective tissue, benign".

    The guidance in the Alphabetic Index (Volume 2) can be over-ridden if a descriptor is present. For example, Malignant adenoma of colon is coded as 153.9 and not as 211.3 because the adjective "malignant" overrides the entry "adenoma - See also Neoplasm, benign".

3. The Neoplasm Table may be consulted directly if a specific neoplasm diagnosis indicates which column of the table is appropriate, but does not delineate a specific type of tumor.

4. Sites marked with an asterisk (*), such as buttock NEC* or calf*, should be classified to malignant neoplasm of skin of these sites if the variety of neoplasm is a squamous cell carcinoma or an epidermoid carcinoma and to benign neoplasm of skin of these sites if the variety of neoplasm is a papilloma (of any type).

5. Primary malignant neoplasms are classified to the site of origin of the neoplasm. In some cases, it may not be possible to identify the site of origin, such as malignant neoplasms originating from contagious sites.

    Neoplasms with overlapping site boundaries are classified to the fourth-digit subcategory .8 "other". For example, code 151.8 "Malignant neoplasm of contiguous or overlapping sites of stomach whose point of origin cannot be determined."

6. Neoplasms which demonstrate functional activity require an additional code to identify the functional activity.

    ### Coding Example

    Cushing's syndrome due to malignant pheochromocytoma

            194.0   Malignant neoplasm of adrenal gland

            255.0   Disorders of adrenal glands; Cushing's syndrome

7.   Two codes in the malignant neoplasm section represent departures from the usual principles of classification in that the fourth-digit subdivisions in each case are not mutually exclusive. These codes are 150 "Malignant neoplasms of the esophagus" and 201 "Hodgkin's disease". The dual axis is provided to account for differing terminology, for there is no uniform international agreement on the use of these terms.

8.   When the treatment is directed at the primary site of the malignancy, designate the primary site as the principal diagnosis, except when the encounter or hospital admission is solely for radiotherapy session(s), code V58.0 or, for chemotherapy sessions.

9.   When surgical intervention for removal of a primary site or secondary site malignancy is followed by adjunct chemotherapy or radiotherapy, code the malignancy using codes in the 140-198 series, or, where appropriate, in the 200-203 series as long as chemotherapy or radiotherapy is being actively administered. If the admission is for chemotherapy or radiotherapy, the malignancy code is listed second.

10.   When the primary malignancy has been previously excised or eradicated from its site and there is no adjunct treatment directed to that site and, there is no evidence of any remaining malignancy at the primary site, use the appropriate code from the V10 series to indicate the site of the primary malignancy. Any mention of extension, invasion or metastasis to a nearby structure or organ, or to a distant site is coded as a secondary malignant neoplasm to that site and may be the principal diagnosis in the absence of the primary site.

11.   If the patient has no secondary malignancy and if the reason for admission or for the visit is follow-up of the malignancy, two codes are used.

Coding Example

Follow-up of breast cancer treated with chemotherapy

> V67.2   Follow-up examination following chemotherapy
>
> V10.3   Personal history of carcinoma of breast

12.   Malignancies of hematopoietic and lymphatic tissue are always coded to the 200.0-208.9 series unless specified as "in remission". "In remission" is coded as V10.60-V10.79.

13.   If the primary malignant neoplasm previously excised or eradicated has recurred, code it as primary malignancy of the stated site unless the Alphabetic Index (Volume 2) directs you to do otherwise.

Coding Examples

Recurrence of prostate carcinoma

> 185   Malignant neoplasm of the prostate

Recurrence of breast carcinoma in mastectomy site

> 192.2 Secondary malignant neoplasm of other specified sites skin of breast

14. Terminology referring to metastatic cancer is often ambiguous, so when there is doubt as to the meaning intended, the following rules should be used:

   A. Cancer "metastatic from" a site should be interpreted as primary of that site.

   B. Cancer described as "metastatic to" a site should be interpreted as secondary of that site.

Coding Examples

Carcinoma in axillary lymph nodes and lungs metastatic from breast

> 174.9 Malignant neoplasm of female breast, unspecified
>
> 196.3 Secondary malignant neoplasm of lymph nodes of axilla
>
> 197.0 Secondary malignant neoplasm of lung

Adenocarcinoma of colon with extension to peritoneum

> 153.9 Malignant neoplasm of colon, unspecified
>
> 197.6 Secondary malignant neoplasm of retroperitoneum and peritoneum

15. Diagnostic statements when only one site is identified as metastatic:

   A. Code to the category for "primary of unspecified site" for the morphological type concerned UNLESS the code thus obtained is either 199.0 or 199.1.

   B. If the code obtained in the above step is 199.0 or 199.1, then code the site qualified as "metastatic" as for a primary malignant neoplasm of the stated site EXCEPT for the sites listed below, which should always be coded as secondary neoplasm of the state site:

bone	*brain*	*diaphragm*
heart	*liver*	*lymph nodes*
mediastinum	*meninges*	*peritoneum*
pleura	*retroperitoneum*	*spinal cord*

   and sites classifiable to 195.

C. Also assign the appropriate code for primary or secondary malignant neoplasm of specified or unspecified site, depending on the diagnostic statement you are coding.

Coding Examples

Metastatic renal cell carcinoma of lung

189.0 Malignant neoplasm of kidney and other unspecified urinary organs, kidney, except pelvis

197.0 Secondary malignant neoplasm of respiratory and digestive systems

Metastatic carcinoma of lung

162.9 Malignant neoplasm of trachea, bronchus, and lung, bronchus and lung, unspecified

199.1 Malignant neoplasm without specification of site, other

This code is assigned to identify "secondary neoplasm of unspecified site" per the instructions in step C above.

16. When two or more sites are stated in the diagnostic statement and all are qualified to be "metastatic", you should code as for "primary site unknown" and code the stated sites as secondary neoplasms of those sites.

Coding Example

Metastatic melanoma of lung and liver

172.9 Malignant melanoma of skin, Melanoma of skin, site unspecified

197.0 Secondary malignant neoplasm of respiratory and digestive systems, lung

197.7 Secondary malignant neoplasm of respiratory and digestive systems, liver, specified as secondary

17. When there is no site specified in the diagnostic statement, but the morphological type is qualified as "metastatic", code as for "primary site unknown". Then, assign the code for secondary neoplasms of unspecified site.

Coding Example

Metastatic apocrine adenocarcinoma

173.9 Other malignant neoplasms of skin, site unspecified

      199.1   Malignant neoplasm without specification of site, other

18.   When two or more sites are stated in the diagnosis and only some are qualified as "metastatic" while others are not, code as for "primary site unknown". However, you should interpret the following sites as secondary neoplasms:

bone	*meninges*
brain	*peritoneum*
diaphragm	*pleura*
heart	*retroperitoneum*
liver	*spinal cord*
lymph nodes	
mediastinum	

Sites classifiable to 195

Coding Example

> *Carcinoma of lung, metastatic, and brain*

>   198.3   Secondary malignant neoplasm of brain and spinal cord

>   197.0   Secondary malignant neoplasm of respiratory and digestive systems, lung

>   199.1   Malignant neoplasm without specification of site, other

PREGNANCY, CHILDBIRTH AND THE PUERPERIUM

Chapter 11 of the Tabular List (Volume 1) uses fifth-digit subclassifications extensively. In general, the fifth-digit is not given in the Alphabetic Index (Volume 2), so each code must be verified in the Tabular List (Volume 1). The codes for Ectopic and Molar Pregnancy, 630-633, do not require the fifth-digit. Note also, that for the codes 634-638, there is a "common" set of fourth-digit subcategory codes to include complications. Be aware of the use of section marks with categories 634-637 to indicate the need for a fifth-digit. All other codes, 640-676 require the use of a fifth-digit with the single exception of code 650.

Coding Example

> *Pregnancy, 3 months gestation complicated by benign essential hypertension*

>   642.03   Benign essential hypertension complicating pregnancy, childbirth and the puerperium

Categories 647 and 648 are used for conditions that are usually classified elsewhere, but which have been classified here because they are complications of pregnancy. The interaction of certain conditions with the pregnant state complicates the pregnancy and/or aggravates the non-obstetrical condition (i.e., diabetes mellitus, drug dependence, thyroid dysfunction) and are the main reason for the obstetrical care being provided.

Coding Examples

Rubella in woman, 7 months gestation

> 647.53 Infectious and parasitic conditions in the mother classifiable elsewhere, but complicating pregnancy, childbirth or the puerperium, rubella

Pregnancy with diabetes mellitus

> 648.03 Other current conditions in the mother classifiable else where, but complicating pregnancy, childbirth or the puerperium, diabetes mellitus

If greater detail is needed for the complication, use an additional code to identify the complication more completely.

USING V-CODES

V-codes are used to identify encounters with the health care setting for reasons other than an illness or injury, for example, immunization. V-codes are also used to identify encounters of persons who are injured or ill and whose injury or illness is influenced by some circumstance or problem classified to the V-codes..... for example, a person with a functioning pacemaker who requires emergency gastrointestinal surgery. V-codes fall into one of three categories; problems, services or facts.

PROBLEM V-CODES

Problem V-codes identify a circumstance or problem that could affect a patient's overall health status but is not itself a current illness or injury. In other words, you may note that a patient has a drug allergy to sulfonamides by using code V14.2.

Although this allergy is not considered an illness or a problem in a healthy person, it may affect how the physician will actually care for the patient. You would only use a problem V-code when the problem has a potential effect on the patient's current diagnosis and the physician's treatment plan for management of the illness or injury.

SERVICE V-CODES

Service V-codes describe circumstances other than an illness or injury which prompt the patient's visit. This type of visit often occurs when the patient has a chronic disease but is not acutely ill. An example would be a patient with a known neoplasm that has sought care to receive chemotherapy. In this instance, you would assign the V-code V58.1 - Maintenance Chemotherapy as the primary code on your claim and list the code to identify the known neoplasm second.

FACT V-CODES

Fact V-codes are used to describe certain facts that do not fall into the "problem" or "service" categories. For example, coding the type of birth using code V30.1 - Single Liveborn prior to admission to hospital.

V-codes can be used as a solo code, a principal code or as a secondary code. It is important to use V-codes properly. If a complication is present, the complication should be coded to categories 001-799 instead of to a V-code.

Coding Example

Colostomy status with colostomy malfunction

569.6   Other specified disorders of rectum and anus, colostomy and enterostomy malfunction

V44.3 Artificial opening status, colostomy, would not be used in this case because of the complication.

Key words found in diagnostic statements which may result in selection of a V code include:

admission for	*health or healthy*
aftercare	*history (of)*
attention to	*maintenance*
care (of)	*maladjustment*
carrier	*observation*
checking or checkup	*problem (with)*
contact	*prophylactic*
contraception	*replacement (by)(of)*
counseling	*screening*
dialysis	*status*
donor	*supervision (of)*
examination	*test*
fitting of	*transplant*
follow up	*vaccination*

USING E-CODES

E-codes permit the classification of environmental events, circumstances and conditions as the cause of injury, poisoning and other adverse effects. The use of E-codes together with the code identifying the injury or condition provides additional information of particular concern to industrial medicine, insurance carriers, national safety programs and public health agencies.

The E-codes may be assigned with any of the codes in the main classification 001-999 to identify the external cause of an injury or condition. E-codes are NEVER used as solo codes or as principal diagnostic codes. When using E-codes, search the Alphabetic Index (Volume 2) for the main term identifying the cause such as "accident", "fire", "shooting", "fall", or "collision". To find the E-code for an adverse reaction to surgical or medical treatment use the main term "reaction".

Coding Example

Burns to right arm, occurred while burning trash

> 943.00 Burn of upper limb, except wrist and hand, unspecified degree
>
> E897 Accident caused by controlled fire not in building or structure

E-codes are important for providing the details of an accident to an insurance carrier to enable them to issue faster and more accurate reimbursement. Most insurance carriers want to be sure they reimburse only for services covered under their policy and not for services covered under Worker's Compensation or Automobile or Homeowner's insurance. A clear understanding of the circumstances will eliminate questions from the insurance carrier which cause delays in reimbursements.

Coding Example

Fractured ribs due to fall from ladder at home

> 807.00 Fracture of ribs, closed, unspecified
>
> E881.0 Fall from ladder
>
> E849.0 Place of occurrence, home

Using the above E-codes to provide important information regarding the circumstances of the injury to the insurance carrier eliminates any doubt about the insurer's responsibility for coverage. When using E-codes, always list the E-codes as secondary or supplemental to the code(s) describing the injury.

FEE SCHEDULE REVIEW AND MANAGEMENT

CHAPTER SUMMARY

Setting fees, or what might be more properly called fee schedule management, involves a lot more than simply deciding the dollar amount associated with a particular service or procedure. Setting fees requires a knowledge of how insurance carriers reimburse, a method for determining the value of your services, an awareness of the going rates, a comprehensive knowledge of Medicare, Medicaid, and Worker's Compensation laws, and private insurance carrier billing rules and regulations.

In today's more competitive market environment, it is important to understand that your fees are part of your marketing strategy. Fees must be reviewed and adjusted periodically. The adjustment is usually in the form of raising fees; however, fee decreases are sometimes appropriate and will become more common as competition increases. In addition, there will continue to be mandatory fee reductions as imposed by Medicare in the recent past.

The objective when reviewing your fees is to set a fair price for your procedures and services, and to be paid that price most of the time. However, neither setting your fees or getting paid is as simple as that.

KEY POINTS REGARDING SETTING FEES

1. Medical professionals are typically reluctant to discuss fees with each other due to the competition issue or the possibility of legal action based on conspiracy.

2. It is difficult to obtain fee information, profiles, relative values, or conversion factors from most private insurance carriers. In addition, medical associations are prevented by Federal antitrust legislation from disclosing the results of their fee surveys.

3. The new Medicare Fee Schedule (MFS) based on the Resource Based Relative Value Scale (RBRVS) will most likely become the method used for reimbursement by all insurance carriers.

4. Charging a fee that is less than an insurance carrier will pay benefits the insurance carrier, not you or your patient.

5. Insurance carriers may be paying you 25-50% less than they are paying your peers for exactly the same service, simply because you have been careless in maintaining your provider profile.

6. Essentially all medical fees are ultimately negotiated (down) or discounted, either voluntarily or involuntarily.

7. Fee schedule management puts you in control of the reimbursement process.

TRADITIONAL METHODS OF ADJUSTING FEES

The consensus among health care management consultants is that most medical professionals generally have no logical basis for fee setting. Medical professionals have used a variety of methods for adjusting fees, some logical and some not. Following is a brief review of some of these methods.

ACROSS THE BOARD BY PERCENT

Increase all fees by a set percentage. This is probably the most common method used because it is simple to calculate and easy to implement. Unfortunately, it also can have an effect on reimbursement that is exactly the opposite of the one intended.

Raising all fees at the same time by the same percentage tends to drive some of your higher priced procedures out of the market, or above the going rates. This can result in price sensitivity by your patients and a reduction in patients referred by your colleagues, which, over time, can result in a loss of income. A typical response to this loss is to raise fees again to compensate, without considering why the loss occurred in the first place.

INFLATION AND INCREASED OPERATING COSTS

While the national economy has been relatively stable for several years, the cost of living has continued to increase slightly every year. The annual increase in the Consumer Price Index (CPI) has been between 3 and 6 percent annually. This of course means that it costs you, and your employees, 3 to 6 percent more each year to purchase basic goods and services.

In order to stay even with this increase, you must increase your income ,and that of your employees if you want to keep them, by an amount equal to the increase in the CPI. These increases must come from either increased income or reduced costs of operating your practice.

Operating costs for the average medical practitioner have been increasing at the rate of about 9% per year for several years. This means that you must increase your revenues by at least 9% per year.... just to stay even. Easy you say! I'll just raise my fees by 9% and that will take care of it. First, consider that raising fees does not necessarily translate into increased revenues. As mentioned above, if you are not careful to consider the going rates when you raise your fees, you may price yourself right out of the market. Plus there are statutory limits on raising fees and/or controls on the increases allowed by Medicare.

Second, consider that with rare exceptions, no one collects 100% of the fees charged. Mandatory reductions such as Medicare and Medicaid disallowances, other insurance write-offs and bad debt reduce the collection possibilities. Third, unless your billing and collections system is well managed, you are probably not collecting 100% of your collectable revenues. As a result your accounts receivable increases each month.

The bottom line is that to offset a 9% increase in operating expenses, you have to achieve a NET 9% increase in revenues. Depending upon the ratios of your discount patient population (Medicare, Medicaid, HMO, etc.) and the effectiveness of your billing and collection system, substantial increases may be required JUST TO STAY EVEN.

INCREASE BY SELECTED PROCEDURE(S)

Rather than implement an across the board increase in fees for all procedures and services, many medical professionals choose to increase fees for selected procedures and services. This is usually done by increasing the fees for the selected procedures and services by a specific percentage or a fixed dollar amount (not necessarily the same amount or percent for all procedures and services). A typical example is a practice that routinely raises its fees for all office and hospital visits by $5.00 every year, or by 10%, or some other formula. This method is better than the across the board method, but it can also have less than optimal results.

The formula used to determine the increase is important. How do we determine which procedures and services to increase? How much of an increase is appropriate or necessary? The key to successful pricing using this method is to pay particular attention to the volume of the specific procedures or services you are reviewing. A small increase in a high volume procedure or service can have a tremendous impact on practice revenues. When using this method, the typical result is that fees for some procedures and services are increased substantially, some are increased a little, many remain unchanged, and some may even be reduced (yes, reduced).

THE GOING RATE

The GOING RATE is a fee for a specific procedure or service that generally represents what most medical professionals charge and what most patients (or third party payors) are willing to pay. Fees that ignore the going rate are self-defeating.

If your fees are significantly above the going rate, price sensitive patients will not choose you as their provider. In addition, your professional referral sources will be reluctant to send patients to you. Consider that the patients will not complain to you about your fees, they will complain to the person or professional who referred them to you.

CATCH UP METHOD

This method is used by providers who find that their fees are hopelessly out of date. After implementing huge increases to CATCH UP, they frequently find that their revenues drop as irate patients leave the practice. The key point to remember is that small, frequent, increases are better than large, infrequent, increases.

RELATIVE VALUES

The use of relative values for setting fees, used by California physicians for almost 20 years before being stopped by the FTC, was and still is, the only logical basis for setting fees in the current economic environment. Contrary to widely held opinion, the use of relative values for fee setting BY INDIVIDUALS has been consistently upheld by the United States Supreme Court. However, the same court has consistently restricted medical associations from creating or publishing relative value studies.

The California Relative Value Study (CRVS), as well as most of its successors, was a charge-based study. The logic used to calculate the relative values was simple. The assumption was made that average fees were an accurate reflection of the value of the services or procedures. The original CRVS was flawed in that it was created by "backing out" fee based data. Once an agreement was reached on what average fee represented a base value, calculation of all other relative values was easy. For example, if a $10.00 procedure was 1.0 units, then a $25.00 procedure must be 2.5 units.

In addition to maintaining, and quantifying, the traditional discrepancy between the value of cognitive services and technical services, these relative value systems provided no mechanism for adjusting the values of procedures or services due to non-charge based factors such as reduced costs, increased risks, etc.

Newer relative value studies, such as the one by Systematics/McGraw-Hill and the Harvard Study (RBRVS), calculate relative values by use of the following factors:

• TIME involved in performing the service or procedure

• SKILL required to perform the service or procedure

• SEVERITY of the patient's condition

- RISK of the service or procedure to the patient

- RISK of the service or procedure to the provider

- COST of operating a medical practice

The relative values presented in these studies provide a far more accurate measurement of the true value of medical procedures and services. Thousands of health care professionals nationwide use the SysteMetrics/Mcgraw-Hill study for fee schedule management. In addition it is used by numerous insurance carriers and HMOs for both reimbursement management and cost analysis.

The Harvard Study (RBRVS) was accepted by the PPRC as the fundamental basis for a new Medicare Fee Schedule (MFS) implemented on January 1, 1992. Ironically, this new fee schedule, based on relative values, was funded and proposed by the government, the same government which forced the California Medical Association to cease publication of the CRVS.

PROSPECTIVE REIMBURSEMENT SYSTEMS

In an effort to control the rapidly increasing costs of providing health care in the United States, many price control mechanisms have been proposed and studied. All of the systems proposed eliminate unrestricted fee-for-service medicine.

DIAGNOSIS DRIVEN REIMBURSEMENT

In a diagnosis driven reimbursement system, your payment is dependent on the final diagnosis. Each diagnosis, or related groups of diagnoses, has a fixed reimbursement rate. The level of service, the quantity of services or procedures, or the cost of providing those services and procedures, is not a factor in determining reimbursement.

This system is essentially identical to the Diagnosis Related Groupings (DRGs) system used by Medicare to reimburse hospitals for the past several years. Some hospitals have done well under this system, actually making a profit on Medicare patients. Others have gone out of business due to the inability to generate enough revenues to cover their operating expenses.

Due to the fact that economic survival depends on code selection, there is obviously a lot of pressure, internal and external, to select diagnosis codes which reimburse at a higher rate. In addition, opponents of this system forecast an increase in costs associated with monitoring and utilization review. In addition, unless the new Medicare Fee Schedule based on RBRVS fails drastically, we do not envision a physician payment system based on diagnosis.

CAPITATION DRIVEN REIMBURSEMENT

In a capitation driven system your reimbursement is dependent on the number of patients who sign up or choose you as their provider. The medical professional is paid a flat rate, per patient, per month, to provide selected services and procedures. The provider may also be responsible for the cost of specialized care and ancillary services.

Capitation driven reimbursement systems makes the medical professional responsible for creating a profit by controlling costs. Profit or loss depends on the efficient and effective delivery of services and procedures in a well-managed environment.

Just like the diagnosis driven system, due to the fact that economic survival depends on cost control, there is obviously a lot of pressure to maximize profits by reducing or limiting services provided to patients. Considering how poorly most HMOs have performed economically, including the biggest, best financed, and supposedly best managed ones, how is it possible that the small group, or single practitioner can make this work?

RELATIVE VALUE BASED FEE SCHEDULE

The general consensus among medical professionals, medical associations, and critics of the health care system is that a fee schedule, based on a more current relative value scale, is the preferred method for determining reimbursement for procedures and services. A two-year study of relative values, financed by HCFA, was completed in August 1988 at Harvard University. The objective of the study was to create a new relative value scale that takes into consideration factors such as time, complexity, amortized value of specialty training and practice costs. A major change from previous relative value studies was the attempt to resolve the discrepancy between cognitive services and technical services.

The final formula from the original 1988 Harvard study was:

RBRV = (TW) (1 + RPC) (1 + AST) where

TW = Total work input

RPC = Index of practice costs

AST = Amortized value of specialty training

The results of the original study were not surprising, finding that:

1) Current charges for procedures and services are not closely related to the costs of providing those procedures and services, and

2) Most cognitive services are undervalued, and

3) Most technical services are overvalued.

Based on continued refinement of the RBRVS under the guidance of the PPRC, this study became the basis for the new Medicare Fee Schedule which became effective January 1, 1992. There are significant differences between the formula above and the one used to implement the Medicare Fee Schedule.

FEE SCHEDULE REVIEW AND MANAGEMENT

The process of fee review includes gathering resource materials, reviewing the procedure and diagnostic codes you use, reviewing the fees charged for each procedure, making decisions regarding fee adjustments, and making sure that the resulting decisions are implemented and followed.

IMPORTANT FEE REVIEW RESOURCE MATERIALS

- Current edition of CPT

- Current edition of HCPCS codes

- Relative Value study

- Medicare Fee Schedule

- Geographic Cost of Practice Indexes

- Insurance carrier Explanation of Benefits (EOBs)

- Other fee data

- Fourth Edition of ICD-9-CM plus most current annual updates

- Copies of all fee listings and superbills

REVIEW PROCEDURE CODES IN THE CURRENT CPT

Review each of the procedure codes from your code listing or superbill in the most current edition of CPT. Pay particular attention to codes that have been added, changed or deleted.

- All CPT codes in the current edition with a small black circle to the left of the code are NEW codes. Review all new codes carefully to see if any of them can be used instead of UNLISTED procedure codes or as replacements for HCPCS codes.

- ▲ All CPT codes in the current edition with a small black triangle to the left of the code are CHANGED codes. Review the description of all changed codes carefully to make sure that your superbills and insurance forms have the same descriptions. Not only will this improve your reimbursement, it will also protect you from audit liability.

- () Next look for codes that have been deleted. These are indicated by parenthesis. CPT includes a referral to a replacement code for all codes that are deleted. Make sure you substitute the replacement codes on your superbills and coding lists.

REVIEW ALL SECTIONS OF THE CPT

Repeat this process for the EVALUATION AND MANAGEMENT, SURGERY, RADIOLOGY, PATHOLOGY and MEDICINE sections of CPT as appropriate for your practice.

EVALUATION AND MANAGEMENT
This section first appeared in the 1992 edition of CPT. All previous visit codes were deleted and replaced by Evaluation and Management codes in preparation for conversion to the Medicare Fee Schedule. As this section is completely new, there will undoubtably be significant changes for the next few years. Review this section carefully each year for changes in office, hospital and other location codes.

SURGERY
Review all portions of this section of CPT which may be appropriate to your practice. Non-surgical practices should review the sections on wound repair, trauma related codes, and any other procedures commonly performed. Pay particular attention to starred (*) procedures and procedures classified as (separate) procedures.

RADIOLOGY
Practices which are performing and/or billing for radiology procedures should review this section of CPT carefully. This section includes procedures that are typically performed on a high volume basis, such as chest x-rays, where a small increase in an individual fee can result in a significant increase in total reimbursement.

LABORATORY
Practices which provide and/or bill for laboratory procedures need to review this section of CPT carefully. This section typically includes procedures that are performed on a high volume basis, such blood counts, urinalysis, etc., where a small increase in an individual fee can result in a significant increase in total reimbursement.

MEDICINE
Review this entire section to update injections, specialty procedures and diagnostic procedures. Changes are usually infrequent in this section. However in the 1992 CPT, all office, hospital and other location visit codes were deleted from this section and replaced by new codes in the new Evaluation and Management section.

REVIEW HCPCS CODES

Review the HCPCS code listings particularly the sections covering supplies, materials and injections. HCFA revises these codes on an annual basis and most Medicare carriers make continual revisions which are published in the form of newsletters. Use of the proper HCPCS codes can make a significant difference in your reimbursement. You need to obtain a copy of the revised codes each year and review it carefully for any changes which may affect your practice.

Remember that while the HCPCS National Level 2 codes are uniform throughout the United States, the method of billing the codes properly varies from one Medicare carrier to another. In addition, each carrier maintains and publishes their own Local Level 3 codes. Check with your local Medicare carrier for proper billing instructions.

REVIEW ICD-9-CM CODES

Due to the Medicare ICD-9-CM coding requirements, most practices have already converted from diagnostic statements to diagnostic coding on insurance claim forms. It is important that you are using the most current diagnosis codes, which is ICD-9-CM, 9th Revision, 4th Edition. In addition, an official addenda is published each year in October. You should obtain the addenda and review it carefully for any code changes which may affect your coding and billing. Keep track of the frequency of ICD-9-CM code usage. Add frequently used codes to your reference listings and superbills. Delete codes that are not being used frequently.

REVIEW YOUR FEES

Review each of your procedures carefully to determine if fees need to be increased, due to increased costs or to maintain your profile, or decreased, in response to changing market conditions or decreased costs. Pay particular attention to the volume of procedures. Small increases in frequently performed procedures and large increases in infrequently performed procedures can usually be implemented without negative results.

RELATIVE VALUE ANALYSIS

Use relative value analysis to calculate a conversion factor for your practice. Then use the calculated conversion factor to determine the appropriate fee for each of your procedures. We recommend using Relative Values for Physicians, published by SysteMetrics/McGraw-Hill. This publication is the only source of current relative values that is not a charge based system.

To perform a relative value analysis, you need a current relative value publication, and a list of your 25 most commonly performed procedure codes from the Medicine, Surgery, Radiology and Pathology sections of CPT, and your fees for the procedures.

- List the 25 codes and fees for each section.

- Look up the relative value and add to your list.

- Total all of the fees.

- Total all of the relative values.

- Divide the total relative values into the total fees.

- The result is your AVERAGE CONVERSION FACTOR.

After you calculate your AVERAGE CONVERSION FACTOR, you can then multiple the relative value for each of the listed procedures by the conversion factor to determine what the fee should be. It is not unusual to find services and procedures both under and over priced based on relative value analysis. Before raising your prices based on relative value analysis, consider that all insurance carriers have a maximum dollar value, based on customary fees, that they will allow for a given procedure. However, the use of relative values gives you a strong argument for a review of a disputed or underpaid claim.

RELATIVE VALUE ANALYSIS - SURGICAL PROCEDURES

The following list represents 25 of the most commonly reported SURGERY procedures along with the 75th percentile fee and a relative value. The relative value is from *Relative Values for Physicians, 3rd Edition* published by SysteMetrics/McGraw-Hill. The conversion factor is calculated by dividing the total relative values into the total charges. Consider that a conversion factor calculated using fees at the 50th percentile would be lower and a conversion factor using fees at the 90th percentile would be higher.

An individual practice would use the actual fees charged for specific procedures to calculate a conversion factor for the practice. Note that the procedures listed below include several surgical specialties whereas procedures of an individual practice would typically be limited to a single area of surgical specialty.

CODE	DESCRIPTION	FEE	RV
43239	Upper GI endoscopy, biopsy	610.00	4.8
36471	Injection therapy of veins	154.00	.6
17000	Destruction of face lesion	100.00	.9
43235	Upper GI endoscopy, diagnosis	644.00	4.2
53670	Insert urinary catheter	35.00	.3
59400	Obstetrical care	3000.00	17.0
45330	Sigmoidoscopy	295.00	1.3
69210	Remove impacted ear wax	50.00	.6
45380	Colonoscopy and biopsy	829.00	7.5
31575	Fiberscopic laryngoscopy	380.00	1.8
49505	Repair inguinal hernia	1412.00	8.5
31500	Insertion of windpipe airway	250.00	1.5
11101	Biopsy, each added lesion	85.00	.7
20550	Injection treatment	60.00	.4
36800	Insertion of cannula	500.00	3.0
45385	Colonoscopy, lesion removal	1300.00	9.0
59025	Fetal non-stress test	100.00	1.0
36830	Artery-vein graft	2100.00	13.0
20610	Inject/drain joint/bursa	100.00	.6
19120	Removal of breast lesion	733.00	5.0
45300	Proctosigmoidscopy	127.00	.7
17100	Destruction of skin lesion	76.00	.6
57452	Examination of vagina	195.00	2.0
35301	Rechanneling of artery	3517.00	15.0
47605	Removal of gallbladder	2718.00	18.0
	TOTALS	19370.00	118.0
	CONVERSION FACTOR		164.15

DETERMINING FEES FOR NEW PROCEDURES

If you perform a service or procedure for the first time and need to determine a fee, the first place to look would be your relative value reference. If the procedure is listed and has a numeric value, then simply multiply the relative value by your conversion factor to determine the appropriate fee. However, if the procedure or service is unlisted, or has a BR (by report) instead of a numeric value, then you can not calculate a fee by this method. The best alternative is to use a comparative procedure as the basis for first determining approximate relative value and then to calculate the proper fee. Review some of the more common procedures you perform and try to find one that requires similar skills, about the same amount of time, and has the same level of complexity and risk as the new procedure.

Use the relative value of the common procedure as a basis for calculating the fee for the new procedure. Watch insurance carrier EOBs carefully to see how much they are allowing for the new procedure and adjust your fee accordingly. You can also request the prevailing charge for the procedure from your local Medicare intermediary.

REVIEW AND REVISE YOUR SUPERBILLS AND FEE SCHEDULES

After you have reviewed all CPT, HCPCS, and ICD-9-CM codes and descriptions and made any necessary revisions to your fees, you need to carefully review all of your superbills and any other documents that may have codes, descriptions or fees printed on them. Make the required changes and then make sure that the revisions are made and the documents printed.

We strongly recommend that you limit the quantity of superbills printed to no more than a six month supply. Inevitably you will change procedure codes, diagnosis codes and/or fees during a six month period and you want to reserve the ability to reprint your superbills without throwing too many away. We also recommend that you do not print fees on your superbills. While it is easier than looking up fees at the cashier's or receptionist's desk, it also causes potential billing errors for interim fee changes.

Distribute copies of the revised superbills and/or fee schedules to all staff members. Consider that not only billing personnel are involved with codes and fees. The person who answers the telephone in response to fee inquiries from potential patients needs to be well informed about your current fee schedules.

STAND BY YOUR FEES

Once your fees are set stand by them. Make few exceptions to your standard fees and always document exceptions by posting full charges followed by an adjustment. This makes billing easier for everyone and provides an accurate record of how much you are discounting.

MEDICARE PARTICIPATION

In the fall of 1984 the Medicare Participation program was created by Congress. Each year, medical professionals must decide to be participating (PAR) or non-participating (NON-PAR) in the program. The national physician participation rate has increased from slightly over 30% for the period ending September 1985 to slightly over 44% for the period ending April 1990. The following table indicates participation rates for selected medical specialties from the period October 1985 through April 1990. Note that participation rates have increased overall and within specific specialty groups. As might be expected, participation rates tend to be higher within those specialties where you would find a larger percentage of Medicare patients.

PHYSICIAN PARTICIPATION RATES, OCTOBER 1985 - APRIL 1990[1]

SPECIALTY	1985	1986	1987	1988	1989	1990
Cardiology	35.6	38.8	43.2	52.8	55.5	60.6
General Surgery	33.9	34.5	37.2	48.5	52.2	55.8
Ophthalmology	27.3	28.7	35.1	46.3	50.5	55.6
Radiology	41.3	39.5	39.8	46.3	49.6	55.6
Orthopedics	29.0	38.3	32.6	44.0	49.2	53.7
Dermatology	34.0	37.8	38.1	45.7	48.7	53.4
Pathology	39.6	37.7	41.2	48.1	50.6	53.4
Neurology	34.8	33.2	39.2	44.1	49.2	53.1
Urology	27.8	29.0	30.9	41.7	45.6	49.6
Internal Medicine	32.5	31.1	33.6	41.2	45.2	48.8
Ob/Gyn	29.1	30.5	31.5	40.4	44.2	48.8
Family Practice	25.5	27.1	27.1	35.6	39.7	47.2
Otorhino-laryngology	24.6	25.1	27.0	36.9	41.2	45.2
Psychiatry	30.0	27.8	28.6	34.4	37.8	41.6
General Practice	27.3	23.6	25.6	32.3	35.8	39.7
Anesthesiology	21.1	21.7	20.3	25.0	28.3	30.8
All Physicians[2]	28.4	28.3	30.6	37.3	40.7	44.1

[1] Source: Health Care Financing Administration
[2] Figures for all physicians include all practioners defined as physicians under the Medicare statute.

In addition to variation in participation rates by medical specialty, there is a significant variation in assignment rates by geographic location as well. The following table indicates the Medicare assignment rates for the 10 HCFA regions for the period ending September 1990. Note that there is a variation of over 69 percent between the lowest assignment area (Seattle region) and the highest assignment area (Boston region).

ASSIGNMENT RATES BY HCFA REGION
OCTOBER 1989 - SEPTEMBER 1990[1]

REGION	PERCENT
Boston	93.4
New York	82.9
Philadelphia	88.6
Atlanta	84.8
Chicago	80.1
Dallas Region	81.4
Kansas City	76.6
Denver	62.7
San Francisco	84.2
Seattle	55.2

ADVANTAGES OF MEDICARE PARTICIPATION

- Payment is made directly to you. This simplifies the billing process, reduces your bad debt, and lowers your billing cost.

- Allowances are based on the Medicare fee schedule.

- You can use a single fee schedule for Medicare and non-Medicare patients.

- Medicare carriers are required to process claims faster for PAR physicians. From a maximum of 30 days in 1987, the processing standard has been reduced to 17 days from 1990 on.

- You are listed in the directory of participating physicians (MEDPARD) published each year by the local Medicare carrier. The directory is supposed to be made widely available to Medicare patients and may have some influence on their choice of physicians.

- Hospitals which refer a patient for outpatient care must provide the patient with the name and address of a qualified PAR physician each time they provide a referral to a NON-PAR physician.

DISADVANTAGES OF MEDICARE PARTICIPATION

- PAR physicians must take assignment on all claims.

- PAR physicians must submit HCFA1500 claim forms for all Medicare patients.

- PAR physicians may charge a maximum of 100% of the Medicare Fee Schedule amount. Medicare pays the first 80% and the remaining 20% must be collected directly from the patient.

ADVANTAGES OF MEDICARE NON-PARTICIPATION

- Under the billing limit you may charge up to 120 percent of the allowed amount for all services in 1992, dropping to 115 percent in 1993 and beyond.

- You have a choice of taking assignment or not on a claim by claim basis.

- You may collect the total billing limit from the patient.

DISADVANTAGES OF MEDICARE NON-PARTICIPATION

- As of October 1990, you must file the HCFA1500 insurance claim form regardless of your participation status or whether or not the claim is unassigned.

- You must maintain more than one fee schedule. One for your non-Medicare patients, and one with the billing limits for Medicare.

- If you do not accept assignment on a claim, the payment goes directly to the patient.

- If you do accept assignment on a claim, the Medicare carrier is allowed more time to process and pay your claim. From a maximum of 30 days in 1987, the Medicare carrier is allowed up to 24 days from 1990 on.

- If you are providing an elective surgery with a charge exceeding $500.00, and you are not taking assignment, you must notify the patient in advance using specified format and terminology

- For services determined to be "not reasonable and necessary", a NON-PAR physician who does not accept assignment may not collect payment from the patient unless a previous notice and agreement exists.

MAKING THE DECISION

In order to make an informed decision regarding Medicare participation you need to obtain several reports from your local Medicare carrier and then perform a financial analysis to determine the economic impact of PAR versus NON-PAR for your practice. You will need a copy of the current Medicare Fee Schedule and the Medicare billing limits for your specialty.

In addition, you will need a list of the common procedures and services that you provide to Medicare patients, plus a report or an estimate of the annual volume of these procedures. To complete the analysis, you make a list of the procedures, with the estimated volume, the MAAC and the allowable charge. You then multiply the billing limit times the volume to get the total billing limit and the fee schedule times the volume to get the total allowable.

After completing your analysis you will be able to determine the financial impact of the PAR versus NON-PAR decision for your practice. However, as mentioned previously, the PAR versus NON-PAR decision must include other criteria. While the majority of physicians (almost 60%) are NON-PAR as of this writing, the majority of Medicare claims (almost 70%) are assigned. In addition, the PAR versus NON-PAR decision tends to be highly influenced by the medical community. In some areas of the United States, almost none of the physicians are PAR. In other areas, almost all of the physicians are PAR. A NON-PAR physician in a community where the majority of physicians are PAR will ultimately be pressured by patients and/or referral sources to become PAR, or will have to replace lost Medicare patients with other types of patients. Perhaps more important than the economic analysis is the answer to two simple questions:

1. If I become (or continue to be) NON-PAR, will I lose some of my existing (or potential) patients to PAR physicians?

2. If I do lose these patients, can I replace them with non-Medicare patients of the same or higher economic value?

MULTIPLE FEE SCHEDULES

It is surprising, when conducting our seminars on fee schedule management, to find out how many health care professionals believe that it is illegal to use multiple fee schedules. Not only is it not illegal, it is absolutely essential to have multiple fee schedules in the wellmanaged practice of the 1990s. The argument can certainly be made that any service or procedure is worth the same, based on relative value calculations, however, all of your potential payors do not use the same method to pay you, or to calculate the value of the services and procedures you perform.

Fees charged for services provided to Medicare patients are highly regulated by Federal law. Fees charged for services provided to Medicaid beneficiaries and Worker's Compensation Carriers are generally based on fixed fee schedules published by state agencies. Many HMOs and PPOs also reimburse based on fee schedules.

None of these rules and regulations or fee schedules applies to services provided to patients paying cash, services rendered to patients in personal injury cases, or for services covered by private insurance carriers. A medical practice with a typical patient mix including Medicare, Medicaid, worker's compensation and private insurance patients would need to use a minimum of two or three different fee schedules for proper billing.

MEDICARE FEE SCHEDULE

Practices which are NON-PARTICIPATING must use the Medicare billing limits when billing for services provided to Medicare patients. Practices which are PARTICIPATING may charge their regular fees for services provided to Medicare patients.

REGULAR FEE SCHEDULE

This is your standard fee schedule representing the fees that you charge for cash patients, private insurance patients, Medicaid patients, and, if you are PARTICIPATING, to Medicare patients also.

WORKER'S COMPENSATION

This fee schedule is used to bill for services related to treating illnesses and injuries related to employment. The fee schedules are generally maintained and published by the state agency responsible for worker's compensation cases.

CONTRACT FEE SCHEDULES

You may have additional fee schedules, based on participating agreements with HMOs, PPOs, etc. that must be used to bill for services provided to beneficiaries of these plans.

THE NEW MEDICARE FEE SCHEDULE

In 1986, the Congress created the Physician Payment Review Commission (PPRC) to advise it on reforms of the methods used to pay physicians under the Medicare program. Since then, the PPRC has conducted analyses of physician payment issues, provided a forum for groups representing physicians, beneficiaries, and other interests to present their views, and worked closely with the Congress to bring about comprehensive reforms in Medicare physician payment policy. Its recommendations formed the basis of 1989 legislation that created a new payment system consisting of a resource-based fee schedule, limits on the amount physicians may charge patients above the fee schedule amount, and Volume Performance Standards, coupled with expanded federal support for effectiveness research and the development of practice guidelines, to control expenditure growth.

While the PPRC's original mandate focused on relative payment and financial protection for beneficiaries, over the years this mandate has been substantially expanded. The PPRC now addresses issues such as private payers and the Medicare Fee Schedule, profiling physician practice patterns, rural health services delivery, and medical malpractice reform.

HISTORICAL INFORMATION

In 1987 when the Physician Payment Review Commission issued its first report, Medicare outlays to physicians were growing at double-digit rates, placing an increasing burden on taxpayers and beneficiaries who share in financing program costs. The program's method of paying physicians on the basis of historical charges had severely distorted the pattern of relative payment across different physician specialties, services, and geographic areas. Concern was also growing about the financial liability of Medicare's 33 million elderly and disabled beneficiaries and their access to care. Physicians, beneficiaries, and policymakers alike agreed that this situation had to be corrected.

Today, the context for reform has changed. In the Omnibus Budget Reconciliation Act of 1989 (OBRA89), the Congress established a new system of payment. It consists of a Medicare Fee Schedule based on resource costs, limits on the amount physicians may charge patients above the fee schedule payment, and Volume Performance Standards (vps) coupled with expanded federal support for effectiveness research and development of practice guidelines to control expenditure growth. This package of reforms built on a series of policy changes enacted since the early 1980s.

CALCULATING REIMBURSEMENT UNDER THE MEDICARE FEE SCHEDULE

After much study and debate, but little effective opposition from organized physician groups, the Medicare Fee Schedule was inacted on January 1, 1992. The final regulations of Public Law 101-239 were published in the Federal Register on November 25, 1991. The conversion is to be completed over a five year period. The current formula for calculating reimbursement amounts under the new Medicare Fee Schedule is as follows:

PAYMENT = [(RVUw x GPCIw) + (RVUpe x GPCIpe) + (RVUm x GPCIm)] x CF

RVU(w)	= physician work relative value units for the service
RVU(pe)	= practice expense relative value units for the service
RVU(m)	= malpractice relative value units for the service
GPCI(w)	= geographic practice cost index value for physician work
GPCI(pe)	= geographic practice cost index value for practice expense
GPCI(m)	= geographic practice cost index value for malpractice
CF	= uniform national conversion factor

To compute a payment amount for a specific service using this intimidating looking formula, you will need a complete Medicare Fee Schedule from your local Medicare carrier (or other source), the geographic cost indexes for your area, and the current national conversion factor. The 1992 conversion factor was set at $31.001. As an example, let's compute the payment amount for a coronary artery bypass, autogenous graft; three coronary grafts performed in Los Angeles, California.

1. Look up the CPT (HCPCS) code for the procedure.

    33512

2. Look up the RVUs for the procedure.

    RVU(w)   = 26.41
    RVU(pe) = 38.61
    RVU(m)   = 6.76

3. Look up the GPCIs for Los Angeles, California.

    GPCI(w)   = 1.060
    GPCI(pe) = 1.196
    GPCI(m)   = 1.370

4. Calculate the adjusted total RVUs for the procedure.

   $(26.41 \times 1.060) + (38.61 \times 1.196) + (6.76 \times 1.370) = 83.43$

5. Multiply the adjusted total RVUs by the conversion factor to obtain the payment amount.

   $83.43 \times \$31.001 = \$2586.41$

If the above procedure was performed in Salt Lake City, Utah, reimbursement would be $2107.76 based on lower cost of practice indexes. As is usual with Medicare, what you see is not what you get. The amount actually paid to a provider is 80 percent of the actual charge or 80 percent of the fee schedule payment amount, whichever is less.

SUMMARY OF THE NOVEMBER 1991 MEDICARE FEE SCHEDULE REGULATIONS

- The global surgery policy excludes the initial evaluation or consultation by a surgeon and all medically necessary return trips to the operating room.

- Global surgery is defined to include: 1) all preop visits, in or out of the hospital, by the surgeon beginning the day before the surgery, 2) usual and customary intraoperative services, 3) all additional services due to complications that do not require additional trips to the operating room, and 4) all services by the primary surgeon during a standard 90-day postop period unless the service is unrelated to the original surgery or is an added treatment other than normal recovery.

- Visits with minor surgeries and "scopies" are not allowed unless a documented, separately identifiable service is performed. Postop services due to recovery from procedures requiring incisions are included for 10 days and no follow-up days are allowed for non-incisional services.

- Certain non-routine supplies are paid under HCPCS National Level 2 code A4550 when performed with specified procedures in the physician's office.

- Services incident to a physician's services are paid as if the physician provided the services.

- For interventional radiology services, the use of CPT complete procedure codes is discontinued. "Supervision and interpretation" codes and the primary non-radiological service (surgery code) are paid at fee schedule amounts. The first additional service is paid at 50 percent, the next three additional services are paid at 25 percent and any other services are paid by report.

- Time units for anesthesia services remain temporarily with the national conversion factor for anesthesiologists set at $13.94 adjusted by GPCIs. For CRNAs, the conversion factors are $10.75 for medically directed services and $15.75 for non-medically directed services.

- Technical components of physician pathology services are 15 percent of the professional component and a new clinical lab interpretation services for 15 codes is established;

- New codes for physician visits and consultations are defined containing elements such as extent of history, extent of examination, level of medical decision making, counseling and/or coordination of care, nature of the presenting problem(s) and time.

- New Evaluation and Management codes for all other visit services replace the existing codes.

- The outpatient limit for physician services is applied to a national list of procedures which are performed at least 50 percent of the time in the office setting. The limit reduces the practice expense RVUs by 50 percent for an average reduction in the overall fee of approximately 21 percent.

- For diagnostic tests with separate professional and technical components, the professional components are treated like other physicians' services.

- RVUs for EKG interpretation are added to visit codes based on the historical frequency associated with office visits, hospital visits and consultations.

- Relative value units are to be reviewed on a yearly basis with proposed and final notices to be printed in the Federal Register.

The only significant variation in the PPRC proposals is that the AMAs version of the new CPT codes for Evaluation and Management services was used instead of the PPRCs proposed version. The PPRCs version was much simpler than the AMA version; using the same five levels of service for all classes of visits, whereas in the AMA version, the number, descriptors, and times in the levels of service for each class. The concern of the PPRC is that with the coding system proposed by the AMA, physicians may focus only on the encounter times in the codes, learn only one set of levels of service but apply them to visits in all classes or locations, or develop arbitrary crosswalks from the "old" codes to the new codes. The AMA "won" the argument in this matter; however, based on interviews with physicians, an analysis of the literature, and actions taken by various medical associations and societies, it appears that the PPRC concerns have validity and we expect future changes to these codes.

TRANSITION PAYMENT RULES

The Medicare Fee Schedule is to be phased in gradually over a period of five years from 1992 to 1996. During the years 1992 through 1995, providers will receive either the fee schedule amount or a blended payment based partially on the adjusted historical payment basis (AHPB) amount and partly on the fee schedule amount. A separate historical payment basis amount is calculated for each procedure in each fee schedule area and is reduced by 5.5 percent to maintain budget neutrality. Medicare carriers were given the task of calculating the AHPBs in the summer of 1991 and then comparing the results to the final fee schedule. In the transition year 1992 payments by carriers will vary as follows:

- If the AHPB amount is between 85 percent and 115 percent of the fee schedule amount, the maximum payment to all providers in the fee schedule area is the fee schedule amount.

- If the AHPB amount is less than 85 percent of the fee schedule amount, the payment will be the APHB amount plus 15 percent of the fee schedule amount.

- If the AHPB amount is more than 115 percent of the fee schedule amount, the payment will be the AHPB amount minus 15 percent of the fee schedule amount.

OTHER INSURANCE CARRIERS AND THE MEDICARE FEE SCHEDULE

The traditional development path in the areas of coding and billing is that policies and procedures mandated by Medicare are implemented shortly thereafter by Medicaid, followed by private insurance carriers. However, there are significant issues which must be dealt with before private insurance carriers can implement a fee schedule.

Private insurance carriers have expressed interest in revising their methods of physician payment. Many support the objectives of Medicare payment reform but have yet to determine the extent to which physician markets will permit changes in relative values. Although few plan to adopt the Medicare Fee Schedule in total, many are contemplating at least marginal changes in relative values to reflect the direction of Medicare changes. Private insurance carriers face limits to the magnitude of change they can institute. Insurers offering indemnity policies are concerned that balance billing for technical procedures will increase. Carriers that contract with physicians are concerned about whether specialists whose fees would fall would agree to participate in sufficient numbers.

More extensive or more rapid changes by private insurance carriers will require public regulation of their payment policies. Under an all-payer system, the Medicare relative value scale could be used by each of the payers. A public body would determine payment rates for the various physician services. While the conversion factors used by different payers need not be the same, the entity that determines rates would have a deliberate policy concerning how they would differ. Conversion factors could be updated through volume performance standards or a similar mechanism. Balance billing would be limited, but again, the limits could differ by class of payer. The entity making these decisions (presumably the U.S. Government) would (try to) balance the interests of physicians, private payers, public payers, and patients.

Based on the time frame outlined above for conversion to the MFS, and the estimated lag for implementation by Medicaid and private insurance carriers, we forecast that ALL medical services and procedures will be billed using a fee schedule based on resource based relative value scales from the year 2000.

IMPLEMENTING YOUR NEW FEE SCHEDULE

Regardless of how carefully you review and set your fees, you will still have complaints from patients. While studies have continued to indicate that most patients do not choose providers of medical care based on fees, it is important to keep in mind that many malpractice cases start out as fee disputes. Fee related complaints tend to fall under the five general categories.

FEE COMPARISON

Patients compare fees among each other. In addition, more and more patients shop fees for elective procedures or routine care. Patients may be well informed regarding the going rates for specific procedures and may ask why your fee is higher than that of other providers. Be prepared to explain your fees for common procedures.

FEE CONSISTENCY

Patients may question what appears to be inconsistencies in your fees from one visit to the next. Patients are not aware of the various levels of service defined by CPT and the fact that some services are packaged or bundled and others are not. Make sure the patient understands exactly what is included in bundled procedures, and is made aware of the levels of care if he/she questions your fees for visits.

TIME SPENT (WITH THE PATIENT)

Patients frequently consider the value of your services to be directly proportional to the time you spent with them. This is logical thinking on the patient's part, as many professional services tend to be rendered and billed based on units of time. Prior to publication of the 1992 edition of CPT, there were very few services or procedures that included time components. Therefore, you could explain simply to the patient that your fees are not based on the amount of time spent but rather the complexity of the situation and the level of care required.

However; with the publication of the 1992 CPT, time became part of the definition of the new Evaluation and Management services. As the definition and understanding of the new coding system becomes widespread among the patient population, you may expect some patients to time your services and compare their time with the time associated with particular Evaluation and Management codes.

RELATIVE VALUE

Due to the lack of knowledge and understanding regarding anatomy, physiology and the difficulties involved in various medical procedures, patients make inappropriate comparisons of procedures. They may not understand why a repair of a hip fracture costs more than life-saving treatment for an acute myocardial infarction. Patients are not aware of the traditional discrepancy between the value of cognitive procedures versus technical procedures. Of interest is the fact that the patients do not recognize any differences in value between cognitive and technical services.

This subjective attitude of the patient population is verified in part by the findings of the Harvard study of Resource Based Relative Values. One of the objectives of the new Medicare Fee Schedule is to legislate away the discrepancy by creating a reimbursement system that is based upon measurable work and cost of practice indexes. If patients question you on this issue, be prepared to explain how your fees for technical services are calculated. Expect Medicare patients to quickly become aware of Medicare Fee Schedule rules, regulations and formulas.

ABILITY TO PAY

In the past it was quite common for health care providers to charge patients based on ability to pay. Therefore, some patients were charged a little more, some a little less, and some nothing at all. It was sort of a private Medicaid system. Now with most patients covered by insurance plans and, more importantly, generally aware of basic fees for the most common procedures and services, the situation is different.

If patients perceive that you are charging them more because they can pay more they will probably not come back. Make sure that your discussion of fees includes assurances that your fees are not based on the patient's ability to pay, but rather on the specific services provided.

DISCUSSING FEES AT THE TIME OF APPOINTMENT SCHEDULING

Some practices discuss fees in advance with patients who call to make an appointment. While this may occasionally cause problems when the bill turns out to be higher than quoted on the phone, the major benefit is that the patient has been informed that there will be a charge, and that they are expected to pay. Any statements regarding fees or amounts made during telephone conversations should be noted on the appointment schedule.

SMALL FEES CAN BE STATED AFTER SERVICES HAVE BEEN RENDERED

Services such as office visits, injections and minor procedures can generally be provided without advance discussion of fees. The provider can fill out the charge slip or superbill including fees and instruct the patient to give it to the receptionist, or the provider can leave the fees blank to be filled out by the receptionist.

When the charge slip is totalled and presented to the patient for payment, the patient has the opportunity to ask questions regarding the services provided and the fees charged. Even if the patient does not pay at the time of service, this presentation of the itemized charge slip makes the patient aware of the fees, which will correspond to the bill received.

DISCUSS LARGER FEES BEFORE PROVIDING SERVICE

Numerous studies have confirmed that when patients are about to undergo major procedures that their first concern is outcome, and their second concern is how much it is going to cost and how are they going to pay for it. Unfortunately, most patients will never express this concern voluntarily.

Most medical professionals already discuss their findings, treatment plans and the probable outcome(s) with their patients, however, many totally neglect any discussion of fees or payment methods. In addition to appreciating the information, discussing the potential cost gives the patient the ability to make an informed decision regarding the service. In order to gain a little perspective on this issue, ask yourself the following questions:

- Would you order a meal in an expensive restaurant from a menu without prices?

- Would you allow a mechanic to perform major service on your car without an estimate of what it was going to cost?

- Would you allow a contractor to begin construction on your new kitchen or bathroom without a bid?

While you answered "no" to each of the above questions, consider that numerous medical procedures have fees that are equivalent or greater than the services referred to. Yet many medical practices expect the patient to receive (and pay for) services without any advance knowledge of their cost. None of this has anything to do with ethics. It is simply a matter of providing professional services with the expectation of being paid for those services. You always have the option to provide services at no charge if that is what you want to do.

OPTIONS FOR INITIATING FEE DISCUSSIONS

Not everyone is comfortable in discussing fees or money with patients. Many medical professionals absolutely refuse to engage in such discussions. It is not necessary for the medical professional to have this fee discussion with the patient, although patient surveys consistently reveal that the patient prefers to discuss fees directly with the medical professional. But it is important that someone representing the practice, the office manager, insurance manager, or the financial counselor, have a discussion with the patient regarding the fees before major services are rendered.

It is important to make the patient aware that your fees are within the going rates for the community, that the fees to this patient are the same as that for every patient, and, for bundled procedures, that your fee includes specific services and procedures. The following statements represent some of the more successful approaches to this subject:

1. *My (our, the doctor's) usual charge for this service is....*

   This lets the patient know what the charge will be and that they are being charged the same as everyone else.

2. *The going rate for this service (around here, in the community)...*

   This opening gives you two options. Either it assures the patient that your fees are in line with those of your colleagues, or it gives you the opportunity to explain why your fees are higher.

3. *My (our, the doctor's) fee covers.....*

   This approach is often used when discussing fees that are global in nature, primarily surgical procedures which include a standard amount of routine follow-up care. Another example would be prenatal care, uncomplicated vaginal delivery and the post-partum visit. This lets the patient know that a single fee covers all of the service.

It is better to state your usual charge first and then explain that any insurance proceeds will be applied against it. By mentioning insurance first, you risk the patient assuming that you will scale your charges based upon insurance payment. Unfortunately, there are still many medical practices which use the following:

   Don't worry. We'll take your insurance as full payment....

- What if the patient isn't covered (but doesn't know it)?

- What about deductibles and coinsurance?

- What about pre-existing conditions and exclusions?

- You can be sued by the patient for breach of contract if you make the above statement and then attempt to collect from the patient any unpaid balance after insurance....even if the insurance pays you nothing!

Many insurance carriers are helping you to protect yourself by requiring precertification before covering services and providing benefits. Many insurance contracts now require preauthorization for non-emergency hospitalization as well as for certain "abused" procedures such as Total Abdominal Hysterectomy. Failure to obtain preauthorization can result in outright denial of claims and/or benefit reductions of up to 50 percent with no appeal! In most cases, the patient does not even know that these requirements exist.

STRATEGIC PRICING

In today's competitive environment the successful practice will learn how to keep its existing patients, attract new patients, and increase its profitability by raising some fees, lowering others, and maintaining enough flexibility to adjust specific fees in response to new opportunities. This process is known as STRATEGIC PRICING and incorporates the following concepts:

MARKET DRIVEN PROCEDURES

Some procedures are price sensitive and patients do call to ask prices of some procedures or services, such as total obstetrical care. It is important that fees for such services be kept comparatively low. On the other hand, consumers know that some procedures are absolutely necessary for them to maintain and they don't shop around for these procedures.

In addition, if your practice provides services that are market driven you want to make sure that the person handling these telephone inquiries is a good salesperson. Ideally, the prospective patient would be "sold" on how good the practice, doctor and/or service is before the requested fee is quoted. This simple technique can significantly increase your new patient volume.

RELATIONSHIP BUILDING

Successful practices are dependent on long-term relationships with patients and/or referral sources. Part of your pricing strategy should be based on attracting new relationships with patients or referral sources and on maintaining and develop existing relationships. How much you charge, whether you charge, and how you bill are all considerations that may impact a relationship.

An example of this component of strategic pricing is the "free" consultation that most pediatricians provide to parents who are interviewing potential physicians for their new (or about to be born) babies. An investment of 30 to 45 minutes late in an afternoon can result in a patient relationship lasting for 20 years! More and more medical professionals are making themselves available for patient interviews.

PRICE SENSITIVITY

Patients are consumers and they expect prices to increase, including yours. However, they do not react positively to sudden or large increases in fees. This happens most often when the practice has held down fees for a long time and then increases fees suddenly, and by large amounts. This is easy to avoid by using more frequent, small increases.

VOLUME CONSIDERATION

Pay particular attention to volume when considering fee increases. A large increase in a fee that is infrequently performed or rarely repeated on the same patient will likely go unnoticed. Likewise, a small increase in your fees for frequent procedures will also be expected by most patients.

PROMOTIONAL PRICING

Fees for certain services and procedures may be used to attract new patients to your practice. Many practices offer "free" screenings, or reduced fees for physical exams, pap smears, and other preventive services. In today's more health conscious society, patients are very receptive to these new marketing techniques. In addition, you or your practice may have particular services, skills, methods, or special office hours, that are not offered elsewhere or close by. Patients do place special value on special services and abilities and are usually willing to pay more for them.

ANALYZING THE FINANCIAL HEALTH OF YOUR PRACTICE

How do you know how well your practice is doing? The following simple formulas can be used to determine how your practice measures up to national standards of performance.

NET CASH FLOW

The first formula is used to calculate your practice's cash flow. The formula looks like this:

Net Cash Flow = Total Payments ÷ Adjusted Charges × 100%

In order to make this calculation, you need the following data:

- Total Payments, year-to-date

- Total Charges, year-to-date

- Total Adjustments, year-to-date

The first step is to calculate what is called "Adjusted Charges". In almost any other business situation, if a bill is presented for $ 100, the payment will be $ 100. This is simply not the case with medical services. Due to Medicare fee limitations, Medicaid fee schedules, bad debt, courtesy and professional discounts, and various other write-offs, the collectible amount of the fee for any given service is significantly reduced.

Adjusted Charges = Total Charges - Total Adjustments

The second step is to divide your Total Payments by the Adjusted Charges as shown in the formula. The following example illustrates the calculation of net cash flow:

Total Payments, year-to-date	=	$ 425,000
Total Charges, year-to-date	=	$ 500,000
Total Adjustments, year-to-date	=	$ 50,000
Adjusted Charges = $500,000 - $50,000	=	$ 450,000

Following the concept discussed above, this means that of the $ 500,000 that was actually billed, $ 450,000 is actually collectible.

Net Cash Flow = $ 425,000 ÷ $ 450,000 × 100% = <u>94.44%</u>

While a Net Cash Flow of almost 95% may seem acceptable, the reality is that this practice just added $ 25,000 (all collectible) to its outstanding accounts receivable for the year. If this example is for only one quarter, and no corrective steps are taken, at the end of the year $ 100,000 in collectible revenues will be languishing in the accounts receivable.

NET CASH FLOW SHOULD BE 100.00%

Your objective is to maintain Net Cash Flow at 100% on a year-to-date basis. The only exception to this objective is for a newly formed practice or one experiencing new growth. The amount of time required to achieve Net Cash Flow of 100% varies with the types of patients you have. If you have a lot of worker's compensation or personal injury cases, it will take you a while longer to reach the 100% goal.

ACCOUNTS RECEIVABLE RATIO

The second formula is used to calculate your practice's accounts receivable ratio. The formula looks like this:

Accounts Receivable Ratio = Accounts Receivable ÷ Adjusted Charges

In order to make this calculation, you need the following data:

- Total Accounts Receivable

- Total Charges, current month

- Total Adjustments, current month

The first step is to calculate the Adjusted Charges as described above; however, for this formula you use monthly totals instead of year-to-date totals. The second step is to divide your Accounts Receivable by the Adjusted Charges as shown in the formula. The following example illustrates the calculation of Accounts Receivable Ratio:

Accounts Receivable   = $ 250,000

Total Charges, current month   = $ 100,000

Total Adjustments, current month   = $ 15,000

Adjusted Charges = $ 100,000 - $ 15,000   = $ 85,000

Accounts Receivable Ratio = $ 250,000 ÷ $ 85,000 = <u>2.94</u>

Accounts Receivable Ratio typically ranges between 2.5 and 3.5 for most medical practices. The ratio varies significantly by specialty and patient mix. Practices which are cash based, such as Plastic surgery and those which collect a lot of cash at the time of service will have much lower ratios, even as low as 0.5 to 1.0. Practices which have a lot of workers' compensation and/or personal injury cases will have a much higher than normal ratio, perhaps as high as 10 or 12. Another way to look at this formula is to convert the ratio to months or days. An Accounts Receivable Ratio of 3.0 translates into three months or 90 days. This means that your average account does not get cleared for three months or 90 days.

THE HARD FACTS REGARDING PAYMENT CYCLES

In the recent past, it was not unusual for medical practices to carry accounts for a long period of time, from several months to years. Long delays by Medicare, Medicaid, and other insurance carriers was the rule rather than the exception. This is no longer the case considering the following:

- As of October 1, 1989, HCFA regulations requires Medicare carriers to pay clean claims within 17 days for participating providers and within 24 days for non-participating providers, or pay interest.

- Medicaid carriers are generally required by state laws to process and pay clean claims within a specified period of time.

- Many states now have statutes requiring private insurance carriers to pay or deny clean claims within a specified period of time, typically 30 days, or pay interest.

- Worker's compensation laws typically contain a requirement to pay, deny or "acknowledge" a claim within a specified period of time, typically 60 days, or pay interest.

- Electronic claims processing, available for Medicare, most Medicaid, many Blue Cross and Blue Shield carriers, and the majority of the large health insurance carriers, can cut processing and payment cycles from weeks to days.

According to the Health Insurance Association of America, more than 70% of all private insurance claims are processed and paid within 30 days. The well-managed practice in the 1990s should be striving for Accounts Receivable Ratios of 1.5 to 2.00 or less, meaning that they are clearing their accounts within 45 to 60 days from the date of billing.

OPTIONS TO INCREASING YOUR FEES

INCREASE PRACTICE PRODUCTIVITY

This doesn't necessarily mean you have to work more, harder or longer. It means simply that you need to look at how you work in order to make sure you are using your time in the most profitable manner. You may need to implement a more formal scheduling and record keeping system for out-of-the-office services in order to keep track of your time better, and to make sure you are billing for all your services.

Maybe its time to bring in an associate to take care of those referrals you have been turning down. Or maybe you are considering extended office hours one evening during the week and Saturday mornings to meet the increasing demands of your patients for more convenient (to them) hours.

Make sure that the time you spend with each patient is appropriate for the level of care you need to provide. This means that you have to provide exactly the right amount of your time, from your perspective, in order to keep your schedule, and, the right amount of your time, from the patient's perspective, to provide the perception of value received.

REDUCE YOUR DISCOUNT BUSINESS

In spite of the continuous national furor over medical fees, the truth is, that with very few exceptions, all medical practices are operated as discount businesses. Some of the more typical types of discounts includes:

- Giving a discount for cash payment at the time of service

- Discounting your services as a professional courtesy

- Accepting insurance payment from a private carrier as payment in full

- Accepting payments on account without interest charges

- Referring accounts to a collection agency

- Writing off an account as a bad debt

- Accepting a capitation payment or discounted payment from an HMO, IPA or PPO.

- Participating in Medicare

- Providing services to Medicaid patients

The simple truth is that you can't accept less (payment) and spend more and still come out ahead. In fact, if you are not extremely careful in managing your discount business, you can find yourself out of business. Altruistic issues aside, you must be able to pay the bills if you want to continue in private practice.

You must take the time to review your practice by revenue sources in order to determine if the types of patients you are attracting and the associations you have with payors are profitable. This review process should include answering the following questions:

- Is Medicare participation in the best interest of my practice?

- Should I implement payment at the time of service?

- Are the contracts I have with HMOs and PPOs profitable?

- Do I have too many Medicaid patients?

- If I reduce my nonprofitable patient categories, can I replace them with profitable ones?

Finding the right answers to these questions for your practice requires an indepth evaluation of your practice economics, patient demographics, the potential patient pool, patient attitudes, and the attitudes, practices and standards of your medical community.

CONTROL PRACTICE COSTS

In addition to increasing profits by increasing revenues, you can also increase profits by controlling and/or reducing practice costs. For any medical practice, costs can be broken down into several basic components.

- Office space, including rent, utilities, etc.

- Non-medical supplies, including furniture

- Medical supplies

- Medical equipment

- Clerical labor, including secretaries, receptionists

- Ancillary (nonphysician) labor, including nurses, lab techs, etc.

- Billing and other management expenses

- Professional liability insurance

Actual expenditures for each of these cost components is under the practice's control. By carefully reviewing these expenditures on a regular basis, and making changes as appropriate, the practice can create a substantial positive impact on profits.

ADD NEW PROFIT CENTERS

Increase revenues by adding new services. These new services do not necessarily (but may) attract new patients. However; they provide more billing (and revenue) per patient visit. Some examples of services currently being provided by medical professionals as "value added" services include:

- Laboratory in office
- X-ray in office
- Weight loss program
- Smoke ending clinic
- Biofeedback
- Office surgery
- Optical dispensary
- Sports and
  Executive Physicals

- Physical therapy
- Dispensing medications
- Nutrition counseling
- Pain management
- Chemical dependency programs
- Hearing aids
- TENS
- Cosmetics

You can debate the ethics and professionalism of these services all you want. The issues here are strategic ones. Patients want these services and may be willing to pay more for these services. Patients prefer to obtain their services from a single provider however they will go elsewhere to obtain wanted services.

MERGERS AND ACQUISITIONS

Merge with another practice. Don't overlook opportunities to acquire good practices from colleagues who are retiring or leaving the area. In addition to expanding your own practice, you will be keeping competitors out of your patient market.

DESIGNING
A BETTER
SUPERBILL

CHAPTER SUMMARY

Whether you call it a Superbill, Charge Ticket, Encounter Form, Visit Slip or whatever, this document is one of the most important when it comes to the billing and coding process. Simply put, a well designed superbill can make a significant difference, positively or negatively, on your reimbursement. The Superbill has been used extensively for the past five to ten years as a substitute for filing insurance claim forms. Even though the current trend is to file claim forms for your patients, you will always need an accurate method of recording the services and procedures you provide.

As of October 1, 1990, new HCFA regulations required that you file HCFA1500 insurance claim forms for all Medicare patients, regardless of your participation status. As of April 1, 1992, Medicare carriers will no longer accept superbills attached to HCFA1500 forms. However, the basic purpose for the superbill is to record, for billing and statistical purposes, the services or procedures performed, the reason(s) for the services, and the fee for each service. In addition, the superbill may be used to record recall and next appointment information, may include a release and assignment statement, and may include patient balance and payment information. This chapter discusses the fundamentals of good superbill design and provides sample superbills for several common medical specialties which can be used as is or modified for your practice.

KEY POINTS REGARDING SUPERBILLS

1.   All medical professionals should use a superbill recording services and procedures, even if they don't use it for billing.

2.   Superbills should include the most common CPT & ICD-9-CM codes used by the practice.

3.   Superbills must have a method to link ICD-9-CM codes to CPT codes in order to comply with Medicare coding requirements.

4.   A well designed superbill can replace several other forms, such as release and assignment, next appointment and receipt.

5.   Fees should never be printed on your superbills.

6.   Due to the frequency and volume of coding changes, you should never print more than a six month supply of forms at a time.

7.   You may not use superbills for Medicare claims after April 1, 1992.

8.   A welldesigned superbill can make a significant difference in your reimbursement.

9.   A welldesigned superbill puts you in control of the reimbursement process.

HCFA ELIMINATES SUPERBILLS FOR MEDICARE

Effective April 1, 1992, Medicare carriers will no longer accept superbills. These are claims submitted with attachments instead of actually completing the HCFA1500 claim form. From April 1, 1992 on, Medicare carriers will accept attachments only for information that cannot be readily entered in designated blocks on the HCFA1500 insurance claim form. These attachments include medical evidence, certifications of medical necessity, and/or other attachments required by law, regulation or by instruction from HCFA.

HCFA is making this change to eliminate costly and inefficient claims processing by Medicare carriers. As of this writing, between 8 and 10 percent of Medicare claims nationwide include superbills. In addition to saving time by standardization, HCFA notes that considerable savings will be achieved due to the elimination of current burdens such as removing staples, batching superbills, microfilming, manual sorting and increased storage, retrieval and document reproduction costs.

It is important to understand that even though you are no longer able to use a superbill to bill Medicare, you still need one to keep track of the services you render.

THE FUNDAMENTALS OF GOOD SUPERBILL DESIGN

DATA ELEMENTS

The basic data elements required on any superbill can be grouped into five general categories:

1.   Practice information

2.   Patient information

3.   Procedures

4.   Diagnoses

5.   Other information

PRACTICE INFORMATION

All superbills or fee tickets should have the following practice information:

*   Practice or physician's name

*   Complete mailing address

*   Telephone Number(s)

*   State license number

*   Federal Employer Identification No. (FEIN), or Social Security No. (SSN)

*   Medicare Group No. (optional depending on group status)

PATIENT INFORMATION

Designing the patient information portion of your superbill properly is dependent on whether or not you use a separate patient registration form. The decision to use a separate patient registration form is usually dependent on whether or not your patients are long-term instead of single visit patients. Examples of single visit situations would be laboratory, radiology, emergency room, and most consulting practices.

REQUIRED PATIENT INFORMATION

All superbills should have the following data elements in the patient information section:

*   Date of service

*   Patient name

- Location of service

- Patient account number

- Practice name, address and telephone number(s)

- Provider's Medicare, Federal Employer Identification Number (FEIN) and state license number

Practices using an inclusive superbill (includes patient registration) would need to add additional data elements to capture all information needed for billing the patient, billing the insurance carrier, and any clinical or financial follow-up activity. These elements include:

- Patient's and/or responsible party's complete address

- Patient's and/or responsible party's home and work telephone numbers

- Responsible party's name, and address if different from patient

- Primary insurance carrier

> Name
> Billing Address
> Member & Group numbers

- Secondary insurance carrier

> Name
> Billing address
> Member & Group numbers

The design of the patient information portion of your superbill will depend on whether or not you have repetitive patients. Take a look at the examples on the facing page to see how you might design this portion if you need an inclusive superbill, which combines patient registration and billing information, or more of a fee ticket form, which identifies a patient for which registration information already exists.

Note the addition of a box to indicate time on the second example. As time is a component of the Evaluation and Management codes first published in the 1992 edition of CPT, we feel that it is important to carefully document the amount of time spent providing a service or performing a procedure. It is also important that face-to-face or unit/floor time be documented in the medical record.

PROCEDURES

When designing your superbill the objective is not to list every procedure that you have ever done or will ever do. What you want on your superbill are the procedures that you do most often, which cover 90-95% of everything you do. Most practices will list basic office visits, basic hospital visits, consultations, some laboratory, some radiology along with the special procedures and services performed by their particular specialty. For most practices, 50-75 procedure listings is sufficient. In a multi-specialty environment, you may need a SUPERBILL for each specialty instead of one for the entire group.

OFFICE VISITS/EVALUATION AND MANAGEMENT

Essentially all medical professionals provide office visits. Even hospital based physicians see patients on an outpatient basis. It is important that you include a full range of codes from this section of CPT on your SUPERBILL. Many professionals put only a few codes, for example brief, intermediate and comprehensive from this section on their SUPERBILL in order to allow space for other procedure codes. This creates a problem because all office visits do not neatly fit one of the three categories provided. However, rather than write in the proper code or description, most professionals will choose one of the listed codes. This creates three potential problems:

1)   By limiting the choice of codes, in some cases the medical professional will be UP CODING the procedure to one of a higher value and in other cases will be DOWN CODING the procedure to one of a lesser value. If you are charging your usual fees for the selected codes, this means that some patients are being overcharged and others are being undercharged even if the net effect to you is zero.

2)   If you are adjusting your fees up and down but not coding appropriately, you are creating havoc with your provider profiles, which may take years to correct.

3)   You may be setting yourself up for an audit based on post-payment review. Medicare as well as private carriers perform statistical analysis of code usage and frequency. They know that all office visits can not be neatly categorized into only a few codes.

TWO SETS OF CODES

Until most insurance carriers have converted to the new Evaluation and Management codes, you will have to include both Visit codes and Evaluation and Management codes on your superbill. The Evaluation and Management codes are used for Medicare patients, and the Visit codes are used for all other carriers. This transition period may last up to a year or more.

MINIMAL SERVICE

All SUPERBILLS should include CPT Visit code 90030 and Evaluation and Management code 99211, defined as "minimal" service. This code is used to record and bill services such as blood pressure checks, suture removal and in addition to routine immunization codes if no other office visit code is used. This code may be used to bill for physician services as well as those provided under the supervision of the physician.

HOSPITAL AND OTHER OUT-OF-OFFICE MEDICAL SERVICES

Unless your practice never or rarely performs hospital visits, you will need a section for these services on your basic SUPERBILL or a separate method of recording hospital and other out-of-office services. The same concerns regarding range of codes and levels of care as described above apply to hospital services as well. Out-of-office services is one of the most frequent areas of poor reimbursement management. Our experience, supplemented by that of most medical management consultants, is that many medical professionals lose significant billable charges by poor record keeping for these services. Various methods used include memory, little scraps of paper, miniature fee tickets, 3 x 5 cards, etc. While the format is important, the most important issue is that you have a system which prevents lost charges. See the sample superbills at the end of this chapter for an example of a method for capturing your out-of-office charges.

CONSULTATIONS

Most medical practices perform consultations, some more frequently than others. The more specialized the practice, the more consultations are performed. Some practices are totally consultative in nature. If you are performing consultations more than occasionally, you need to include a full range of consultation codes from the Visit codes 90600-90654 and the Evaluation and Management codes 99241-99263 on your SUPERBILL. It is also important that you include a space to record the name of the physician who requested the consultation. For Medicare you will also need the license number of the physician who requested the consultation.

OFFICE PROCEDURES

Most medical professionals provide a variety of office procedures to patients either as part of the office services or in addition to office services. In order to record and bill these services properly, the most frequently performed office procedures should be included on your SUPERBILL.

IMMUNIZATIONS & THERAPEUTIC INJECTIONS

Therapeutic injections are among the most frequently performed office medical procedures. In addition to including CPT code 90782, Therapeutic or diagnostic injection, which you would use to record and bill this service to private insurance carriers, you should also list HCPCS codes for frequently performed therapeutic injections provided to Medicare beneficiaries. HCPCS codes must be used to bill these services to Medicare. Listing them on your SUPERBILL will reduce the amount of time required to process the codes for billing and will reduce the chance of choosing the incorrect code(s). Frequently performed immunizations should be listed on your SUPERBILL. Remember to include HCPCS codes when appropriate.

90701   Immunization; DTP
90702   Immunization; DT
90703   Immunization; Tetanus Toxoid

DIAGNOSTIC PROCEDURES

Many primary care practice provide diagnostic medical, radiology and laboratory procedures in addition to basic medical services. In addition, there are specific CPT codes for special diagnostic procedures performed by specialists as well. All frequently performed diagnostic services should be included on your SUPERBILL, however, remember that OBRA 1987 placed severe restrictions on global billing of certain diagnostic tests provided to Medicare beneficiaries as of March 1988. Unless you are providing the global service, or the professional component (modifier -26), you should not bill these services to Medicare patients.

93000	Electrocardiogram	85031	CBC
94010	Spirometry	88150	PAP Smear
71020	X-ray, chest, two views	80019	Lab Panel
81000	Urinalysis		

MISCELLANEOUS SERVICES

If you frequently provide services defined in this section of CPT (99000-99090), include selected codes from this section on your SUPERBILL. Commonly used miscellaneous service codes include:

99000   Handling and/or conveyance of specimen

99024   Postoperative follow-up visit, included in global service

99025   Initial (new) patient visit when starred (*) surgical procedure constitutes major service at that visit

99050   Services requested after office hours in addition to basic service

99052   Services requested between 10:00 p.m. and 8:00 a.m. in addition to basic service

90054   Services requested on Sundays and holidays in addition to basic service

99058   Office services provided on an emergency basis

99070   Supplies and materials provided by the physician over and above those usually included with the office visit or other services rendered

As we discussed in the chapter on CPT coding, CPT provides 28 specific codes for recording and billing supplies and materials provided by the physician. However, most of the supplies and materials used by physicians that are not included in the definition of the basic service, would be classified to a single CPT code, namely 99070.

All SUPERBILLS should include the code 99070 with a space to identify the specific supply or material provided. This code is used to bill private insurance carriers. In addition, frequently used HCPCS codes for supplies and/or materials such as catheter sets, sterile/surgical trays, etc., which must be used to bill Medicare, should be included if you have any significant Medicare volume.

AN IMPORTANT NOTE ABOUT TELEPHONE CALLS

Many private insurance carriers will reimburse telephone calls made to, received from, or about patients. Medicare will not due to the [Medicare] rule that you must be able to visualize the patient in order to charge for a service. Reading x-rays, interpreting lab reports and EKGs are considered visualization. In today's litigious environment, perhaps a more important issue regarding telephone calls is to make sure that you document all of your calls to protect yourself legally. While many practices have specific telephone call logging policies and procedures in the office, many have no such system for recording and filing calls made after hours and on weekends. Consider a situation in which you give a patient specific instructions during an after hours call, the patient misunderstood or ignored your instructions with fatal results, and the patient's spouse sues you for malpractice.

What if you can't prove that you made or returned the call? What if you can't provide documentation which not only proves you made the call, but has notes regarding specific complaints and your recommendations? Many practices now use special forms for recording after hours visits and telephone calls. The sample form below is an example of one possible solution to this problem:

DOCTORS ON-CALL RECORD	DATE			TIME	A M P M	PHONE				LEVEL OF CARE						
	DR						☐ CALL	☐ VISIT		NO CHARGE	ADMIT / DC	BRIEF	LIMITED	INTERMED.	EXTENDED	COMPREN.
PATIENT																
ADDRESS																
LOCATION / PHARMACY						PHONE										
PROBLEMS SYMPTOMS COMPLAINTS																
INSTRUCTIONS PRESCRIPTION PROCEDURE																

☐ NEW PATIENT   ☐ BILL   FeeSaver 1990 PMI

FEE

SURGICAL PROCEDURES

Surgical procedure codes may be used by any physician, not only by those classified as surgeons. All frequently performed surgical procedure codes should be listed on your SUPERBILL. Starred procedures should be identified as such by placing the star (*) to the right of the procedure code on the SUPERBILL. This alerts the physician that there are coding options for any office medical services provided in addition to the surgical procedure. See the **SURGERY** section of **Procedure Coding with CPT** for a complete discussion of starred procedures.

PROCEDURE MODIFIERS

If your practice tends to properly use modifiers frequently, you should leave a column next to the procedure code for entering modifiers when appropriate. If your practice uses modifiers infrequently, leave a modifier section under your "unlisted procedure" space and use this when you need to record a modifier.

QUICK CODES

Many practices use what we call QUICK codes instead of CPT or HCPCS codes. These codes may be either alpha, numeric or alphanumeric. Many practices which use a ledger card system use alphabetic codes such as **OV** for Office Visit or **HV** for Hospital Visit when posting their ledgers. While this may be simple, easy to remember, and acceptable to patients receiving your bills, this coding system can not be used for insurance billing and typically does not distinguish levels of care.

Many computer systems allow the use of QUICK codes instead of CPT codes for input. Most provide a means of cross-referencing the input code to a CPT or HCPCS code. The QUICK code is what you enter into the computer and the cross-reference CPT or HCPCS code is what is printed on the insurance claim form. Another use for this type of QUICK code is as "administrative codes" to annotate the computer history with commonly used notes or comments, such as "insurance claim filed" or "sent to collection".

Examples of how a practice might assign QUICK codes:

CODE	DESCRIPTION	CPT/HCPCS
1	Office visit, intermediate	90060
2	Hospital visit, intermediate	90260
3	Electrocardiogram	93000
50	Immunization, tetanus toxoid	90703
51	Immunization, tetanus toxoid (Medicare)	J3180
90	Insurance claim filed	*****
99	Sent to collection	*****

While there is no question that QUICK codes can be input faster than CPT codes, there are potential problems which can develop if these codes are not carefully managed. The most obvious problem occurs due to the fact that CPT codes are revised every year. If your QUICK codes are not carefully reviewed and revised as soon as the new CPT is available, you may create a reimbursement problem which may take some time to discover and correct.

The second problem with QUICK codes is based on the fact that it is easier to make up a QUICK code, than to look up and choose the correct CPT or HCPCS code. If you are not carefully reviewing and managing the assignment of QUICK codes you may find yourself billing insurance carriers with procedures codes that do not exist, causing unnecessary delays, denials and rejections.

The use of QUICK codes for administrative purposes may be helpful to the practice following considerations: 1) the capacity of your computer system (or that of your billing service) must accommodate the use of these codes (which will dramatically increase the volume of stored data), and 2) you MUST have the ability to suppress these codes from insurance claim forms and/or patient statements.

TYPICAL PROCEDURES SECTION DESIGN

□ NEW PATIENT	□ ASSIGNED?	DX #1		DX #2		DX #3		DX #4	

✓	CODE	DESCRIPTION	DX	FEE	✓	CODE	DESCRIPTION	DX	FEE	✓	CODE	DESCRIPTION	DX	FEE
	OFFICE VISITS NEW PATIENT	E/M				INJECTIONS AND IMMUNIZATIONS					LABORATORY (Cont'd)			
	90000	Brief 99201				90702	Immunization; DT				84295	Blood Sodium		
	90010	Limited 99202				90703	Immunization; Tetanus Toxoid				84450	SGOT		
	90015	Intermediate 99203				90724	Immunization; Influenza				84460	SGPT		
	90017	Extended 99204				90782	Injection, IM/SQ				84478	Blood Triglycerides		
	90020	Comprehensive 99205				90784	Injection, IV				85014	Hematocrit		
	OFFICE VISITS ESTABLISHED PATIENT					90788	Injection, Antibiotic				85022	Automated Hemogram		
	90030	Minimal 99211									85031	Manual Hemogram		
	90040	Brief 99212									85048	White Blood Cell Count		
	90050	Limited 99213									85580	Blood Platelet Count		
	90060	Intermediate 99214				RADIOLOGY					85610	Prothrombin Time		
	90070	Extended 99215				71010	X-Ray Exam Chest				85651	RBC Sedimentation Rate		
	90080	Comprehensive				71020	X-Ray Exam Chest				86585	Skin Test, TB		
	CONSULTATIONS INITIAL										87060	Culture, Throat or Nose		
	90605	Intermediate 99242												
	90610	Extended 99243												
	90620	Comprehensive 99244				LABORATORY								
						80019	Lab Panel 19+ Tests				SUPPLIES			
						80052	Premarital Profile				99070	Supplies & Materials		
						80070	Thyroid Panel							
	PROCEDURES					80072	Arthritis Panel							
	10060*	Drain Skin Lesion				80060	Hypertension Panel				MISCELLANEOUS			
	20550*	Injection, Tendon Sheath				80061	Lipid Profile				99361	Med Conference, 30 Min		
	36415*	Routine Venipuncture				81000	Urinalysis				99362	Med Conference, 60 Min		
	45330	Sigmoidoscopy				82270	Stool for Occult Blood				99371	Telephone Call, Brief		
	93000	EKG Complete				82310	Calcium				99372	Telephone Call, Intermediate		
	93040	Rhythm EKG with Report				82465	Serum Cholesterol				99000	Specimen Handling		
	94010	Spirometry Complete				82565	Blood Creatinine				99080	Special Reports		
						82643	Ria for Digoxin							
						82951	Glucose Tolerance Test							
						83718	Blood Lipoprotein							
						84075	Alkaline Phosphatase							
	UNLISTED PROCEDURE	CODE		DESCRIPTION									FEE	

Note that this sample has a special row at the bottom of the procedures section, with plenty of space, to write in and code any procedures or services which are not listed on the form.

DIAGNOSIS CODES & DESCRIPTIONS

The tendency in the past has been to simply leave a few lines somewhere on the bottom of the superbill to write in a diagnostic statement; however, that is no longer sufficient. You need to provide a space on your superbill to record up to four diagnosis CODES using the ICD-9-CM coding system. Take a look a the same superbills to see how we recommend placing the four ICD-9-CM codes on your superbill. It really doesn't matter where you put the codes, only that they are there, that they are numbered and that you can link the procedure to the diagnosis.

The problem is providing a ready reference to the codes that go in the boxes. There are over 19,000 ICD-9-CM codes, however; most practices use from a few dozen to one hundred codes within a year. The number of codes used usually corresponds to how specialized the practice is. For example, a pediatric cardiology practice would use fewer codes than an internal medicine practice.

While there is no problem listing from 50 to 100 ICD-9-CM codes and descriptions on your superbill using the format of our sample superbill, there is a problem with listing any more than that. You also do not want to be in a situation of having to look up the code from the ICD-9-CM book every time you see a patient. As with procedures, the idea is to list the most common diagnosis codes that would cover 90-95% of the patients seen. If you can not fit all of your ICD-9-CM codes on the front of your superbill, then you have two options:

1)   Print several hundred ICD-9-CM codes and descriptions on the back of your superbill. The downside of this is that printing both sides of a form costs more than printing only one side, but the time saved and coding accuracy obtained will more than justify the additional expense.

2)   Print a list of several hundred ICD-9-CM codes and descriptions on reference lists which you keep on your desk in a binder or document protectors. Use the reference list to code from.

Below is an example of a superbill which can have up to 120 ICD-9-CM codes printed on the front. The codes applicable to the patient's visit or services should either be numbered 1, 2, 3 and 4 or should be written into a linking field as illustrated immediately following.

Note that this sample has a special row at the bottom of the diagnosis section, with plenty of space, to write in and code any diagnoses which are not listed on the form.

LINKING DIAGNOSIS TO PROCEDURES

To comply with the new Medicare regulations, your superbill must have a means for you to link the procedures and services to specific diagnosis codes. It is not acceptable to simply write out diagnostic statements somewhere on your superbill. The best way to do this is to leave a column next to your procedure code titled "DX" or "ICD" that you may use to record the "link number" of the diagnosis which corresponds to the procedure or service.

INTERNAL MEDICINE GROUP   **4186**
4727 Wilshire Boulevard
Los Angeles, CA 90010
(708) 920-0700
LICENSE: P12345
FEIN: 95-4210732

DATE OF SERVICE	ACCOUNT NUMBER
03	22	92 4372	

ACCOUNT NAME (LAST, FIRST)
HEARNE, ALAN

TIME   12"

☐ NEW PATIENT   ☐ ASSIGNED?

DX #1	DX #2	DX #3	DX #4
599.0			

✓	CODE	DESCRIPTION	DX	FEE	✓	CODE	DESCRIPTION	DX	FEE	✓	CODE	DESCRIPTION	DX	FEE
	OFFICE VISITS NEW PATIENT		E/M			INJECTIONS AND IMMUNIZATIONS					LABORATORY (Cont'd)			
	90000	Brief	99201			90702	Immunization; DT				84295	Blood Sodium		
	90010	Limited	99202			90703	Immunization; Tetanus Toxoid				84450	SGOT		
	90015	Intermediate	99203			90724	Immunization; Influenza				84460	SGPT		
	90017	Extended	99204			90782	Injection, IM/SQ				84478	Blood Triglycerides		
	90020	Comprehensive	99205			90784	Injection, IV				85014	Hematocrit		
	OFFICE VISITS ESTABLISHED PATIENT					90788	Injection, Antibiotic				85022	Automated Hemogram		
	90030	Minimal	99211								85031	Manual Hemogram		
X	90040	Brief	99212	1	45						85048	White Blood Cell Count		
	90050	Limited	99213								85580	Blood Platelet Count		
	90060	Intermediate	99214			RADIOLOGY					85610	Prothrombin Time		
	90070	Extended	99215			71010	X-Ray Exam Chest				85651	RBC Sedimentation Rate		
	90080	Comprehensive				71020	X-Ray Exam Chest				86585	Skin Test, TB		
	CONSULTATIONS INITIAL										87060	Culture, Throat or Nose		
	90605	Intermediate	99242											
	90610	Extended	99243											
	90620	Comprehensive	99244			LABORATORY								
						80019	Lab Panel 19+ Tests				SUPPLIES			
						80052	Premarital Profile				99070	Supplies & Materials		
						80070	Thyroid Panel							
	PROCEDURES					80072	Arthritis Panel							
	10060*	Drain Skin Lesion				80060	Hypertension Panel				MISCELLANEOUS			
	20550*	Injection, Tendon Sheath				80061	Lipid Profile				99361	Med Conference, 30 Min		
	36415*	Routine Venipuncture			X	81000	Urinalysis	1	18		99362	Med Conference, 60 Min		
	45330	Sigmoidoscopy				82270	Stool for Occult Blood				99371	Telephone Call, Brief		
	93000	EKG Complete				82310	Calcium				99372	Telephone Call, Intermediate		
	93040	Rhythm EKG with Report				82465	Serum Cholesterol				99000	Specimen Handling		
	94010	Spirometry Complete				82565	Blood Creatinine				99080	Special Reports		
						82643	Ria for Digoxin							
						82951	Glucose Tolerance Test							
						83718	Blood Lipoprotein							
						84075	Alkaline Phosphatase							

UNLISTED PROCEDURE	CODE	DESCRIPTION	FEE

The above example illustrates an effective means of linking diagnosis codes with procedures.

OTHER INFORMATION

In addition to the essential items mentioned above, many practices add other items to their superbill which may be useful. Some of the other items commonly found on superbills include:

RELEASE AND ASSIGNMENT

Printing a release and assignment statement on your superbill is highly recommended, particularly for the single visit type of practice, unless you are using a lifetime release and assignment form. Printing the release and assignment on your superbill eliminates one form, however, it is very important that you instruct, encourage and observe the patient signing the release and assignment portion before they leave your office, unless you collected payment at the time of service.

RECALL AND/OR NEXT APPOINTMENT

Providing a space on your superbill to indicate recall in days, weeks months can encourage the patient recall process. In addition, having a space to indicate the patient's next appointment eliminates one more form or piece of paper and reduces forgotten appointments and no-shows.

ACCOUNTING INFORMATION

All superbills or fee tickets, even those used only internally, should have a space to record prior balance, today's charges, payments received today and new balance. For practices which collect payment at the time of service, this portion of the superbill serves as your statement, invoice and receipt. Several studies have indicated that patients are sometimes embarrassed for the doctor to know that they owe him/her money, so they will take care of the previous balance to avoid this situation.

For practices which use the form for computer input, this accounting information is used for batch control purposes, for example balancing your computer input. By carefully considering the specific needs of your practice and your patients, you can design a superbill which combines, and therefore eliminates, other forms and duplication of effort. For example, your superbill could contain all of the above elements, combining a patient registration, charge slip, release and assignment form, recall form and function as a receipt as well. The following example shows how the bottom, or other information portion of a superbill might be designed.

☐ Asthma w/o status 493.90	☐ Convulsions, seizures 780.3	☐ Hematuria benign ess 599.7	☐ Lymphomas NEC 202.8	☐ Peptic ulcer unsp 533.9	☐ Thyrotoxicosis NOS 242.9
☐ Atherosclerosis gen 440.9	☐ Cough 786.2	☐ Hemiplegia 342.9	☐ Malaise & fatigue 780.7	☐ Periph vasc dis unsp 443.9	☐ Trans cereb isch unsp 435.9
☐ Atrial fibrillation 427.31	☐ Cystitis unsp 595.9	☐ Hemorr GI tract unsp 578.9	☐ Melena blood in stool 587.1	☐ Pernicious anemia 281.0	☐ Unsp septicemia 038.9
☐ Atrial flutter 427.32	☐ Dehydration 276.5	☐ Hemorr rectum & anus 569.3	☐ Mitral valve disord 424.0	☐ Pharyngitis acute 462	☐ Unsp sinusitis chr 473.9
☐ backache unsp 724.5	☐ Depress disord NEC 311	☐ Hemorrhoids unsp 455.6	☐ Mixed hyperlipid 272.2	☐ Phlebitis unsp 451.9	☐ Urinary tract infection 599.0
☐ B hypertensive hrt dis 402.1	☐ Diabetes w/comp NOS 250.00	☐ Herpes zoster 053.9	☐ Myalgia unsp 729.1	☐ Pleurisy unsp 511.9	

UNLISTED DIAGNOSIS	CODE	DESCRIPTION
REMARKS OR INSTRUCTIONS		

RELEASE & ASSIGNMENT	RECALL & RETURN	ACCOUNTING INFORMATION	
I authorize release of any information necessary to process my insurance claim and assign and request payment directly to my physicians.	RETURN ☐ DAYS ☐ WEEKS ☐ MONTHS	PRIOR BALANCE	
		TODAY'S CHARGES	
SIGNED DATE	NEXT APPOINTMENT	TOTAL DUE	
	DATE _____ TIME _____ AM PM	AMOUNT PAID	
_____		NEW BALANCE	

© 1992 PMIC   REV. 01/92

FORMAT AND DESIGN ISSUES

FORMAT

The most typical format is a superbill that is divided into the four basic sections previously described, namely: patient identification, procedure codes, diagnoses codes and supplemental information. The sample superbill on the facing page illustrates a design that includes these four basic sections, however, there are a variety of potential design formats which may be used.

When choosing a format, you should design a form which matches the specific needs of your practice. Practice characteristics which may need special design consideration include:

• Practices with a lot of procedure codes and few diagnosis codes

• Practices with a lot of diagnosis codes and few procedure codes

• Practices with a lot of procedure codes and a lot of diagnosis codes

The first two problems can be solved by simply reallocating columns and spaces appropriately. The third situation may require a longer form [standard multi-part forms can be obtained up to 14 inches long] or may require that you print the diagnosis codes on the back of the form.

SUPERBILL DESIGN FORMATS

The three most common superbill formats, illustrated below, include:

Standard Format In this format there are typically three vertical spaces of identical size for procedures and one horizontal space for diagnosis codes. The diagnosis section is typically typeset in a smaller font (type size) than the procedures so that more codes can be listed.

Procedures Dominant In this format there are typically two vertical spaces extending from the "patient information" section to the "other information" section for procedures, and a third vertical space of the same size divided between procedures and diagnosis codes.

Diagnosis Dominant In this format there is typically only one vertical space for procedures and either two vertical spaces or one large vertical space for diagnosis codes.

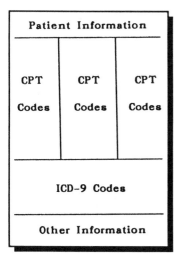
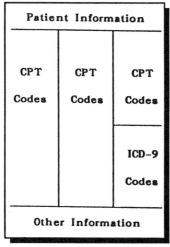
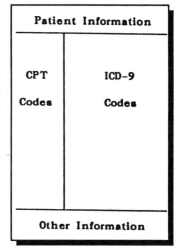

Standard Format   Procedures Dominant   Diagnoses Dominant

SIZE

Most superbills are printed on 8 1/2 x 11 inch (letter size) paper. Common variations include 8 1/2 by 14 (legal size) and 8 1/2 x 7 inch. The larger sizes are used most frequently simply because they have more space to record information and list procedures and diagnoses plus they are easier to file.

NUMBER OF COPIES

You need to consider how many "parts" your superbill will have based on the specific needs of your practice. The most common option is a two-part form, with three-part and one-part being the second and third most common. For multi-part forms, such as two-part and three-part, you should always use carbonless copies. This type of stock is commonly known as "NCR" and printers carry it in standard color combinations. Two-part is typically white (first copy) and yellow (second copy), while three-part is typically white (first copy), yellow (second copy) and green (third copy).

You can also get multi-copy forms in any specified color, with all copies white, or with any sequence of color copies you want. Keep in mind that "standard" color sequences are stock items for the printer. Non-standard sequences means the printer has to print the colored copies individually and then re-sequence them to your specifications, which means more cost for you. The single copy superbill is used when the practice does its own billing in-house and always bills insurance for their patients. There is no need for a second copy to give the patient or any other outside entity such as a computer service bureau.

SUPERBILL CONTROL NUMBERS

All superbills should be imprinted with a control number sequence that you specify. Strict supervision of the superbills and control numbers should be maintained. The purpose of the control number is to make sure that you account for every superbill issued, whether it is used or not. A "lost" superbill could be a patient who did not show up, or services totalling thousands of dollars that are under a pile of papers on someone's desk! Medical practices lose millions of billable charges every year simply because they do not account for all of their superbills.

CHOICE OF CODING SYSTEMS

In our opinion, you should use standard coding systems on your superbill instead of office or QUICK codes as previously discussed. This eliminates the need for multiple code columns and reduces the possibility of coding problems when using the superbill for insurance claims. Procedure codes should be CPT and HCPCS and diagnosis codes should be ICD-9- CM.

TERMINOLOGY

Procedure and diagnostic terminology are important. Due to the space limitations you will have to reduce the number of characters which describe each procedure or diagnosis. This is another good reason to use CPT and ICD-9-CM codes. The codes have a universal definition, based upon the CPT and ICD-9-CM publications. In the chapter **Procedure Coding with CPT & HCPCS**, we suggested that you should eliminate procedure descriptions from your insurance claims in order to prevent insurance carriers from "down-coding" your claim. Due to the fact that your patient does not understand or have the ability to interpret the codes on your form, you can not do this on your superbill. What you can do however, only if you are submitting insurance claims for all patients and all services, is to print patient oriented descriptions on your superbill instead of precise medical terminology. This will minimize patient questions and complaints about what services were provided.

SAMPLE SUPERBILLS

On the following pages you will find examples of superbills for several medical specialties. While the codes have been carefully reviewed prior to publication, due to the fact that CPT, HCPCS and ICD-9-CM codes are reviewed on an annual basis, the reader should verify codes in the most current editions of these publications before using the sample superbills.

CARDIOLOGY

DATE OF SERVICE	ACCOUNT NUMBER		**CARDIOLOGY MEDICAL GROUP**	**1186**
			4727 Wilshire Boulevard	
ACCOUNT NAME (LAST, FIRST)			Los Angeles, CA 90010	
			(708) 920-0700	TIME
			LICENSE: P12345	
			FEIN: 95-4210732	

☐ NEW PATIENT ☐ ASSIGNED?	DX #1	DX #2	DX #3	DX #4

✓	CODE	DESCRIPTION	DX	FEE	✓	CODE	DESCRIPTION	DX	FEE	✓	CODE	DESCRIPTION	DX	FEE
	OFFICE VISITS NEW PATIENT	E/M				PROCEDURES (Cont'd)					LABORATORY (Cont'd)			
	90000	Brief	99201			93501	Right Heart Cath				83718	Blood Lipoprotein		
	90010	Limited	99202			93503	Insert Heart Catheter				84075	Alkaline Phosphatase		
	90015	Intermediate	99203			93547	Heart Cath & Angiogram				84295	Blood Sodium		
	90017	Extended	99204			93798	Cardiac Rehab/Monitor				84450	SGOT		
	90020	Comprehensive	99205			94010	Spirometry Complete				84460	SGPT		
	OFFICE VISITS ESTABLISHED PATIENT										84478	Blood Triglycerides		
	90030	Minimal	99211								85022	Automated Hemogram		
	90040	Brief	99212								85031	Manual Hemogram		
	90050	Limited	99213			INJECTIONS AND IMMUNIZATIONS					85580	Blood Platelet Count		
	90060	Intermediate	99214			90782	Injection, IM/SQ				85610	Prothrombin Time		
	90070	Extended	99215			90784	Injection, IV				85651	RBC Sedimentation Rate		
	90080	Comprehensive				90788	Injection, Antibiotic							
	CONSULTATIONS INITIAL													
	90605	Intermediate	99242								SUPPLIES			
	90610	Extended	99243								99070	Supplies & Material		
	90620	Comprehensive	99244			RADIOLOGY								
	90630	Complex	99245			71010	X-Ray Chest One View							
						71020	X-Ray Exam Two Views							
											MISCELLANEOUS			
	PROCEDURES										99361	Med Conference, 30 Min		
	93000	EKG Complete				LABORATORY					99362	Med Conference, 60 Min		
	93010	EKG Report				80019	Lab Panel 19+ Tests				99371	Telephone Call, Brief		
	93015	Cardiovascular Stress Test				80060	Hypertension Panel				99372	Telephone Call, Intermediate		
	93040	Rhythm EKG with Report				80061	Lipid Profile				99000	Specimen Handling		
	93042	Rhythm EKG Report				80062	Cardiac Evaluation Panel				99080	Special Reports		
	93224	ECG Monitor/Report 24 Hrs				80073	Renal Panel							
	93230	ECG Monitor/Report 24 Hrs				81000	Urinalysis							
	93235	ECG Monitor/Report 24 Hrs				82465	Serum Cholesterol							
	93307	Echo Exam of Heart				82565	Blood Creatinine							
	93320	Doppler Echo Exam, Heart				82643	Ria for Digoxin							

UNLISTED PROCEDURE	CODE	DESCRIPTION				FEE

DIAGNOSIS	ICD-9 CM					
☐ Abd.aortic aneurysma	441.4	☐ Cardiac arrest	427.5	☐ Diabetes uncomp adult	250.00	☐ Hypoglycemia NOS 251.2

☐ Cardiac dysrhythm NEC 427.8 · ☐ Dizziness and giddiness 780.4 · ☐ Hypopotassemia 276.8 · ☐ Observ cardiovasc dis V71.7 · ☐ Respiratory arrest 799.1
☐ Abnormal EKG 794.31 · ☐ Cardiac murmurs NEC 785.2 · ☐ Edema 782.3 · ☐ Hposmolality 276.1 · ☐ Observ for unsp cond V71.9 · ☐ Respiratory failure 518.81
☐ Acute bronchitis 466.0 · ☐ Cardiac pacemaker stat V45.0 · ☐ Edema lung, acute unsp 518.4 · ☐ Hypotension unsp 458.9 · ☐ Retention urine 788.2
☐ Acute renal fail NOS 584.9 · ☐ Cardiogenic shock 785.51 · ☐ Emphysema other 492.8 · ☐ Hypothyroidism unsp 244.9 · ☐ Oth unsp comp care 999.9 · ☐ Rhythm disorders 427.89
☐ Acute URI NOS 465.9 · ☐ Cardiomegaly 429.3 · ☐ Esophagitis 530.1 · ☐ Intermed cor synd 411.1 · ☐ Pacemaker malfunct 996.01 · ☐ Screen-cardiovas NEC V81.2
☐ Acute MI ant wall NEC 410.1 · ☐ Cardiomyopathies 425.4 · ☐ Heart block oth 426.6 · ☐ Isch heart dis acute 411.0 · ☐ Painful respiration 786.52 · ☐ Sinoatrial node dys 427.81
☐ Acute MI inf wall NEC 410.4 · ☐ Carotid artery 433.1 · ☐ Heart dis unsp 429.9 · ☐ Isch heart dis unsp chr 414.9 · ☐ Palpitations 785.1 · ☐ Subendocard infarct 410.7
☐ Anemia unspec 285.9 · ☐ Cerebral art occ unsp 434.9 · ☐ Heart dis ischemic NEC 411.8 · ☐ Isch heart dis chr 414.0 · ☐ Pancreatitis acute 577.0 · ☐ Sx: abdomen & pelvis 789.0
☐ Angina Unspec 413.9 · ☐ Cellulitisleg 682.6 · ☐ Heart failure, congest 428.0 · ☐ Left heart failure 428.1 · ☐ Parkinson disease 332.0 · ☐ Sx: bruit/weak pulse 785.9
☐ Anxiety state NOS 300.00 · ☐ Chest pain NEC 786.59 · ☐ Heart failure NOS 428.9 · ☐ Lower extremity emb 444.22 · ☐ Parox ventric tach 427.1 · ☐ Sx: rapid heart beat 785.0
☐ Aortic valve disord 424.1 · ☐ Chest pain unsp 786.50 · ☐ Hematuria benign 599.7 · ☐ Malaise and fatigue 780.7 · ☐ Pericard dis NOS 523.9 · ☐ Sx: nausea/vomiting 787.0
☐ Aortocoronary bypass V45.81 · ☐ Chr airway obst NEC 496 · ☐ Hemiplegia 342.9 · ☐ Malfunct CABG 996.03 · ☐ Periph vasc dis unsp 443.9 · ☐ Sx: headache, face pain 784.0
☐ Apoplexia 436 · ☐ Chr blood loss anemia 280.0 · ☐ Hemorrhage GI unsp 578.9 · ☐ Mitral stenosis 396.1 · ☐ Pernicious anemia 281.0 · ☐ Sx: apnea/SOB 786.09
☐ Arrhythmia 427.9 · ☐ Chr ischemic hrt ds 414.8 · ☐ Hypercholesterolemia 272.0 · ☐ Mitral valve dis NEC 394.9 · ☐ Premature beats unsp 427.60 · ☐ Syncope & collapse 780.2
☐ ASCVD 429.2 · ☐ Chr renal failure 585 · ☐ Hyperlipidemia NEC 272.4 · ☐ Mitral valve incomp 424.0 · ☐ Prinzmetal angina 413.1 · ☐ Trans cerebral isch 435.9
☐ Atherosclerosis unsp 440.9 · ☐ Conduction disord unsp 426.9 · ☐ Hyperpotassemia 276.7 · ☐ Mitral/aortic stenosis 396.0 · ☐ Pulmonary congestion 514 · ☐ Unsp anomaly heart 746.9
☐ Atrial fibrillation 427.31 · ☐ Convulsions 780.3 · ☐ Hypertension benign 401.1 · ☐ Mitral/aortic insuff 396.3 · ☐ Pulmonary collapse 518.0 · ☐ Unsp septicemia 038.9
☐ Atrial flutter 427.32 · ☐ Coronary art anomaly 746.85 · ☐ Hypertension essent 401.0 · ☐ MI unsp 410.90 · ☐ Pulmonary embolism 415.1 · ☐ Ventric prem beats 427.69
☐ Atrial prem beats 427.61 · ☐ Dehydration 276.5 · ☐ Hypertens hrt dis NOS 402.90 · ☐ MI old 412 · ☐ Pul heart dis unsp 416.9
☐ AV block first degree 426.11 · ☐ Diab w/comp NOS adult 250.90 · ☐ Hypertroph cardiomyop 425.1 · ☐ Obesity 278.0 · ☐ Renal failure NOS 586

UNLISTED DIAGNOSIS	CODE	DESCRIPTION	

REMARKS OR INSTRUCTIONS	

RELEASE & ASSIGNMENT	RECALL & RETURN	ACCOUNTING INFORMATION
I authorize release of any information necessary to process my insurance claim and assign and request payment directly to my physicians.	RETURN ☐ DAYS ☐ WEEKS ☐ MONTHS	PRIOR BALANCE
		TODAY'S CHARGES
SIGNED DATE	NEXT APPOINTMENT	TOTAL DUE
		AMOUNT PAID
	DATE _____ TIME _____ AM PM	NEW BALANCE

©1992 PMIC

REV. 01/92

GENERAL SURGERY

GENERAL SURGERY GROUP — 3186

4727 Wilshire Boulevard
Los Angeles, CA 90010
(708) 920-0700
LICENSE: P12345
FEIN: 95-4210732

DATE OF SERVICE	ACCOUNT NUMBER		TIME

ACCOUNT NAME (LAST, FIRST)

☐ NEW PATIENT   ☐ ASSIGNED?

DX #1	DX #2	DX #3	DX #4

✔	CODE	DESCRIPTION	DX	FEE	✔	CODE	DESCRIPTION	DX	FEE	✔	CODE	DESCRIPTION	DX	FEE
	OFFICE VISITS NEW PATIENT	E/M				PROCEDURES (Cont'd)					LABORATORY			
	90000	Brief	99201			19000	Aspiration Breast Cyst				80019	Lab Panel 19+ Tests		
	90010	Limited	99202			19100*	Breast Biopsy				81000	Urinalysis		
	90015	Intermediate	99203			19120	Excision Breast Lesion				82270	Stool For Occult Blood		
	90017	Extended	99204			45300	Proctosigmoidoscopy				82951	Glucose Tolerance Test		
	90020	Comprehensive	99205			45305	Proctosigmoidoscopy BX				83718	Blood Lipoprotein		
	99025	Initial Visit, Starred Procedure				45330	Sigmoidoscopy				85014	Hematocrit		
	OFFICE VISITS ESTABLISHED PATIENT										85022	Automated Hemogram		
	90030	Minimal	99211								85031	Manual Hemogram		
	90040	Brief	99212								85048	White Blood Cell Count		
	90050	Limited	99213			SCALP, NECK, TRUNK & EXTREMITIES					85580	Blood Platelet Count		
	90060	Intermediate	99214			12001*	Repair Wound Simple To 2.5				85651	RBC Sedimentation Rate		
	90070	Extended	99215			12002*	Repair Wound Simple 2.6-7.5							
	90080	Comprehensive				12004*	Repair Wound Simple 7.6-12.5							
	99024	Postop Visit												
	CONSULTATIONS INITIAL										SUPPLIES			
	90605	Intermediate	99242			FACE, EARS, EYELIDS, NOSE & LIPS					99070	Surgical Tray		
	90610	Extended	99243			12011*	Repair Wound Simple to 2.5				99070	Supplies & Materials		
	90620	Comprehensive	99244			12013*	Repair Wound Simple 2.6-5.0							
						12014	Repair Wound Simple 5.1-7.5							
											MISCELLANEOUS			
	PROCEDURES										99361	Med Conference, 30 Min.		
	10060*	Drain Skin Abcess				INJECTIONS AND IMMUNIZATIONS					99362	Med Conference, 60 Min.		
	10080*	Drain Pilonidal Cyst				90702	Immunization; DT				99371	Telephone Call, Brief		
	10120*	Remove Foreign Body Subcut				90703	Immunization; Tetanus Toxoid				99372	Telephone Call, Intermediate		
	11000*	Debride Infected Skin				90782	Injection, IM/SQ				99000	Specimen Handling		
	11200*	Excise Skin Tags				90784	Injection, IV				99080	Special Reports		
	17000*	Destroy Face Lesion 1st				90788	Injection, Antibiotic							
	17001*	Destroy Face Lesions 2nd & 3rd												
	17002*	Destroy Face Lesions >3 Each												
	17100	Destruction Skin Lesion												

UNLISTED PROCEDURE	CODE	DESCRIPTION										FEE		

DIAGNOSIS   ICD-9 CM

☐ Abd aortic aneurysm 441.4	☐ Cellulitis leg 682.6	☐ Edema 782.3	☐ Int hemorr w/o comp 455.0	☐ Mastopathy cystic 610.1	☐ Symptoms in breast 611.7
☐ Abd or pelvis swelling 789.3	☐ Cellulitis trunk 682.2	☐ Emphysema other 492.8	☐ Int hemorr w/comp NEC 455.2	☐ Myalgia unsp 729.1	☐ Sx: abd pain, cramps 789.0
☐ Abn findings, breast 793.8	☐ Cholecystitis acute 575.0	☐ Enlarge lymph nodes 785.6	☐ Intest obstr NOS 560.9	☐ Neoplasm unsp skin 238.2	☐ Sx: bruit, weak pulse 785.9
☐ Abn loss weight 783.2	☐ Cholecystitis NEC 575.1	☐ Esophagitis 530.1	☐ Intest adhes w/obstr 560.81	☐ Obesity 278.0	☐ Sx: nausea & vomiting 787.0
☐ Acute vasc insuff intest 557.0	☐ Cholelithiasis NEC 574.10	☐ Essent hypertension 401	☐ Keratoderma acquired 701.1	☐ Osteoarthrosis unsp 715.9	☐ Sx: headache, face pain 784.0
☐ Anal & rectal abscess 566	☐ Chr airway obst NEC 496	☐ Gastritis acute 535.0	☐ Leg varicosity w/ulcer 454.0	☐ Osteoarthrosis gen 715.0	☐ Syncope & collapse 780.2
☐ Anal fissure 565.0	☐ Chr renal failure 585	☐ Gastritis unsp 535.5	☐ Lipoma unsp site 214.9	☐ Other unsp comp care 999.9	☐ Trans cer isch unsp 435.9
☐ Anal or rectal pain 569.42	☐ Chr ulcer leg 707.1	☐ Heart failure 428.0	☐ Local infection skin 686.9	☐ Other dermatoses 702	☐ Umbilical hernia 553.1
☐ Anemia unsp 285.9	☐ Chr ulcer unsp site 707.9	☐ Hematuria benign ess 599.7	☐ Lower extr embolism 444.22	☐ Pain in limb 729.5	☐ Unilat inguinal hernia 550.90
☐ Apoplexia 436	☐ Comp device NEC 996.7	☐ Hemiplegia 342.9	☐ Lumbago 724.2	☐ Pancreatitis acute 577.0	☐ Unsp disorder skin 709.9
☐ Arthropathy unsp 716.9	☐ Constipation 564.0	☐ Hemorr GI tract unsp 578.9	☐ Lump/mass breast 611.72	☐ Peptic ulcer unsp 533.9	☐ Unsp septicemia 038.9
☐ Backache unsp 724.5	☐ Circ sys discord unsp 459.9	☐ Hemorr rectum & anus 569.3	☐ M.neoplasm sig colon 153.3	☐ Peri vasc dis unsp 443.9	☐ Urinary tract infection 599.0
☐ B.neoplasm breast 217	☐ Cyst sebaceous 706.2	☐ Hemorrhoids unsp 455.6	☐ M.neoplasm breast unsp 174.9	☐ Pernicious anemia 281.0	☐ Varicose leg ulcer 454.2
☐ B.neoplasm lrg bowel 211.3	☐ Decub ulcer bed sore 707.0	☐ Hist breast malig V10.3	☐ M.neoplasm cecum 153.4	☐ Postsurg states NEC V45.89	☐ Varicose vein lower ext 454.9
☐ B.neoplasm oth sites 229.8	☐ Dehydration 276.5	☐ Hist colon malig V10.05	☐ M.neoplasm colon unsp 153.9	☐ Prostate hyperplasia 600	☐ Venous insuff NOS 459.81
☐ Biliary inguinal hernia 550.92	☐ Diabetes uncomp adult 250.00	☐ Hypertension benign 401.1	☐ M.neoplasm lung 162.9	☐ Rectal prolapse 569.1	☐ Ventral hernia NOS 553.20
☐ Breast hypertrophy 611.1	☐ Diaphragm hernia 553.3	☐ Hypertension essential 401.0	☐ M.neoplasm rectum 154.1	☐ Renal failure NOS 586	
☐ Ca in situ breast 233.0	☐ Diverticulitis colon 562.11	☐ Hypertension NOS 401.9	☐ M.neoplasm panc unsp 157.9	☐ Rotator cuff syn 726.1	
☐ Calc kidney/ureter 595.0	☐ Diverticulosis colon 562.10	☐ Hypothyroidism unsp 244.9	☐ M.neoplasm prostate 185	☐ Stricture artery 447.1	
☐ Calc gallbladder 574.0	☐ Duodenal ulcer unsp 532.9	☐ Incisional hernia 553.21	☐ Mastodynia 611.71	☐ Surgery follow-up V67.0	
	☐ Dysphagia 787.2	☐ Ing hernia w/o obst 550.9		☐ Swelling head & neck 784.2	

UNLISTED DIAGNOSIS	CODE	DESCRIPTION

REMARKS OR INSTRUCTIONS

RELEASE & ASSIGNMENT	RECALL & RETURN	ACCOUNTING INFORMATION

I authorize release of any information necessary to process my insurance claim and assign and request payment directly to my physicians.

SIGNED _____ DATE _____

RETURN
☐ DAYS   ☐ WEEKS   ☐ MONTHS

NEXT APPOINTMENT

DATE _____ TIME _____ AM / PM

PRIOR BALANCE	
TODAY'S CHARGES	
TOTAL DUE	
AMOUNT PAID	
NEW BALANCE	

REV. 01/92

INTERNAL MEDICINE

DATE OF SERVICE	ACCOUNT NUMBER		INTERNAL MEDICINE GROUP	4186
			4727 Wilshire Boulevard	
ACCOUNT NAME (LAST, FIRST)			Los Angeles, CA 90010	TIME
			(708) 920-0700	
			LICENSE: P12345	
			FEIN: 95-4210732	

☐ NEW PATIENT ☐ ASSIGNED?	DX #1	DX #2	DX #3	DX #4

✓	CODE	DESCRIPTION	DX	FEE	✓	CODE	DESCRIPTION	DX	FEE	✓	CODE	DESCRIPTION	DX	FEE
OFFICE VISITS NEW PATIENT		E / M			INJECTIONS AND IMMUNIZATIONS					LABORATORY (Cont'd)				
	90000	Brief	99201			90702	Immunization; DT				84295	Blood Sodium		
	90010	Limited	99202			90703	Immunization; Tetanus Toxoid				84450	SGOT		
	90015	Intermediate	99203			90724	Immunization; Influenza				84460	SGPT		
	90017	Extended	99204			90782	Injection, IM / SQ				84478	Blood Triglycerides		
	90020	Comprehensive	99205			90784	Injection, IV				85014	Hematocrit		
OFFICE VISITS ESTABLISHED PATIENT						90788	Injection, Antibiotic				85022	Automated Hemogram		
	90030	Minimal	99211								85031	Manual Hemogram		
	90040	Brief	99212								85048	White Blood Cell Count		
	90050	Limited	99213		RADIOLOGY						85580	Blood Platelet Count		
	90060	Intermediate	99214			71010	X-Ray Exam Chest				85610	Prothrombin Time		
	90070	Extended	99215			71020	X-Ray Exam Chest				85651	RBC Sedimentation Rate		
	90080	Comprehensive									86585	Skin Test, TB		
CONSULTATIONS INITIAL											87060	Culture, Throat or Nose		
	90605	Intermediate	99242		LABORATORY									
	90610	Extended	99243			80019	Lab Panel 19+ Tests							
	90620	Comprehensive	99244			80052	Premarital Profile			SUPPLIES				
						80070	Thyroid Panel				99070	Supplies & Materials		
						80072	Arthritis Panel							
PROCEDURES						80060	Hypertension Panel							
	10060*	Drain Skin Lesion				80061	Lipid Profile			MISCELLANEOUS				
	20550*	Injection, Tendon Sheath				81000	Urinalysis				99361	Med Conference, 30 Min		
	36415*	Routine Venipuncture				82270	Stool for Occult Blood				99362	Med Conference, 60 Min		
	45330	Sigmoidoscopy				82310	Calcium				99371	Telephone Call, Brief		
	93000	EKG Complete				82465	Serum Cholesterol				99372	Telephone Call, Intermediate		
	93040	Rhythm EKG with Report				82565	Blood Creatinine				99000	Specimen Handling		
	94010	Spirometry Complete				82643	Ria for Digoxin				99080	Special Reports		
						82951	Glucose Tolerance Test							
						83718	Blood Lipoprotein							
						84075	Alkaline Phosphatase							

UNLISTED PROCEDURE	CODE	DESCRIPTION		FEE

DIAGNOSIS   ICD-9 CM

☐ Abnormal loss weight 783.2	☐ Diaphragmatic hernia 553.3	☐ Hypercholesterolemia 272.0
☐ acute bronchitis 466.0	☐ Diverticula colon 562.1	☐ Hyperlipidemia 272.4
☐ Acute URI NOS 465.9	☐ Diverticulitis colon 562.11	☐ Hypertension benign 401.1
☐ Allergic rhinitis 477.9	☐ Diverticulosis colon 562.10	☐ Hypertension essential 401.0
☐ Alzheimer's disease 331.0	☐ Dizziness & giddiness 780.4	☐ Hypertension NOS 401.9
☐ Anemia iron def unsp 280.9	☐ Duodenal ulcer unsp 532.9	☐ Hyperten heart dis NOS 402.90
☐ Anemia unsp 285.9	☐ Dyspepsia 536.8	☐ Hypopotassemia 276.8
☐ Anemia protein def 281.9	☐ Edema 782.3	☐ Hypothyroidism unsp 244.9
☐ Angina pectoris unsp 413.9	☐ Emphysema other 492.8	☐ Impacted cerumen 380.4
☐ Anxiety state NOS 300.00	☐ Esophagitis 530.1	☐ Intermed cor syndrome 411.1
☐ Aortic valve disord 424.1	☐ Gastritis unsp 535.5	☐ Intest obstruction NOS 560.9
☐ Aortocoronary bypass V45.81	☐ Gen osteoarthrosis 715.09	☐ Intracereb hemorr 431
☐ Apoplexia 436	☐ Gout NOS 274.9	☐ Irritable colon 564.1
☐ Arrhythmia 427.9	☐ Gouty arthritis 274.0	☐ Isch heart dis unsp chr 414.9
☐ Arthropathy unsp 716.9	☐ Heart dis isch NEC 411.8	☐ Isch heart dis chronic 414.0
☐ ASCVD 429.2	☐ Heart fail congestive 428.0	☐ Kidney disord unsp 593.9
☐ Asthma w / o status 493.90	☐ Heart failure NOS 428.9	☐ Lumbago 724.2
☐ Atherosclerosis gen 440.9	☐ Hematuria benign ess 599.7	☐ Lymphomas NEC 202.8
☐ Atrial fibrillation 427.31	☐ Hemiplegia 342.9	☐ Malaise & fatigue 780.7
☐ Atrial flutter 427.32	☐ Hemorr GI tract unsp 578.9	☐ Melena blood in stool 587.1
☐ backache unsp 724.5	☐ Hemorr rectum & anus 569.3	☐ Mitral valve disord 424.0
☐ B.hypertensive hrt dis 402.1	☐ Hemorrhoids unsp 455.6	☐ Mixed hyperlipid 272.2
	☐ Herpes zoster 053.9	☐ Myalgia unsp 729.1

☐ B.neoplasm lg bowel 211.3	☐ Myeloma multiple 203.0	☐ Pneumonia, org NOS 486
☐ Bronchitis NOS 490	☐ MI unsp 410.90	☐ Polycythemia vera 283.4
☐ Bronchitis obstr chr 491.2	☐ MI old 412	☐ Polymyalgia rheum 725
☐ Calculus kidney 595.0	☐ Nasopharyngitis acute 460	☐ Preop chest xray/EKG V99.99
☐ Cardiomyopathies 425.4	☐ Neuralgia, neuritis 792.2	☐ Prostate hyperplasia 600
☐ Cataract NOS 366.9	☐ Obesity 278.0	☐ Pul heart dis unsp 416.9
☐ Cerebrovasc dis other 437.0	☐ Osteoarthrosis unsp 715.90	☐ Pyrexia unk origin 780.6
☐ Cerebral Thrombosis 434.0	☐ Osteoporosis NOS 733.00	☐ Renal failure 586
☐ Cerebrovasc dis NOS 437.9	☐ Osteoarthrosis gen 715.0	☐ Rheumatoid arthritis 714.0
☐ Chest pain NEC 786.59	☐ Other abn blood chem 790.6	☐ Rhythm disord, other 427.89
☐ Chest pain unsp 786.50	☐ Other comp med care 999.9	☐ Senile dementia 290.0
☐ Chr sirway obstr NEC 496	☐ Other bursitis 727.3	☐ Sx: abd pain, cramps 789.0
☐ Chr isch heart dis NEC 414.8	☐ Other cellulitis unsp 682.9	☐ Sx: nausea & vomiting 787.0
☐ Chr renal failure 585	☐ Pain in limb 729.5	☐ Sx: headache face pain 784.0
☐ Cirrhosis liver 471.5	☐ Painful respiration 786.52	☐ Sx: shortness breath 786.09
☐ Constipation 564.0	☐ Palpitations 785.1	☐ Syncope & collapse 780.2
☐ Contact dermatitis 692.9	☐ Parkinson disease 332.0	☐ Systemic lupus eryth 710.0
☐ Convulsions, seizures 780.3	☐ Peptic ulcer unsp 533.9	☐ Thyrotoxicosis NOS 242.9
☐ Cough 786.2	☐ Periph vasc dis unsp 443.9	☐ Trans cereb isch unsp 435.9
☐ Cystitis unsp 595.9	☐ Pernicious anemia 281.0	☐ Unsp septicemia 038.9
☐ Dehydration 276.5	☐ Pharyngitis acute 462	☐ Unsp sinusitis chr 473.9
☐ Depress disord NEC 311	☐ Phlebitis unsp 451.9	☐ Urinary tract infection 599.0
☐ Diabetes w / comp NOS 250.00	☐ Pleurisy unsp 511.9	

UNLISTED DIAGNOSIS	CODE	DESCRIPTION

REMARKS OR INSTRUCTIONS	

RELEASE & ASSIGNMENT	RECALL & RETURN	ACCOUNTING INFORMATION
I authorize release of any information necessary to process my insurance claim and assign and request payment directly to my physicians.	RETURN ☐ DAYS ☐ WEEKS ☐ MONTHS	PRIOR BALANCE
SIGNED		TODAY'S CHARGES
		TOTAL DUE
DATE	NEXT APPOINTMENT	AMOUNT PAID
	DATE _____ TIME _____ AM PM	NEW BALANCE

© 1992 PMIC   REV. 01 / 92

OBSTETRICS & GYNECOLOGY

DATE OF SERVICE	ACCOUNT NUMBER		**OBSTETRICS & GYNECOLOGY GROUP**	**5186**
			4727 Wilshire Boulevard	

ACCOUNT NAME (LAST, FIRST)

Los Angeles, CA 90010
(708) 920-0700
LICENSE: P12345
FEIN: 95-4210732

TIME

☐ **NEW PATIENT** ☐ **ASSIGNED?**	DX #1	DX #2	DX #3	DX #4

✓	CODE	DESCRIPTION	DX	FEE	✓	CODE	DESCRIPTION	DX	FEE	✓	CODE	DESCRIPTION	DX	FEE
	OFFICE VISITS NEW PATIENT	E/M				PROCEDURES (Cont'd)					LABORATORY (Cont'd)			
	90000	Brief	99201			58100*	Endometrial Biopsy				80070	Thyroid Panel		
	90010	Limited	99202			58102	Endometrial Currettage				81000	Urinalysis		
	90015	Intermediate	99203			58120	Dilation and Curettage				84702	Gonadotropin, Quantitative		
	90017	Extended	99204			58140	Remove Uterus Lesion				84703	Gonadotropin, Qualitative		
	90020	Comprehensive	99205			58300*	Insert IUD				85014	Hematocrit		
	99025	Initial Visit Starred				58301	Remove IUD				85022	Automated Hemogram		
	OFFICE VISITS ESTABLISHED PATIENT					59000*	Amniocentesis				85031	Manual Hemogram		
	90030	Minimal	99211			59025	Fetal Non-stress Test				85025	CBC with WBC		
	90040	Brief	99212			59050	Fetal Monitor w/Report				85580	Blood Platelet Count		
	90050	Limited	99213			59400	Obstetrical Care				85610	Prothrombin Time		
	90060	Intermediate	99214			59420	Antepartum Care				85651	RBC Sedimentation Rate		
	90070	Extended	99215			59430	Postpartum Care				86082	Blood Typing, ABO & RHO(D)		
	90080	Comprehensive				59840	Abortion, Induced				86592	Blood Serology, Qual		
	99024	Postop Visit N/C									87086	Culture, Urine		
	CONSULTATIONS INITIAL					INJECTIONS AND IMMUNIZATIONS					87110	Culture, Chlamydia		
	90605	Intermediate	99242			90706	Immunication, Rubella				87210	Smear, Stain & Interp		
	90610	Extended	99243			90731	Immunization, Hepatitis B				88150	Cytopathology, Pap Smear		
	90620	Comprehensive	99244			90782	Injection, IM/SQ				88155	Cytopathology, Pap Smear		
	90630	Complex	99245			90784	Injection, IV				SUPPLIES			
						90788	Injection, Antibiotic				99070	Diaphragm		
	PROCEDURES										99070	Supplies & Materials		
	10060*	I&D Abcess				RADIOLOGY								
	56420	Drainage of Vulva Abscess				76805	Echo Exam Pregnant Uterus				MISCELLANEOUS			
	56501	Destruction, Vulva Lesion(s)				76816	Echo Exam F/U or Repeat				99361	Med Conference, 30 Min		
	56600*	Biopsy of Vulva				76856	Echo Exam Pelvis				99362	Med Conference 60 Min		
	57020*	Colpocentesis				76946	Echo Guide Amniocentesis				99371	Telephone Call Brief		
	57170	Fitting of Diaphragm				LABORATORY					99372	Telephone Call Intermediate		
	57410*	Pelvic Exam Under Anesth.				80019	Lab Panel 19+ Tests				99000	Specimen Handling		
	57452*	Colposcopy				80052	Obstetric Profile							
	57500*	Biopsy of Cervix				80056	Amenorrhea Profile							
	57511*	Cryocautery of Cervix												

UNLISTED PROCEDURE	CODE		DESCRIPTION			FEE

DIAGNOSIS	ICD-9 CM		
☐ Abd/pelvic mass	789.3	☐ Candidal vulvovaginitis 112.1	☐ Gastritis unsp 535.5

☐ Abd/pelvic mass 789.3	☐ Candidal vulvovaginitis 112.1	☐ Gastritis unsp 535.5	☐ M.neoplasm vagina 184.0	☐ Pap smear abnormal 795.0	☐ Unsp disorder skin 709.9
☐ Abscess vulva NEC 616.4	☐ Cervitis 616.0	☐ Genital herpes 054.1	☐ M.neoplasm vulva NOS 184.4	☐ Polypcorpus uteri 621.0	☐ Unsp ovarian dysfunc 256.9
☐ Absence menst 626.0	☐ Cervix disorders unsp 622.9	☐ Genital prolapse NEC 618.8	☐ M.neoplasm breast unsp 174.9	☐ Postablat ovarian fail 256.2	☐ Unsp sympt fem gen 625.9
☐ Acute URI NOS 465.9	☐ Cervix erosion 622.0	☐ Genital prolapse NOS 618.9	☐ M.neo cerv uteri unsp 180.9	☐ Postmenopaus bleed 627.1	☐ Urinary tract infection 599.0
☐ Anemia iron def unsp 280.9	☐ Cervix inflam dis 616.8	☐ Gynecologic exam V72.3	☐ M.neoplasm corp uteri 182.0	☐ Postop vag prolapse 618.5	☐ Urethral caruncle 599.3
☐ Anemia unsp 285.9	☐ Corpus luteum cyst 620.1	☐ Hemorr rectum & anus 569.3	☐ M.neoplasm corp 183.0	☐ Postsurg states NEC V45.89	☐ Urethritis unsp 597.80
☐ Apoplexia 436	☐ Cyst sebaceous 706.2	☐ Hemorrhoids unsp 455.6	☐ M.neoplasm ovary 183.0	☐ Prolapse vaginal walls 618.0	☐ Urethrocele 623.2
☐ Atrophic vaginitis 627.3	☐ Cystitis unsp 595.9	☐ Hist uterus malig NEC V10.42	☐ Mastodynia 611.71	☐ Pruritus genitalia 698.1	☐ Urination frequency 788.4
☐ Atrophy vulva 624.1	☐ Diabetes uncomp adult 250.00	☐ Hyperestrogenism 256.0	☐ Mastopathy cystic chr 610.1	☐ Routine med exam V70.0	☐ Uterine leiomyoma NOS 218.9
☐ Backache unsp 724.5	☐ Diverticulitis colon 562.11	☐ Yperplas endomet 621.3	☐ Melena 578.1	☐ Screen M.neopl cervix V76.2	☐ Uterovag prolap comp 618.3
☐ Barth gland cyst 616.2	☐ Dysmenorrhea 625.3	☐ Hypertension benign 401.1	☐ Menopaus disord NEC 627.8	☐ Screen M.neo rectum V76.41	☐ Uterovag prolap incomp 618.2
☐ B.neoplasm cerv uteri 219.0	☐ Dyspareunia 625.0	☐ Hypertension NOS 401.9	☐ Menopaus disord NOS 627.9	☐ Second syphilis skin 091.3	☐ Uterovag prolapse 618.4
☐ B.neoplasm corp uteri 219.1	☐ Dysplasia cervix 622.1	☐ Hypothyroidism unsp 244.9	☐ Menopause art state 627.4	☐ Senile osteoporosis 733.01	☐ Uterus disorders unsp 621.9
☐ B.neoplasm ovary 220	☐ Dysuria 788.1	☐ Incontinence urine 788.3	☐ Menstrual disord NEC 626.8	☐ Solitary cyst breast 610.0	☐ Vaginal disord noninfl 623.8
☐ B.neoplasm vagina 221.1	☐ Endocrine disord NOS 259.9	☐ Intestinal obstr NOS 560.9	☐ Mucous polyp cervix 622.7	☐ Surgery follow-up V67.0	☐ Vagina dysplasia 623.0
☐ Bladder disorders 596.8	☐ Endometriosis NOS 617.9	☐ Irreg menstrual cycle 626.4	☐ Obesity 278.0	☐ Sx: abd pain, cramps 789.0	☐ Vag enterocele congen 618.6
☐ Bleed uncont to menses 626.6	☐ Examination NEC V72.8	☐ Irritable colon 564.1	☐ Observ susp cond V71.9	☐ Syncope & collapse 780.2	☐ Vaginitis 616.10
☐ CA in situ fem gen NEC 233.3	☐ Excess menstruation 626.2	☐ Lab exam V72.6	☐ Osteoarthrosis unsp 715.9	☐ Treatment f/u NEC V67.5	☐ Viral warts 078.1
☐ CA in situ uterus NEC 233.2	☐ Female gen sympt NEC 625.8	☐ Leukoplakia vagina 623.1	☐ Osteoporosis NOS 733.00	☐ Trichomonal vaginitis 131.01	☐ Vulva dystrophy 624.0
☐ Calculus kidney 595.0	☐ Female stress incont 625.6	☐ Lump/mass in breast 611.72	☐ Oth comp med care 999.9	☐ Trigonitis 595.3	
☐ Cancer uterus in situ 233.1	☐ Fibroscler breast chr 610.3	☐ Malaise & fatigue 780.7	☐ Ovarian cyst 620.2	☐ Ulceration vulva unsp 616.50	
	☐ Follow-up exam NEC V67.59	☐ M.neoplasm uterus NOS 179	☐ Ovarian failure NEC 256.3	☐ Unsp bleeding 626.9	
			☐ Pain in limb 729.5		

UNLISTED DIAGNOSIS	CODE		DESCRIPTION

REMARKS OR INSTRUCTIONS	

RELEASE & ASSIGNMENT	RECALL & RETURN	ACCOUNTING INFORMATION
I authorize release of any information necessary to process my insurance claim and assign and request payment directly to my physicians.	RETURN ☐ DAYS ☐ WEEKS ☐ MONTHS	PRIOR BALANCE
SIGNED DATE	NEXT APPOINTMENT AM	TODAY'S CHARGES
	DATE _____ TIME _____ PM	TOTAL DUE
		AMOUNT PAID
		NEW BALANCE

©1992 PMIC

REV. 01/92

DEALING WITH INSURANCE CARRIERS

CHAPTER SUMMARY

Most health care professionals would prefer to practice medicine and leave the subject of insurance to their staff. But medical insurance, with its regulations, forms and terminology is here to stay. Nearly 200 million Americans, 88 percent of the population, are now covered in one way or another by health insurance. Insurers currently pay about 70 percent of all health care costs in the United States. Depending upon your specialty, from 60 to 90 percent of your practice income will be from insurance carriers. While it is not necessary for health care professionals to know the precise details of preparing insurance claims, it is very important that they know the general concepts of third party payment systems and whether or not their staff is fully aware of, and handling diligently, the necessary details.

Unfortunately, the relationship between providers of health care and the payers of health care has traditionally been an adversarial one. One of the main reasons for this adversarial relationship is that the providers and payers have different missions. Your economic mission is to provide your services and be paid your entire fee as soon as possible. With the exception of government and other nonprofit carriers, the mission of the private insurance carriers appears to be to pay you less, pay you later, or pay you nothing. The reason for this is simple. Most of the insurance carriers are publicly held companies or subsidiaries of publicly held companies. Their other mission, other than administering insurance claims, is to provide a profitable return on investment for their shareholders.

Taking away the profit motive doesn't necessarily improve the relationship. For the most part, Medicare and Medicaid carriers are bottomless pits of bureaucratic inefficiency drowning in a sea of constantly changing rules and regulations. A telephone call regarding a specific coding or billing problem to six different provider relations representatives of the same Medicare carrier may result in six different answers to the same question!

Blue Cross organizations are known as slow payers, however, in a non-profit environment, if you don't have money to pay claims or to hire staff to process claims, what choice do they have? Rumors abound (many confirmed) of claims examiners tossing claims by the handful into wastebaskets to eliminate claims backlogs. Are these claims examiners maliciously trying to hurt you? No, they are simply trying to reduce pressure from their supervisors, who are in turn being pressured by their managers, and so on and so on.

It is possible to WIN the insurance game, but you have to know the rules, have the right tools, and play the game well. This chapter provides a comprehensive overview of what health insurance is, the relationships of providers, beneficiaries and carriers, claims processing, electronic claims, and some useful tips for maximizing your reimbursement from insurance carriers.

KEY POINTS REGARDING HEALTH INSURANCE

1. Virtually all insurance carriers now accept or require CPT and ICD-9-CM codes for procedures and diagnosis.

2. Virtually all insurance carriers now accept or require the HCFA1500 insurance claim form.

3. Filing insurance claim forms for patients is the number one practice marketing tool according to recent surveys.

4. NON-PAR physicians will be required to file HCFA1500 forms for all Medicare patients, even unassigned claims, effective October 1990.

5. The December 1990 revision of the HCFA1500 insurance claim form is mandatory for all Medicare claims as of April 1, 1992.

6. Proper insurance claims management can make a significant difference in your reimbursement.

7. Accurate insurance claims processing puts you in control of the reimbursement process.

WHO'S WHO IN HEALTH INSURANCE

Before we get into a detailed description of how health insurance works, it is appropriate that we identify the major participants.

THE CARRIER

The insurance company which writes and administers the policy is commonly referred to as the CARRIER. It is also known as the insurer, underwriter or administrative agent. Carriers are responsible for providing coverage as outlined in the contract between the company and the insured or contracting group. The carrier cannot be expected to provide reimbursement for which coverage has not been purchased.

Each insurance company offers many different plans. Also, most government health care programs are administered by insurance companies (with the notable exception of most Medicaid programs, which are managed by data processing companies). Thus, a single carrier may sell individual policies and group plans, and administer a government program such as Medicare. These plans fall into three basic groups:

Group Policies: are often benefits of employment that are provided by the employer with little or no cost to the insured. Coordination of Benefits is a clause in most group policies which limits the amount that will be paid to a patient who has coverage under more than one group policy.

Individual Policies: are those purchased by individuals. There are also health care benefits provided under individuals' policies, such as home owners and auto insurance. There is no coordination of benefits under individual policies.

Government Programs: are designed to provide benefits and health care for individuals who would not otherwise be able to afford them.

THE PROVIDER

The provider is the person in relation to the insurance program who provides covered services and supplies to the beneficiaries. The provider may be a physician, chiropractor, physical therapist or other health care professional who treats the patient. The provider may also be the pharmacist who fills the prescription, the outside laboratory which conducts tests, or the medical supply house that rents or sells the patient equipment such as a wheelchair or walker. In the medical office, when the nurse or in-house laboratory provides services under the physician's supervision, the physician is still considered the provider.

THE BENEFICIARIES

The beneficiary is the person eligible to receive benefits under a health insurance policy. In the medical office, these are the patients.

THE INSURED

The insured is the person who represents the family unit in relation to the insurance program. This may be the employee, whose employment makes this coverage possible. This person may also be known as the enrollee, certificate holder, policy holder, or subscriber.

DEPENDENTS

Dependents include the spouse (husband or wife) and children of the insured as defined in the contract. The following is an example of how dependents are defined:

- The insured's spouse who is not legally separated from the insured and who is not a member of the Armed Forces.

- The insured's unmarried child (including any stepchild, legally adopted child or foster child) who is not a member of the Armed Forces, provided that any child over 19, but less than 23, shall be considered a dependent only if he is not employed on a full-time basis and if he has the same home address as the insured.

- A child who is physically or mentally incapable of self-support upon reaching the age of 23 may be continued under the plan while remaining incapacitated and unmarried, subject to the insured's coverage continuing in effect.

MAJOR TYPES OF INSURANCE CARRIERS

There are currently over 2000 health insurance carriers in the United States, with three or four times as many plans. The types of health insurance coverage fall neatly into seven categories: Commercial, Blue Cross and Blue Shield, Medicare, Champus, Medicaid, Worker's Compensation and Health Maintenance Organizations (HMOs).

COMMERCIAL CARRIERS

Commercial carriers offer contracts to individuals and groups, mostly groups, under which payments are made to the beneficiary (or to the providers if they have accepted assignment of benefits) according to an indemnity table or schedule of benefits for specified medical services. In general most plans conform to one of three basic types:

BASIC MEDICAL PLANS

These pay total costs up to a maximum (usually around $5,000) for all but a few exclusions such as cosmetic surgery and mental disorders. There may or may not be a deductible, which is an amount the beneficiary must pay. The costs may be incurred in the hospital, home or office.

MAJOR MEDICAL PLANS

These policies are designed for catastrophic situations only, and there is no payment under such plans for minor health problems. They usually take up where basic plans leave off, and almost always have a large deductible and copayment.

COMPREHENSIVE MEDICAL PLANS

These plans consist of combinations of BASIC and MAJOR MEDICAL.

BLUE CROSS AND BLUE SHIELD

BLUE CROSS

BLUE CROSS plans are nonprofit, community service organizations providing health care services to their subscribers. They are called "prepayment" plans because individuals pay in advance for the health services they may need. BLUE CROSS was initially founded for the purpose of covering hospital stays and remains as such in some states. In many states, the BLUE CROSS and BLUE SHIELD plans have effectively merged, to provide comprehensive coverage for hospital and non-hospital services.

BLUE SHIELD

BLUE SHIELD plans are nonprofit voluntary associations originally established so that subscribers may pay in advance for expenses incurred for surgery, in-hospital medical care, and in some plans, outpatient emergency services. As subscribers pay a premium in advance to receive these benefits, BLUE SHIELD plans are also "prepayment" plans.

BLUE SHIELD is not a commercial insurance company. A person becomes a member by entering into a contract with his or her local Blue Shield Plan, and by paying regular dues. He or she becomes a subscriber, not a policyholder, and retains a certificate, not a policy, which tells him or her what to expect when medical services are required. Under a contract in which the patient has both Blue Shield and Blue Cross coverage, the Blue Cross plan (typically) pays for hospital services and the Blue Shield plan (also typically) pays for professional services.

Blue Cross and Blue Shield also administer Medicare, Medicaid, and CHAMPUS programs in many states. In addition, Blue Cross and Blue Shield plans across the country are developing joint ventures, merged care programs, prepaid group practices and health maintenance organizations (HMOs).

MEDICARE

Medicare is a health insurance program under the Social Security Administration's Health Care Financing Administration (HCFA) and consists of two parts.

MEDICARE PART A

Medicare Part A is hospital insurance (including skilled nursing facilities and home health care in certain cases) for almost everyone over the age of 65, the permanently disabled, and those with chronic renal disease. Coverage under Part A Medicare is automatic.

MEDICARE PART B

Medicare Part B, also known as Supplementary Medical Insurance (SMI) covers physician services, laboratory tests and x-rays. Although a voluntary program, almost all who are eligible sign up. Those who are receiving social security benefits and some others have the low premium for Part B coverage deducted from their monthly checks, while the rest pay their premium directly to the Social Security Administration. There is an annual deductible and a 20 percent copayment. Many Medicare patients maintain supplemental MEDI-GAP coverage which pays (to some degree) the difference between what Medicare pays and the total charges.

MEDICARE-MEDICAID (CROSS-OVERS)

A cross-over patient, frequently referred to as a MEDI-MEDI patient is a patient who has Medicare as primary coverage and Medicaid as secondary coverage due to low-income status. Due to continuous cutbacks in Medicaid programs, many providers will no longer accept MEDI-MEDI patients unless they agree to be treated as if they were covered by Medicare only.

CHAMPUS

CHAMPUS, which stands for Civilian Health and Medical Program of the Uniformed Services, is a program that makes health care benefits available to dependents of active military personnel, as well as retired military personnel and their families. Under the CHAMPUS program, these people can go to civilian (non-military) physicians for medical care and have part of the cost of care paid by the Federal government. At age 65, all CHAMPUS beneficiaries are transferred to the Medicare program. CHAMPUS is similar to Medicare, but there are differences in the deductible and copayment.

WORKER'S COMPENSATION

Worker's Compensation covers medical expenses and disability benefits for workers whose injuries or illnesses are the result of doing their jobs. Anyone who employs more than a specific number of workers is required to carry worker's compensation insurance with a carrier of the employer's choice. When handling worker's compensation cases, special information is required such as the date of injury, employer, case number, and adjuster's name. In addition, fee allowances for various kinds of medical care are set by the state and paid directly to the doctor by the insurance carrier. Worker's compensation carriers typically use special coding systems or older versions of

Relative Value Studies (such as California Relative Value Studies) so you have to pay particular attention to coding.

Treatment for worker's compensation cases must be authorized and there is a lot of second opinion type review involved in some cases where it is not exactly clear that the injury or illness is indeed work related, or, there is a dispute about the level of disability. In addition, there are a variety of additional reports and forms which must be filed such as the "Initial Medical Report" or "First Report of Injury".

MEDICAID

Medicaid is a health care assistance program administered jointly by the federal and state governments. Each state sets up and operates its own program within the general guidelines set down by the federal government. Some states offer only the minimum services required by the program while other states offer expanded services financed by a combination of federal and state funds.

Medicaid is the most difficult health insurance carrier to deal with. The reimbursement, currently running between 30 and 33 percent of billed charges, in many cases does not even cover the cost of doing the paperwork, much less the cost of providing the care. The biggest problem with Medicaid is the program itself and the way it is administered. Regulations limit the diagnostic procedures performed, the type of treatment given, and the medications prescribed. Decisions regarding hospitalization are restricted.

The claim forms used must be those designated by the carrier. They must be submitted within certain dates, complete in every detail, and routed first to all other possible sources of payment. Claims are frequently rejected and / or denied outright and payment, when it comes, if it comes, runs from 30 to 33 percent of the amount charged. With the exception of physicians whose practices are located within, or in close proximity to, areas where the population includes a large percentage of Medicaid patients, many physicians no longer accept Medicaid patients.

HEALTH MAINTENANCE ORGANIZATIONS (HMOs)

The previous six listings deal with organizations which pay for medical services but do not provide it. Health maintenance organizations are prepaid group practice plans where the patient or the patient's employer pays monthly premiums, services are rendered, and the patient either does not pay any additional payment or pays small co-payments and any deductibles required by the plan. Health maintenance organizations are the most popular of all the prepaid health plans.

An HMO is a plan or program where specific health care services are rendered to enrolled groups of patients, with fixed payments made in advance by the patient or patient's employer. There are four types of HMOs.

PREPAID GROUP PRACTICE MODEL

In this type of program, the HMO delivers medical services at one or more locations through a group of physicians who contract with the HMO to provide care or through its own physicians, who are employees of the HMO. Kaiser-Permanente is the most well known HMO of this type.

STAFF MODEL

This type of plan hires physicians directly and pays them a salary instead of contracting with a medical group.

INDEPENDENT PRACTICE ASSOCIATION (IPA)

In this type of plan the physicians are not employees and are not paid salaries. They are paid fees for their services out of a fund drawn from the premiums collected by the organization that markets the health plan. An IPA makes contractual arrangements with physicians in the community who provide services from their own offices.

NETWORK HMO

In this type of plan the HMO contracts with two or more group practices to provide health care services to its members.

UNDERSTANDING HEALTH INSURANCE COVERAGE

LIMITATIONS OF COVERAGE

When health insurance coverage is purchased, the benefits are spelled out clearly in the terms of the contract. The limits of coverage under a given contract are a business agreement based on economic reasoning, i.e. the more limits, the less coverage, and the lower the cost to the purchaser. The amount of benefits a patient is entitled to receive is determined by the terms of the contract. The insurance carrier is obligated to provide coverage (reimbursement) only for those services specified in the contract. If you ask most patients about their insurance coverage, they will tell you that it covers everything. They probably have never read the insurance contract and are generally unaware of the deductibles, limitations, coinsurance requirements, and exclusions.

EXCLUSIONS

LISTED EXCLUSIONS

Specific exclusions in terms of services, procedures and/or supplies may be listed. Anything listed as an exclusion is not covered under the terms of the policy, which means that no benefits will be paid for these conditions.

PREEXISTING CONDITIONS

Depending upon the terms of the policy, coverage for treatment of pre- existing conditions may also be excluded or limited.

MAXIMUMS

Most insurance policies have specific maximum dollar amounts that they will pay. These may be annual maximums, lifetime maximums, or maximums for a specific illness.

ANNUAL MAXIMUM

Under an annual maximum insurance policy, benefits become available again at the beginning of the next benefit year or calendar year depending upon the terms of the policy.

LIFETIME MAXIMUM

Some conditions are not totally excluded; however, coverage is discontinued after a specific limitation has been reached.

MENTAL AND ADDICTIVE DISORDERS

The most common limitation is a separate schedule of benefits that covers mental, psychoneurotic and personality disorders, and the treatment of drug and alcohol addiction. They may be excluded completely, or be subject to limitations.

BENEFIT PERIOD LIMITATION

The term "benefit period" may be used to describe maximums allowed for a specific illness. This limitation most often applies to hospitalization; however, there are similar limitations on payment for outpatient treatment of alcoholism, drug addiction and mental illness.

DEDUCTIBLES

A deductible is a specified amount which the covered person must pay toward the cost of medical treatment, before the benefits of the insurance policy go into effect. Most insurance policies contain deductible clauses; however, the amount and type of deductible depends upon the specific plan. The amount of the deductible is generally related to the premium. The insured may elect a higher deductible in exchange for lower premiums. Or, the insured may elect no deductible in exchange for seeking care only from specified providers.

INDIVIDUAL/FAMILY DEDUCTIBLE

Under some policies, the deductible must be met on each individual family member. Others are written so that the first family expenses meeting the specified dollar value will satisfy the deductible for the following year.

DEDUCTIBLE CARRYOVER

This means that the insured may apply some or all of the deductible for health care expenses incurred in the last three months of the year to deductibles for the following year.

COINSURANCE (COPAYMENT)

Also referred to as copayment, coinsurance is a provision of an insurance plan which requires the insured to share the cost of certain covered services on a percentage basis. The majority of health insurance policies include some form of coinsurance.

DUAL COVERAGE

A patient may have coverage under more than one health insurance policy. This is known as dual coverage. With respect to dual coverage, it is important to consider the three basic types of health insurance policies as they each have different ways of dealing with dual coverage.

INDIVIDUAL PLANS

Individual plans are required by law to pay full benefits as specified by the health insurance policy regardless of any other health insurance coverage the patient may have. There is no coordination of benefits under individual health insurance policies. It is not unusual to find patients with two, three, or even more private health insurance plans. Quite often these patients receive reimbursement of two to three times the actual cost of the care. In other words, they make a profit on their illness or injury!

GROUP PLANS

Group health insurance plans most often include a coordination of benefits clause. Also known as non-duplication of benefits, it is a provision of a group health insurance plan that specifies that when a patient is covered by more than one group health insurance plan, total benefits paid by all policies are limited to 100 percent of the actual charges. No group plan pays more than it would without the coordination of benefits clause.

It is now law in some states that when a dependent is covered under multiple group insurance plans, the insured's date of birth is to be used to determine which insurance coverage is primary. In other words, in these states, if a child is covered as a dependent under insurance plans where the mother is the insured on one and the father the insured on the other, the insurance plan of the older parent is to be considered the primary carrier.

GOVERNMENT PLANS

If a patient has dual coverage which includes a government health care plan, such as Medicaid, the government plan is always considered supplementary to private or group health insurance plans. Medicare is the major exception to this rule as many of its insureds also have supplemental health insurance policies, known as MEDI-GAP plans, to help with uncovered expenses.

MEDICARE AS SECONDARY PAYER (MSP)

With mandatory retirement against federal law, many people are working long after the Medicare age of 65. These people are often covered by group plans through their employers, and for these patients, Medicare is the supplementary plan. In addition, Medicare is the secondary payer in cases involving job related accidents, automobile and other accidents, the first 12 months of treatment for end stage renal disease (ESRD) and for certain disabled individuals. It is YOUR responsibility to determine whether Medicare is the primary or secondary payer. Failure to make this determination, and bill appropriately, can mean significant delays in your reimbursement. The following categories are individuals subject to Medicare MSP requirements:

- Working individual 65 or over [covered by employer group health plan (EGHP)].

- Spouse 65 or over of working individual of any age [covered by EGHP].

- Individuals in employer prepaid plan.

- Individuals receiving treatment for end stage renal disease (ESRD) [covered by EGHP].

- "Active [employed] individuals" under 65 with a disability [covered by EGHP].

- Work related injuries or illnesses.

- Injuries or illnesses related to automobile accidents.

- Other injuries or illnesses covered by homeowner's, malpractice, product liability or general casualty insurance.

KEY POINTS FOR BILLING MSP PROPERLY

1. For EGHP situations the group health plan is billed first. If your agreement with the EGHP is to accept their payment as payment in full, then you may not bill Medicare at all.

2. The payment from the EGHP may exceed the Medicare prevailing charge and/or MAAC. Regardless of your participating status, you may keep the full amount of the payment in this case.

3. If you are NON-PAR, you may bill the EGHP using the Medicare MAAC or your higher fees for non-Medicare patients. Frequently, billing your private fees to the EGHP and writing off the unpaid balance results in the highest reimbursement.

4. An explanation of benefits (EOB) from the EGHP showing any payments made (or lack of payment) must be submitted with the HCFA1500 when billing Medicare as the secondary payor.

5. For situations involving automobile/no fault coverage, bill the automobile/no fault carrier first.

6. For liability situations, PAR physicians are REQUIRED to bill Medicare first for conditional primary payments. You are not allowed to bill the liability carrier instead of Medicare, however, you may bill the EGHP first and Medicare second as described above.

ICD-9-CM CODES WHICH MAY TRIGGER AN MSP INVESTIGATION

The following ICD-9-CM codes are issued by HCFA to Medicare carriers for potential MSP investigation.

800.0 - 800.99	Fracture of vault of skull
801.0 - 801.99	Fracture of base of skull
802.0 - 802.99	Fracture of face bone
803.0 - 803.99	Other and unqualified skull fractures
804.0 - 804.99	Multiple fractures involving skull or face with other bones
805.0 - 805.98[1]	Fracture of vertebral column without mention of spinal cord injury
806.0 - 806.99[1]	Fracture of vertebral column with spinal cord injury
807.0 - 807.69	Fractures of rib(s), sternum, larynx, and trachea
810.0 - 810.3	Fracture of clavicle
811.0 - 811.19	Fracture of scapula
812.49	Multiple fractures of lower end trachea
828.0 - 828.1	Multiple fractures involving both lower limbs, lower with upper limb, and lower limb(s) with rib(s) and sternum
839.0 - 839.3	Other multiple and ill-defined dislocations
839.7 - 839.9 & 847.0	Sprains and strains of the neck (whiplash)
850.0 - 850.9	Concussion
851.0 - 851.99	Cerebral laceration and contusion
852.0 - 852.59	Subarachnoid, subdural, and extradural hemorrhage following injury
854.0 - 854.19	Intracranial injury of other and unspecified nature
860.0 - 860.5	Traumatic pneumothorax and hemothorax
862.8	Injury to multiple and unspecified intrathoracic organs, without mention to open wound into cavity (crushed chest)
866.0 - 866.13	Injury to kidney
868.0 - 868.19	Injury to other intra-abdominal organs
869.0 - 869.1	Injury to unspecified or ill-defined organs
887.0 - 887.7	Traumatic amputation of arm and hand
896.0 - 896.3 [2]	Traumatic amputation of foot
897.0 - 897.7 [2]	Traumatic amputation of leg(s)
900.0 - 900.9	Injury to blood vessels of head and neck
925	Crushing injury of face, scalp, and neck
929.0 - 929.99	Crushing injury of multiple and unspecified sites
940.0 - 949.5	Burns

[1] Carriers are instructed to override the 805 and 806 series codes when accompanied by a diagnosis of either 733.0, osteoporosis, or 733.1, pathological fracture.

[2] Carriers are instructed to override the 896 and 897 series codes when accompanied by a diagnosis of 250.00, adult onset diabetes mellitus without mention of complication.

UNDERSTANDING YOUR PROVIDER PROFILE

All the actual charges you have filed with an insurance carrier during the previous calendar year are accumulated and used to develop customary charges for the current year. Charge data are obtained from both the insurance claims you submit on behalf of your patients, and from claims submitted directly by your patients. Generally, it takes a minimum of three charges to develop your "usual charges" for a specific procedure.

Your usual charge is the MEDIAN (50th percentile) of your range of charges for a specific procedure. For example, let's assume that you have filed five claims for CPT code 90060, Office Visit, Intermediate, during the previous calendar year. And let's say that your charges, if listed in ascending order by fee, would look like the following list:

90060	Office medical service, intermediate	$ 50.00
90060	Office medical service, intermediate	$ 50.00
90060	Office medical service, intermediate	$ 55.00 <--- **MEDIAN**
90060	Office medical service, intermediate	$ 60.00
90060	Office medical service, intermediate	$ 60.00

In this example, the median charge of the office visit, your "usual charge", is calculated to be $55.00, the point at which one-half of your charges are above and one-half of your charges are below.

Taking this example a step further, let's presume that instead of a list of five procedures, that the list is 500, or 5,000, or 50,000, or 500,000 procedures, and represents all of the 90060, Office medical service, intermediate charges filed by providers of your specialty in your city or county. While the median charge is still $ 55.00, most carriers would use the 90th percentile, in this case $ 60.00, as the "customary charge", which is the maximum that they would pay to any provider, in your area, for this procedure.

The importance of "maintaining" your profile with the insurance carriers should be obvious from the above example. It is critical that your charges are consistent so that you do not negatively affect your profile. This includes making sure that you do not charge less than your "usual charge" very often, as well as avoiding submission of "zero" charges.

HOW INSURANCE CARRIERS PAY

There are four basic methods of payment employed by the various health insurance plans; namely, UCR, Schedule of Benefits, Maximum Allowances, and Capitation. As many health insurance carriers offer a variety of plans which create different relationships between the carrier, the provider, and the patient, you may find that you are reimbursed by different methods for different plans of the same carrier.

USUAL, CUSTOMARY AND REASONABLE (UCR)

This is a concept to determine benefits approximating the physician's actual charge and is commonly referred to as UC & R.

USUAL FEE

The usual fee is what you charge most of the time for a specific procedure or service for the majority of your patients.

CUSTOMARY FEE

The customary fee is determined by insurance carrier profiles. The typical customary fee is based on the 90th percentile of all fees charged by providers with the same specialty in the same geographic location for a specific procedure or service.

REASONABLE FEE

The reasonable fee is the lesser of the billed fee, the usual fee, the customary fee, or is justifiable due to special circumstances of the particular case.

HOW UCR WORKS

As explained above, the insurance carriers determine the customary fees for providers within the same grouping and geographic area. Fees for surgeons are compared with those of other surgeons in the area, etc. Unless justified by special circumstances, the carrier will never pay more than the customary fee for a specific procedure or service. However, if the charge is lower than the customary fee, the carrier will pay the usual fee (or billed fee if less than the usual fee).

The coinsurance clause affects the amount which the carrier actually pays. The following examples illustrate how UCR and coinsurance would work for a hypothetical procedure billed by three different providers in the same geographic area. Let's presume that the customary fee for the procedure, as determined by the insurance carrier, is $ 225.00.

- Dr. Katz submits a claim for his usual fee of $ 220.00. As this is his usual fee, and lower than the customary fee, the carrier "allows" the $220.00 fee.

- Dr. McKellar submits a claim for her usual fee of $ 250.00. As this is her usual fee, but higher than the customary fee, the carrier "allows" $225.00.

- Dr. Williams submits a claim for his fee of $ 250.00 which is higher than his usual fee but is considered reasonable by the carrier because of special circumstances. After a review of the claim, the carrier "allows" $250.00.

If the insurance plan in these examples had no coinsurance clause, each provider would be paid the "allowed" amount. However, if the plan had an 80 percent coinsurance clause, Dr. Katz would be paid $176.00; Dr. McKellar would be paid $180.00; and Dr. Williams would be paid $200.00.

The insured is required to make up the difference, unless the provider is accepting insurance benefits as payment in full either voluntarily or as part of a preferred provider agreement.

The importance of maintaining a current fee schedule in terms of "going rates" should be obvious. If your fees are consistently below the customary fees, the insurance carriers will be more than happy to continue paying you less than they are paying your colleagues.

SCHEDULE OF BENEFITS

A schedule of benefits is a list of specified amounts which the health insurance carrier will pay toward the cost of medical services provided. It is also known as Table of Allowances, Table of Benefits, Indemnity Schedule or Schedule of Allowances. The dollar amounts listed on the Schedule of Benefits represents the total obligation of the health insurance carrier with respect to payment for a specific procedure, service or supply. It does not in any way relate to the doctor's actual fee.

Most plans which use a Schedule of Benefits to determine payments also include a coinsurance clause. The insured is responsible for the coinsurance amount, typically 20 percent, plus the difference, if any, between the actual charge and the amount "allowed" by the schedule.

MAXIMUM FEE SCHEDULE

A Maximum Fee Schedule is a payment plan in which the participating provider agrees to accept the Maximum Fee Schedule amount for a given procedure, service or supply as his or her total reimbursement for a covered service. Government programs, such as Medicaid, are the most common examples of this type of reimbursement plan.

As of January 1, 1992 payments for Medicare services are based on a maximum fee schedule instead of prevailing charges. We anticipate that Medicaid and most other insurance carriers will convert to a fee schedule system in the near future.

CAPITATION

A Capitation plan is a prepaid plan wherein the carrier pays the contracted provider a specified amount, usually on a monthly basis, for each of the carrier's insureds who have selected the provider for their health care. This type of reimbursement system is being seen more often as physicians in private practice are "subcontracted" by Health Maintenance Organizations (HMOs) to provide services to their subscribers.

A capitation form of payment system for Medicare was favored by the Reagan administration, however, the proponents of a fee schedule calculated using a resource based relative value scale, won the political battle for payment reform.

DETERMINING ELIGIBILITY AND VERIFYING BENEFITS

It is very important to make a determination that a patient is indeed eligible for benefits (covered) prior to filing a claim for service to the health insurance carrier. Ideally, eligibility should be determined before treatment is initiated, except in emergencies of course. Patients change jobs, lose jobs, and change marital status and dependent status. Any of these changes may result in the loss of or a substantial change in health insurance coverage.

KEY POINTS REGARDING VERIFYING BENEFITS

1. For all new patients, ask to see his or her insurance identification card(s). All carriers issue cards to their beneficiaries and many of the cards have valuable information such as special telephone numbers or even an explanation of basic coverage provided in addition to patient identification.

2. Make a photocopy of the card(s) and use it to verify the member number and/or group number recorded on the patient registration form. Insurance identification cards usually have the effective date of coverage. It is important to note that these cards are frequently issued and distributed to the beneficiaries in advance, sometimes as much as 30 days in advance, of the effective date. If you provide service prior to the effective date on the card, the patient, not the carrier, is responsible to pay you.

3. Obtain employment information including length of employment. Most group health insurance plans have a waiting period of at least 30 days and frequently 60 or 90 days before the employee is eligible for coverage.

4. Update employment and insurance information frequently. Unless a patient is being seen with unusual frequency, ask him or her if there have been any changes in address, employment or insurance coverage since his or her last visit.

5. Patients with Medicaid are required by federal law to provide current Proof of Eligibility when seeking medical care. Eligibility in these programs changes quickly and benefits are not paid without adequate proof of eligibility at the time of treatment.

6. Termination of benefits. In an individual policy, benefits are terminated when the policy is canceled by either the insured or the carrier. Also, coverage will automatically lapse in most plans after 30 days if the insured fails to make a premium payment. In a group policy, benefits usually terminate when the insured ceases to be a full-time employee and/or the employer or carrier terminates the plan.

7. Extension of Benefits. Under certain circumstances, benefits are extended for a limited period after termination of the policy. This varies considerably and is determined by the specific policy.

PRECERTIFICATION AND PREDETERMINATION

More and more health insurance carriers are requiring, as a condition of their policies, precertification before they will agree to reimburse for certain hospital admissions, inpatient or outpatient surgeries, and elective procedures. The purpose of precertification is to reduce health care costs by reducing or eliminating unnecessary services.

PRECERTIFICATION

Precertification (also known as preauthorization) refers to the process of getting permission from the health insurance carrier, in advance, before providing certain services to the beneficiary. In general, the process involves informing the carrier of your plans and the carrier granting permission for the procedure if covered under the patient's plan.

Most Medicaid programs have rigid precertification programs for all non-emergency hospitalization and surgeries. Many commercial health insurance plans now require precertification for non-emergency hospitalization and/or specific surgical procedures such as total abdominal hysterectomy. With over 2,000 commercial and government insurance carriers it is impossible to determine in advance the specific requirements with regard to precertification and predetermination for them all. Unfortunately, you will learn about the specific requirements of some carriers by trial, and mostly, error.

An important point is to note that precertification is usually required for non-emergency hospitalizations, some elective surgeries, and certain diagnostic procedures. Precertification may also result in a demand or request for a second opinion by the carrier prior to them granting permission for the procedure. Many health insurance carriers now offer reduced premiums in return for revised plans which include some precertification. As mentioned previously, there is no way, other than by previous experience, that you would know about precertification requirements. However; this requirement is stated clearly in the insured's policy and it is the insured's responsibility to inform you of the requirement.

The first attempt at precertification should be with the insured's employer. Call the insured's place of work and ask for the Health Plan Manager or the Personnel Director. Be prepared to discuss procedures, diagnosis, etc. If you are unable to obtain the necessary information from the employer, or choose to bypass the employer, call or write the insurance carrier. Some carriers will precertify over the telephone, others will require a written request. Follow whatever instructions you are given precisely to avoid claims problems later on.

Make sure you have a signed release of information before you discuss the diagnosis and treatment of the patient with the patient's employer or health insurance carrier. To do otherwise is to create a potential for an "invasion of privacy" suit by the patient against you. It is also strongly advised that for diagnoses of a sensitive nature, such as mental illness, alcoholism, drug addictions, and AIDS, that you bypass the employer totally if possible and deal directly with the insurance carrier.

We suggest that you create a Precertification Form for use in your practice. Either use our sample form from the chapter on FORMS AND DOCUMENTS, modify it to suit the specific needs of your practice, or design a form precisely suited to what you do and how you do it. Whenever precertification is required, fill out a copy of the form, and have it available when calling the employer and/or the insurance carrier. If the insurance carrier doesn't want to precertify over the telephone, mail them a copy of the form with a cover letter.

PREDETERMINATION

Predetermination refers to the process of requesting from the carrier the maximum dollar amount(s) that will be paid for services, procedures or supplies, in advance of performing the service. The primary purpose of predetermination is for the provider and the beneficiary to be informed of the portion of the provider's charge(s) that will be reimbursed by the carrier.

Predetermination is helpful to the provider because it gives him or her assurance that a certain portion of his or her fee(s) will be paid by the insurance carrier. In addition to avoiding surprises, predetermination allows the provider and the insured to make arrangements for any difference between actual and allowed amounts before the service is rendered.

QUESTIONS TO ASK THE INSURANCE CARRIER

When you are ready to do a predetermination (also known as verify coverage or verify benefits), call the insurance carrier and inform them that you want to verify eligibility for inpatient and/or outpatient benefits. After responding to any questions they ask about the beneficiary, ask the carrier the following questions:

1. Is there a deductible on this plan?

    A. How much?

    B. Has the deductible been met?

2. Is a portion covered under major medical benefits?

3. Is a portion covered under basic benefits?

4. What are the benefits for inpatient?

5. What are the benefits for outpatient or office?

6. What percentage do you reimburse?

    A. Is that of fee or UCR?

    B. If UCR: can you give me a rough estimate of your reimbursement for our charge of _____ for a _____ (code)?

7. Is there a yearly maximum?

    If yes, how much has been used?

SHOULD YOU SUBMIT CLAIM FORMS FOR YOUR PATIENTS?

Before we discuss how to complete and submit an insurance claim, it is important that you ask yourself the question: Should I do insurance claim forms for my patients? Several years ago, before HMOs, PPOs, Medicare freezes, MAACs, RBRVS, Medicare Fee Schedules, etc., the majority of practice management consultants would have recommended that you let patients do their own claim forms using an itemized statement "fee ticket" or "superbill" provided by you at the time of service. Now most would strongly recommend that you complete insurance claim forms for all of your patients.

IT IMPROVES COLLECTIONS AND CASH FLOW

If you use "assignment of benefits" for your claims, the insurance carrier payment (in most cases) will come directly to you instead of the patient. In many cases, patients won't pay you until the insurance carrier pays him or her. Filing claim forms for patients and using "assignment of benefits" means you are in control of your cash flow, at least with respect to insurance carriers.

IT IMPROVES PATIENT RELATIONS

Patients don't like to go to the doctor, and they don't like to pay for it either. Not to mention that they think you charge too much. Filing claims on behalf of your patients makes good sense. They appreciate your effort to help them pay for services or get reimbursed from their insurance carrier. By helping patients in this manner, you prove that you recognize them as people as well as patients, and that we care enough to assist them.

Think about some of the HMO ads you have read or seen on television. Were they pushing benefits, selection or location? No! They were pushing the end to claim forms! This trend will continue. If medical professionals in private practice expect to compete successfully with managed care operations, they must increase their level of service to include filing insurance claims for their patients. In a recent survey, Medical Economics magazine asked health care professionals to rank their marketing activities in descending order of importance. The number one ranked marketing activity was "doing claim forms for our patients".

MANDATORY SUBMISSION FOR MEDICARE CLAIMS

Since October 1, 1990, submission of the HCFA1500 insurance claim form is mandatory for ALL Medicare claims, PAR or NON-PAR, assigned or unassigned. As of April 1, 1992 you may no longer submit a superbill attached to a HCFA1500 claim form.

HOW TO COMPLETE INSURANCE CLAIM FORMS

As with coding systems, historically there have been a variety of insurance claim forms to deal with, the so-called "universal" or "standard" claim form of the American Medical Association, various incarnations of Medicare forms, Blue Shield forms, Medicaid forms, and many, many other forms printed by various insurance carriers. Needless to say, just keeping track of the proper form to use was a major job. Most practices depended on their patients to provide the proper claim form, which the patient usually obtained from their employer.

The American Medical Association recognized the need to simplify and standardize the reporting of physician services under the various types of government programs and third party policies. A task force was established to develop a uniform physician reporting form acceptable to the various government agencies and health insurance carriers. The result of this effort is the Uniform Health Insurance Claim Form, also known as the HCFA 1500 form, or Standard Claim Form. As of this writing, the Standard Claim Form is accepted by Medicare, Blue Cross and Blue Shield, the majority of commercial carriers, and most Medicaid plans.

Most of the exceptions to the use of the Standard Claim Form for submitting Medicaid claims occur where computer companies, instead of health insurance carriers, serve as the fiscal intermediary for the Medicaid program. A specific example of this is the Form 401C used to process California Medicaid (Medi-Cal). The Form 401C is designed for what is called optical scanning (machine read) and is very difficult to complete without using a computer.

Note that there are currently two versions of the HCFA1500 insurance claim form which may be required or accepted by insurance carriers. On the following pages you will find examples of both forms with detailed instructions for their completion.

HCFA1500 (10/84 Version)

CARRIER

HEALTH INSURANCE CLAIM FORM

PICA | PICA

1. MEDICARE MEDICAID CHAMPUS CHAMPVA GROUP HEALTH PLAN FECA BLK LUNG OTHER
(Medicare #) (Medicaid #) (Sponsor's SSN) (VA File #) (SSN or ID) (SSN) (ID)

1a. INSURED'S I.D. NUMBER (FOR PROGRAM IN ITEM 1)

2. PATIENT'S NAME (Last Name, First Name, Middle Initial)

3. PATIENT'S BIRTH DATE MM DD YY SEX M F

4. INSURED'S NAME (Last Name, First Name, Middle Initial)

5. PATIENT'S ADDRESS (No., Street)

6. PATIENT RELATIONSHIP TO INSURED Self Spouse Child Other

7. INSURED'S ADDRESS (No., Street)

CITY STATE

8. PATIENT STATUS Single Married Other
Employed Full-Time Student Part-Time Student

CITY STATE

ZIP CODE TELEPHONE (Include Area Code) ( )

ZIP CODE TELEPHONE (INCLUDE AREA CODE) ( )

9. OTHER INSURED'S NAME (Last Name, First Name, Middle Initial)

10. IS PATIENT'S CONDITION RELATED TO:

11. INSURED'S POLICY GROUP OR FECA NUMBER

a. OTHER INSURED'S POLICY OR GROUP NUMBER

a. EMPLOYMENT? (CURRENT OR PREVIOUS) YES NO

a. INSURED'S DATE OF BIRTH MM DD YY SEX M F

b. OTHER INSURED'S DATE OF BIRTH MM DD YY SEX M F

b. AUTO ACCIDENT? PLACE (State) YES NO

b. EMPLOYER'S NAME OR SCHOOL NAME

c. EMPLOYER'S NAME OR SCHOOL NAME

c. OTHER ACCIDENT? YES NO

c. INSURANCE PLAN NAME OR PROGRAM NAME

d. INSURANCE PLAN NAME OR PROGRAM NAME

10d. RESERVED FOR LOCAL USE

d. IS THERE ANOTHER HEALTH BENEFIT PLAN? YES NO *If yes*, return to and complete item 9 a-d.

READ BACK OF FORM BEFORE COMPLETING & SIGNING THIS FORM.
12. PATIENT'S OR AUTHORIZED PERSON'S SIGNATURE I authorize the release of any medical or other information necessary to process this claim. I also request payment of government benefits either to myself or to the party who accepts assignment below.

SIGNED DATE

13. INSURED'S OR AUTHORIZED PERSON'S SIGNATURE I authorize payment of medical benefits to the undersigned physician or supplier for services described below.

SIGNED

PATIENT AND INSURED INFORMATION

14. DATE OF CURRENT: ILLNESS (First symptom) OR INJURY (Accident) OR PREGNANCY(LMP) MM DD YY

15. IF PATIENT HAS HAD SAME OR SIMILAR ILLNESS GIVE FIRST DATE MM DD YY

16. DATES PATIENT UNABLE TO WORK IN CURRENT OCCUPATION MM DD YY FROM TO MM DD YY

17. NAME OF REFERRING PHYSICIAN OR OTHER SOURCE

17a. I.D. NUMBER OF REFERRING PHYSICIAN

18. HOSPITALIZATION DATES RELATED TO CURRENT SERVICES MM DD YY FROM TO MM DD YY

19. RESERVED FOR LOCAL USE

20. OUTSIDE LAB? $ CHARGES YES NO

21. DIAGNOSIS OR NATURE OF ILLNESS OR INJURY. (RELATE ITEMS 1,2,3 OR 4 TO ITEM 24E BY LINE)
1. ___ 3. ___
2. ___ 4. ___

22. MEDICAID RESUBMISSION CODE ORIGINAL REF. NO.

23. PRIOR AUTHORIZATION NUMBER

24.

A DATE(S) OF SERVICE From MM DD YY To MM DD YY	B Place of Service	C Type of Service	D PROCEDURES, SERVICES, OR SUPPLIES (Explain Unusual Circumstances) CPT/HCPCS MODIFIER	E DIAGNOSIS CODE	F $ CHARGES	G DAYS OR UNITS	H EPSDT Family Plan	I EMG	J COB	K RESERVED FOR LOCAL USE
1										
2										
3										
4										
5										
6										

25. FEDERAL TAX I.D. NUMBER SSN EIN

26. PATIENT'S ACCOUNT NO.

27. ACCEPT ASSIGNMENT? (For govt. claims, see back) YES NO

28. TOTAL CHARGE $

29. AMOUNT PAID $

30. BALANCE DUE $

31. SIGNATURE OF PHYSICIAN OR SUPPLIER INCLUDING DEGREES OR CREDENTIALS (I certify that the statements on the reverse apply to this bill and are made a part thereof.)

SIGNED DATE

32. NAME AND ADDRESS OF FACILITY WHERE SERVICES WERE RENDERED (If other than home or office)

33. PHYSICIAN'S, SUPPLIER'S BILLING NAME, ADDRESS, ZIP CODE & PHONE #

PIN# GRP#

PHYSICIAN OR SUPPLIER INFORMATION

790-0117 (12/90) (OCR) 2 pt.

(APPROVED BY AMA COUNCIL ON MEDICAL SERVICE 8/88) **PLEASE PRINT OR TYPE** FORM HCFA-1500 (12-90) FORM OWCP-1500 FORM RRB-1500

THE HCFA1500 INSURANCE CLAIM FORM

The HCFA1500 (10/84 version) insurance claim form is separated into two major sections, patient information and physician information. The patient and insured (subscriber) section contains 11 data elements and two spaces for signatures. Basically, this section captures patient name and address, insured's identification number(s), and patient's and insured's signatures. The physician or supplier information section consists of 20 data elements; however, there are few situations in which all of these elements need to be completed.

A brief description of each element and its applicability to the requirements of Medicare, Medicaid and private carriers is listed below. Please note that the term "insured" as used below is the same as the terms "policy holder" or "subscriber".

HCFA1500 "OLD" VERSION

PATIENT INFORMATION

1. **PATIENT'S NAME**

   Enter the patient's full name....do not use nicknames or abbreviated names. The form specifies that the name be entered in last name, first name, middle initial order; however, our experience indicates that listing the name in the more normal order of "first name, middle initial, last name" has no detrimental affect.

2. **DATE OF BIRTH**

   Enter the patient's date of birth in month, day, year format.

   MEDICARE: May be left blank.

3. **INSURED'S NAME**

   Enter the full name of the insured, unless the patient is the insured.... then enter the word "SAME".

   MEDICARE: If the patient or spouse is age 65 through 69, employed, and covered by an employer health plan, show the insured person's full name.

4. **PATIENT'S ADDRESS**

   Enter the patient's complete address. Enter the street address on one line followed by the city, state and zip code on the next line.

5. **PATIENT'S SEX**

   Check the appropriate box. Note that this information is used to validate sex specific procedures.

6.   INSURED'S IDENTIFICATION NUMBER

Enter the insured's primary identification number including any letters. The number is usually obtained from the patient's or insured's insurance identification card.

MEDICARE: Enter the Medicare number and suffix.

MEDICAID: Enter the Medicaid number from the patient's current Medicaid card.

COMMERCIAL: Enter the insured's "member number" or "subscriber number" or "certificate number" from the insurance identification card. Most often this is the insured's social security number.

7.   PATIENT'S RELATIONSHIP TO INSURED

Check the appropriate box.

8.   INSURED'S GROUP NUMBER

For commercial carriers, enter the "group number" or "group name" from the insurance identification card if the patient is covered by an employer sponsored health insurance plan.

9.   OTHER HEALTH INSURANCE COVERAGE

If the patient is covered by another insurance plan, enter the name and address of the other insurance carrier, and the appropriate member and/or group numbers.

10.   CONDITION RELATED TO EMPLOYMENT OR ACCIDENT

Check appropriate box(es) if you are treating the patient for either a work related injury or accident related injury. Note that worker's compensation claims are filed with insurance carriers designated by the patient's employer and is not the same carrier as the patient's health insurance carrier. Likewise, accident related claims, such as automobile accidents, are frequently processed by automobile insurance carriers and/or private attorneys.

11.   INSURED'S ADDRESS

Enter insured's street address, city, state and zip code. If same as patient's, enter "SAME".

12.   RELEASE OF INFORMATION

Either have the patient, or his or her representative sign the claim form, or attach your own release form to the claim and enter "SEE ATTACHMENT" in this space. If the patient is a minor, the signature must be that of a parent or legal guardian.

MEDICARE: For the Medicare program, the beneficiary's signature in this space also authorizes direct payment to the provider. For Medicare, you may obtain a "lifetime" authorization one time, which you must keep on file in your office. Enter "SIGNATURE ON FILE" in this space if you have such an authorization on file.

13. ASSIGNMENT OF BENEFITS

The insured's signature in this space directs the insurance carrier to pay any benefits directly to the provider. You may also use a form which combines release of information and assignment of benefits, attached to the claim form.

PHYSICIAN INFORMATION

14. DATE OF (ILLNESS, INJURY OR PREGNANCY)

Enter, if known, the date of onset for illnesses, the date of injury or, for pregnancy, the date of the last menstrual period (LMP). The carriers like to have this information to assist them in determining coverage or exclusions for preexisting conditions; however, in our experience, lack of the information rarely affects processing of a claim.

MEDICARE: Leave blank.

15. DATE FIRST CONSULTED

Enter, if known, the date the patient first came to see you for the condition for which you are submitting the claim. We recommend that you leave this space blank, or, if you do enter the information, do so only on the first claim for the condition.

MEDICARE: Leave blank.

16. DATE(S) OF SAME/SIMILAR ILLNESS OR INJURY

Handle same as item 15.

17. DATE PATIENT ABLE TO RETURN TO WORK

Enter only if the patient is entitled to disability benefits, or is being treated for a work related injury.

MEDICARE: Leave blank.

18. DATES OF TOTAL DISABILITY

Handle same as item 17.

19. **REFERRING PHYSICIAN**

Enter name of referring physician if your service(s) includes a visit or evaluation and management consultation code. Generally required only for the first claim listing a consultation.

MEDICARE: As of this writing Medicare has issued requirements to include the Medicare license number of the rendering or ordering physician in this space in addition to the name. Actual implementation has been indefinitely delayed. Consult your local Medicare carrier for current information.

20. **HOSPITALIZATION DATES**

Enter dates of admission and/or discharge if services are rendered as a result of or subsequent to a hospitalization.

21. **FACILITY NAME AND ADDRESS**

Enter name and address of the hospital, clinic, emergency room, etc. if services were provided at a location other than the provider's office or the patient's home.

22. **OUTSIDE LABORATORY WORK**

If you are billing for laboratory work performed by an outside laboratory, check the "yes" box and enter the amount of the charges. If you are billing for laboratory work performed in your own laboratory, check the "no" box or leave blank.

MEDICARE: Leave blank. You are no longer allowed to bill the Medicare program for work performed by an outside laboratory.

23. **DIAGNOSIS**

PART A

Enter diagnosis description(s) and/or diagnosis code(s) using ICD-9-CM. If codes are entered in section 24 D, leave blank.

MEDICARE: Enter up to four (4) ICD-9-CM codes in this space. Descriptions are optional and will be ignored by the carrier. The first code is to define the reason for the current visit or service.

PART B

For Medicaid claims only, complete spaces for "EPSDT" (Early and Periodic Screening for Diagnosis and Treatment of Children) and "Family Planning" if appropriate. Include prior authorization number for services which require it.

24. DATE(S) AND PLACE(S) OF SERVICE

Column A Date of Service

Enter the month, day and year that the service or procedure was performed, or supply provided. If using "from" and "to" dates, the number of services should appear in Column F.

Column B Place of Service

Enter the place of service code (POS) using the codes listed on the back of the claim form. Note that there are two coding systems for place of service. For Medicare, use only the alphabetic codes, for Medicaid, use the codes specified by your local Medicaid intermediary, for all other carriers, use the numeric codes.

POS	ALPHA	NUMERIC
Office	O	3
Home	H	4
Inpatient Hospital	IH	1
Outpatient Hospital	OH	2
Emergency Room	OH	2
Ambulatory Surgery	ASC	B
Birthing Center	OL	0
Skilled Nursing	SNF	8
Nursing Facility	NH	7
Custodial Care	OL	0
Hospice	OL	0
Inpatient Psychiatric	OL	0
Community Mental Health	--	5 or 6
ESRD Treatment	COR	E

Column C Procedure Code and Description

Procedure Code

MEDICARE: Enter the proper procedure code, using the appropriate level of the HCPCS codes. Make sure you use Evaluation and Management codes for all office visits, hospital visits, skilled nursing visits, home visits, domiciliary visits, emergency department services and consultations provided to Medicare beneficiaries on or after January 1, 1992.

MEDICAID: Enter the proper procedure code from the most current edition of CPT or other codes as instructed by your MEDICAID carrier.

COMMERCIAL: For all commercial insurance carriers, enter the proper procedure code from the most current edition of CPT.

WORKER'S COMP: Use the coding system specified by your State Worker's Compensation Board.

Procedure Description

For all carriers, enter precise procedure description from current edition of CPT, or, leave procedure description blank.

Column D Diagnosis Code

Enter appropriate diagnosis code using ICD-9-CM. Enter at least one primary diagnosis code for each claim and more if appropriate. You may also use the option described below for Medicare.

MEDICARE: Enter the number between 1 and 4 of the ICD-9-CM codes listed in box 23 which corresponds to the visit or service listed.

Column E Charges

Enter the charge for the service, procedure or supply.

Column F Days or Units

For Medicare only, if "from" and "to" dates are used in Column A for a series of identical services, such as hospital visits, the number of these services should be entered in this column.

Column G Type of Service

MEDICARE: List the type of service code from the back of the HCFA1500 claim form.

ALL OTHERS: Leave blank unless otherwise instructed by insurance carriers.

Column H Leave Blank

This column is provided for carrier use and should be left blank.

MEDICARE: Many Medicare carriers are using this column to identify the provider number of the "rendering" physician when the billing entity is a group practice.

25. SIGNATURE OF PHYSICIAN OR SUPPLIER

The physician or supplier, or his or her authorized representative must sign the provider's name and enter the date in this space. For most carriers, impressions such as rubber stamps are acceptable.

MEDICARE: There is a portion of the statement in this space which refers to information on the back of the claim form. Medicare carriers are not allowed to process claims which do not have this information printed on the on the back. Keep this is mind if you are having your own claim forms printed.

26. **ACCEPT ASSIGNMENT**

The provider should check the appropriate box to indicate whether or not he or she accepts assignment under Medicare. With the exception of a few other government funded programs, not including Medicaid, there is no need to complete this space.

27. **TOTAL CHARGE**

Enter the total of all charges listed in Section 24 Column E.

28. **AMOUNT PAID**

For all private carriers, enter zero or none in this space. This assures that your total charges will be processed for determination of benefits and the resulting payment. Any overpayments resulting can be handled between you and your patient.

MEDICARE: If you are the first provider of service for a Medicare beneficiary at the beginning of a new benefit year, you should collect the deductible and indicate the payment in this space.

29. **BALANCE DUE**

Enter the amount from space 27 unless you have collected payment from a Medicare beneficiary as specified under 28 above.

30. **YOUR SOCIAL SECURITY NUMBER**

Enter the provider's social security number if not billing under a group provider number.

31. **PROVIDER INFORMATION**

If your claim forms are not already preprinted with this information, enter the provider number(s), the provider name(s), provider street, city, state, zip code and telephone number.

32. **PATIENT ACCOUNT NUMBER**

If you use a patient account number system, enter the patient account number in this space. Most Medicare and Medicaid intermediaries, and some commercial carriers, include this information on their Explanation of Benefits, making it easier for you to identify patients for posting of payments, particularly if you use a computer or service bureau.

33. **EMPLOYER IDENTIFICATION NUMBER**

Enter this information if the provider is providing services in a group practice or is employed by a hospital or other institution and has been assigned an employer identification number.

HCFA1500 (12/90 Version)

PLEASE
DO NOT
STAPLE
IN THIS
AREA

HEALTH INSURANCE CLAIM FORM

PICA   PICA

1. MEDICARE	MEDICAID	CHAMPUS	CHAMPVA	GROUP HEALTH PLAN	FECA BLK LUNG	OTHER	1a. INSURED'S I.D. NUMBER (FOR PROGRAM IN ITEM 1)
(Medicare #)	(Medicaid #)	(Sponsor's SSN)	(VA File #)	(SSN or ID)	(SSN)	(ID)	

2. PATIENT'S NAME (Last Name, First Name, Middle Initial)
3. PATIENT'S BIRTH DATE MM DD YY   SEX M☐ F☐
4. INSURED'S NAME (Last Name, First Name, Middle Initial)

5. PATIENT'S ADDRESS (No., Street)
6. PATIENT RELATIONSHIP TO INSURED   Self☐ Spouse☐ Child☐ Other☐
7. INSURED'S ADDRESS (No., Street)

CITY   STATE
8. PATIENT STATUS   Single☐ Married☐ Other☐
CITY   STATE

ZIP CODE   TELEPHONE (Include Area Code) ( )
Employed☐ Full-Time Student☐ Part-Time Student☐
ZIP CODE   TELEPHONE (INCLUDE AREA CODE) ( )

9. OTHER INSURED'S NAME (Last Name, First Name, Middle Initial)
10. IS PATIENT'S CONDITION RELATED TO:
11. INSURED'S POLICY GROUP OR FECA NUMBER

a. OTHER INSURED'S POLICY OR GROUP NUMBER
a. EMPLOYMENT? (CURRENT OR PREVIOUS) YES☐ NO☐
a. INSURED'S DATE OF BIRTH MM DD YY   SEX M☐ F☐

b. OTHER INSURED'S DATE OF BIRTH MM DD YY   SEX M☐ F☐
b. AUTO ACCIDENT?   PLACE (State) YES☐ NO☐
b. EMPLOYER'S NAME OR SCHOOL NAME

c. EMPLOYER'S NAME OR SCHOOL NAME
c. OTHER ACCIDENT? YES☐ NO☐
c. INSURANCE PLAN NAME OR PROGRAM NAME

d. INSURANCE PLAN NAME OR PROGRAM NAME
10d. RESERVED FOR LOCAL USE
d. IS THERE ANOTHER HEALTH BENEFIT PLAN? YES☐ NO☐ *If yes,* return to and complete item 9 a-d.

READ BACK OF FORM BEFORE COMPLETING & SIGNING THIS FORM.
12. PATIENT'S OR AUTHORIZED PERSON'S SIGNATURE I authorize the release of any medical or other information necessary to process this claim. I also request payment of government benefits either to myself or to the party who accepts assignment below.

SIGNED _____ DATE _____

13. INSURED'S OR AUTHORIZED PERSON'S SIGNATURE I authorize payment of medical benefits to the undersigned physician or supplier for services described below.

SIGNED _____

14. DATE OF CURRENT: MM DD YY   ILLNESS (First symptom) OR INJURY (Accident) OR PREGNANCY(LMP)
15. IF PATIENT HAS HAD SAME OR SIMILAR ILLNESS GIVE FIRST DATE MM DD YY
16. DATES PATIENT UNABLE TO WORK IN CURRENT OCCUPATION MM DD YY   MM DD YY FROM   TO

17. NAME OF REFERRING PHYSICIAN OR OTHER SOURCE
17a. I.D. NUMBER OF REFERRING PHYSICIAN
18. HOSPITALIZATION DATES RELATED TO CURRENT SERVICES MM DD YY   MM DD YY FROM   TO

19. RESERVED FOR LOCAL USE
20. OUTSIDE LAB? YES☐ NO☐ $ CHARGES

21. DIAGNOSIS OR NATURE OF ILLNESS OR INJURY. (RELATE ITEMS 1,2,3 OR 4 TO ITEM 24E BY LINE)
1. _____   3. _____
2. _____   4. _____

22. MEDICAID RESUBMISSION CODE   ORIGINAL REF. NO.
23. PRIOR AUTHORIZATION NUMBER

24. A DATE(S) OF SERVICE From MM DD YY To MM DD YY	B Place of Service	C Type of Service	D PROCEDURES, SERVICES, OR SUPPLIES (Explain Unusual Circumstances) CPT/HCPCS MODIFIER	E DIAGNOSIS CODE	F $ CHARGES	G DAYS OR UNITS	H EPSDT Family Plan	I EMG	J COB	K RESERVED FOR LOCAL USE
1										
2										
3										
4										
5										
6										

25. FEDERAL TAX I.D. NUMBER   SSN☐ EIN☐
26. PATIENT'S ACCOUNT NO.
27. ACCEPT ASSIGNMENT? (For govt. claims, see back) YES☐ NO☐
28. TOTAL CHARGE $
29. AMOUNT PAID $
30. BALANCE DUE $

31. SIGNATURE OF PHYSICIAN OR SUPPLIER INCLUDING DEGREES OR CREDENTIALS (I certify that the statements on the reverse apply to this bill and are made a part thereof.)

SIGNED _____ DATE _____

32. NAME AND ADDRESS OF FACILITY WHERE SERVICES WERE RENDERED (If other than home or office)

33. PHYSICIAN'S, SUPPLIER'S BILLING NAME, ADDRESS, ZIP CODE & PHONE #

PIN# _____   GRP# _____

(APPROVED BY AMA COUNCIL ON MEDICAL SERVICE 8/88)   **PLEASE PRINT OR TYPE**   FORM HCFA-1500 (12-90) FORM OWCP-1500   FORM RRB-1500

790-0117 (12/90) (OCR) 2 pt.

CARRIER

PATIENT AND INSURED INFORMATION

PHYSICIAN OR SUPPLIER INFORMATION

NEW HCFA1500 CLAIM FORM

Below is a copy of the "new" HCFA1500 insurance claim form. Under development since 1986, the final version was approved as of December 1990. The form has been accepted since November of 1991 and is mandatory for all Medicare claims filed on or after April 1, 1992. In addition to increased emphasis on secondary payers, the new form increases the requirement for accurate procedure and diagnosis coding because there is no space on the new form to describe procedures or diagnoses. All services, procedures and diagnoses will be reported by code.

The new form also requires medical professionals to report additional information such as marital status, employment and student status. This means that tens of thousands of computers will have to be reprogrammed not only to print the new form, but also to collect the additional data required.

HCFA1500 "NEW" VERSION

PATIENT INFORMATION

1. **PROGRAM**

   Enter an "X" in the appropriate box to indicate proper carrier. This is optional and redundant if your computer system includes the insurance carrier name and address on the form.

1a. **INSURED'S IDENTIFICATION NUMBER**

   Enter the insured's primary identification number including any letters. The number is usually obtained from the patient's or insured's insurance identification card.

   MEDICARE: Enter the Medicare number and suffix.

   MEDICAID: Enter the Medicaid number from the patient's current Medicaid card.

   COMMERCIAL: Enter the insured's "member number" or "subscriber number" or "certificate number" from the insurance identification card. Most often this is the insured's social security number.

2. **PATIENT'S NAME**

   Enter the patient's full name....do not use nicknames or abbreviated names. The form specifies that the name be entered in last name, first name, middle initial order; however, our experience indicates that listing the name in the more normal order of "first name, middle initial, last name" has no detrimental affect.

3.   DATE OF BIRTH AND SEX

Enter the patient's date of birth in month, day, year format. Enter an "X" in the appropriate box to indicate male or female.

4.   INSURED'S NAME

Enter the full name of the insured, unless the patient is the insured.... then enter the word "SAME".

MEDICARE: If the patient or spouse is age 65 through 69, employed, and covered by an employer health plan, show the insured person's full name.

5.   PATIENT'S ADDRESS

Enter the patient's complete address. Enter the street address on one line followed by the city, and state on the next line, and the zip code and telephone number on the last line.

6.   PATIENT'S RELATIONSHIP TO INSURED

Check the appropriate box.

7.   INSURED'S ADDRESS

Enter insured's street address, city, state and zip code and telephone number. If same as patient's, enter "SAME".

8.   PATIENT STATUS

Enter patient's marital status, employment status, and student status in the appropriate boxes.

9.   OTHER INSURED'S NAME

If the patient is covered by a secondary insurance plan, enter the name of the insured party in this field.

9a.   OTHER INSURED'S POLICY OR GROUP NUMBER

Enter the policy number for the secondary insurance plan.

9b.   OTHER INSURED'S DATE OF BIRTH

Enter the date of birth and sex of the secondary insured.

9c.   EMPLOYER'S NAME OR SCHOOL NAME

Enter the employer or school name of the secondary insured.

9d.   INSURANCE PLAN NAME OR PROGRAM NAME

Enter the plan or program name of the secondary insurance.

10.   CONDITION RELATED TO EMPLOYMENT OR ACCIDENT

Check appropriate box(es) if you are treating the patient for either a work related injury or accident related injury. Note that worker's compensation claims are filed with insurance carriers designated by the patient's employer and is not the same carrier as the patient's health insurance carrier. Likewise, accident related claims, such as automobile accidents, are frequently processed by automobile insurance carriers and/or private attorneys.

11.   INSURED'S POLICY GROUP OR FECA NUMBER

For commercial carriers, enter the "group number" or "group name" from the insurance identification card if the patient is covered by an employer sponsored health insurance plan.

11a.   INSURED'S DATE OF BIRTH

Enter the date of birth and sex of the primary insured.

11b.   EMPLOYER'S NAME OR SCHOOL NAME

Enter the employer or school name of the primary insured.

11c.   INSURANCE PLAN NAME OR PROGRAM NAME

Enter the name of the primary insurance carrier.

11d.   IS THERE ANOTHER HEALTH BENEFIT PLAN?

Enter an "X" in the YES box if the patient is covered by a THIRD insurance plan.

12.   RELEASE OF INFORMATION

Either have the patient, or his or her representative sign the claim form, or attach your own release form to the claim and enter "SEE ATTACHMENT" in this space. If the patient is a minor, the signature must be that of a parent or legal guardian.

MEDICARE: For the Medicare program, the beneficiary's signature in this space also authorizes direct payment to the provider. For Medicare, you may obtain a "lifetime" authorization one time, which you must keep on file in your office. Enter "SIGNATURE ON FILE" in this space if you have such an authorization on file.

13. ASSIGNMENT OF BENEFITS

The insured's signature in this space directs the insurance carrier to pay any benefits directly to the provider. You may also use a form which combines release of information and assignment of benefits, attached to the claim form.

PHYSICIAN INFORMATION

14. DATE OF CURRENT (ILLNESS, INJURY OR PREGNANCY)

Enter, if known, the date of onset for illnesses, the date of injury or, for pregnancy, the date of the last menstrual period (LMP). The carriers like to have this information to assist them in determining coverage or exclusions for preexisting conditions; however, in our experience, lack of the information rarely affects processing of a claim.

MEDICARE: Leave blank.

15. DATE(S) OF SAME/SIMILAR ILLNESS OR INJURY

Enter, if known, the date the patient first came to see you for the condition for which you are submitting the claim. We recommend that you leave this space blank, or, if you do enter the information, do so only on the first claim for the condition.

MEDICARE: Leave blank.

16. DATES PATIENT UNABLE TO WORK IN CURRENT OCCUPATION

Enter only if the patient is entitled to disability benefits, or is being treated for a work related injury.

MEDICARE: Leave blank.

17 NAME OR REFERRING PHYSICIAN OR OTHER SOURCE

Enter name of referring physician if your service(s) includes a visit or evaluation and management consultation code. Generally required only for the first claim listing a consultation.

17a. I.D. NUMBER OF REFERRING PHYSICIAN

MEDICARE: Enter the Medicare license number of the rendering or ordering physician in this space. For all other carriers, leave blank.

18. HOSPITALIZATION DATES RELATED TO CURRENT SERVICES

Enter dates of admission and/or discharge if services are rendered as a result of or subsequent to a hospitalization.

19. RESERVED FOR LOCAL USE

Enter information in this space only if advised to do so by local insurance carriers.

20. OUTSIDE LABORATORY WORK

If you are billing for laboratory work performed by an outside laboratory, check the "yes" box and enter the amount of the charges. If you are billing for laboratory work performed in your own laboratory, check the "no" box or leave blank.

MEDICARE: Leave blank. You are no longer allowed to bill the Medicare program for work performed by an outside laboratory.

21. DIAGNOSIS OR NATURE OF ILLNESS OR INJURY

Enter up to four (4) ICD-9-CM codes in this space. There is no space for diagnosis descriptions on this form. The first code listed should clearly define the reason for the current visit or service.

22. MEDICAID RESUBMISSION

For Medicaid resubmission claims only, enter the resubmission code and the original reference number.

23. PRIOR AUTHORIZATION NUMBER

Enter the prior authorization number if required by Medicare or Medicaid.

24. DATE(S) AND PLACE(S) OF SERVICE

Column A Date(s) of Service

Enter the month, day and year that the service or procedure was performed, or supply provided. If using "from" and "to" dates, the number of services should appear in Column F.

Column B Place of Service

Enter the place of service (POS) code using the codes listed on the back of the claim form. Note that the previous alpha or numeric codes have been completely revised for the new form.

POS	NEW CODES
Office	11
Home	12
Inpatient Hospital	21
Outpatient Hospital	22
Emergency Room - Hospital	23
Ambulatory Surgical Center	24
Birthing Center	25
Military Treatment Facility	26
Skilled Nursing Facility	31
Nursing Facility	32
Custodial Care Facility	33
Hospice	34
Ambulance - Land	41
Ambulance - Air or Water	42
Inpatient Psychiatric Facility	51
Psychiatric Facility Partial Hospitalization	52
Community Mental Health Center	53
Intermediate Care Facility/Mentally Retarded	54
Residual Substance Abuse Treatment Facility	55
Psychiatric Residential Treatment Center	56
Comprehensive Inpatient Rehabilitation Facility	61
Comprehensive Outpatient Rehabilitation Facility	62
End Stage Renal Disease Treatment Facility	65
State or Local Public Health Clinic	71
Rural Health Clinic	72
Independent Laboratory	81
Other Unlisted Facility	99

Column C Type of Service Code

MEDICARE: List the type of service code from the back of the HCFA1500 claim form.

ALL OTHERS: Leave blank unless otherwise instructed by insurance carriers.

Column D Procedures, Services or Supplies

Procedure Code

MEDICARE: Enter the proper procedure code, using the appropriate level of the HCPCS codes. Make sure you use Evaluation and Management codes for all office visits, hospital visits, skilled nursing visits, home visits, domiciliary visits, emergency department services and consultations provided to Medicare beneficiaries on or after January 1, 1992.

MEDICAID: Enter the proper procedure code from the most current edition of CPT or other codes as instructed by your MEDICAID carrier.

COMMERCIAL: For all commercial insurance carriers, enter the proper procedure code from the most current edition of CPT.

WORKER'S COMP: Use the coding system specified by your State Worker's Compensation Board.

Procedure Description

There is no space available on this form for a procedure description.

Column E Diagnosis Code

Enter the number between 1 and 4 of the ICD-9-CM codes listed in box 21 which corresponds to the visit or service listed.

Column F Charges

Enter the charge for the service, procedure or supply.

Column G Days or Units

For Medicare only, if "from" and "to" dates are used in Column A for a series of identical services, such as hospital visits, the number of these services should be entered in this column.

Column H EPSDT Family Plan

MEDICAID: Complete if appropriate

ALL OTHERS: Leave blank

Column I EMG

Column J COB

Column K Reserved for local use

This column is reserved for definition by the local carriers. Leave blank unless instructed otherwise by local carriers.

25. **FEDERAL TAX I.D. NUMBER**

Enter the Social Security Number (SSN) or Federal Employer Identification Number (FEIN) and also mark an "X" in the appropriate box to indicate which number you are using.

26. **PATIENT ACCOUNT NUMBER**

If you use a patient account number system, enter the patient account number in this space. Most Medicare and Medicaid intermediaries, and some commercial carriers, include this information on their Explanation of Benefits, making it easier for you to identify patients for posting of payments, particularly if you use a computer or service bureau.

27. **ACCEPT ASSIGNMENT**

The provider should check the appropriate box to indicate whether or not he or she accepts assignment under Medicare. With the exception of a few other government funded programs, not including Medicaid, there is no need to complete this space.

28. **TOTAL CHARGE**

Enter the total of all charges listed in Section 24 Column F.

29. **AMOUNT PAID**

For all private carriers, enter zero or none in this space. This assures that your full charges will be processed for determination of benefits and the resulting payment. Any overpayments resulting can be handled between you and your patient.

MEDICARE: If you are the first provider of service for a Medicare beneficiary at the beginning of a new benefit year, you should collect the deductible and indicate the payment in this space.

30. **BALANCE DUE**

Enter the amount from space 28 unless you have collected payment from a Medicare beneficiary as specified under 29 above.

31. **SIGNATURE OF PHYSICIAN OR SUPPLIER**

The physician or supplier, or his or her authorized representative must sign the provider's name and enter the date in this space. For most carriers, impressions such as rubber stamps are acceptable.

MEDICARE: There is a portion of the statement in this space which refers to information on the back of the claim form. Medicare carriers are not allowed to process claims which do not have this information printed on the on the back. Keep this is mind if you are having your own claim forms printed.

32. **NAME AND ADDRESS OF FACILITY WHERE SERVICE WERE RENDERED**

If the services were provided at a location other than the provider's office or the patient's home, enter the name and address of the facility in this space.

33. **PROVIDER INFORMATION**

If your claim forms are not already preprinted with this information, enter the provider number(s), the provider name(s), provider street, city, state, zip code and telephone number.

HOW INSURANCE CARRIERS PROCESS YOUR CLAIM

Have you ever wondered exactly what happens to a claim form once it arrives at the insurance carriers location? The following flow diagram illustrates the basic steps that your claim goes through after it arrives at the insurance carriers processing center.

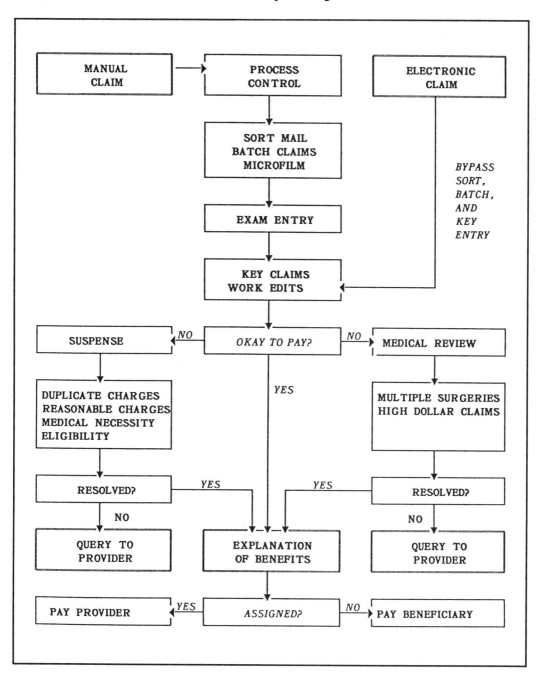

ELECTRONIC (PAPERLESS) CLAIMS

Private health insurance claims are increasing at the rate of over 15 percent yearly. The accompanying labor costs are rising even higher for both the providers submitting the claims, and the insurance carriers processing them. Many providers long ago decided to let patients file their own insurance claims using "superbills" or something similar, or charged a fee for filing the insurance claim form, which often accomplished the same result. With increasing volumes of claims to process, and increased competition among providers for patients, as well as HMOs marketing "the end of claim forms" as one of their major benefits, many providers find themselves "going backward" and reversing their policies of not completing claim forms for patients.

Making sure insurance claims are processed quickly and accurately can help you keep your patient base. It can also contribute significantly to the growth and success of your practice. At the same time, the additional burden of processing paper claims can be very costly in terms of additional time and labor. This is where the benefits of electronic (paperless) claims processing are realized.

WHAT IS AN ELECTRONIC CLAIM?

Filing insurance claims electronically, instead of manually, requires that claim data be entered into a computer system (either your own, or that of a computer service bureau). After the claims data is entered, your office (or the service bureau) places a telephone call to the insurance carrier's computer system, using a piece of equipment called a modem. The claims data is transmitted directly from your computer to theirs.

Many providers already have experience with electronic claims because that is how they submit their Medicare claims. The Health Care Financing Administration (HCFA), one of the chief proponents of electronic claims processing, states that its carriers currently receive almost 30 percent of Part B Medicare claims electronically and their goal is to increase that figure to 50 percent by the early 1990s. All Medicare intermediaries provide electronic claims processing.

In addition, many Medicaid programs, and some Blue Cross and Blue Shield programs have their own electronic claims systems. There are two national clearinghouses which provide electronic claims service to various Medicare and Medicaid agencies as well as about 40 major commercial carriers.

BENEFITS TO INSURANCE CARRIERS

Electronic claims processing saves insurance carriers money. When a manual claim is processed it is handled by many people. It is handled the longest by the claims examiner, who must enter the claim into the insurance carriers computer system. By using electronic claims processing, claims go directly into the insurance carriers computer system, without human intervention. Each time this occurs, the carrier saves from 50 cents to a dollar.

BENEFITS TO PROVIDERS

The benefits of electronic claims processing for providers include faster payment, fewer rejected claims, reduced paperwork, and greater consistency.

FASTER PAYMENT

Electronic claims bypass the time consuming claims examination process and enter the insurance carrier's computer system faster. Faster entry, combined with the fact that electronic claims are "cleaner" than manual claims, allows the insurance carrier to process and pay the claim faster.

Electronic claims are paid faster, but the cashflow benefit to an individual provider occurs only once.....when you change from manual to electronic processing. As an example, let's say your practice now gets paid on the average in four weeks for manual claims and that switching to electronic claims processing would mean that you would get paid in two weeks instead of four. If your insurance payments averaged $ 10,000 weekly, you would have a one-time cash flow benefit of $ 20,000.

FASTER PAYMENT ANYWAY

As of October 1, 1989 Medicare intermediaries are required by law to pay all clean claims within 17 days to PAR providers and 24 days to NON-PAR providers, or they must pay interest. In some states, there are laws governing insurance claims processing by commercial carriers. In California for example, clean insurance claims must be paid or rejected within 30 days by carriers based in the state or they must pay you interest.

FEWER REJECTED CLAIMS

Most electronic claims software provided by computer vendors or computer service bureaus includes extensive "editing" features which assure that claims processed for electronic submission are properly coded, complete and accurate. This results in fewer rejections or requests for additional information from the insurance carrier and less work for the provider.

REDUCED PAPERWORK

One of the major benefits of electronic claims processing is reduced paperwork and a concurrent reduction in claims costs due to the decrease in time and labor. Claims paperwork is a very time-consuming, and therefore labor intensive process. Regardless of whether claims are typed or printed by a computer, they must be checked, separated, sorted, collated, signed, and mailed. Copies must be filed and maintained. The cost of completing a form is about the same for any service. It is just as costly to complete a form for a $ 15 injection as it is for a $ 1500 procedure. Electronic claims processing eliminates these manual steps (at least in theory), resulting in a considerable labor savings.

Many providers and their staffs are reluctant to trust the electronic claims process totally. They print paper "copies" of electronic claims which they then check, separate, sort, file, etc. This duplication of effort reduces the desired labor savings, but there is some benefit. Electronic claims do "get lost". Either the transmission fails, or the electronic claims are not processed by the carrier. In addition, many providers prefer to compare insurance claims to the carrier's explanation of benefits before posting payments. Unless you have an "open item" system, this is difficult without some kind of paper trail, either a claim form or a report.

STILL IN DEVELOPMENT PROCESS

Electronic claims processing is still in the developmental stage. Medicare carriers are generally far ahead of all the other carriers in providing this service. This is due to congressional mandates, not because HCFA is more technologically advanced or efficient.

The National Electronic Information Corporation (NEIC), founded in 1981 by 11 major private commercial insurance carriers, provides clearinghouse services to 34 of the major commercial carriers for private and/or group claims as well as claims to some Medicare Part B carriers. NEIC wisely chose the national Medicare data set (HCFA 1500) for its claims format. Medicare intermediaries on the other hand were allowed to develop their own versions of the format; therefore, the fact that you may be sending electronic claims to Medicare, does not mean that you can use the same program to transmit claims to private carriers.

As of this writing, the following insurance carriers, which represent over 85% of the nation's private commercial group health claims reimbursement dollars are actively receiving, or preparing to receive, electronic claims via NEIC:

Aetna Life & Casualty Co.	Life Insurance Co. of Georgia
American General Corporation	Metropolitan Life Insurance Co.
Benefit Trust Life Insurance Co.	Modern American Life
California-Western States Life	The New England
CIGNA (Connecticut General)	New York Life Insurance Co.
CNA Insurance Co.	Pacific Mutual Life Insurance Co.
Confederation Life Ins. Co.	Philadelphia American Life
EQUICOR	Pacific Mutual Life Insurance Co.
General American Life Ins.	Philadelphia American Life
Great-West Life Assurance Co.	The Phoenix
The Guardian Life Ins.Co.	Principal Mutual Life Insurance
Gulf Group Services	Provident Life & Accident
Jefferson-Pilot Life Insurance	Republic National Life Insurance
Liberty Life Assurance Boston	State Mutual Life Assurance Co.
	The Travelers

For more information regarding electronic claims processing with NEIC, contact them directly at 500 Plaza Drive, Secaucus, NJ 07096, or call (201) 902-7000.

LACK OF UNIVERSAL ELECTRONIC CLAIM FORMAT

Ironically, the standard or universal claim form was developed to standardize insurance claims processing by eliminating separate forms for Medicare, Medicaid, Blue Cross & Blue Shield and Commercial carriers. Due to the lack of a coordinated national standard for electronic claims processing we are "regressing" to an electronic version of the same problem. Medicaid programs, being administered by a totally different group of insurance carrier intermediaries, or in some states, computer service bureaus, have developed their own electronic claims systems totally independent of the local or national Medicare programs. Likewise, various Blue Cross and Blue Shield plans have either implemented, or are developing electronic claims processing on a totally independent basis.

To process all claims electronically, a provider may have to acquire four different programs, one for Medicare, one for Medicaid, one for Blue Cross and one for Commercial Carriers. In addition, the provider will most likely wind up with four different data sets, four different user's guides, and four different operating formats. Integrating these programs with an existing computer billing system may be difficult if not impossible.....resulting in the need to re-enter data for these other programs.

There are already new businesses, known as "clearinghouses" which exist solely because of the lack of a national standard for electronic claims processing. These firms collect all of your insurance data in a specific format, then they reprocess the information into the specific claim format required by Medicare, Medicaid, Blue Cross and the various private carriers.

WHY INSURANCE CLAIMS ARE REJECTED

At a recent hearing of the U.S. House & Senate Health Committees, the Associate Administrator for Operations of the Medicare Program indicated that 30 percent of all Medicare claims filed required additional work due to missing information or improper completion. In other words, only 70 percent of claims submitted to Medicare are submitted as required. As Medicare requirements are less forgiving that those of many of the commercial carriers, we would estimate that more than 30 percent of non-Medicare claims filed would be missing information or incomplete.

COMMON REASONS FOR INSURANCE CLAIM REJECTION

- The patient's (or insured's) subscriber number and/or group number is incorrect or missing.

- The physician's signature (or facsimile) is missing.

- Dates are obviously incorrect. For example, surgery is dated prior to preop exam, or discharge date is before admission date, or date(s) are missing entirely.

- The diagnosis does not correspond with or support the services or procedures.

- The diagnosis is missing or incomplete.

- Reasons for multiple visits made the same day are not listed on the claim.

- The charges are not itemized.

- Necessary information about prescription drugs or durable medical equipment prescribed by the physician is not included.

- The procedure codes are missing or incorrect.

- The patient did not answer all questions on his or her portion of the form.

- The fee column is left blank. Many insurance carriers will not process a claim which has blank fees.

- The diagnosis is not coded using ICD-9-CM. This is now mandated for all Medicare claims.

- The claim is difficult to read due to smudges or handwriting.

INSURANCE CLAIMS MANAGEMENT

We strongly recommend that you have a designated "insurance claims reviewer" checking claims before they are mailed. This reviewer should be someone other than the person who filled out the claim. It may not be necessary, or practical, to review every claim. You may wish to have only claims exceeding a certain dollar amount reviewed, or all surgeries, or whatever a spot check of claims indicates.

Many practices which do a lot of surgeries have the claims reviewer review operative reports to make sure the proper procedure codes were used. While this may occasionally result in the correction of coding errors, it mandates that operative reports be made available to the reviewer shortly after the procedure so that billing is not delayed.

We also recommend that you institute your review process BEFORE the procedures are processed for insurance claims. Reviewing your fee tickets or superbills for accuracy and completeness before posting will allow you to correct coding and provide missing information before insurance claims are produced. This pre-billing review process assures that any insurance claims produced will be accurate and complete and minimizes the need for claims review.

MONITORING CLAIMS STATUS

File copies of claim forms in an accordion file. We recommend that you file alphabetically by patient last name as that is what you are going to be looking for when you get the Explanation of Benefits (EOB). As the EOBs are received, pull the claim copy from the file and compare the EOB to the original claim. Look for any procedures which are listed on the claim form which are not listed on the EOB. Look for procedures where the amount "allowed" is less than expected.

Review all claims where reimbursement was less than expected to make sure no mistakes were made in coding procedures or diagnosis. If mistakes are found, correct them and refile the claim with a cover letter to the insurance carrier. If no coding mistakes are found and you still believe that payment was less than it should have been, file a request for review with the insurance carrier. Maintain a separate accordion file for claims that have been refiled or submitted for review. Follow up these claims no less than once a month.

INSURANCE LOGS

Some practices use insurance logs or claims registers where they record the date and amount each claim was filed along with the insurance carrier name, total charges and other items of interest. When payments arrive, they are recorded on the insurance log. If the payment is less than expected, an appeal can be instituted as described above. Review of the log allows you to quickly spot unpaid claims as the payment column is blank.

Insurance logs can quickly get out of hand in a busy practice. Imagine typing or writing claim information on such a log for 100 claims a day! Consider the amount of time required to match

EOBs to the log and post payments. At 100 claims a day, you would have over 3,000 claims logged every six work weeks. Think about how long it would take to locate an individual claim after 30 to 45 days.

Some computer systems provide the ability to do what is called "open item" posting, which means that you post payments, usually directly from the EOB, for each individual procedure instead of as a lump sum. These systems usually allow you to print out all procedures for which no payment has been received which gives you a tool for claims follow-up. If you can do this with a computer.....fine. Otherwise, we strongly recommend using a copy of the claim form as your follow- up system.

CLAIMS INQUIRIES

Once you have identified claims that need to be followed up, you may develop either a telephone based system or a written system for requesting information from the insurance carriers. While a telephone system has the advantage of speed, tracking down the right person to answer your questions may be difficult, plus unless you keep track of it, there is no record of the telephone call for future reference.

Most practice management consultants recommend that claims inquiries be in writing, using either a letter or inquiry form developed for this specific purpose. Many Medicare and Medicaid intermediaries have specific forms which they supply for the purpose of doing claims follow-up. We highly recommend getting your patient involved in claims follow-up activities, as in many cases the patient will be far more successful than the provider in getting information, and payment, from the insurance carrier.

HOW TO GET PAID BETTER AND FASTER

To maximize the reimbursement you receive from insurance carriers and to make sure your patients are receiving all of the benefits possible, consider some of the following suggestions.

MANAGE YOUR FEE SCHEDULE

Fee schedule management involves far more than the amount you charge for a given procedure, service or supply. Fee schedule management includes proper coding, good data collection methods, efficient claims processing, strategic pricing, patient and peer relations, and marketing and promotional opportunities.

Make sure your fee schedule review includes an analysis of the going rates. To charge less than insurance carriers will pay results in lower reimbursement to you and is a disservice to your patient. To charge significantly more than the going rates invites the criticism of your referral sources and the potential loss of price sensitive patients.

CODE PROPERLY

We've said this before, but it bears repeating again. Purchase a new copy of the CPT code book yearly. Hundreds of procedure codes are added, changed and deleted each year. Failure to review and incorporate these changes in your fee schedule may seriously affect your reimbursement from third party carriers as well as create audit liability.

Code review is simple. All new codes are preceded by a black circle. Codes which have changed descriptions are preceded by a black triangle. Codes which have been deleted are enclosed in parenthesis () along with a reference to the proper code to use. First review your specialty section of the CPT. Then review the other sections as necessary. Don't forget to review the Laboratory and Radiology sections if you have an in-house lab and/or your own x-ray facilities.

Make sure your fee ticket or visit slip includes the proper codes for your most frequently performed procedures and most common diagnoses. Designate at least one staff member to be(come) an expert coder and send this person to coding seminars to learn the most current coding techniques. Use the appropriate HCPCS codes; CPT, National codes or Local codes for your Medicare claims. Use the coding system specified by your state for Worker's Compensation claims and use CPT codes for Medicaid and all commercial carriers. Use ICD-9-CM diagnosis codes for all claims.

ELIMINATE DOWN-CODING BY ELIMINATING DESCRIPTIONS

Down-coding, which is the process of changing the procedure code you submitted to one of a lower value, costs physicians and their patients millions of dollars annually. Insurance claims examiners are trained to match codes and descriptions. If they don't match, the claims examiner has an opportunity to substitute a code with a lower value.

You can minimize this process by making sure your procedure descriptions are the same as those listed in the CPT. Even better, you can eliminate down-coding by submitting all your claims without procedure descriptions. With no description to match, the claims examiner must allow full value for your procedure code. As we discussed earlier in this chapter, the December 1990 revision of the HCFA1500 insurance claim form has no space for procedure or diagnosis descriptions. Once all carriers have converted to this new form, you won't have this problem anymore.

RANK PROCEDURES BY ORDER OF IMPORTANCE

When completing your claim forms list all procedures performed on the same date in order from the highest to the lowest charge. Insurance carriers will reduce the values of all procedures listed after the primary procedure. By listing your highest charge first, followed by the next highest, etc. you are making sure that the carrier's reduction will result in the maximum reimbursement. Always list your full charge for all procedures. Let the insurance carriers perform the reduction.

USE MODIFIERS APPROPRIATELY

In our experience, modifiers are used too frequently and often incorrectly resulting in unnecessary reimbursement delays and claim reviews. Use modifiers when necessary to provide additional information regarding a procedure, such as assistant surgeon, multiple procedures, right side, left side, etc. Avoid whenever possible the use of modifiers 22 (Unusual Services) and 52 (Reduced Services). Use procedure codes of higher or lower value instead.

CODE PROCEDURES INSTEAD OF TIME

One of the most common reimbursement problems results from the discrepancy, in terms of procedure values, between "technical" services and "cognitive" services. This discrepancy is the result of the way that the original California Relative Value Study was performed in 1956. As all current coding and reimbursement systems can be traced back to the CRVS, this discrepancy has been maintained by tradition. Until adoption of a fee schedule calculated with resource based relative values, you will probably achieve higher reimbursement by choosing CPT codes based on technical services (procedures), instead of cognitive services (time) when presented with a choice.

DON'T SEND DOCUMENTATION UNLESS ASKED TO

Unless you are using a procedure code for an "unlisted" procedure or are indicating unusual circumstances by use of the modifier 22, do not routinely send operative reports or other documentation with your claims. If the insurance carriers need additional documentation, they will request it. However, as most procedures are relatively common, they won't ask very often. When they do ask for documentation, respond promptly.

SEND CLAIMS PROMPTLY AND FREQUENTLY

File your insurance claims as quickly and frequently as possible. Many providers with large claims volume file claims daily. Filing claims weekly for the current week is the minimum acceptable standard. The rationale is simple: the faster you get the claim to the insurance carrier, the faster you, or your patient, get paid. Even for hospitalized patients, insurance carriers prefer to receive frequent, small claims instead of one big one following discharge.

While you may be holding hospital charges as a consideration to the hospitalized patient; consider that the patient's second most important concern (the first is result) is how he or she is going to pay for their care. Filing interim claims results in interim payments which can help reduce the patient's anxiety about the financial consequences of his or her illness. In addition, holding claims throughout a long hospitalization is risky. You may find that when you finally get around to filing your claim, that the patient's benefits are exhausted.

USE THE INSURANCE CARRIER'S DOLLAR WHENEVER POSSIBLE

FREE PHONE CALLS

What is the first thing that happens when you call an insurance carrier? You get put on hold. Who is paying for the call? You are! Whenever possible use toll-free 800 numbers for insurance carriers or local access numbers. Another of our publications, the *Health Insurance Carrier Directory*, lists over 1,000 toll-free telephone numbers for insurance carriers.

All Medicare carriers are required to have toll-free 800 numbers, however, many of them are busy all the time. What they do is install enough lines to meet the requirement, knowing that most people will get tired of getting a busy signal and call the regular number.

FREE CLAIM FORMS

Some insurance carriers still provide free insurance claim forms, however, the practice is declining due to the general acceptance of the HCFA1500 as the standard claim form.

FREE MAILING ENVELOPES

Many insurance carriers, including some Medicaid carriers, will provide free envelopes upon request for mailing claims.

FREE OR INEXPENSIVE SOFTWARE

Many insurance carriers, including Medicare, Medicaid and private insurance carriers provide free or low cost software for electronic claims filing. Unfortunately, as we explained above, there is little compatibility among these programs and usually no way to integrate these programs with existing billing and accounting software. However, if you have a significant volume of a particular patient type, Medicaid for example, the reduction in claim errors and the improved claims processing speed may justify the extra work of duplicate data entry.

FREE TRAINING & SEMINARS

Most Medicare and Medicaid carriers provide seminars explaining how their programs work and supplying valuable billing information. These programs are usually free.

FREE USERS GUIDES

Most Medicare and Medicaid carriers provide free or inexpensive guides and work books that tell you how to file claims and handle inquiries. These guides can be an invaluable source of claims processing information.

FILE CLAIMS BY FAX

Even though you pay the cost of the phone call, sending insurance claims by FAX results in you getting paid faster. While claims sent by mail may take a week (or more) to be delivered, claims transmitted by FAX are delivered in seconds or minutes. In addition, transmitting claims by FAX reduces the problem of claims "lost in the mail" or "never received". The *Health Insurance Carrier Directory*, revised and published annually by PMIC, lists over 500 FAX numbers for filing claims with insurance carriers.

REVIEW YOUR INSURANCE PAYMENTS

The explanation of benefits (EOB) you receive from insurance carriers with your payments (when you have indicated assignment of benefits) is one of the most valuable sources of difficult to obtain fee data. Unfortunately, it is also frequently ignored and discarded.

The first use of the EOB is to make sure that the insurance carrier processed your claim properly. The copy of the insurance claim is pulled from the pending file and the claim is carefully reviewed against the EOB.

- Are all charges listed on the insurance claim listed on the EOB?

- Is there an explanation for any unpaid or unprocessed charges?

- Are all of the codes on the EOB exactly the same as those on the insurance claim?

- Does the payment for each procedure meet with your expectation or agree with your pre-certification form?

If your answer to each of the previous questions is not yes, you need to carefully review the claim and file an immediate appeal with the insurance carrier.

Another very important use for the EOB is to determine where your fees are in relation to the customary fees used by a particular insurance carrier. If insurance carriers are *allowing* 100 percent of your usual charge for a given procedure in determining their payment to you, then your charge is less than or equal to the customary (going rate) charge. If insurance carriers are paying *100* percent of your usual charge for a given procedure, then your charge is far below the going rates.

USE YOUR PATIENT AS A COLLECTION TOOL

Getting the patient involved is one of the best ways to resolve problems with insurance carriers. The insurance contract is between the insurance carrier and the patient. The provider is an outside party. If you are not getting a response from an insurance carrier regarding an unpaid claim, let the patient know you are having a problem and ask him or her to contact the insurance carrier. In many cases this will result in a quick resolution of the problem.

INSURANCE COMMISSIONERS

Insurance carriers always respond quickly to investigations started by the state insurance commissioner. This can be an effective tool but should be used only after regular appeal processes have failed. In some states, the insurance commissioner will act only at the request of the consumer (patient). In others, the insurance commissioner will also act on the request of the consumer advocate. When requesting assistance from your state insurance commissioner, you should send a cover letter along with copies of claims and copies of any correspondence sent to or received from the insurance carrier.

MEDICARE FRAUD AND ABUSE

Due to the rapidly escalating costs of health care, and the underlying assumption, correct or not, that physicians are responsible for the major portion of this escalation, there is increased activity on the part of Medicare, Medicaid and private insurance carriers to detect cases of fraud and abuse. We stated in the introduction to this book that for every single case of overbilling or up-coding that the insurance carriers can find, we can produce nine cases of physicians who are underbilling and down-coding their own services. However, the emphasis, due to the publicity value and the possible deterrent affects on others, is to vigorously detect, pursue, punish and publish all cases of fraud and abuse.

While a complete review of Medicare policies and procedures regarding fraud and abuse is beyond the scope of this work, the following listings from the *Medicare Carrier's Manual* will provide an understanding of the types of situations that are considered either fraud or abuse by Medicare. A careful review of these lists and your own billing policies and procedures should provide sufficient protection against Medicare fraud and abuse accusations.

MEDICARE FRAUD

- Billing for service or supplies that were not provided. This includes billing for "NO SHOWS".

- Provider claim forms which have been altered to obtain a higher reimbursement amount.

- Provider's deliberate application for duplicate reimbursement. This would include billing Medicare and the beneficiary for the same service or billing both Medicare and another insurance carrier to attempt to be paid twice.

- Soliciting, offering, or receiving a kickback, bribe or rebate.

- False representation with respect to the nature of the services rendered, charges for the services rendered, identity of the person receiving the services, dates of service, etc.

- Claims for non-covered services billed as covered services. For example, routine foot care billed as a more involved form of foot care to obtain reimbursement.

- Claims involving collusion between a provider and a beneficiary, resulting in higher costs to the Medicare program.

- Use of another person's Medicare card to obtain medical care.

- Alteration of claims history records to generate fraudulent payments.

- Repeated violations of the participation agreement, assignment agreement or billing limits.

- Use of the adjustment payment process to generate fraudulent payments.

MEDICARE ABUSE

The *Medicare Carriers' Manual* states that the type of abuse to which Medicare is most vulnerable is overutilization of Medicare and health care services. The following are examples of what Medicare considers possible abusive situations:

- Excessive charges for services or supplies.

- Claims for services not medically necessary, or, if medically necessary, not the extent rendered.

- Breaches of assignment agreements which result in beneficiaries being billed for amounts disallowed by the carrier on the basis that such charges exceeded the reasonable charge criteria.

- Provider exceeds billing limit.

- Provider bills Medicare patients at a higher and different fee schedule than non-Medicare patients.

- Improper billing practices such as submitting bills to Medicare instead of other insurance carriers which are primary insurers.

- Violations of Medicare participation agreements by physicians or supplies.